Trusts and Foundations in Europe

A comparative survey
Edited by Klaus Neuhoff and Uwe Pavel

Published for the Stifterverband für die Deutsche Wissenschaft by the Bedford Square Press of the National Council of Social Service, 26 Bedford Square London WC1

The German version of this book (Stiftungen in Europa—Eine vergleichende Übersicht) was published in 1971 as No. 5 of the 'Schriftenreihe zum Stiftungswesen' (Studies on Foundations) by the Stifterverband für die Deutsche Wissenschaft e.V. (Donors' Association for the Promotion of Sciences and Humanities in Germany), Essen.

Printed in England by Alden and Mowbray Ltd at the Alden Press, Oxford

Contents

Foreword

At the suggestion of the Fondation Européenne de la Culture, the Ford Foundation and the Fritz Thyssen Stiftung, a conference of representatives of European foundations together with the Ford Foundation was held in Berlin on 10th and 11th November 1964. At this conference it was resolved to instruct competent persons to examine the legal position and the legal effect of foundations in the Western European countries and to report thereon. On the basis of the results of these studies a further conference should be convened to consider what stimulus could be given to the advancement of a liberal foundation concept particularly in the areas of education and the natural and social sciences, including activities appropriate to foundation operations related to human advancement.

For this purpose the conference set up a committee made up of the signatories to this foreword under the guidance of R. Goerdeler of Frankfurt, Germany.

The committee's first task was to find competent persons in the various countries who were prepared to make a report on foundations and the law relating thereto in their own country. This proved to be more difficult and time-consuming than was originally anticipated. In addition, the finished report had later to be translated into two, sometimes three, languages since the reports of the various countries were to be published in English, French and German. This explains the considerable period of time which has elapsed since the project was initiated.

The committee is now in a position to submit the reports to the foundations which were invited to the Berlin conference and also to publish the said reports. In doing so, the committee wishes to thank the authors of the reports who have carried out the task assigned to them with great diligence and who were also ready to give consideration to the committee's wishes and suggestions.

The efforts of a number of suitably qualified translators have made it possible to submit the reports, which in most cases were originally written in the author's native language, in the three languages as was intended. The committee is also indebted to the European Cultural Foundation, Amsterdam, for its valuable contribution to the preparation and initial stages of the project and in particular to the Stifterverband für die Deutsche Wissenschaft (Donors' Association for the Promotion of Sciences and Humanities in Germany), Essen, which played an important part in the work connected with the issue of the reports and which also supervised a considerable part of the translation work. Special thanks are due to Mr. Klaus Neuhoff and Mr. Uwe Pavel for their editorial work.

At the commencement of their task the authors of the national reports were given a list of issues which, having regard to legal and taxation differences in the various countries, were to form the basis of the examination and which have accordingly been dealt with in most of the reports. Thus each report was to deal with foundations with legal status as well as foundations without legal status and other institutions in a form similar to a foundation. The description of the effect of foundations was intended to include, in addition to information relating to the establishment of a foundation, details of the manner in which they are provided with property. In this connection consideration was, where possible, also to be given to the case of continuing transfer of funds from commercial enterprises. In dealing with questions of taxation, particular emphasis has been given to the description of the principles which apply to foundations for the advancement of science and research, to those for the advancement of culture and to those for general purposes. Finally, the changes in foundations and the law relating thereto which have occurred in the course of time have in most cases been referred to as well as the reforms which appear to be desirable at present or which may be expected in the future.

In many cases (but not in all) the national reports include information relating to the foundations which exist in the countries concerned. A complete survey was not, however, necessary since in many countries more or less detailed reviews on the effect of foundations are now available and the Giovanni Agnelli Foundation, Turin, has, in the meantime, published a handbook on European foundations (Directory of European Foundations, Turin 1969). Further sources of information are given at the end of each of the national reports.

It is intended by means of the reports to give as comprehensive a review as possible of the effect of foundations and their legal status in the various countries. Nevertheless, the committee is aware that further work remains to be done. It is hoped that this can be based on the national reports and that the evaluation of the collected material will provide further food for thought and will give rise to new discussions on a variety of questions. In this connection, the reports appear to be particularly suitable to stimulate suggestions for the co-ordination of the tax treatment of foundations. In addition, the reports could also provide a starting point for a further analysis and legal comparison of the problems which have been indicated. This would be particularly desirable in the interest of the advancement of the foundation concept at both the national and international level.

In order to ensure that the sequence in which the different entries appear is the same in all three versions (English, French, German—see Nomos Verlagsgesellschaft, Baden-Baden 1971), their order of presentation has been determined in accordance with a customary international system.

Autumn 1970

P. Ansiaux,   R. Goerdeler,   J. D. Livingston Booth,   S. Petrén,   M. Pomey
Brussels   Frankfurt   London   Stockholm   Paris

Austria*

Gunter Beinhauer

I. THE CONCEPT OF THE FOUNDATION

There is no legal definition in Austrian law of the concept of the foundation. The attempt of the legislature of the *Land* (the State of) *Vorarlberg* to define, in an Act relating to foundations and funds in the *Land Vorarlberg*[1], foundations as assets destined for a specific purpose and vested with legal status was frustrated by a decision of the Constitutional Court (*VerfGH*)[2], which declared as unconstitutional the section of the Act (para.2) containing this particular legal definition. In this decision, the Constitutional Court stated that the *Land Vorarlberg* had certainly not been obliged or compelled to preface its regulation with a legal definition of the term 'foundation'. It could just as well simply have presupposed the concept of the foundation as already established in Austrian law. If, however, the said Act intended to lay down such a legal definition, it should take as its point of departure the concept devised by Austrian law, since this concept was based on the distribution of competences provided for by the *B-VG*[3] (Federal Constitution) and since the distribution of competences between the Federal Government and the *Länder* (States) in matters relating to foundations seemed to be comprehensible and practicable only in relation to this definition developed in conformance with Austrian law. According to Sec.646 of the *ABGB* (General Civil Code), it was part of the nature of the foundation that the dedicated assets be destined either for purposes beneficial to the community (non-profit purposes) or for the support of specific persons, and this for all future time.

Through its decision, the Constitutional Court rejected a legal definition

* Translated from the German.

[1] LGB No. 10/1947 (Official Gazette).
[2] Decision of 16th June, 1952, G 2/52, Slg. No. 2319/1952.
[3] Bundesverfassungsgesetz (Federal Constitution) of 1929 (*Federal Law Gazette, No. 1/1930*).

I

of the foundation without, however, itself undertaking to provide in its stead a comprehensive definition of the concept—albeit, of course, it was under no obligation to do so. What then is the concept of the foundation as 'devised by Austrian law'? Both jurisdiction and legal theory consider essential characteristics of the concept to be: dedication of assets, juridical personality, serving the public interest, and perpetuity. With regard to each of these characteristics the following can be stated:

1. The dedication of assets

The availability of assets and their incorporation by an act of dedication are incontestably basic components of the concept of the foundation. Already Sec.646 of the *ABGB* considers it an essential characteristic of a foundation that the income from capital, real estate or rights shall be destined for institutions serving the public interest or for the support of specific persons for all future time.

The foundation comes into being by dedication[4]. Such dedication can be effected by means of a unilateral act *inter vivos* or *mortis causa*[5]. However, since the end of the monarchy, no regulations have been issued concerning the dedication and investment of the assets of the foundation.

The question as to whether the regulations issued at that time still constitute part and parcel of Austrian law and, if so, as to whether they constitute a part of federal law or of the law of the individual *Länder*, in accordance with the federal structure of Austria, cannot be answered without undertaking studies in the field of the transition of laws which are attended by considerable difficulties. The problems in this field are all the more difficult since foundations are neither exclusively the concern of the Federal Government, nor exclusively the concern of the *Länder*. In accordance with Art.10 para.1 No. 13 of the *B-VG* (Federal Constitution) foundations are, as regards the enactment of laws and their application, the concern of the Federal Government only if their purposes transcend the range of interests of a particular *Land* and if they have not already previously been autonomously administered by the *Länder*[6].

---

[4] Klang, *Kommentar zum Allgemeinen bürgerlichen Gesetzbuch*, 2nd. Ed., Vol. III, Vienna 1952—hereinafter abbreviated to Klang, p. 473; Gschnitzer, Allgemeiner Teil des bürgerlichen Rechts, 1966—hereinafter abbreviated to Gschnitzer, p. 105; Adamovich, *Handbuch des österreichischen Verwaltungsrechts*, 5th Ed., Vol. II, 1953—hereinafter abbreviated to Adamovich, p. 53.

[5] It is doubtful whether the dedication can also be effected by an act of State, for instance by a law.

[6] Until the entry into force of the articles re jurisdiction on 1st October, 1925.

2. The foundation as a legal entity

Although, especially in the literature on civil law, certain 'institutions' without legal status are also designated as foundations, namely as so-called 'nonrecognised' foundations[7], the manuals of both public and private law classify the foundation among the legal entities[8]. Hence, it is certainly not erroneous to maintain that, if one talks in general terms about foundations in Austria, they are understood to be a form of organisation with a legal status of its own, i.e. a legal entity.

As to the beginning of the foundation's legal existence, Adamovich[9] puts forward the view that the foundation only emerges as a legal entity upon official recognition by the State[10].

3. Serving the public interest as a purpose of the foundation

If one takes Sec.646 of the ABGB as one's starting point, foundations are destined either

(a) as institutions serving the public interest (e.g. schools, hospitals or almshouses) or

(b) for the support of specific persons for all future time.

That the purpose of the foundation shall be such that it will be of benefit to the community is a view which one finds almost unanimously supported by the older literature and older judicial decisions; this also applies in regard to those foundations that are intended 'for the support of specific persons', although the wording of Sec.646 of the ABGB would, as regards this point, clearly allow for another interpretation.

In his work *Das österreichische Stiftungsrecht*, 1896, Herrnritt[11] writes on p. 49 et s.: 'The Government must seek to ensure that the foundation's assets are preserved intact and that the will of the founder is duly complied with; and, should this become impossible, it must take the appropriate measures towards saving the foundation's existence. Thus the foundation must rely at all stages of its life on active promotion by the public authorities, while, in turn, the prescriptions laid down by the founder provide these authorities

---

[7] Gschnitzer, p. 105; Klang, p. 475.

[8] Antoniolli, *Allgemeines Verwaltungsrecht*, 1954—hereinafter abbreviated to Antoniolli, p. 139; Ehrenzweig, *System des österreichischen allgemeinen Privatrechts*, 2nd. Ed., Vol. I, 1951—hereinafter abbreviated to Ehrenzweig, p. 199; Adamovich, p. 53; Gschnitzer, p. 94.

[9] p. 53 et s.

[10] cf. however, the decision of the OGH (Austrian Supreme Court) cited below, Glaser-Unger, N.F., Vol. IV, 1903, No. 1363; cf. infra the statements in Chapter II.

[11] Hereinafter abbreviated to Herrnritt.

with the opportunity to assume a multitude of positive administrative tasks of the most diverse nature which are absolutely essential both to the security and effective operation of the foundation. From this, however, it necessarily follows that the purpose of the foundation must be of a specific nature, for the founder must encourage the State to take an active interest in his foundation by ascribing to it a purpose with which the State can appropriately associate itself. Such a purpose must transcend the interest of individual persons; it must fall within the framework of the administrative tasks of the State, for the State cannot intervene in support of any and every purpose. The State will always remain, in all its activities, the representative of the common interest of its citizens. Hence it can intervene in a positive and active manner only if the public interest requires it to do so. It goes without saying, however, that there are also certain legitimate purposes which not only have nothing to do with the public interest but whose promotion may even be detrimental to it.

'Consequently, the characteristic of being legitimate or legally acceptable is not a sufficient justification for the purpose of the foundation; only such purposes may be realised in the form of a foundation as transcend the individual interest. Such purposes, however, are described as serving the public interest. Hence, in contrast to the purpose of a corporation, the purpose of a foundation must be to benefit the community. Since the concept of what is beneficial to the community has its source in its coincidence with the tasks of the Government, it is by no means constant but subject to continuous modification and change, depending on the current conception of the role of the State. The decision, therefore, as to whether the purpose intended by the founder can be realised in the form of the foundation, as to whether the latter is acceptable, must be taken in the light of the view currently held of Government's role. A firm ruling in this connection is out of the question from the start, and the decision as to whether the establishment of a foundation is acceptable is generally left to the discretion of the competent administrative authority.'

In Mayrhofer's *Handbuch für den politischen Verwaltungsdienst*[12] it reads as follows: 'Such an activity, aimed at the permanent withdrawal of certain assets from public circulation cannot, however, be undertaken by the State in relation to every purpose desired by the founder, but only if the public is interested in it, and if the purpose is one that is beneficial to the community.'

Decisions of the *Verwaltungsgerichtshof* (*VerwGH*—Administrative Court) during the nineteenth century point in the same direction: 'The essential

---

[12] 5th. Ed., 1901, Vol. V, p. 184, hereinafter abbreviated to Mayrhofer.

characteristics of a foundation are, generally speaking, that it is by nature permanent and enduring, as well as legitimate and beneficial to the community[13]. From the provision set out in Sec.646 of the *ABGB*, it follows that the nature of a foundation generally includes the characteristic of being legitimate and beneficial to the community as well as being permanent and lasting[14].'

In a fundamental decision[15], the *Oberste Gerichtshof* (OHG—Supreme Court) has stated that the establishment of a foundation requires (1) the availability of assets destined to achieve autonomously and in a legitimate manner, a purpose that is beneficial to the community and (2) a provision of law which vests these assets with legal status. The *OHG* then continues: 'It is true that in the present case assets are available for the endowment of the projected foundation and that there is no need to issue for each particular case a provision of law which would vest such assets with legal status, as Sec.26 of the *a.b.G.B.* contains a general provision of law for corporations vesting them with legal status, and under Secs. 646, 694 and 778 of the *a.b.G.B.* such a general provision of law can be assumed to exist for foundations. Consequently, the only issue at stake is whether the purpose of the projected foundation as declared by the testator to the *Stiftungsbehörde*, i.e. the authority of the *Land* competent to approve the establishment of a foundation, appears to be acceptable. In the case under review the political authority of the *Land* has declined, in a manner leaving no room for doubt, to concern itself in any way with the projected foundation because it cannot consider the said declaration to be relevant to the establishment of a foundation within the meaning of Sec.646 of the *a.b.G.B.* This pronouncement of the political authority of the *Land* which, in accordance with the *Hofdecret* (Imperial Decree) of 7th June 1841, J.G.S. No. 541, is competent to decide on the acceptability of the projected foundation, shows that the purpose intended by the testator, namely to earmark assets and to withdraw them from free circulation, is incompatible with the conditions and regulations governing the organisation and operation of the institutions of the State. If it appears to the political authority, which is the sole power competent to examine the question of approval, that the intended purpose of the foundation is unsuitable for establishing such foundation, then the law does not vest the intended endowment with legal status, and the designation of the foundation as heir cannot be considered as valid.'

[13] Decision of the VerwGH (Administrative Court) of November 27, 1883, Z. 2719, B. 1926.
[14] Decision of the VerwGH (Administrative Court) of February 5, 1884, Z. 238, B.200 g.
[15] See Glaser-Unger, N.F., Vol. IV,1903, No.1363.

This decision is of great importance, especially because it tries to demonstrate the relationship between the benefit which the foundation promises to bring to the community and its legal status. In the opinion of the OHG the legal status of the foundation is conditional on its potential value to the community, and the administrative authority decides whether such potential is in fact present. In addition, the decision holds that the foundation does not require official bestowal of legal status, but that its legal status already derives from the *ABGB*.

So-called private family foundations (*Familienstiftungen*), i.e. foundations existing for the promotion of the interests of certain families[16], are therefore not foundations for the purposes of Sec.646 of the *ABGB*. A Proclamation by the Imperial and Royal *Statthalter* (Governor) of 14th July 1897, Z. 9495, relating to the Regulations for the formal Establishment and the profitable Investment of the Assets of the Foundation for the Purpose of such Establishment (*Stiftsbriefnormale*[17]—Regulation relating to the Charter of Foundations), expressly states that direction entitling the members of certain families to exclusively enjoy the yield of specific assets without such right being made conditional on any further qualification relating to the promotion of purposes that are beneficial to the community (so-called private family foundations) do not fall within the legal concept of the foundation and are, therefore, excluded from the jurisdiction of the government authorities competent to deal with foundations.

Nor are *politische Verordnungen* (political regulations), referred to in Sec.646 of the *ABGB*, applicable to private family trusts. Such trusts—provided they can still be established at all—are governed by other provisions[18]. According to Mayrhofer[19] these family trusts are, however, to be distinguished from those trusts which are intended to promote a specific administrative task (relief of poverty, study) within a specific family; such foundations which, because of their being confined to the members of a specific family or to the inhabitants of a certain place, are also called foundations *jure sanguinis aut loci*, are actually foundations under administrative law and are, with certain exceptions, governed by the same provisions as are the other foundations.

The *VerwGH* (Administrative Court) states with regard to such foundations[20]: 'Family trusts (in this sense) can already not be judged exclusively from the angle of civil law because in that case, they would have to be considered

---

[16] Mayrhofer, p. 185.

[17] Gesetz- und Verordnungsblatt für die gefürstete Grafschaft Tirol und das Land Vorarlberg No.28/1897 (Official Gazette for Tirol and Vorarlberg).

[18] See Sec. 849 of the ABGB. [19] p. 185.

[20] Decision of the VerwGH (Administrative Court) 10th November 1877, Z.1485, B.150.

substitutes for entailed estates Sec.608 *ABGB*, which are barred by Secs. 612 and 652 of the same act. Just as a family entail can be established only with the special approval of the legislative power Sec.627 of the *ABGB*, a foundation can exist only if it has been declared admissible and acceptable by the political authority and established with its approval[21].' 'A foundation is in no way less subject to the political provisions existing for foundations, merely by virtue of its being family trust—Sec.646 of the *ABGB* refers to foundations in general without making any exceptions in favour of family trusts.'

However, the question as to whether such family trust would be recognised today as beneficial to the community is problematical, and would probably have to be answered in the negative.

It does not seem to be excluded as a possibility that, through the provisions of Sec.34 et ss. of the *Bundesabgabenordnung (BAO)* (Federal Revenue Code)[22], the concept of benefit to the community has been determined as a legal concept not only for the field of revenue law but also for the whole legal system of Austria—at least—for its federal sector. Now, under Sec.35 para.1 of the *BAO* only such purposes are deemed beneficial whose realisation promotes the public good, and under Sec.36 of the same Act a group of persons cannot be considered the general public, if it is defined by closer ties such as membership of a family. In spite of this the authority competent for dealing with foundations recently approved a foundation called 'Islamic Centre' whose intended beneficiaries are primarily persons of the Mohammedan faith. In view of Sec.34 et ss. of the *BAO*, it is therefore not surprising that a special Federal Act[23] was passed for the purpose of exempting donations to this particular foundation from the donation tax. For the tax lawmakers obviously considered that this foundation did meet the requirements of being beneficial to the community as laid down in Sec.15 para.1 No.14 of the *Erbschafts- und Schenkungsgesetz* (Act relating to the Death Duty and Gift Tax)[24] and by the *BAO* (Federal Revenue Act).

Although the scope of this concept is by no means rigidly defined, benefit to the community is an essential characteristic of Austrian concept of the foundation. The contemporary literature supports this. Antoniolli[25] accordingly defines the foundation as assets vested with legal status which permanently serve purposes beneficial to the community. Adamovich[26]

[21] Decision of the VerwGH of 11th May 1895, B. 8656.
[22] BGBl. (Federal Law Gazette) No.194/961.
[23] Federal Act of 6th March 1968, under which donations to the foundation 'Islamic Centre' are exempt from the gift tax, BGBl. No.11/1968.
[24] BGBl. No.141/1955, new wording in BGBl. No. 15/1968.
[25] p. 139.   [26] p. 53.

considers the foundation a special-purpose fund having its own legal status, which by a declaration of intent on the founder's part has been permanently devoted to specific purposes which are beneficial to the community. Ehrenzweig[27] points out that the purpose of the foundation must be a religious one or one beneficial to the community; Klang[28] too stresses the requirement of being beneficial to the community.

4. The perpetuity of the foundation

The characteristic of perpetuity in the concept of the foundation is stressed in particular in the literature on civil law. Ehrenzweig[29] considers the perpetual purpose of the foundation to be the characteristic distinguishing it from a collecting charity (*Sammelvermögen*) which raises funds by means of a public collection by one or more persons (a committee) for a temporary, non-profit purpose, and Geschnitzer[30] emphasises that it is essential for the foundation that its purpose is not merely a temporary, but an enduring one. Even Antoniolli[31] and Adamovich[32], in their manuals on administrative law, have included the characteristic of perpetuity in their concept of the foundation.

Another view, however, is held by Herrnritt[33] who considers that those definitions of the foundation which include the characteristic of perpetuity are going too far. He writes verbatim 'Quite apart from the fact that the foundation, even if it rests on an extremely secure basis, must ultimately share the fate of everything that is human—either because its assets pass into some other fund or because they are absorbed into the general national income—there is no denying that even a foundation life that is *a priori* of limited duration is compatible with the concept of the foundation. For even the assured fulfilment of a temporary purpose may depend on organisation as a foundation. Here, again one can imagine various possibilities: the date of dissolution of the foundation may either be fixed by the founder, or else be dictated by the nature of the purpose itself; in the latter case it may depend either on the occurrence of a specific event, or the purpose of the foundation may draw on the foundation's own capital and cause it to be gradually consumed.'

However, as the aforementioned theories indicate, Herrnritt's opinion has not prevailed.

II. TYPES OF FOUNDATIONS

Herrnritt[34] divides foundations into
(a) secular and purely ecclesiastical foundations

[27] p. 200.   [28] p. 476.   [29] p. 201.
[30] p. 105.   [31] p. 139.   [32] p. 53.
[33] p. 51.   [34] p. 52.

(b) poor relief, educational, military or other foundations designated according to their purposes

(c) operational foundations and foundations employing only the revenue derived from their assets.

Moreover, in the German literature, a distinction is made between foundations under public law and foundations under civil law.[35] Has such a distinction also validity for the Austrian system of law? According to Wolff[36] a foundation under civil law comprises assets which have become independent from an organisational point of view and owe their individuality as a legal entity to the private autonomy (of a donor), the Act of State (i.e. entry in a register) recognising this fact not being the reason for but only the condition for the effectiveness of the legal status.

A foundation under public law, however, comprises assets having become independent from an organisational point of view which owe their individuality as a legal entity not to the private autonomy but to a law or an Act of State based on a law which is then not merely the condition for the effectiveness of, but the reason for, the legal status. The reason for the legal status thus constitutes the criterion for classification.

If one takes this distinction as a basis the question arises whether under Austrian law the foundation based on a private act 'owes to private autonomy its individuality as a legal entity'. The answer depends on whether in Austrian law there can be found a rule of civil law which may be considered the 'source' of the legal status. The OGH (Supreme Court) in its already cited decision[37] holds Secs.646, 694 and 778 of the ABGB to be a general rule of law conferring legal status on foundations.

This legal opinion, however, cannot be concurred with unquestioningly. The cited provisions of the ABGB cannot, as the OGH believes, be compared with Sec.26 of the ABGB from which such general rule of law with respect to corporations can clearly be deduced. Sec.646 of the ABGB merely defines foundations as compared with entailed estates and substitutions for entailed estates, while there is nothing at all in Secs.694 and 778 that would suggest a provision conferring legal status. By referring to 'political regulations' (regulations to be promulgated by the Länder), Sec.646 of the ABGB seems to leave it to public law to resolve the question of the legal status of foundations[38].

---

[35] e.g. W. Jellinek, *Verwaltungsrecht*, 3rd. Ed., 1931, pp. 176 and 178; H. J. Wolff, *Verwaltungsrecht I*, 6th. Ed. 1965, p.188 et s.

[36] p. 188.   [37] See p. 5.

[38] A different approach is, of course, to be found in the German Civil Code (BGB) which not only contains detailed provisions in regard to foundation in Sec. 80 et ss.,

Herrnritt[39], after making a thorough study and putting forward detailed arguments, also comes to the conclusion that the legal status of the foundation is based on the act of recognition by the administrative authority.[40] Hence, with regard to the question raised above, it follows that the foundation which can be traced back to a private act does not owe its legal status to private autonomy, but that it is also a foundation under public law in the sense stated by H. J. Wolff, and that a distinction between foundations under public law and foundations under civil law according to Wolff's criterion for the definition of foundations cannot be obtained for Austrian law.

Nor can Gschnitzer's distinction[41] between legal entities under public law and legal entities under civil law, according to which the latter are based on a private charter—on a private founding act—while the former may originate by law or through an administrative act, or be recognised by such act, serve as a suitable starting point for a distinction between foundations under public law and foundations under civil law. For, as has just been shown, a foundation 'based' on a private act indeed comes into being through an administrative act.

According to Antoniolli's concept of the legal entity under public law[42], a foundation would come under public law if it were vested with sovereign powers, if it performed tasks within the framework of public administration, and if its existence were compulsory. However, it is not difficult to prove that the two last-mentioned characteristics also apply in Austria to a foundation based on a private act. As already mentioned above[43], it was stressed in the older literature that the Austrian foundation 'is an incumbent of a specific administrative function'[44], that it performs tasks relating to public administration. Compulsory existence is also referred to, since only the State can invalidate a foundation once it has been established. True, the foundations are generally not vested with sovereign powers, yet this fact would not prevent the federal lawmakers or the lawmakers of the *Länder* from vesting them with such powers. The potential capacity of the foundation to hold sovereign powers, however, seems to be sufficient for Antoniolli as well as for Adamovich to classify it exclusively among the legal entities coming within the scope of public law.

III. THE ESTABLISHMENT OF THE FOUNDATION

The private act on which the foundation is based is a unilateral act *inter vivos* but in addition, by explicit reference to foundations under public law in Sec. 89, qualifies those which it regulates as foundations under civil law.

[39] p. 119 et ss.   [40] p. 128.   [41] p. 96.
[42] p. 136.   [43] pp. 3, 4.   [44] Herrnritt, p. 3 et s.

or *mortis causa*. The founding act or the declaration of intent *inter vivos* is a legal act not requiring any specific form[45]. The preparation of the charter, i.e. of the rules and regulations of the foundation, is not considered part of the founding act as such. During the monarchy this was the subject of numerous provisions issued by the *Länder*[46]. As regards the founding declaration *mortis causa*, the provisions of the law of succession issued for such legal acts must be complied with.

The question whether approval of the foundation by the administrative authority is a discretionary or a mandatory act is subject to dispute in the relevant literature. Gschnitzer[47] maintains that the administrative authority must approve the foundation if the legal requirements have been met, i.e. if the purpose of the foundation is legitimate and the means for its continuous operation have been secured. The same opinion is held by Klang[48]. The relevant passage reads: 'If the political authority has determined that the legal requirements for a foundation have been met, according to the prescriptions of the testator, it must approve such foundation. Nowhere there is to be found any power of the authority to refuse approval by pleading its discretion, which frequently conceals political interests, i.e. interests that are outside the law.'

Ehrenzweig[49] on the other hand, referring to the *Hofkanzleidekret* of 7th June 1841, talks of a discretionary act, and so do Adamovich[50] and Mayrhofer.[51] During the time of the monarchy, the *HVerwGH* (Administrative Court) also, assumed that the authorities had discretionary power[52].

It seems, however, that formerly the approval of the foundation by the authorities was considered a discretionary act because, as Mayrhofer[53] writes, 'only such foundations appear to be acceptable as are beneficial to the community, but benefit to the community is a concept which changes in accordance with the current view held by the State concerning its tasks'.

Hence the decision on the acceptability of foundations had to be left to the discretion of the authority competent in matters regarding foundations. A legal concept as vague as that of benefit to the community does not, accord-

[45] Gschnitzer, p. 105; Klang, p. 473; also Herrnritt, p. 133.
[46] See examples enumerated by Herrnritt, p. 147, note 1 and Sec. 34 and the Stiftbriefnormale (Regulation relating to the Charter of Foundations) for Tirol and Vorarlberg of 1897.
[47] p. 106.   [48] p. 474.
[49] p. 210.   [50] p. 53.
[51] p. 191.
[52] Cf. Decisions of the VerwGH (Administrative Court) of 2nd May 1894, Z 1729, B 7879 and of 28th January, 1897, Z 556, B 10328.
[53] p. 191.

ing to current opinion, leave any room for discretion. Hence discretion cannot be inferred merely from the concept of benefit to the community.

IV. THE SUPERVISING AUTHORITIES

The *Hofkanzleidekret* of 1841, already mentioned in the previous section and which even today is still considered a valid source of the law relating to foundations[54], is worded as follows: 'The decision on the acceptability of a projected foundation, on its modification or dissolution, on the investment and the administration of its assets, and further the obligation to ensure that the political authority and those benefiting from the foundation, shall comply with their duties, rest with the administrative authorities; in the case of ecclesiastical foundations, with the administrative authorities in co-operation with the *Ordinariat* (supreme administrative authority of the respective bishopric). The civil judge, on the other hand, shall intervene if the person who, as founder or on the founder's behalf, is obliged to fund the foundation, or pay out the proceeds of the foundation, must be compelled to comply with obligations which he has failed or even expressly refused to fulfil.

Furthermore, he shall also intervene if, because of non-compliance or incomplete compliance with the instructions of the founder, someone seeks to secure any rights to the assets of the foundation, or if, on the basis of some civil claim, the surrender of assets dedicated to a foundation is demanded. However, as regards the question as to whether the prescriptions of the founder have been complied with, the civil judge shall be satisfied with confirmation by the political authorities initially entrusted with the supervision of the foundation. The person considering himself to be put at a disadvantage by such confirmation may appeal against it to the higher political authorities. Disputes, however, on the question as to whether someone is entitled to the enjoyment of a foundation or to be barred therefrom, and, further, as to the terms under which such usufruct may be granted, shall be decided by the civil judge only if such disputes arise from a civil claim, or if it is important to obtain evidence for judicial proceedings.'

Which administrative authorities, however, are competent in matters regarding foundations, in addition to the 'civil judge'? With regard to this question, Adamovich[55] states quite rightly that the exercise of executive powers regarding those foundations which, under Art.10 para.1 No.13 of the *B-VG* (Federal Constitution), come within the competence of the Federal Government rests in the first instance with the *Landeshauptmann* (Prime

---

[54] Klang, p. 473; Gschnitzer, p. 105 et ss.; Ehrenzweig, p. 210.
[55] p. 54.

Minister of a *Land*) and, in the second instance, generally with the Federal Minister of the Interior (in the case of educational foundations, however, with the Federal Minister of Education), whereas in the case of those foundations which come within the competence of the *Länder* the exercise of such powers rests exclusively with the government of the respective *Land*. Hence, Klang is incorrect in mentioning the government of the *Länder* as authorities competent in matters regarding foundations.

He apparently disregards the fact that the system of foundations in Austria is divided in accordance with the distribution of competences between the Federal Government and the *Länder*. Under Art.10 para.1 No.13 of the *B-VG* (Federal Constitution) the Federal Government is competent to deal only with those foundations whose purposes go beyond the range of interests of a particular *Land* and which were not previously (before 1st October 1925) autonomously administered by the *Länder*.

Which are the purposes of the foundation which go beyond the range of interests of a particular *Land*? The distribution of competences laid down in the *B-VG* (Federal Constitution) offers a legally comprehensible and sensible guideline for answering this question[56]. For every distribution of competences is at the same time a distribution of interests. Hence the Federal Government would be competent in regard to those foundations, whose purposes relate to the matters referred to in Arts.10 and 14 of the *B-VG*. With regard to all other foundations, the competence rests with the *Länder*[57]. Thus, the administrative competence of the Federal Government in the field of education (scholarship or research foundations) is provided for in Art.14 of the *B-VG*, that of the *Länder* in the field of relief of poverty (almshouses, orphanage foundations) in Art.12. para. 1 No 2.

V. INSTITUTIONS RESEMBLING FOUNDATIONS

The first type of organisation that presents itself for attaining purposes similar to those followed by foundations is the *ideeller Verein* (non-profit association) to which the provisions of the *Vereinsgesetz* (Act relating to Associations) of 1951[58] apply. One can safely say that in Austrian practice the association pursuing purposes beneficial to the community has completely superseded the foundation as an organisational form. The extensive latitude which Austrian law allows to the associations (the State barely interferes with

---

[56] Arts. 10–15.
[57] See on this point Decision of the VerfGH (Constitutional Court). Slg. No. 2668/1954 and 3685/1960.
[58] BGBl. (Federal Law Gazette) No. 233/1951, new wording in BGBl. No.102/1962.

associations, whereas foundations have at all times been subject to rigid controls) is probably the most important reason for this fact[59].

Other institutions resembling foundations are funds with their own legal status which play an important role especially in the field of commerce and industry, e.g. as benevolent funds for salaried employees. The legal basis of such funds comprises very few provisions[60]; there is a complete lack in Austria of provisions of substantive law regulating such funds.

As far as those institutions which resemble foundations but which have no legal status are concerned, the following statements in Klang[61] concerning the endowments without legal personality (*unselbständige Stiftung*) are applicable: 'Where such an endowment is involved, the founding act may be so effected that the assets of the foundation are allocated to a third party as trustee together with an obligation comparable to the purpose of a foundation (Sec.709 et ss. of the *ABGB*). In this case the allocation becomes part of the assets of the trustee, but is tied to the purpose of the trust. However, there is another kind of allocation conceivable, namely one which is effected in such a way that the assets of the foundation are assigned to a person who is obliged only in a personal capacity (under the law of contract) to administer the same, accounting for them separately.

The foundation will then be a separate fund distinct from the other assets of the trustee. This fund is out of the reach of his private creditors and may not be estranged from its purpose either in such manner or by inclusion in the trustee's estate in the case of bankruptcy. There exists a right of separation with regard to these assets, because they are assets not belonging to the bankrupt[62]. On the other hand, if there is no guilt on his part, the trustee's liability for debts for the foundation is limited to the amount of the separate fund.'

VI. THE FISCAL TREATMENT OF FOUNDATIONS

Foundations are generally subject to unlimited tax liability. Their income is

[59] An important example of an association with a purpose resembling that of a foundation which may be cited here, is the Internationale Stiftung Mozarteum in Salzburg. Its function is to ensure the preservation of the Mozart memorials and their appurtenances, to promote research in relation to Mozart's life and work and to encourage the performance and enjoyment of the latter.

[60] For instance, Art. 24 of the Verwaltungsentlastungsgesetz (Act relating to Relief of the Administration), BGBl. 277/1925.

[61] p. 475.

[62] See Sec. 11 of the Konkursordnung (Bankruptcy Act).

subject to corporation tax[63]. They have to pay property tax on their assets. If they run a business they are liable to business tax[64]. Gratuitous contributions *inter vivos* or *mortis causa* are subject to gift tax or death duty[65]. For real estate land tax is payable.

Foundations which exclusively serve purposes beneficial to the community, or charitable or ecclesiastical purposes, are exempt from practically all taxes, or at least obtain considerable tax benefits. What this means in detail is specified in Sec.34 et ss. of the BAO (Federal Revenue Code). Purposes beneficial to the community are those whose fulfilment promotes the spiritual, cultural, moral or material well-being of the community.[66] This means in particular the promotion of the arts and sciences, of public health, of child and juvenile welfare and the care of the aged and sick, of education and teaching in all fields as well as the support of cultural institutions. In this connection the range of persons assisted must not be too small[67].

Charitable (*gemeinnützig*) purposes are those which are aimed at assisting persons in need[68]. Finally, ecclesiastical purposes are involved when legally recognised churches and religious communities are promoted[69]. The *BAO* deals in great detail with the question of exclusiveness. It presupposes that no other purposes than the privileged ones are followed, that no profit is aimed at, that no person employed by the foundation will receive unduly high remuneration for his services, and that in the event of the dissolution of the foundation the remaining funds will be applied to the said privileged purposes[70].

The tax privileges are granted only if the foundation meets the requirements described above both as regards its charter and the actual conduct of its affairs[71]. In the latter respect the operation of an industrial or of a commercial enterprise is always prejudicial. If a commercial enterprise is the means for achieving the privileged purposes the foundation is liable for taxation only with regard to such enterprise[72]. There is no tax liability if the operational scope of the enterprise is deemed to be essential to the achievement of these privileged purposes[73].

[63] See Sec. 1 para. 1 No. 5 of the Körperschaftsteuergesetz (Corporation Tax Act).
[64] See Sec. 1 paras 1, 4 of the Gewerbesteuergesetz (Business Tax Act).
[65] See Sec. 2 para. 2 No. 1, Sec. 3 para 1 No. 7 of the Erbschaft- und Schenkungsteuergesetz (Act relating to the Death Duty and the Gift Tax).
[66] Sec. 35 paras 1, 2 of the BAO (Federal Revenue Code).
[67] As for instance membership in a family or a family group, an association (Verein), Sec. 36 of the BAO.
[68] Sec. 37 of the BAO.   [69] Sec. 38 of the BAO.
[70] Sec. 39 of the BAO.   [71] Secs 41, 42 of the BAO.
[72] Sec. 45 para. 1 of the BAO.   [73] Sec. 45 para. 2 of the BAO.

If the requirements of Sec.34 et ss. of the BAO have been met, the tax liability ceases completely under most of the tax laws[74]. Nor will the gift tax be levied in the case of contributions *inter vivos* if goods and chattels or pecuniary claims are involved[75]. Other contributions *inter vivos* or *mortis causa* are subject to a tax of 5%[76], irrespective of their amount; if real estate is involved the tax will be increased by another 2%, apparently to compensate for the exemption from the transfer tax[77].

Contrary to other countries, the Austrian tax law grants no privilege to anybody establishing a foundation beneficial to the community, or to charitable or ecclesiastical foundations, or to anybody making a contribution to such foundation from his property. It excludes the possibility of a deduction from the taxable income[78]. This regulation is likely to thwart many initiatives for establishing foundations.

VII. THE IMPORTANCE OF FOUNDATIONS

To give an opinion on the present importance of the foundation in Austria is fraught with considerable difficulties. It is impossible to give any estimates concerning the number of Austrian foundations or their nature or size which can be guaranteed to be even approximately exact or reliable. There is no central register in which each duly approved foundation would have to be entered, and even the various ratifying and supervisory authorities of the Federal Government and the *Länder* apparently have no official lists of the foundations falling within the scope of their respective competences, hence, all that is possible is to make cautious estimates based on information supplied by the authorities.

It is certain, however, that the foundation in Austria is of little importance today when compared with foundations in other countries—for instance in Switzerland or Germany. Such a comparison, however, would not always have yielded so disproportionate a picture. For up to the end of the First World War there existed a multitude of, in particular, small or medium-

---

[74] Cf. Sec. 4 para. 1 No. 6 of the Körperschaftsteuergesetz (Corporation Tax Act), Sec. 3 para. 1 No. 7 of the Vermögensteuergesetz (Property Tax Act), Sec. 2 No. 6 of the Gewerbesteuergesetz (Business Tax Act), Sec. 2 No. 3 lit. b of the Grundsteuergesetz (Land Tax Act).

[75] Sec. 15 para. 1 No. 14 of the Erbschaft- und Schenkungsteuergesetz (Act relating to the Death Duty and the Gift Tax).

[76] Sec. 8 para. 3 of the Erbschaft- und Schenkungsteuergesetz.

[77] Sec. 8 para. 4 of the Erbschaft- und Schenkungsteuergesetz.

[78] Sec. 16 No. 4 of the Körperschaftsteuergesetz; Sec. 4 para. 4 No. 16, Sec. 10 of the Einkommensteuergesetz (Income Tax Act).

sized foundations. The purpose of most of them was to give aid to poor and needy persons as well as to grant scholarships. It seems that at that time a considerable number of pupils and students were assisted in this way. Soon after the end of the war, however, the foundations experienced their first great decline. Most of the foundations whose means consisted mainly of liquid assets or securities became victims of the general economic crisis and of the financial collapse. The majority of those that survived did so because they also, or primarily, owned real estate.

Another extremely critical point was reached during the years following the incorporation of Austria in the German Reich. In accordance with the Law of 14th May 1938[79], all foundations which on 13th March 1938, were domiciled in Austria (except the ecclesiastical foundations) were dealt with by the so-called *Stillhaltekommissar* (Controller) for *Vereine* (associations), organisations and federations, or on his recommendation to this effect, by the Ministry of Internal and Cultural Affairs. As a result of the process foundations were either kept alive and only the charters changed in accordance with the wishes and dictates of the national-socialist authorities or else—and this happened in the majority of the cases—they were dissolved. The assets of the dissolved foundations were either confiscated in favour of the *Stillhalte-kommissar* or allocated to another legal entity (a local authority, a corporation, an institution or even a foundation with the same or a similar purpose that had been maintained).

Thus at the end of the Second World War the lowest ebb had been reached, for not many foundations had survived the national-socialist era. Soon after, however, the so-called *Rückstellungsgesetze* (restitution laws) were passed, under which, among other things, those foundations that had suffered damage could submit a claim for restitution of the assets of which they had been deprived. The proceedings in relation to the restitution cases were as a rule both late in getting under way and in being terminated—in the territories under Russian occupation not until the signing of the State Treaty in 1955. The recovery of former assets of the foundations was then rendered possible by the fact that all alienation transactions effected during the occupation under political pressure were nullified by law. During the mid-fifties the Federal Government and the *Länder* subsequently issued the so-called *Stiftungs Reorganisationsgesetze* (Acts relating to the Reorganisation of Foundations) under which many of the foundations eliminated after 1938 were reconstituted.

Leaving these events aside an upward trend has manifested itself since 1945, characterised by the establishment of a number of new foundations. That the

[79] GBl. f.d.Land Österreich, No. 136 (Official Gazette for Austria).

idea of the foundation has, in the meantime, even gained a certain popularity is certainly due in large measure to the names borne by some of the newly established foundations which have attracted the attention of the public and thus achieved a kind of publicity effect (e.g. the Theodor Körner Foundation, the Dr. Karl Renner Foundation and the Cardinal Innitzer Foundation).

When talking of Austrian foundations reference can also appropriately be made to a large number of funds. These are institutions which have practically all the essential characteristics of a foundation without being theoretically defined by the law and without being clearly distinguishable from the foundation. In practice, the licensing and supervisory authorities on which they depend, in the same way as the foundations, have sometimes held the view that a foundation is established for all time, while the life of a fund is limited from the outset. The validity of this view cannot, however, be proved; when one considers their stated purposes, one finds that the life of most funds is no more or less limited than that of the majority of foundations. Thus as far as assets that have been rendered legally independent are concerned, the funds, too, are, in essence, genuine foundations.

As already mentioned, statistical data on the foundations in Austria are not available. With a great deal of caution, however, estimates can be made of the number of foundations, albeit not of the assets available to them for their purposes, since not even the vaguest indications exist in this connection. It seems that nobody has so far given serious attention to this matter.

The Austrian Ministry of the Interior today supervises 130 foundations and funds, the funds constituting more than one-half of this number. Approximately 25 foundations and funds are supervised by the Ministry of Education. The competent government agency of the *Land* of Lower Austria estimates that in this largest Austrian federal state there are perhaps 80 to 100 foundations under its tutelage. If one assumes that the other eight *Länder* supervise, on an average, 50 foundations and funds each, we arrive at a total number of approximately 660.

The vast majority of the Austrian foundations serve charitable purposes. Some of them have conventional purposes[80], others again quite individual and unusual ones[81].

A large number of foundations serve educational purposes, in particular

[80] Operation of hospitals, asylums for the blind and homes for children, support of the poor and the needy, of widows and orphans.

[81] e.g. the Reinhold and Anna Rostock Foundation for young farmers designed to improve the economic situation of farmers' living in the mountains; the Duke of Savoy Foundation for Ladies of Rank designed to maintain unmarried ladies of noble birth in circumstances consistent with their station; the Haas von Langenfeld Foundation designed to procure dowries for girls marrying sons of farmers.

nearly all those which come under the supervision of the Ministry of Education. Examples which may be cited are the *Julius Raab-Stiftung zur Schulung von Wirtschaftstreibenden* (Julius Raab Foundation for the Education of Tradesmen), the Scholarship Foundation of the Theresianum which was established about ten years ago by former students of that academy, as well as the Count Hardegg Foundation, a foundation assisting students writing a doctor's thesis, which receives approximately S.1.5 million a year from forestry estates in Lower Austria; however, more than two-thirds of this income still goes to the Federal Government which apparently has made further funds available to the foundation for additions to its estates.

Among the foundations for educational purposes there are some which, in view of the specific tasks they have set themselves, may simultaneously be considered as foundations for the promotion of science and research, such as the Dr. Adolf Schärf-Fonds which, by granting scholarships, seeks especially to serve the interests of science. Foundations having a scientific or research programme of their own set up by the founder are, however, relatively rare[82].

It is noteworthy that there are also in Austria a number of funds whose purpose is staff welfare[83]. However, it is also impossible in this case to make any statements as regards the nature and the assets of these institutions. Finally, ecclesiastical foundations are widespread in Austria. The best known among them is the Cardinal Innitzer Foundation to which reference has already been made.

Family trusts play practically no significant role in Austria, at least not today, since they lack the characteristic of being beneficial to the community so that, in accordance with present-day practice, the authorities withhold their approval. Exceptions are only made where specific family purposes are pursued in conjunction with other purposes that are beneficial to the community[84].

Only a modest part is played in Austrian foundation practice by the so-called *Stiftungsunternehmen* (enterprises constituted in the form of a foundation). The idea of combining an industrial enterprise with the legal form of the foundation has, as far as we know, only been realised in one case, that of

---

[82] By way of example we would cite a foundation under the supervision of the Federal Ministry of the Interior whose purpose is research in relation to incurable diseases.

[83] e.g. the pension fund for workers and salaried employees of the Schoeller-Bleckmann Stahlwerke AG which is under the supervision of the Federal Ministry of the Interior.

[84] e.g. the Scheidl-Schüller Foundation of Johann Scheidl and Katharina Scheidl-Schüller intended to assist those relatives of the founders who are still alive as well as to support the relief of poverty in Donnerskirchen in the Burgenland and Waidhofen on Thaya.

the Carl Huber Foundation in Vienna. In 1941 its founder, Carl Huber, transformed his enterprise, manufacturing good quality vinegars, liqueurs and fruit juices, into a foundation along the lines of the German Carl Zeiss Foundation. In doing so, however, he initially encountered considerable difficulties with the authorities of that time, since the idea of continuing an enterprise as a foundation was new in Austria and such a move was at first suspect as being communist inspired. Again, after the war this and other such enterprises which were eventually granted official recognition by the national-socialist regime, ran the risk of being nationalised as so-called national-socialist enterprises and had great difficulty in escaping this fate.

The purposes of such foundations are to secure the continuation of the enterprise, the advancement of its workers and salaried employees through payments over and above the normal salary rates, as well as the granting of scholarships to students at the University of Vienna.

Furthermore, it appears that the requirement of benefit to the community and, in particular, the fear of government supervision, have so far constituted an obstacle to the establishment of similar foundations. It is true that there is an important foundation in Steiermark which, out of the income derived from 110 ha (approximately 272 acres) of forest land belonging to a large forestry enterprise, assists the latter's workers and salaried employees by granting housing loans on favourable terms[85]. Such an institution, however, cannot be considered a genuine *Unternehmensstiftung*.

To sum up, it can be stated that foundations in Austria have gained in importance and that a certain upward trend is noticeable. It appears, however, that there are frequently not sufficient means available to put into practical effect the idea of establishing a foundation. That is why of late foundations have often only been approved subject to the condition that they first allow their assets to accumulate up to a certain specified amount before becoming operational. On the other hand, there are no doubt a number of assets which could reasonably be made available for the establishment of new foundations. However, the State would first have to intervene actively by carrying out a comprehensive reform of the extremely complicated and, for the most part, outdated law relating to foundations.

[85] Adolph Prince of Schwarzenberg Housing Foundation at Murau, Steiermark.

LITERATURE

Adamovich. Handbuch des österreichischen Verwaltungsrecht 5th Ed., Vol. II, p. 53 et ss.
Antoniolli. Allgemeines Verwaltungsrecht, 1954, p. 139.
Ehrenzweig. System des österreichischen allgemeinen Privatrechts, 1951, page 199 et ss.
Gschnitzer. Allgemeiner Teil des bürgerlichen Rechts, 1966, p. 105 et ss.
Herrnritt. Das österreichische Stiftungsrecht, Vienna 1896.
Itzinger. Reform des Stiftungsrechts, ÖVB. 1934, p. 55 et ss.
Klang. Kommentar zum Allgemeinen bürgerlichen Gesetzbuch, 2nd. Ed., Vol. III, Vienna 1952, p. 471 et ss.
Mischler-Ulbrich. Stiftungen, in: Österreichisches Staatswörterbuch, 2nd. Ed., Vol. IV, Vienna 1909, p. 484 et ss.
Reeger-Stoll. Kommentar zur Bundesabgabenordnung, Vienna 1966, p. 174 et ss.
Das Stiftungswesen. in: Ernst Mayrhofer's Handbuch für den politischen Verwaltungsdienst, Vol. V, Vienna 1901, p. 184 et ss.
Stiftungen. in: Österreichisches Rechts-Lexikon, Vol. IV, Prague 1898, p. 451 et ss.

OTHER DATA

Authorities competent in matters regarding foundations

Federal Ministry of the Interior

Section IV—Head: SektChef Dr. Willibald Liehr
Department 36 (Vienna 16, Herbststraße 57)
MinRat Dr. Johann Fischer
MinSekr. Otto Stammer

Federal Ministry of Education

Präsidial- und Rechtssektion—Head: SektChef Dr. Leo Kövesi
Schuladministrative Abteilung
Matters of the Department relating to foundations and funds:
Supervision of the Theresianum (Theresian Academy)
MinRat Dr. Josef Bousek
SektRat Felix Hosch-Merkl

Federal Ministry of Defence

Section I—Head: SektChef Dr. Lothar Steiner
Legal Group—Head: MinRat Dr. Oskar Zlamala
Legal Department A
Legal matters relating to military foundations, institutions and funds
MinRat Dr. Franz Sailer
SektRat Dr. Josef Zimmerl
MinKmsr Dr. Peter Lausch
Kmsr Dr. Hans Penkler

Offices of the Governments of the Länder (States)

Burgenland   Amt der Burgenländischen Landesregierung
                  Landhaus
                  A 7010 Eisenstadt
Kärnten   Amt der Kärntner Landesregierung
                  Arnulfplatz 1
                  A 9010 Klagenfurt
Niederösterreich Amt der Niederösterreichischen Landesregierung
                  Herrengasse 9
                  A 1010 Vienna
Oberösterreich   Amt der Oberösterreichischen Landesregierung
                  Klosterstr. 7
                  A4010 Linz
Salzburg   Amt der Salzburger Landesregierung
                  Chiemseehof
                  A 5010 Salzburg
Steiermark   Amt der Steiermärkischen Landesregierung
                  Hofgasse
                  A 8010 Graz
Tirol   Amt der Tiroler Landesregierung
                  Landhaus, Maria Theresienstr. 43
                  A 6010 Innsbruck
Vorarlberg   Amt der Vorarlberger Landesregierung
                  Montfortstr. 4 und 12
                  A 6900 Bregenz
Wien   Magistrat der Stadt Wien
                  Friedrich Schwidt—Platz 5
                  1010 Vienna

Belgium[*]

Pierre Ansiaux and Francis Allard

A. Definition

A foundation is an endowment made available and earmarked in accordance with the wishes of the donor, or founder, for a specified purpose of general benefit to the community and vested with the status of a juristic person in order that it may pursue its prescribed objectives (De Page, Vol. I—Droit Civil 1939, No. 528, p. 591).

Foundations have only enjoyed legal recognition in Belgium since the law of 27th June 1921, was promulgated. Chap. II, Secs 27 to 43 of this law deals with foundations, and designates them as non-profit bodies serving the public interest—'*etablissements d'utilité publique*' (De Page, Vol. I, 1939, No. 528, p. 591).

The '*établissement d'utilité publique*' (EUP) is a private foundation of general interest to the community set up by a private individual. The creation of a foundation can thus be defined as the act whereby a private person earmarks all or part of his property for the establishment of a private institution of benefit to the community which is endowed with the status of a legal person (Buttgenbach No. 319, p. 283).

B. Characteristics of 'Etablissements d'utilité publique' (Foundations)

A foundation is essentially the expression of the will of an individual which remains in force even after the latter's decease and serves as the fundament or base for a juristic person (R.P.D.B. No. 25).

It is this will which calls the foundation into being and is perpetuated within the framework of the approved statutes (R.P.D.B. No. 23). Just as an

[*] Translated from the French.

'*association sans but lucratif*' (A.S.B.L.), i.e. a non-profit making association falling under civil law, is created by the will of its members, a foundation is the embodiment of the creative will of a single person acting on his own behalf and beyond the bounds of any contractual agreement (R.P.D.B. No. 23; Travaux préparatoires, Pas. 1921, p. 389).

A non-profit association is a group of persons whereas a foundation is set up by one person whose explicit will constitutes the foundation charter with whose execution the competent bodies, i.e. the administrators or trustees, are entrusted and which they must respect (Buttgenbach 1959, No. 320, p. 283).

A foundation is a private undertaking created by a private person. This is what distinguishes it from an '*établissement public*' which is created by the Government and is therefore a public facility.

This also explains why the State disposes of far more extensive rights of intervention *vis-à-vis* the latter than *vis-à-vis* the former.

I. PRIVATE UNDERTAKINGS SERVING THE PUBLIC INTEREST—THE CONCEPT AND ITS HISTORICAL DEVELOPMENT

1. *General observations*

In Belgium, there is a profusion of charitable and benevolent bodies, associations and foundations pursuing philanthropic, scientific, cultural and artistic purposes created by private persons for the common weal.

Founded, managed and administered as they are by private individuals, they are not of governmental origin nor placed under the supreme control of the State nor governed by the same legal system as applies to public services. They form part of the private sector of society (Buttgenbach No. 302, p. 268).

2. *Historical development*

It is impossible to grasp the significance and importance of the law of 27th June 1921 on associations and foundations unless one views it within the whole context of jurisdiction affecting associations and private foundations, of which the said law was the culmination, and unless one briefly outlines the historical evolution of the status of charitable organisations and of their legal personality from their origins in Roman law until the present day (Buttgenbach 1959, No. 303, p. 269).

The history of the legal status of associations and foundations revolves around two questions of decisive importance:

(1) Are private persons freely entitled to establish such undertakings?

(2) If so, should they be vested with legal personality? (Buttgenbach 1959, No. 303, p. 269).

Roman law acknowledged the existence of associations and charitable foundations, which were run exclusively by the Church—the only institution in a pagan world to take any interest in poor relief. Such organisations could only be founded if the public authorities granted them permission; but once such authorisation was given they automatically possessed legal personality under civil law and were not obliged to secure any special concession or licence from the State. Indeed, the Romans could not imagine an association that did not have an endowment of its own and they viewed legal personality as a natural concomitant of the association, forming an integral part of its very existence (Buttgenbach No. 303, p. 269).

This concept was taken over by mediæval lawmakers both in Belgium and France. However, the influence engendered by a number of factors such as the Church's monopoly of public relief and assistance, the abuse inherent in the possession of such a monopoly, the proliferation of ecclesiastic foundations and the disadvantages of the system of mortmain, gradually brought about a change both in terms of circumstances and of attitudes.

In the first place the monarchy started to compete with the Church by setting up 'royal foundations'. This led to significant changes both in attitudes and in legislation because the monarchy began to adopt an increasingly restrictive approach in regard to granting the necessary authorisation for setting up an association or foundation. In this way general authorisation gave way to special authorisation for each individual case, and this could, of course, always be refused.

Thus confusion crept into men's minds and the end result was that the *ancien régime* vested the public authorities with the power to confer (or withhold) legal personality, which Roman and mediaeval law had considered to be the normal attribute of any association or foundation (Buttgenbach 1959, No. 303, pp. 269-70).

This erroneous viewpoint was translated into a basic guiding principle by the French Revolution and as such it continued to hold sway throughout the nineteenth and early twentieth centuries. The legislation enacted during the Revolution emphasized the State's distrust of associations and foundations. The revolutionary lawmakers were hostile to the existence or formation of any groups or associations as intermediaries between the State and the individual because (or at least allegedly so), by becoming part of a group, the individual runs the risk of sacrificing too great a measure of his freedom.

This basic hostility and the drawbacks of the system of mortmain explain

the two important measures taken by the legislature:
(a) The dissolution of all ecclesiastic endowments acquired through mort-
    main and the abolition of the right of private persons to set up founda-
    tions. This right was not re-established in Belgium until the law enacted
    on 27th June 1921;
(b) The introduction of a restrictive law on associations. If they comprised
    more than twenty members, they had henceforth to obtain prior
    authorisation from the Government (Art. 29 of the Penal Code of 1910)
    and even then they did not enjoy legal personality (Buttgenbach 1959,
    No. 303, p. 270).

Thenceforward, associations had to operate under men of straw or
figureheads and face all the inconvenience and risks which this entailed:
the possible dishonesty of their man of straw; potential legal action on the
part of creditors; and practical difficulties in the event of the figurehead's
death (Buttgenbach, op. cit.).

Art. 20 of the Belgian constitution of 1831 re-established liberty of association. On the other hand, since the French Revolution and even following
the reinstatement of the monarchy, legal personality, i.e. the capacity to act,
was not considered an association's natural right, but as the result of special
concession by the State, a favour which it could grant or refuse as it chose
(Buttgenbach, op. cit.).

Haunted by their old fears of mortmain and, admittedly, preoccupied
by other political problems, parliamentary circles long retained their hostility towards any move in favour of granting associations special rights; on
3rd April 1851, a law was promulgated to limit the powers of Mutual Aid
Societies (sociétés de secours mutuel); in 1841, the plan for granting the Universities of Brussels and Louvain a separate existence in law was defeated whilst
in 1857, the 'law on convents' caused a commotion on the political scene.

At the end of the nineteenth century and the beginning of the twentieth,
new ideas and attitudes came to the fore and the doctrine was propounded
that associations should be acknowledged as juristic persons[1].

Parliament continued to take a reserved attitude and legislation in this
field remained scant, and limited to certain associations or kinds of association:

9th August 1889   Law permitting the establishment of building
                     societies for inexpensive workmen's dwellings.

---

[1] Vanden Heuvel: La liberté d'association et la personnalité civile (1894); Marcq: La
personnalité civile des associations en Allemagne (1907); Errera: La personnification civile des
associations (1907) and Traité de Droit Public (1910).

30th March 1891	Law granting legal personality under civil law to the Belgian Red Cross.
23rd June 1894	Law on mutual aid societies.
31st March 1898	Law on professional associations.
21st August 1911	Law granting legal personality under civil law to the Universities of Brussels and Louvain.

(Buttgenbach 1959, No.303, p.271)

Following the First World War, the process was speeded up and parliamentary resistance weakened. In 1919 and 1920, Parliament conferred legal personality on a number of charitable associations whose good works had been recognised for some time:

7th August 1919	Law on the *Société Royale Protectrice des Enfants Martyrs*.
7th August 1919	Law on the *Œuvre du Grand Air pour les Petits*.
12th March 1920	*Œuvre des Asiles des Invalides Belges*.
25th May 1920	Law on the *Société Royale de Philanthropie*.
25th October 1919	Law granting general recognition to international societies pursuing scientific aims.

The year 1921 witnessed the culmination of this line of development. An overwhelming majority in the 'House of Commons' (*Chambre*) and a unanimous vote in the Senate passed the law of 27th June 1921, on non-profit associations and foundations (Buttgenbach, No. 303, p. 271).

II. TERMINOLOGICAL DIFFICULTIES

Prior to the promulgation of the law of 27th June 1921, no distinction was made either by the legislator or by legal theory between an '*établissement public*' and an '*établissement d'utilité publique*', i.e. between government institutions and private foundations which had been given legal personality under the terms of a special law.

It was not until the law of 27th June 1921, was passed that a clear distinction was finally made between the '*établissement public*', i.e. a foundation set up by the public authorities, and the *établissement d'utilité publique*,' i.e. a private foundation (Buttgenbach 1950, No. 322, p. 284).

The will of the founder can only become effective and lasting provided that certain conditions are observed which the lawmakers have established in regard to the content of his expressed wishes, the form in which they are manifested, and a number of extrinsic factors (R.P.D.B. No. 24).

The following prerequisites must be fulfilled if an institution is to enjoy the status conferred by the law of 27th June 1921:

(1) It must be clearly shown that it was the founder's will that a foundation should be established;

(2) The beneficial effects of the foundation must be within the framework stipulated by the lawmakers: philanthropy, religion, science, art and teaching; there must be no pursuit of material gain (Art. 27);

(3) It must be clearly shown that it was the founder's will that certain of his assets be allocated to the organisation set up by him;

(4) The founder must have made provisions for the administration of the said organisation (acp 30 R.P.D.B. No. 25, De Page, Vol. I, 1939, No. 530, p. 593).

The list contained in Art. 27, is a limited one (De Page, Vol. I, 1939, No. 528, p. 592, *Travaux préparatoires*, Pas. 1921, p. 362).

The aim of a foundation must, by definition, be of a general nature. But the law has stated precisely what is meant by this. '... only such organisations shall be considered as being of benefit to the community which renounce the pursuit of material gain and attempt to implement a scheme of a philanthropic, religious, scientific, artistic or educational nature' (Art. 27 para. 2).

The declaration of intent to set up a foundation is a formal and official act. A foundation could not exist if it were not created by a person's declaration of will expressed in an official document or holographic testament (Art. 27; R.P.D.B. No. 27; De Page, T.I., 1939, No. 530, p. 593). The deed must be authenticated by a notary public. This requirement in respect of an authentic declaration of intent is considered to be a guarantee of the institution's legality, i.e. its viability as a foundation (Buttgenbach 1959, No. 324, p. 285).

The existence of a declaration of intent must also be accompanied by the fulfilment of certain extrinsic conditions, i.e. which have nothing intrinsically to do with the founder's will or the form in which it is manifested. These are:

(1) Government approval (Art. 30);

(2) Official recognition of the charitable nature of the purpose for the pursuance of which the foundation was established (R.P.D.B. No. 28).

Without the official approval of the declaration of intent (Art. 27) and of the statutes which must be contained therein (Art. 30), an institution cannot enjoy legal personality. In such a case, a foundation has not come into existence (R.P.D.B. No. 29).

But unlike the will (or wishes) of the founder, which creates the institution, the Government has no such creative powers. It is not the concurrence of the founder's and the Government's wishes that calls a foundation into existence. The Government's act is of a juridical nature: the Government checks the full purport of the founder's expressed will which becomes binding for the public authorities from the moment that it satisfies the requirements of the law both in terms of substance and form (R.P.D.B. No. 29; Buttgenbach No. 326, p. 287).

An unjustified refusal of approval could lead to an appeal to the Council of State to have the decision quashed (Buttgenbach No. 326, p. 287).

The Government's powers in this sphere are not arbitrary. The Government must approve foundation deeds or statutes which are submitted to it in conformity with legal requirements (R.P.D.B. No. 29) and which do not infringe the rights of the founder's creditors or heirs (Buttgenbach No. 326, para. 4, p. 287).

Although the law prohibits the setting up of a foundation whose object is the pursuit of material gain (Art. 27), it does not prohibit the allocation of assets in the form of a commercial or industrial enterprise to an institution whose object is of a philanthropic, scientific or similar nature (R.P.D.B. No. 143).

C. General Rules Governing Foundations

These general rules relate to:
  —the establishment of the foundation:
  —administration;
  —dissolution of foundations.

They were laid down by the law of 27th June 1921, and although some of them are not explicitly formulated in the law, they follow from *combinatoris* of the individual rules and regulations contained therein or from their interaction with general legal principles.

I. THE ESTABLISHMENT OF THE FOUNDATION

1. *Number*

Every foundation is based on one or several foundation deeds or declarations of intent. But when there are several such declarations, they have to complement each other or stem from the same founder(s) since the essence of one or several foundation deeds is that they must express a unilateral declaration of will or consistent unilateral declarations of will (R.P.D.B. No. 112).

No supplementary declaration of will or intent to set up a foundation is possible after a first declaration has been approved by royal decree or after the death of the founder. Once royal approval has been granted or the founder has died, it is only possible to modify the statutes in accordance with Art.31 (R.P.D.B. No. 113). On the other hand, until the founder actually receives the requisite approval, he is at liberty to withdraw his declaration of intent (De Page, Vol. I, 1939, No. 530, p. 593).

2. Content

Government approval revolves around the very essence of a foundation, i.e. does it conform to the legal definition of foundation and has it been organised by the founder in such a way as to be viable?

In addition, the law requires that the request for approval must be accompanied by the foundation's statutes which must clearly state:
(1) The object of the foundation;
(2) Its designation and seat;
(3) The surnames, Christian names, profession and domicile of the administrators and the provisions established for their replacement;
(4) The disposal of the foundation's assets in the event of its dissolution (Art. 30).

The foundation deed must contain a declaration of the intention to set up a foundation (Arts. 17 and 28) together with the statutes (Art. 30). The declaration and statutes may be laid down in one document or in separate deeds. No precise delimitation has been fixed between the contents of the declaration and those of the statutes (R.P.D.B. No. 114).

But a distinction must be made between the essential components of the declaration of intent, in the absence of which Government approval will not be granted, and the non-essential components (R.P.D.B. No. 115). The essential components comprise the minimum of precision in the founder's declaration of intent needed in order that it may satisfy the requirements of the law and, in particular, that it may be duly submitted for approval (R.P.D.B. No. 119).

Moreover, the will expressed must be authentic and unequivocal. This is considered to be the case if at least the four requirements indicated above are satisfied.

GENERAL CHARACTERISTICS OF FOUNDATION STATUS

The status of foundations is slightly less liberal than that of the non-profit associations in that they are subject to wider powers of intervention and control on the part of the State. These powers may be witnessed at the birth of the foundation (official approval of statutes), during its existence (Government control of its management and accounts, and also State intervention in the case of amendment of the statutes), and, finally, in the event of its dissolution (determination of the disposal of assets).

The justification for this government intervention is to be found in the fundamental difference between a foundation and the non-profit association (*association sans but lucratif*).

(a) First of all, it is understandable that the State can only permit the will or declaration of intent of a single individual to bring about the creation of an institution, the duration of whose existence is, in principle, unlimited and which may be the recipient of substantial assets, if it is able to verify that the purposes for which the foundation is intended are compatible with the interests of the community as a whole and the requirements of law and order and that the founder is not impairing the legitimate interests of his creditors or heirs by transferring part of his fortune to the said foundation.

(b) Moreover, in view of the absence of permanent control, such as that wielded by the members of an association, the Government sees itself obliged to exercise supervisory control over the persons administering the body concerned and ensure that the assets vested in it by the founder are not used for any purposes other than those he has designated.

It will, however, be seen that the law of 1921 took the necessary precautions to prevent Government control and action in respect of foundations from being either arbitrary or too one-sided. All in all, this enactment proved to be very liberal towards foundations, the idea behind it not being to thwart the founder's will but, on the contrary, to make sure that it is carried out once it has been deemed to be in conformity with the requirements of the law (Buttgenbach 1959, No. 323, p. 284).

The essential requirements are as follows:

(1) Selecting certain property for the creation of the foundation;
(2) The intention of earmarking this property for the formation of a new foundation;
(3) A specification of the objects of the foundation;
(4) The designation of at least one administrator or trustee (R.P.D.B. No. 117).

In other words, it is in principle the founder who has to specify in the foundation deed the nature and the volume of the assets which he has earmarked for the creation of a foundation. He may, however, simply decide to appoint a third party to select them from the property he leaves, just as he can entrust a third party with the task of selecting the first administrator or trustee (Art. 33; Report of the Consultative Commission, Pas. 1921, pp. 362–3; R.P.D.B. No. 118).

As regards the nature of the declaration of intent, it is neither a donation (since there is nobody who actually accepts it) nor a legacy. None the less, it does have certain similarities with these concepts and the declaration of intent is in fact deemed to constitute a gift (R.P.D.B. No. 119).

As far as the form of the declaration of intent is concerned, the Government draft only authorised foundations to come into existence on the basis of a certified deed (*par acte authentique*). The *Section centrale*, however, added to the text: 'or by a holograph will, because circumstances may have rendered this necessary' (R.P.D.B. No. 125). It follows, therefore, that if the foundation is established during the founder's lifetime, its creation must be effected 'by a certified declaration of intent'. If its creation is effected by last will and testament, it may be done through a will drawn up before a notary or, equally, through a private testament² or a testament *sous seing privé*² (Art. 27).

This raises the question as to who must seek Government approval:

(a) When the foundation is set up during the founder's lifetime, it is incumbent upon the latter to transmit to the Government the certified deed including the statutes for official approval. The founder may, moreover always retract his declaration of intent as long as royal approval has not been accorded (Arts. 28–30).

(b) If the founder dies before he has forwarded the deed to the Goverment or if the foundation is set up by testament, the executor of the will or the heirs are obliged to transmit to the Government the certified or private will instituting the foundation (Art. 28; Buttgenbach 1959, No. 326, para. 2, p. 286).

Any declaration of intent in any form whatsoever must be submitted to the Government, i.e. in practice to the Ministry of Justice. This submission is subject to different rules depending on whether it has been made by the founder himself, his heirs or other interested parties (R.P.D.B. No. 129).

The founder is not bound by any time limit. After having had a deed setting out his wishes drawn up and certified, he may postpone the communication thereof to the Government for an indefinite period of time. Art. 27, para. I, only vests the founder with rights, not with duties. But this only applies in the case of a foundation *inter vivos*. Otherwise the testator may submit the (public or holograph) will to the Government, but it cannot be approved until after his decease (R.P.D.B. No. 130).

² This means that the will has not been signed before a notary or other official witness.

The heirs or other interested parties named by the founder are obliged to submit the declaration of intent to the Government except in two cases:
(1) If the founder himself has already submitted the deed to the Government in some form other than a testamentary one.
(2) If the deceased has nominated one or several executors of the will whose task includes the duty to either submit the declaration of intent to the Government in a form other than that of a will or the testamentary provisions constituting the declaration of intent (R.P.D.B. No. 131).

Moreover, the heirs or interested parties must submit the declaration of intent to the Government as soon as they are aware of the said declaration. They are held responsible for any prejudicial delay (R.P.D.B. No. 132).

3. Government approval

The establishment of any foundation is subject to Government approval. This is in fundamental contradistinction to the provisions governing a non-profit association. The latter are vested with legal personality without any intervention on the part of the Government, by the mere fact of their existence and their acceptance of the general conditions laid down by the law and the announcement of their existence in the official gazette (*Le Moniteur Belge*). On the other hand, a foundation may only come into existence and enjoy legal personality with explicit Government approval (Buttgenbach 1959, No. 326, p. 285).

This basic difference is justified by the different natures of the association and the foundation. The wishes of one person may indeed have been the origin of the former, but the association must nevertheless also respect those of its members, i.e. living persons in the present and the future whose joint will may at any time adapt the association's aims and activities to conform with social needs and exigencies.

Thus the non-profit association is in the constant position of being able to adjust itself to changing circumstances.

This is the opposite of a foundation where the will of one person can call into existence a juristic person—the foundation—which disposes of a permanent endowment in accordance with his or her instructions.

It is, therefore, quite understandable that the Government reserves for itself the right of approving a decision which may have prolonged effects and tie up assets for an indefinite period of time and for specific aims (Buttgenbach 1959, No. 326, p. 285).

(a) Government powers

The Government may not arbitrarily refuse to grant approval to the declaration of intent nor to statutes which fulfil the conditions laid down by the law (R.P.D.B. No. 134).

However, the Government has the right of assessment and it exercises similar controls to those accorded to courts and tribunals under Art. 41. Government approval may be withheld when:

—a foundation is incapable from the outset of fulfilling its prescribed function;

—a foundation is in a position where creditors or heirs to their legal portion would be legally entitled to terminate it pursuant to Art. 37 (R.P.D.B. No. 134) because it is evident that the foundation may prejudice the legitimate rights of its creditors and the founder's creditors (Buttgenbach No. 326, p. 286).

The Government's approval does not deprive creditors and lawful heirs[3] of the right to take legal action under the terms of Art. 37. The founder's creditors and lawful heirs may always apply to the Government who will then have to refuse approval to the foundation if it impairs their rights. If the Government ignores their claim, they may then turn to the tribunals to ask them to quash whatever acts may have been committed in contravention of their rights (for example, a reduction in the capital donated), and even, if it is necessary, to dissolve the foundation and have its assets liquidated (Art. 37; Buttgenbach No. 326, 3, p. 286).

As for the other persons who may be involved, the report from the *Section centrale* (Arts. 19 and 23) does not authorise them to contest Government approval in the courts even if their claims were to be based on the invalidity of the declaration of intent (R.P.D.B. No. 135).

(b) The consequences of governmental approval

With the exception of the reservation stemming from the application of Art. 37, royal approval puts the seal of State approbation on the foundation, which is then classified as belonging to this special category of juristic persons (R.P.D.B. No. 137).

This approbation is definitive since the Belgian legal system does not contain any provision for retracting this approval by Government action (R.P.D.B. No. 137).

The legal personality accorded under civil law to a foundation by Government approval is universally binding from the time indicated in Art. 29 of the law, i.e. from the date on which the Government duly received the decla-

---

[3] These heirs are entitled to the *réserve légale*, i.e. that portion of an estate which a testator may not freely dispose of to the prejudice of the heirs.

ration of intent, provided it was not in the form of a testament, and, otherwise, from the date of the founder's death (R.P.D.B. No. 138).

Government approval records the founder's creative will as expressed in the declaration of intent, if necessary after an adjustment or clarification has been introduced to complete the document in question, i.e. in cases where its contents have been confined to the basic essentials (in default whereof there can, of course, be no approval because there is no legally valid deed). The Government may, and indeed must, make its approval dependent on the adoption of such complementary measures as may be necessary for the proper functioning of the institution even though they do not constitute part of the essential components of the declaration of intent (R.P.D.B. No. 140).

It is not only the foundation's legal personality which commences to take effect as from the time indicated in Art. 29 para. 2, but also its rights. It is at this moment that the transfer of the assets earmarked for the foundation by the founder is effected (R.P.D.B. No. 143).

(c) The form of governmental approval

The royal decrees of approval must be published in full in *Le Moniteur Belge* since their inclusion in this official gazette is in the public interest (Law of 18th April 1819, amended 28th December 1909 and 3rd August 1924, Arts. 5 and 6; R.P.D.B. No. 148).

The statutes and the amendments thereto are published in the supplements to *Le Moniteur Belge* (Law of 27th June 1921, Art. 32).

II. THE ADMINISTRATION OF FOUNDATIONS

The Law of 27th June 1921, contains only few provisions on the administration of foundations. The rules which the law contains in this connection are partly the application of the principles of common law. Moreover, these principles must be referred to every time that the law or the foundation's statutes depart from them (R.P.D.B. No. 150).

A foundation is subject to the provisions of common law in civil cases both in respect of civil acts (such as contracts) or illegal acts (R.P.D.B. No. 151).

The foundation is liable for its debts, whatever their cause, to the extent of its total assets just like any other private person in pursuance of Art. 7 of the Law of 16th December 1951 (R.P.D.B. No. 151).

The powers of the administrators are usually defined in advance by the statutes. If the latter contain no provisions in regard to this aspect, the administrators must be accorded the widest possible powers within the framework of the object for which the foundation was created (Buttgenbach No. 328, p. 287).

The administrators represent the foundation in legal matters. They possess the capacity to take every legal step necessary for applying the assets to the pursuit of the foundation's prescribed purpose (Buttgenbach No. 328, p. 287). The basic rules in this connection are contained in Arts. 38 and 39 of the Law of 27th June 1921.

A foundation is able to dispose of its assets like any other natural person pursuant to Arts. 537 paras. I and 544 of the Civil Code. In view, however, of the specified purpose(s) for which the assets were earmarked, a number of important rules have been introduced in order to ensure a certain degree of control over the administration of the foundation on the part of the public and the Government (R.P.D.B. No. 152).

The composition and augmentation of the endowment are subject to the provisions of Arts. 35, 36 and 37 and 40 of the Law of 27th June 1921 (R.P.D.B. No. 153).

There are restrictions in regard to the ownership of real estate; any acquisition of real estate which is not necessary for the realization of the foundation's goal is prohibited (Buttgenbach No. 328, p. 287).

Gratuitous acquisitions require the Government's permission. In such cases, the creditors of the donors and testators concerned have the right under common law to take proceedings to reduce an unconscionable obligation or to deprive an agreement of any legal effect due to the existence of a defect (R.P.D.B. No. 153).

1. *Government control of the administration of foundations*

Art. 40 of the Law of 27th June 1921 entrusts the Government with the supervision of foundations. But the Government's right of supervision is virtually restricted to watching over or 'keeping an eye on' foundations. It cannot interfere in the running of the foundation or modify, reform or annul the decisions taken by the administrators. All it can do is in cases where such decisions appear to constitute an infringement of the law or the statutes, is to ask the Courts to apply the appropriate sanctions. In reserving the right of punitive action to the Courts, the lawmakers were actuated by the concern —as with the associations—to remove the danger of governmental caprice or despotism *vis-à-vis* foundations.

Government supervision of foundations could be increased by the introduction of additional controls which would function in accordance with conditions established by the founder himself, for example he might provide for the designation of commissioners and determine their mode of nomination. This precaution would be perfectly justifiable since there is always a danger that remote and centralized supervision by the Government is not always very effective (Buttgenbach 1958, No. 329, p. 288).

Government supervision is mainly exercised through the inspection of the accounts and budget which have to be submitted each year (Art. 34) and published in *Le Moniteur Belge* (R.P.D.B. No. 156). They must be submitted by the administrators within two months of their being drawn up. It is worth noting that all that is essentially involved is a simple communication of information, designed to facilitate the supervisory task of the central authorities. If the Government were to discover irregularities as a result of this inspection, it could not take any punitive action; it could only request the Courts to apply the appropriate sanctions (Buttgenbach 1959, No. 331, p. 288).

The fundamental rule which the administrators must observe is to ensure that the assets are applied for the purpose for which the foundation was created (Art. 40). The Public Prosecutor has the right to apply to the Court to have the appointments of the administrators cancelled. It is then up to the Court to decide whether their successors are to be nominated by the Government (R.P.D.B. No. 158).

The administrators, who are named in the statutes which also set out the arrangements for replacing them (Arts. 30 and 33), may be dismissed in cases of negligence, e.g. if they do not respect the obligations enumerated in the statutes, if they dispose of the foundation's assets in a manner which is contrary to their proper purpose or for purposes which are contrary to law and order (Buttgenbach No. 330, p. 288).

But this right of dismissal does not come within the scope of the Government's powers; it is the prerogative of the courts. The Government may only ask the Courts to pronounce sentence accordingly and, in so doing, it must state the reasons for its request; the judge then reaches his decision in complete independence.

And if the latter decides in favour of dismissal, it is also his task to decide whether the new administrators are to be named in accordance with the provisions laid down in the statutes or by the Government. Here again one finds clear evidence of the legislator's concern to avert any danger of arbitrary action on the part of the executive (Buttgenbach No. 330, p. 288).

2. Regulations in regard to publicity

The law stipulates that the following information must be published in the supplements of *Le Moniteur Belge*:

(a) the foundation's statutes which, like those of associations, must mention any envisaged amendments pursuant to Arts. 30 and 33 of the Law, i.e.

   (1) the aim(s) of the foundation;

   (2) the surnames, Christian names, profession, domicile and nationality of the administrators;

   (3) the provisions made for future appointments and/or replacements of administrators;

   (4) the name and seat of the institution; and

   (5) the use to which the assets will be put if the institution is dissolved.

(b) any amendments made in the statutes;

(c) nominations, resignations, and dismissals;

(d) accounts and annual budgets (Buttgenbach 1959, No. 332, p. 289).

The justification of these regulations in regard to publicity is the same as that obtaining for the non-profit associations.

With regard to punitive measures in the event of non-observance of this rule, if these facts are not published or only inadequately so, the foundation in question may not avail itself of its legal personality *vis-à-vis* third parties. The latter's security in the event of the foundation running into their debt consists not only of the foundation's whole assets, but also the personal assets of those administrators with whom they had dealings.

On the other hand, however, the administrators and the foundation cannot take advantage of an absence of legal personality, due to failure to publish in *Le Moniteur Belge*, in order to evade the fulfilment of their obligations (Buttgenbach Nos. 334 and 310, pp. 289 and 270).

3. *Amendments to the statutes of foundations*

It can, and does, happen that the statutes of a foundation need to be amended. For example, the statutes specify the location of the foundation's registered offices, but it may subsequently prove expedient to transfer them elsewhere, or it may happen that the foundation has acquired assets which are of disproportionate importance in relation to its prescribed aims.

The statutes of an association can always readily be modified by a general meeting of its members. But a foundation has no members and the founder may be dead. Who, then, should be given the right to act in such a case? (Buttgenbach 1959, No. 335, p. 289)

The solution provided by the Law is that the amendment(s) to foundations' statutes must be jointly agreed by the Government and a majority of administrators. If such agreement proves impossible, it is the task of the legislator to stipulate which amendments are deemed to be indispensable (Art. 31; Buttgenbach 1959, No. 336, p. 260).

III. DISSOLUTION OF FOUNDATIONS

The Law of 27th June 1921, only mentions one reason for the dissolution of a foundation (Art. 41), but it does not exclude (and even postulates) the existence of other situations where a foundation may be dissolved (R.P.D.B. No. 160).

A foundation may be temporary and the limited period of time for which it has been created may be laid down in precise terms in the statutes. This might ensue from the very object of the foundation. In this case, the administrators—acting in accordance with their obligation to observe the statutes—will have to arrange for the foundation to be dissolved. This is called a statutory dissolution.

If a founder has not stipulated either expressly or implicitly a certain date by which the foundation must be dissolved, the latter's duration is in principle perpetual by virtue of its creator's will. A founder cannot allow the administrators to decide of their own accord that there are grounds for dissolving the foundation. It is for the founder and for him alone to decide how the endowment is to be applied and, consequently, how long this undertaking should endure (R.P.D.B. No. 162); and the creative will of the founder remains paramount for the foundation in all circumstances and all decisions affecting its life (Buttgenbach 1959, No. 337, p. 240, 290 and 291).

A foundation can only be dissolved by court decision if it can be proved that it can no longer fulfil the tasks for which it was founded. This might for instance be due to the exhaustion of its assets or to the fact that the needs which it was designed to meet no longer exist.

Here again, it should be observed that the Law has given the right to enforce a dissolution to the judiciary, and not to the Government, so as to avert the danger of any arbitrariness (Buttgenbach 1959, No. 338, p. 290).

When it is not temporary, a foundation created in accordance with the Law by the will of the founder can only be terminated in accordance with the provisions of the Law. Art. 41 of the Law of 27th June 1921, which is a general provision, envisages such an eventuality and lays down the procedure to be followed. This procedure is judicial and not administrative. The Government has no power to retract the approval it has given to the declaration of intent and to the statutes (R.P.D.B. Nos. 137 and 164).

The circumstance that the Law can even terminate the existence of a foundation for reasons other than those envisaged in Art. 31 (e.g. alteration of statutes) is because it is the task of the legislator to ensure that the will and general interest of the nation prevail over the individual will of the founder (R.P.D.B. No. 166).

The dissolution of a foundation in a certain sense opens the path to a

D

successor and imposes an obligation to decide who is to receive its assets. These persons are, in principle, named in the statutes. It should be recalled that this is a matter which must be settled in the declaration of intent (Buttgenbach 1959, No. 339, p. 290). If the provisions for settling this matter cannot be put into practice, it is the State which acquires the assets (R.P.D.B. No. 167).

The tribunal authorises the liquidators to transfer the assets to the Government which then earmarks them for a purpose as closely related as possible to the object for which the institution was created (Buttgenbach 1959, No. 339, p. 290).

This is yet another instance of the concern to respect the founder's wishes and obviate the danger of governmental despotism. It is in fact the judiciary and not the Government who are the sole arbiters of whether the object set out in the statutes can or cannot be achieved (Buttgenbach 1959, No. 339, p. 290).

SUMMARY: A LIBERAL ATTITUDE TOWARDS FOUNDATIONS

The Law of 27th June 1921 has given foundations a considerable measure of freedom. Admittedly, governmental control is a little stricter than it is with associations: authorisation required at the time of establishment, permanent supervision of the management, and possible intervention in the appointment of administrators to replace those recalled by the Courts, in the amendment of statutes, in the allocation of the foundation's assets if the object for which they are earmarked in the statutes can no longer be achieved.

However, it should be noted that such interventions are the exception, not the rule: when they do occur, the law obliges the Government to respect at all times the expressed or presumed wishes of the founder.

Finally, any penalties inflicted on foundations are always imposed by the Courts, never by the Government, a situation which constitutes a very effective guarantee of impartial treatment.

D. The Fiscal Treatment of Foundations

I. TAXES ON REVENUES (C.I.R., ARTS. 136 TO 138)

In principle, the juristic persons tax (*impôt des personnes morales—IPM*) applies to all juristic persons under private or public law which do not pursue profit-making activities, which have their registered offices, principal branch or administrative seat in Belgium, and which are not subject to company tax[4].

Charitable foundations or institutions which are exclusively engaged, in conformity with the rules laid down by the law or by their statutes, in administrative activities or in tasks of general benefit to the community which are not essentially of a commercial, industrial or agricultural nature and which do not involve the employment of industrial or commercial methods, cannot be considered as profit-making and they are therefore subject to the IPM (*Impôts et Taxes, Guide Pratique No. 194/125*).

The following cases must be considered in regard to both foundations and associations.

(1) The association or foundation does not engage in any profit-making activities. In this case, it escapes liability to company tax and is subject to the IPM.

(2) The association or foundation contravenes its statutes and engages as its principal activity in industrial, commercial or agricultural operations or other profit-making pursuits. In this case, it is liable to company tax.

(3) The association or foundation engages in such activities but only as a subsidiary operation. Here, the profits realised by such activities are exempt if the conditions imposed by previous jurisdiction are observed, i.e.: the work undertaken for pecuniary gain must be essential for the realisation of the tasks of communal benefit, which represent the object for which the association was set up and the latter must dedicate the whole of its revenue to implementing the said object. (Decision of 22nd January 1952, Pas. 1952 I 285; G. van Fraeyenhofen, op. cit. No. 211, p. 180; G. van den Avyle, *Guide Fiscal Permanent* No. 273/7; Simon and Neesen, op. cit. p. 248.) IPM rests applicable.

II. ASSESSMENT OF TAXES

Juristic persons are liable to taxation only in respect of the revenues and income derived from capital and movables which they possess or benefit from, as well as their income from landed property provided that such receipts are not exempt by virtue of special legal arrangements or of Art. 41 para. I No. 2 (Simon et Neesen, p. 249; Tiberghien No. 233, p. 122; C.I.R. 137).

Taxes are deemed to correspond to the payments made in respect of:—

[4] *Impôts et Taxes, Guide Pratique* 136/I; G. van Fraeyenhoven *La Réforme des Impôts sur les Revenus*, p. 228, No. 253; G. van den Avyle: *Guide Fiscal Permanent*, No. 273/I.

tax credits (*crédit d'impôt*); tax on dividends and on real estate (précomptes *mobiliers et immoviliers*) (Simon et Neesen, p. 249; Tiberghien No. 234, p. 122).

But juristic persons other than the State, the provinces, the Government, the C.A.P. (Public Welfare System) and the intermunicipal associations are equally taxable in respect of the value added to landed property on which no buildings have been constructed in the same way as the same added-value enjoyed by natural persons is taxable (Tiberghien, No. 234, p. 122).

III. REGISTRATION AND DONATION TAX

1. *Creation of the foundation*

The Law of 27th June 1921 on associations and foundations makes no provision for the registration of their constituent acts. However, the latter are governed by the provisions of common law.

To acquire legal personality, these acts must be officially published in *Le Moniteur*; this is tantamount to a requirement for registration (Feye: *Traité de droit fiscal des Associations et Sociétés*, T.I., No. 274, p. 332).

For the constituent act the organization in question is only liable to the standard fixed charge (M. Feye, op. cit. No. 275, p. 333).

2. *List of members*

The lists of members, which pursuant to the Law of 921, have to be deposited with the registrar of a Civil Court, must also be registered in advance (Art. 42 of the Law). Here again the standard fixed charge is levied (M. Feye, op. cit. No. 277, p. 334).

3. *Donations*

Donations are, in principle, subject to a proportional tax of 6.6% in the case of foundations and 8.8% for associations.

Testamentary gifts are subject to taxation at the same rate.

A gift in the form of movables, of which the value does not exceed 50,000 francs, does not require any authorisation. If it is transferred without any document being drawn up, it is not subject to any requirement for registration either.

Subject to these reservations, gifts given *inter vivos* or by testament to foundations are governed by the provisions of Arts. 28 and 29 of the Law of 1921.

(a) Donations

Unless and until the Royal Decree of approval provided for in Art. 16 has been given, gifts to foundations cannot be legally accepted by the latter. As a result, until then the donation remains a mere promise and a proportional registration fee can accordingly not be levied. In the case of such an offer, only the standard charge is applicable. The proportional rate is only payable when the institution has been duly authorised and has formally accepted the gift (M. Feye, op. cit. No. 288, p. 341).

(b) Testamentary gifts

Gifts given to foundations by means of a will are not recognised until Government approval has been granted. Notwithstanding this rule, the foundation has a right to the bequeathed item immediately after the testator's death.

Hence the authorities levy an inheritance tax regardless of the question of authorisation. An exception is made to this practice only in cases where a new declaration is deposited or where refusal of the right to accept the legacy necessitates a reallocation of the item involved (M. Feye op. cit. No. 286 b, p. 341).

(c) Donations made by the founder for setting-up of foundation

Gifts covered by Arts. 27 et ss. are earmarked for an as yet non-existent entity and are invalid unless and until the formalities and preconditions laid down by the Law of 1921 have been fulfilled. These relate both to the recognition of the legal existence of the foundation (Art. 30) and to the official authorisation of the transfer of assets (Arts. 27 to 29).

So far, the act of donation is only subject to the standard fixed charge since it still only constitutes a promise. The liability to pay the proportional tax on the gift in question does not arise until Government approval has been granted.

Inheritance tax is levied on a provisional basis, regardless of whether the foundation is finally set up. Once Government approval is given, the ordinary time limits come into play either for depositing a corrected inheritance tax declaration and paying the supplementary charges or for instituting claims for restitution (M. Feye, op. cit. No. 287, pp. 342, 343).

4. Dissolution

As we have already noted, the assets of a foundation even after its liabilities have been paid, cannot be shared out amongst its members and beneficiaries.

They must, however, be handled as set out in the relevant provisions of the statutes or, in the absence of such provisions, by the general assembly or the liquidator(s).

Any transfer of assets affected in this way does not fall into the category of those which are exempt under Art. 53 and, as regards registration, they are subject to the regulations of common law.

In general, the donation will be subject to the charge on gratuitous transfers. However, each individual case must be examined in order to determine its character and to determine the amount of tax to be charged (M. Feye, op. cit. No. 288, p. 343).

Above all, it is necessary to determine and assess the obligations in regard to the foundation's capital and which will have to be assumed by the organisation to which these assets are transferred. If the obligations stipulated by the founder are equal to, or greater than, the value of the gift, the contract is no longer of a gratuitous nature: it represents a transfer which is not subject to the charge on donations but to the charge applicable in the case of contracts of a remunerative character (J. Schicks, *Traité de Droit Fiscal*, No. 138; Maton T. II, No. 620).

If none of the provisions mentioned above have been made, Art. 4 of the Law stipulates that the liquidators must transfer the assets to the Government which then assigns them to a purpose as close as possible to the aim for which the foundation was set up.

In this case, the transfer is registered free of charge in pursuance of Art. 70 para. 2 No. I, of the Law governing registrations of *22nd Frimaire of Year VII* (= 12th December 1800) (M. Feye op. cit. No. 289, p. 344).

IV. TAX ON PUBLIC ENTERTAINMENTS AND AMUSEMENTS

The associations and foundations in question benefit from tax exemption or reduction on presentation of the requisite documentary evidence that their object is philanthropic, or in the field of the arts, literature or the sciences or of interest to the community as a whole (Law of 28th February 1920, Art. 2; A.R. 4th January 1922; M. Feye op. cit. No. 292, p. 344).

LITERATURE

Buttgenbach, A. Manual de Droit Administratif, Brussells, Larcier 1959.

Cardyn, C. Répertoire Fiscal.

Dembour, J. Les Actes de la Tutelle Administrative en Droit Belge, Brussells, Larcier 1955.

Feye, M. Traité de Droit Fiscal des Sociétés et Associations, Brussells, Bruylant 1934.

Goedsels, J. La Personnalité Civile des A.S.B.L. et E.U.P., Brussells, Hauchamps 1921.

Goedsels, J. Traité Juridique des A.S.B.L. et des E.U.P., Brussells, 1935.

De Guertechin, Ch. Léonhard L'Impôt des Personnes Physiques, Brussells, Larcier.

Hallet, M. Loi du 27 juin 1921 accordant la personnalité civile aux A.S.B.L. et aux E.U.P., Brussells, Bruylant 1922.

't Kint, J. Les A.S.B.L., Brussells, Larcier 1961.

Neve, L. Commentaires Pratiques de la Loi du 27 juin 1921, Gand 1922.

De Page, A. Traité Elémentaire de Droit Civil Belge: Vol. I, 2nd Ed. Brussells, Bruylant 1939. Vol. I, 3rd Ed. Brussells, Bruylant 1962.

Raucq, D. A. L'Enregistrement des Actes de Sociétés, Brussells, Larcier 1966.

Schliks, A. and Van Itterbeek, A. Les A.S.B.L. et les E.U.P. Extrait du traité formulaire de la pratique notariale.

Simon, L. and Neesen, U. La Réforme des Impôts sur les Revenus (L. du 20. II. 1962), Farciennes, Hénin.

Teege Associations et Fondations en Belgique, Brussells, 1942.

Tiberghien, A. Manuel de Droit Fiscal, Brusselles, Institut Fiscal et Financier 1967, 2nd Ed.

Vauthier, M. Etude sur les personnes morales, Brussells-Paris 1887.

Wibault, H. L'Evolution de la Notion de Revenu Imposable en Droit Fiscal Belge, Brussells, Bruylant 1965.

Van Wynendaele, J. R. Principes de Droit Fiscal des Sociétés, Brussells, Bruylant 1963.

R.P.D.B. Vol. IV-Etablissements Publics et d'Utilité Publique, Brussells, Bruylant.

Switzerland*

Uwe Pavel

I. INTRODUCTION

A foundation in common parlance occurs whenever an asset is dedicated to a specific purpose. This might appear, at first glance, to be a precise definition, but one should realise that already such common occurrences as the donation of extremely small sums of money to a collection or the award of a prize for some contest could, in that case, be defined as foundations. Formally speaking, however, there can be no question of foundations being present in the two aforementioned examples under the Swiss law currently in force. The lawmakers enacting the German Civil Code of 1900 (BGB) accepted the conclusion reached by the legal theorists during the second half of the past century that the foundation is an institution enjoying legal status, and the fathers of the ZGB (Swiss Civil Code) have in this particular instance followed the example furnished by the German Civil Code. Thus the concept of the foundation was limited in the same way as in Germany by excepting from any special legal regulation the original form of the foundation which today is loosely termed the dependent foundation, endowment or foundation without legal status (*unselbständige Stiftung*). Such foundations which lack a legal status of their own are to be qualified legally as donations or as bequests with an obligation (Art. 245 of the OR—Act relating to the Swiss Law of Contract; Art. 482 of the ZGB), as mandates of a special kind (Art. 394 of the OR) or as bilateral contracts; although they are still as widespread today as are foundations with legal status.

When looking at the legal position of the foundation prior to the enactment of the ZGB, it seems astonishing that the private initiative to establish foundations as a manifestation of a particular social and philanthropic disposition still developed so strongly during the second half of the past century, since the Cantonal law of that time dealt with the foundation in as

* Translated from the German.

49

niggardly a manner as the authoritative foreign codes hitherto in force as the Code Civil (1804) and the Austrian General Civil Code (1811). Relevant provisions existed only in a few Cantons, and they were, in these instances, contained in the law relating to donations and in the law of succession. The foundation came predominantly within the scope of public law and in special laws which showed mistrust towards it; the establishment of a foundation always required the permission of the government which was frequently granted only for a limited period of time. The only exceptions were the excellent *Zürcher Gesetzbuch* (Zurich Code) drafted in 1853–5 by Bluntschli, a code conscious of tradition but at the same time progressive and modern, as well as the subsequently enacted *Bündnerische Privatgesetzbuch* (Civil Code of Graubünden). Both these codifications adopted a positive attitude towards foundations. While Zurich provided for permission by the *Regierungsrat* (Governing Council) only with regard to foundations following ecclesiastical or public purposes, Graubünden granted complete freedom to establish foundations. This principle of freedom to establish foundations has been adopted by the ZGB.

II. THE FOUNDATION WITH LEGAL STATUS

1. *The foundation as an institution under civil law*

The ZGB distinguishes, in the case of legal entities, between corporations or associations and independent institutions (*Anstalt*) which are intended for a specific purpose (Art. 52 para. 1 of the ZGB). Among the institutions one must again make a distinction between the institutions under public law (cf. Art. 59 para 1 of the ZGB) and the foundations, including the ecclesiastical foundations as well as the private family trusts, which are subject to special regulations. While under Swiss law the 'institution' is characterised by the fact that independent endowments are dedicated to a specific purpose[1], the foundation is to be understood as an institution under civil law[2].

2. *Legal sources of the law relating to foundations*

The core of the law relating to foundations is formed by the general provisions of the ZGB dealing with legal entities which aim at the greatest possible assimilation of the legal position of the legal entities to that of the natural person (Arts. 52 to 59 of the ZGB)[3] as well as by the special provisions

[1] Cf. Hafter. Kommentar zum Schweizerischen Zivilgesetzbuch, Personenrecht, 2nd Ed., Bern 1919, Art. 52, Mar Nos. 7, 8.

[2] Tuor, Das Schweizerische Zivilgesetzbuch, 8th Ed., Zurich 1968, p. 101.

[3] Cf. Tuor, op. cit. p. 98.

on foundations contained in the third chapter of the said work (Arts. 80 to 89 *bis* of the ZGB). Family trusts are governed by the additional provision of Art. 335 of the ZGB, and the authority to establish a foundation *mortis causa* only derives from the provision of the law of succession contained in Art. 493 of the ZGB. Special provisions relating to *Personalfürsorgestiftungen* (pension funds) are to be found in Art. 89 *bis* of the ZGB and in the law of Master and Servant (Art. 343 *bis* of the *Obligationenrecht*—OR). Other provisions of federal law which are of importance are Arts. 101 to 104 of the *Verordnung über das Handelsregister* (HRVO—Commercial Register Regulation) of 7th June 1937.

The Cantonal law primarily regulates the supervision of foundations. It specifies the authorities competent to exercise such supervision and—mainly in special ordinances—the tasks of such authorities.

In spite of its relatively extensive regulations, there are some gaps in the Swiss statutory law relating to foundations.

Many questions not dealt with by statutory law have, however, been resolved by common law, by the decisions of courts, especially the *Bundesgericht* (Swiss Federal Supreme Court) and by law created by the authorities[4]. In this way the Swiss law relating to foundations is, on the whole, distinguished by its lucidity and clarity.

3. *The concept of the foundation*

The concept of the foundation is not legally defined. While it is true that Art. 80 of the ZGB states that the establishment of a foundation requires the dedication of assets for a specific purpose, this provision covers only one essential element of the concept of the foundation which identifies the foundation, as far as its nature is concerned, as an institution in the sense of Art. 52 para. 1 of the ZGB. The establishment of the foundation requires initially a formal declaration of intent to be entered in a public record or in a testament or in a contract of inheritance (family settlement)[5]. The founding act, being the germ cell and charter of the foundation, must manifest the intention to establish a foundation. It must contain a dedication of assets and state the specific purpose which the assets vested in the foundation shall serve. In addition, it should contain provisions for organising the foundation.

4. *The dedication of assets*

The dedication consists in the settling of any assets, whose nature shall be

---

[4] Cf. Egger, Kommentar zum Schweizerischen Zivilgesetzbuch, Vol. I, Einleitung und Personenrecht, 2nd Ed., Zurich 1930, Preliminary remarks to Art. 80. Mar. No. 7.

[5] Art. 81 para. 1 of the ZGB.

determined by the founder, which are to serve the specified purpose of the foundation. This, however, does not require the direct transfer of the ownership of goods and chattels; it is sufficient to secure a specific contribution of assets by the founder or by a third party, which may also consist of a pecuniary claim[6], as is always the case when assets are dedicated by bequest.

The vesting of claims as a form of endowing the foundation with assets plays a significant role in the case of *Personalfürsorgestiftungen* (pension funds)[7] which are established by the employers for the purpose of providing for the welfare of workers and salaried employees. However, mere arrangements for procuring the assets to be subsequently contributed to the foundation, such as collections or lotteries[8], are not deemed to constitute adequate provision.

5. *The determination of the purpose*

The requirement of determining a 'specific purpose'[9] prescribes no limitation of the purposes that foundations may pursue. The wording used by the lawmakers merely aims at urging founders to specify the purpose as clearly as possible so as to avoid general and meaningless phrases such as 'promotion of tasks beneficial to the community' or 'fight against poverty'. In all other respects there prevails—within the usual limits—the principle of the free determination of purpose. Hence, only those purposes are inadmissible which are deemed to be impossible, illegal or immoral[10]. Foundations having such purpose(s) are subject to dissolution by law[11] or on request[12].

Despite the requirement to give a clear designation of the purpose, concise wording or summary descriptions in the charter are admissible and frequently appropriate[13]. For details or detailed regulations can be left to special by-laws or a special set of rules which, as distinct from the charter of the foundation, require no specific form and can be freely amended and thus permit the foundation to adjust its activity to changing times and circumstances[14]. However, in so doing compliance with the founder's intention as laid down in the charter must always be maintained[15].

[6] BGE 51 II 469 et s.; 75 I 271 (Decisions of the Federal Supreme Court).
[7] Egger, op. cit., Art. 83, Mar. No. 6; BGE 51 II 465 et ss.
[8] Hafter, op. cit. Art. 80, Mar. No. 4.
[9] Cf. Art. 80 of the ZGB.
[10] Art. 52 para. 3 of the ZGB.
[11] In the case of impossibility, cf. Art. 88 para. 1 of the ZGB.
[12] In the other two cases, see Art. 88 para. 2 of the ZGB.
[13] Hindermann, Der Stiftungszweck, ZSR 47 (1928), p. 225 et ss., p. 235.
[14] Cf. BGE 76 I 78 et s.
[15] Cf. Hindermann, op. cit. p. 235. Hafter, op. cit. Art. 83, Mar. No. 4.

The principle of freedom to establish a foundation comprises the power of the founder to give directions, to impose conditions, and to make reservations. This power is based on the idea that anybody who is prepared to give up his property or any part thereof in order to pursue specific purposes shall be entitled to make this dependent on the occurrence of specific or of uncertain events or to do so subject to certain—perhaps even selfish—reservations. Thus there exist foundations whose founder has reserved the right to dissolve them[16]. Such rulings, however, appear questionable in the light of the basic idea of the foundation as a definitive, permanent and voluntary renunciation of one's property.

Finally, the principle of freedom to establish a foundation naturally allows for the determination of several purposes, whether parallel or successive ones. There is agreement on this point today, although the question as to whether parallel purposes should be admissible was for a time the subject of controversy owing to the possible difficulties that might arise in deciding in what ratios the available funds should be used for the different purposes[17].

6. The organisation of the foundation

Although the foundation by virtue of its being a legal entity can neither exist nor act without at least one organ (administrator, administrative board), the designation of an organ together with the specification of rules relating to the administration of the foundation does not belong to the essential, indispensable components of the founding act.

Admittedly, the law states: 'the organs. . .and the nature of the administration are determined by the charter[18].' The lawmakers, however, express in this respect only an expectation[19]. The founder may thus lay down the relevant provisions in a special set of rules or he may leave this task to third parties (such as heirs, executors or intended beneficiaries). If he fails to do so or makes only inadequate arrangements 'the supervisory authority shall make the necessary dispositions[20]', in which case, however, it has to make as much allowance as possible for the intentions of the founder[21]. If the founder is still alive, the supervisory authority will come to an understanding with him.

The founder has complete latitude in organising the foundation. He may appoint several organs instead of only one and thus already set up a controlling agency inside the foundation. He can also exercise his discretion as to

---

[16] A well-known example is reported by Hindermann, op. cit. p. 242.
[17] Cf. Hindermann, op. cit., pp. 243 and 244.
[18] Art. 83 para. 1 of the ZGB.   [19] Hafter, op. cit., para. 83 Mar. No. 2.
[20] Art. 83 para. 2 of the ZGB.   [21] Egger, op. cit., Art. 83 Mar. No. 2.

the persons he wishes to appoint as members of such organs, except in the case for pension funds (Art. 89 para. 3 of the ZGB). In the event of any organs being composed of several members, and lacking special prescriptions for the decision-making process, the relevant provisions of the law relating to *Vereine* (associations) shall apply analogously[22]. The founder may also issue special rules for the appointment, the supplementation and the removal of organs or of their members. Finally, the power to make any kind of arrangements he chooses for changing the organisation, offers him an opportunity to render the foundation flexible and adaptable so as to allow for changing circumstances[23].

A special case which, however, is of very little practical importance arises where the establishment of a suitable organisational structure proves impossible for one reason or the other. For instance, the foundation's funds might be completely inadequate for this purpose. In such instances, the authority supervising foundations has the power to allocate the assets to another foundation which, as far as this is possible, has a similar purpose, unless the founder is explicitly opposed to such an arrangement or his opposition thereto can be deduced from the charter[24].

7. The emergence of the legal entity—registration

If the declaration of intent conforms to the minimum legal requirements, the foundation will—unless it is an ecclesiastical foundation or a family trust[25]—come into being as a legal entity as soon as it has been entered in the commercial register. The registration will be effected upon the application of the administrator of the foundation or, in the case of a body consisting of several members, upon the application of all the members[26]. In the event of the administrator's (administrative board's) failure to act, the supervising authority will take the necessary measures[27]; it has power, if necessary, to order the administrator (administrative board) to effect the registration[28].

Prior to registration, the Registrar merely examines whether the requisite legal requirements have been met and, in particular, whether the purpose of the foundation is not unlawful or *contra bonos mores*; the purpose of a foundation is also unlawful *inter alia* if its realisation is completely impossible, but not simply if the funds contributed to the foundation are inadequate for such

---

[22] Egger, op. cit., Art 83 Mar. No. 5.   [23] Cf. BGE 76, 78 et s.
[24] Art. 83 para. 3 of the ZGB.
[25] This question will be dealt with separately later on.
[26] Egger, op. cit., Art. 81 Mar. Nos. 7, 8.   [27] Art. 81 para. 2 of the ZGB.
[28] BGE 40 I 262.

purpose[29]. On the other hand, a foundation for the purpose of promoting space flights to neighbouring systems of the Milky Way might, accordingly, be deemed unlawful.

The *Bundesgericht* (Federal Court) had, in the course of time, to deal repeatedly with foundations which, in view of their declared function, could be described as 'foundations for their own sake'[30]. By exploiting the freedom to establish foundations, such foundations were designed primarily to obtain tax advantages. In such instances the founder, by cleverly arranging the appointments to the organs of the foundation—not infrequently by appointing himself as its administrator—usually retained complete freedom to dispose both of the 'dedicated' assets and of their proceeds so that in the end the foundation was his *alter ego*, frequently with only another domicile. Since in these cases the *Bundesgericht* always concerned itself solely with the question as to the competence in tax matters[31], it could not explicitly express an opinion on the validity of such foundations under civil law. Had it, however, been obliged to render a decision on this particular issue, it would have had to deny validity in all these cases since the requirement that the purpose of the foundation must—at least in part—be an altruistic one is one of the indispensable basic characteristics of the foundation, and this requirement had not been met in any of the cases in question. A foundation which does not meet this requirement is unlawful.

If the foundation applying for registration has no legal shortcomings, the Registrar has to enter it in the commercial register. In this context, the question arises whether in the event of a foundation being entered in spite of legal defects such defects are remedied by the entry. This question is not answered in a uniform way. The decisions of the courts show a certain tendency to answer it in the affirmative with the emphasis, as in the Corporation Law, on the idea of protecting innocent third parties[32].

The prevailing opinion is against the remedying effect of registration. The position of a foundation in law is not to be compared with that of a stock corporation. Besides, the foundation does not acquire legal status because of registration but because it fulfils the legal requirements[33].

---

[29] Hafter, op. cit., Art. 80, Mar. no. 8; cf. Art. 83 para. 3 of the ZGB.

[30] Ackermann, Der besondere Zweck der Stiftung unter spezieller Berücksichtigung des Zweckes der Familienstiftung, Thesis submitted to the Faculty of Law, University of Fribourg (Switzerland) 1950, pp. 17, 21, 28 et s.

[31] e.g. BGE 53 I 440 et ss.; 55 I 373 et ss., 380; 71 I 268.

[32] BGE 33 II 161; also a decision of the Appellationshof (Court of Appeal) of Bern, cited by Hindermann, op. cit. pp. 231, 232. Hafter, op. cit., Art. 52, Mar. No. 13.

[33] Hindermann, op. cit.; Egger, op. cit., Art. 81, Mar. No. 9.

8. *The supervision of foundations*[34]

The foundation with legal status is subject to supervision by the public agency under whose authority it falls according to its purpose[35]. An exception exists in this respect again for private family foundations and ecclesiastical foundations.

The public bodies exercising this supervision are, depending on the purpose of the foundation and the local area to which it appertains, the Federal Government, the Canton and the local authority and possibly also the *Bezirk* (District) or certain administrative associations serving two or more local authorities and established for a specific purpose. The competent supervisory authority is notified by the Registrar responsible for maintaining the commercial register that the foundation has been entered therein, and the authority in turn confirms to the Registrar that it has assumed the supervisory responsibilities[36]. In the event of conflicting competence, the Registrar has to ask for a decision by the Cantonal Government or—in the case of foundations coming under the authority of the Federal Government—by the Federal Department of the Interior. Against such decision is the possibility of recourse (administrative appeal) *vis-à-vis* the *Bundesgericht*.

The ZGB only lays down the principle of the exercise of supervision. It leaves the regulations regarding competence as to the subject matter as well as the stipulation of provisions for the nature and scope of exercise of supervision to the public law of the Swiss Confederation and the Cantons.

Thus it follows that the Cantons can issue repressive but not preventive regulations and take action accordingly. Consequently coercive cantonal regulations in regard to the investment of the foundation's assets are to be regarded as running contrary to federal law[37].

The task of the supervisory authority is to ensure that the assets of the foundation are utilised in accordance with its declared purposes[38]. It performs this task by keeping a continuous check on the soundness of the annual budgets, the funds paid out and the investment of the foundation's assets[39].

---

[34] Cf. Wirz, Hans Gerold, Die Personalwohlfahrtseinrichtungen der Schweizerischen Privatwirtschaft—ihre Stellung im Steuerrecht und ihre Beaufsichtigung, Ed. B, Stäfa 1955, pp. 179–351, 223 et ss. (cited hereinafter as Wirz, Beaufsichtigung).

[35] Art. 103 para. 1 of the ZGB.

[36] Art. 103 para. 1 of the HRVO (Commercial Register Regulation).

[37] Cf. Wirz, Beaufsichtigung, pp. 266 et ss., 328 et ss.; Wirz, Vermögensanlage von Personalfürsorgestiftungen aus der Sicht der Aufsichtsbehörden, in: Personalfürsorge, Vol. 5, No. 3, May 1970 (cited hereinafter as Wirz, Vermögensanlage).

[38] Art. 84 para. 2 of the ZGB.

[39] This power, however, is frequently disputed by the administrative organs of the foundations, especially by those of pension funds.

In so doing it must also see to it that special prescriptions of the founder are adhered to. Within the scope of its activity, it may issue warnings and instructions to the organs of the foundation; the supervisory authority may even disband completely unsuitable organs and restaff them anew in accordance with the charter[40]. Its measures, however, must never exceed the scope of mere tutelage[41]. Thus it is neither authorised to reserve to itself the approval of actions carried out by the organs of the foundation, nor may it itself act in their stead[42].

The supervisory authority is furthermore the authority to which complaints can be made against all actions carried out by the organs of the foundation[43]. A complaint can be filed by anybody who can prove a legal interest, including the founder and his heirs, a possible executor to an estate appointed by the founder, other organs of the foundation, or members of such organs, the intended beneficiaries and such persons who, according to the charter, may come under consideration as intended beneficiaries[44]. Each complaint obliges the supervisory authority to carry out a pertinent investigation; in so doing it has to examine whether the action about which complaint has been made is admissible according to the law and to the charter. Discretionary decisions must be investigated for abuse of powers or arbitrariness. Civil claims, however, cannot be submitted in the form of a complaint[45].

In addition to this civil law supervision there is a cantonal supervision by the cantonal tax authorities in order to check periodically with pension funds that the regulations concerning the charitable status of these funds are observed[46].

9. The legal position of the beneficiaries

The charter and/or any other available regulations determine who is the intended beneficiary of a foundation, i.e. who shall benefit from the funds of a given foundation. If, in this connection, no specific category of persons has been named or described, it will frequently only be possible to identify the intended beneficiaries by means of interpretation. Their selection may also be left entirely to the discretion of the organs of the foundation or even to outside third parties; in any case, their identification is frequently quite complicated.

---

[40] Egger, op. cit., Art. 84, Mar. No. 9.
[41] Hindermann, op. cit., p. 254.
[42] Cf. BGE 40 I 263.   [43] BGE 40 I 261.
[44] Hindermann, op. cit., p. 260.
[45] Egger, op. cit., Art. 84, Mar. No. 10.
[46] Wirz, Beaufsichtigung, p. 328 et ss.

E

The legal position of the intended beneficiaries is characterised by the fact that they generally have a right to benefit and, consequently, an enforceable claim. This right is considered to be correlative with the necessity of fulfilling the purpose on which the recognition of the foundation as an independent legal entity is based[47]. On the other hand, from the principle that the founder has complete freedom to organise the foundation within the limits of what is legally and morally admissible, it also follows that an enforceable claim to the usufruct of the foundation may be excluded[48]. Such exclusion need not be prescribed explicitly, it may again follow from an interpretation of the statements made by the founder, or from other circumstances.

Special regulations apply to pension funds.

10. *Alteration of the foundation*

In order to assure the continued existence of the essentially rigidly defined foundations through the vicissitudes of time, the law of Switzerland also provides for the possibility of a transformation so as to adapt the foundation to changing circumstances. This may require both the modification of the organisation[49] and a change of purpose[50]. In both cases, the transformation is effected by the competent authority of the relevant public agency, and after hearing the supreme organ of the foundation. This is the only, though under the circumstance quite extensive, deviation from the principle that the intention of the founder shall constitute the principal guideline governing the foundation's existence. However, it is precisely because of this principle that, even where the requirements of Secs. 85 and 86 are fulfilled, these provisions may only be applied if the founder himself has not made arrangements for an eventual alteration.

But even without any special arrangements on the founder's part, his intention is never left completely out of account. Thus no regulation may be established which it may be assumed would have run counter to the wishes of the founder; in particular, no arbitrary measures may be taken. In the event of a purpose being changed, the new purpose must, as far as possible, be similar to the original one[51]. In order to ensure this, the co-operation of two public authorities is required[52].

---

[47] Egger, op. cit., Art. 83, Mar. No. 10.

[48] BGE 61 II 289 et ss., 293, 296; Decision of the Zivilgericht des Kantons Baselstadt (Civil Court of the Canton of Baselstadt) SJZ 37, 18 et s. 19.

[49] Art. 85 of the ZGB.   [50] Art. 86 of the ZGB.

[51] Art. 57 para. 2 of the ZGB.   [52] Egger, op. cit., Arts. 85 and 86, Mar. No. 10.

Because of its far-reaching implications, the change of the purpose of the foundation is subject to stricter requirements than a mere restructuring of its organisation. On the one hand, it must be incontrovertibly demonstrated that the original purpose has, with the passage of time, acquired quite another meaning or effect, and, on the other, that the foundation has obviously ceased to conform to the intentions of the founder[53].

The first requirement is as a rule relatively easy to determine; it is mostly the consequence of a too narrow specification of the purpose[54]. It will, *inter alia*, have been met also, if the dedicated assets prove to be in excess of the means required for the realisation of the original purpose[55]. The determination of the second requirement is frequently more difficult. It is not enough to conclude that because the meaning or effect of the foundation has changed due to changing conditions, the foundation has inevitably evolved into something different from what the founder intended it to be. One should rather ask what he would want, if he were in a position to consider the new situation. In this connection, one should take into account all circumstances which might help to provide an answer, even those that are not evident from the charter[56].

A less serious effect on the existence of the foundation is exercised by a change of its organisation. Therefore it is subject to less stringent requirements. Admittedly, even in this case a change should not be brought about if perhaps a better or more practical organisational alternative offers itself. The preservation of the assets or of the purpose of the foundation constitute a justification for so drastic a measure[57]. If, however, the better or more practical organisational structure is at the same time much less complicated or expensive, the requirements for such intervention may already have been met.

II. *Revocation of a foundation*

The provision of Art. 82 of the ZGB deserves special attention. Under this provision, a foundation may be revoked by the heirs or the creditors of the founder, just as in the case of an unsolicited donation or gift.

This means that on the one hand, even in the case of a foundation established *inter vivos*, the heirs may start an action to reduce the endowment under Art. 522 of the ZGB, if their right to their legitimate portion has been infringed[58].

---

[53] Art. 86 para. 1 of the ZGB.
[54] Egger, Arts. 85 and 86, Mar. No. 5.
[55] Egger, with further references.
[56] Egger, Art. 86, Mar. No. 6.
[57] Art. 85 of the ZGB.
[58] Art. 257 Nos. 3 and 4 of the ZGB.

The right of revocation is governed by Art. 185 et ss. of the *Bundesgesetz über Schuldbetreibung und Konkurs (SchKG*—Federal Act relating to Recovery of Debts and Bankruptcy). The question whether the founder himself has a right of revocation is not regulated in the law relating to foundations. However, one may unhesitatingly assume that the general provisions relating to revocation are applicable[59]. It is doubtful, whether, in addition, a right of revocation according to the principles of the law of donation[60] may be recognised which could be of importance, if a right of revocation, because for instance, of a mere error in motive, is not available.

According to what is probably the prevailing opinion, the right of revocation is admitted[61], although the reference to the law of donation in Art. 82 of the ZGB is in the nature of an exception. This means that the founder may revoke the foundation at any time, at least to the extent to which it benefits persons who have gravely misconducted themselves *vis-à-vis* the founder[62]. Where the foundation has not yet been registered and can thus be virtually considered as a donation which has not been duly effected, a revocation will be possible if, in the meantime, the pecuniary circumstances of the founder have changed to such an extent that the foundation would be a serious burden on him, or if, since the drawing up of the charter, he has incurred substantial obligations under family law[63]. In all the cases enumerated, revocation will, however, be barred, if the foundation was established in fulfilment of a moral obligation[64].

12. Private family foundations and ecclesiastical foundations

When dealing with family foundations and ecclesiastical foundations, the Swiss law relating to foundations deviates, in part, to a considerable extent from what has been stated hitherto. Both types of foundations are characterised by their specific purpose. Thus, we are dealing with a family trust if the purpose is 'defraying the costs of the education, the dowries, or the support of members of the family', or 'a similar purpose'[65]. On the other hand, a foundation cannot be termed ecclesiastical simply because its funds are to benefit, for

[59] Arts. 7 of the ZGB, 23 et ss. of the OR
[60] Art. 250 of the OR.
[61] Cf. Egger, op. cit., Art. 80, Mar. Nos. 17, 18.
[62] Arts. 250 para 1 No. 1, 249 of the OR.
[63] Art. 250 para. 1 Nos. 2 and 3 of the OR.
[64] Art. 239 para. 3 of the OR.
[65] Art. 335 para. 1 of the ZGB; for a detailed exposition: Gerhard, Die Familienstiftung nach ZGB, ZSR 49, 1930, p. 137 et ss., p. 142.

example, the adherents of a certain faith or if the foundation is administered by clergymen[66]. The decisive factor is that its purpose should serve ecclesiastical interests or needs[67]. Whether the foundation is a family trust or an ecclesiastical foundation is a matter to be decided by the supervisory authority. A dispute in relation thereto is heard in administrative proceedings, not before the civil courts[68].

Private family trusts and ecclesiastical foundations are primarily subject to two special regulations. Firstly, they do not have to be entered in the commercial register in order to be established, but already come into being as legal entities through the founding act done in the form prescribed by law[69]. Secondly, they are not subject to government supervision[70]. This not only facilitates the establishment of such foundations, but the latter enjoy the greatest measure of freedom imaginable as regards their activities.

Family foundations and ecclesiastical foundations are thus left almost entirely to themselves and are frequently unknown to the public at large. The supervisory authority does not interfere in their affairs either in the case of an unsatisfactory organisation[71], or in the case of a conversion[72, 73]. All this, however, does not apply to so-called mixed foundations serving other purposes besides specifically ecclesiastic or family interests, because the said privileges are based on the assumption that family trusts and ecclesiastical foundations never or hardly ever come to the notice of the general public and take part but rarely in private legal dealings[74]. However, modest ancillary purposes such as, for instance, tasks that are beneficial to the community shall not be to their disadvantage in this respect[75].

These privileges naturally provide an incentive for abuses. Thus, family foundations have repeatedly been established in order to circumvent the progressive scale of taxation or, by means of an appropriate selection of domicile, to make use of the favourable tax rates of another Canton. In such foundations 'for their own sake' the founders have, by means of astute

[66] Egger, op. cit., Art. 87, Mar. No. 2.
[67] Hindermann, op. cit., p. 251; Egger, op. cit.
[68] BGE 40 I 261.
[69] Art. 52 para. 2 of the ZGB.
[70] Art. 87 para. 1 of the ZGB.
[71] Art. 83 paras. 2 and 3 of the ZGB.
[72] Arts. 85 and 86 of the ZGB.
[73] Hafter, op. cit., Art. 87, Mar. Nos. 9–11; Egger, op. cit., Art. 87.
[74] Egger, op. cit., Art. 87, Mar. No. 5 with further references.
[75] Egger, Kommentar zum Schweizerischen Zivilgesetzbuch, 2nd Ed., Vol. 2, Das Familienrecht, 2nd Chapter: Die Verwandtschaft Art. 335, Mar. No. 14.

organisational arrangements, on the whole always retained the power to dispose of the assets and the income of the foundation[76].

Frequently, they have reserved the right to dissolve the foundation. Fiscal authorities and courts, however, have in such cases denied the existence of legal status[77] as far as tax liability is concerned. If, without a sufficient objective reason, the administration of a foundation as described above is transferred to a Canton with more favourable tax conditions, the foundation in question will nevertheless be taxed at the domicile of the founder, the assets and the income of the foundation and the founder being taxed together[78]. Although the *Bundesgericht* has sometimes questioned the seriousness of such foundations[79] it has still not invalidated them in these cases, because it has always confined itself to dealing with the question as to competence in tax matters. In the relevant literature, however, it is held that such foundations are also invalid under civil law, since they do not meet the requirements of Art.335 para.1 of the ZGB[80].

The *Bundesgericht* has also held so-called *Unterhaltsstiftungen* (family maintenance funds) to be inadmissible and invalid. These are foundations whose sole purpose is to provide the means for the support of a family and its issue. The inadmissibility of such foundations is derived from the prohibition to establish entailed estates[81] and from the time limit in regard to the appointment of a residuary legatee[82]; both these regulations, it has held, are based on the principle that property should not be tied up for several generations[83].

The Federal Court has occasionally examined the question as to whether an *Unterhaltsstiftung* might not acquire validity through alteration. In this connection alteration by the appointment of a residuary legatee has been deemed to be invalid[84]. In another case, however, the *Bundesgericht* accorded validity to a foundation established as a family trust, but not meeting the requirement of Art.335 para.1 of the ZGB, after the purpose of this foundation had been modified on its recommendation[85].

Family trusts or ecclesiastical foundations may also voluntarily apply for

[76] Cf., for instance, the case in BGE 53 I 440 et ss., 447, 448.

[77] see *supra*, p. 55.

[78] Egger, op. cit., Art. 335, Mar. No. 9; BGE 45 I 190; 46 I 175; 52 I 372; 53 I 440 et ss.; 55 I 380; 71 I 268.

[79] e.g. BGE 53 I 447.

[80] Gerhard, op. cit., p. 143; Müller, Die Besteuerung der Familienstiftung, SJZ 28, 1931/32, p. 180.

[81] Art. 335 para. 2 of the ZGB.

[82] Art. 488 para. 2 of the ZGB.

[83] BGE 73 II 86; 75 II 24, 90; 79 II 118; Egger, op. cit., Art. 335, Mar. Nos. 9, 14, 17–19; Gerhard, op. cit., pp. 153–56.

[84] BGE 89 II 437.   [85] BGE 75 II 81 et ss., 91 et s.

entry in the commercial register[86]. They must apply for entry, if, in order to fulfil their specific purposes, they operate a commercial, manufacturing or other business enterprise[87].

Complaints under civil law are—as in the case of all other foundations—decided by civil courts in accordance with Art.87 para.2 of the ZGB. This reference has been considerably developed by the courts with regard to family trusts and ecclesiastical foundations, so as to provide—in view of the absence of government supervision and therefore of administrative proceedings—the parties concerned with the same safeguards which are otherwise guaranteed by the right to have recourse to complaint proceedings. Thus it is possible to bring an action for establishing the attributes of the intended beneficiaries, or an injunction against administrative acts which amount to dereliction of duty or which damage or endanger the assets of the foundation or against decisions contrary to the charter, or an action for damages[88]. This type of action is available not only to interested outsiders but also to the organs of the foundation or its members, for instance in the case of acts or measures prejudicing their position as laid down in the charter.

The privilege under Art.87 para.1 of the ZGB of exemption from government supervision is granted with the reservation that the provisions of public law must be adhered to. Although the purport of this reservation is difficult to determine, it is certain that it means a limitation, or at least the possibility of a limitation, of this privilege by provisions of public law established by the Federal Government or by the Cantons. Hence, the Federal Government and the Cantons may, under public law, subject private family foundations and ecclesiastical foundations to a certain control. This, however, must not lead to supervision by the State thereby being reintroduced contrary to the principle of exemption laid down in Art.87 para.1 of the ZGB[89]. Foundation control under public law, should, therefore, hardly come into consideration as far as strictly private family trusts and ecclesiastical foundations are concerned[90].

13. *Pension funds*[91]

Some special provisions of the law apply also to specific welfare foundations

---

[86] Egger, op. cit., Art. 335, Mar. No. 10.

[87] Arts. 61 para. 2 of the ZGB, 934 of the OR.

[88] BGE 40 I 266; 50 II 423 (26); 61 II 295, 296.

[89] BGE 50 II 424; Hindermann, op. cit., p. 252 Egger, Personenrecht, Art. 87, Mar. No. 6.

[90] Cf. thereon in detail Egger, op. cit., Art. 87, Mar. Nos. 6, 7.

[91] cf. Wirz, Beaufsichtigung (Literature, p. XL et ss.), Helbling, Personalfürsorge Bern 1964.

established for the benefit of workers and salaried employees. The provision of Company Law, laid down in Art.673 para 2 of the OR and valid till 1958, specified that those parts of the assets which are clearly earmarked for welfare purposes, shall be separated from the overall assets of the corporation and be transferred to a foundation. This provision applied also to *Kommanditgesellschaften* (limited partnerships)[92], *Gesellschaften mit beschränkter Haftung* (limited liability companies)[93] and co-operative societies[94]. Foundations established under these provisions are generally described as *Personalfürsorgestiftungen* (staff welfare funds or pension funds).

However, theory and practice were essentially in agreement that, as regards the establishment of welfare funds under the above provisions, the lawmakers who had passed the *Obligationsrecht* (Act relating to the Swiss Law of contract) of 1937 not only had had in mind the legal form of the foundation with legal status within the meaning of Art.80 et ss. of the ZGB but also, by using the word *Stiftung* (foundation), only wanted to make explicit the obligation to endow the contributed assets with legal autonomy[95]. Thus it was also to be permissible to use the forms of the *Verein* (association) or perhaps of the co-operative society, a procedure that was quite common in practice. However, already at that time genuine foundations predominated by far[96].

In the meantime, the above-mentioned provisions of Company Law have been repealed by the *Gesetz betreffend die Ergänzung des Dienstvertrags- und des Stiftungsrechts* (Act relating to the Supplementation of the Law of Master and Servant and the Law relating to Foundations) of 21st March 1968, and by the general provision of Labour Law contained in Art.343 of the OR. Under these provisions only the foundation and the co-operative society can be the institutions responsible for assets dedicated by an employer for welfare purposes. The establishment of special facilities for the administration of assets, which today still predominantly take the form of the foundation, is legally required if an employer has clearly dedicated a considerable part of his assets to welfare purposes, i.e. if it is certain that specific funds are intended to benefit his employees in the form of retirement pensions or in the event of death or disablement[97]. The endowment may vary. Both cash and pecuniary

[92] Through Art. 764 para. 2 of the OR.   [93] Art. 805 of the OR.

[94] Art. 862 para. 2 of the OR in its old wording.

[95] Bürgi, Kommentar zum Schweizerischen Zivilgesetzbuch, Zurich 1947, Vol. 5, Obligationenrecht, 5th Part, Art. 673, Mar. Nos. 40, 44.

[96] Of 581 pension funds in 1928 527 were foundations, 44 co-operative societies and 10 associations; cf., Bürgi, op. cit., Mar. No. 45.

[97] Arts. 343 *bis* para. 1 of the OR; cf. in detail Bürgi, op. cit., Art. 673 Mar. No. 37 et ss.

claims may be contributed. Contributions by the employees may be added. Often even insurance policies are taken out under which the foundation is both the insured party and the beneficiary. Thus the foundation transfers all risks or part of them to an insurance company. Also many pension funds assume the risks themselves (so-called autonomous pension funds). In recent years, particularly in the case of smaller foundations the system of a savings scheme linked to a death benefit insurance policy has been developed.

If the employer is a company, it is also conceivable that a right to participate in it may be granted. However, in view of the tasks generally entrusted to the welfare organisations, as a rule recurrent annual or monthly contributions are made which in financially profitable years are increased by contributions from the annual surpluses.

The lawmakers have granted the intended beneficiaries special rights. They can request the employer to furnish them with information as regards their claims *vis-à-vis* the welfare fund[98]. Where a foundation is involved, its organs have to provide information about its organisation, its activities and its financial situation[99]. If the intended beneficiaries are themselves contributors, they shall participate in the administration in proportion to the amount of their contributions[100]. In this case, the assets of the foundation shall, in proportion to the amount of such contributions by the staff, not consist of unguaranteed claims against the employer[101]. Finally, the intended beneficiaries are normally entitled to start legal action to secure their due benefits[102].

In addition, the general provisions of the law relating to foundations shall apply. Pension funds, in particular, are also subject to government supervision[103].

14. *The dissolution of the foundation*

A foundation may be dissolved by virtue of an intention of the founder to this effect laid down in the charter, by operation of law[104] or by the court[105].

If grounds for a dissolution or termination are provided for in the charter itself, such grounds are of legal importance only if they appear to be justified by the nature of the foundation as it is at the time or by the specific purpose of the foundation. Thus dissolution may, for instance, be provided for in the event that the purpose of the foundation has been fulfilled, or that the State

[98] Art. 343 *bis* para. 2 of the OR.   [99] Art. 89 *bis* para. 2 of the ZGB.
[100] Art. 89 *bis* para. 3 of the ZGB.   [101] Art. 89 *bis* para. 4 of the ZGB.
[102] Art. 89 *bis* para. 5 of the ZGB.
[103] Cf. Wirz, Beaufsichtigung, pp. 179–351, 223 et ss.
[104] Art. 88 para. 1 of the ZGB.
[105] Art. 88 para. 2 of the ZGB.

takes over the tasks of the foundation, or that the purpose of the foundation itself is taken over by the State, or that—in the case of a *Personalfürsorgestiftung*—the founding firm goes out of existence. The founder may not reserve to himself an arbitrary right of dissolution, nor may he grant such right to the organs of the foundation; this would be incompatible with the nature of the foundation[106].

The foundation will be dissolved by operation of law, as soon as the purpose of the foundation has become unattainable. Such impossibility to fulfil the purpose does not exist as long as a reasonable activity on the part of the foundation can still be achieved by way of alteration. An alteration is frequently impossible if the foundation still has assets. A further or alternative activity of the foundation may, as a rule, be considered impossible only if all funds have been exhausted and there is no prospect of replenishing them, or if no more intended beneficiaries exist.

Dissolution by a court order will take place, if the purpose of the foundation becomes unlawful or immoral. Both may be the consequence of mere lapse of time; especially unlawfulness may result from unforeseen legislative measures.

Dissolution takes place *eo ipso* if there exists a ground provided for in the charter, or if the purpose of the foundation cannot be attained. In the other cases it is brought about by a court order. Anybody having a justifiable interest has the right of action.

Failing any determination by the founder to the contrary, the assets of a dissolved foundation shall pass to the public authority under whose tutelage the foundation, according to its purposes, has been placed. The same shall use it as far as possible for the previous purpose. If the dissolution took place, because the purpose of the foundation was unlawful or immoral, its assets will pass to the local authority irrespective of any specific provisions made by the founder[107].

After the dissolution of the foundation, its entry in the commercial register will be cancelled.

III. THE IMPORTANCE OF THE FOUNDATION WITH LEGAL STATUS

1. *The essential forms of activity of foundations with legal status and their importance*

In order to explain the importance of the foundation in Switzerland, let us

---

[106] Egger, Personenrecht, Arts. 88 and 89, Mar. No. 1; Art. 81, Mar. No. 11.
[107] Art. 57 paras. 1–3 of the ZGB.

first quote a few figures. According to information given by the Federal Commercial Register Office at the end of 1969 84,032 individually owned firms, 60,746 stock corporations, 18,537 foundations, 13,518 co-operative societies, 10,986 partnerships, 3,940 limited partnerships, 2,714 limited liability companies and 1,607 associations were entered into the Swiss Commercial Register. There is perhaps hardly any country in the world, in which the foundation plays a comparable part in mere numerical terms. Add to this that family trusts and ecclesiastical foundations require no entry in the commercial register and are, therefore—except for the undoubtedly few cases of voluntary registration—not included in the figure quoted above. However, it is precisely family trusts that have been established in Switzerland in large numbers and, although they have sometimes been abused for tax purposes and are excluded as being mere *Unterhaltsstiftungen* (family maintenance funds), their special importance lies in the fact that in numerous cases they have prevented the impoverishment of once wealthy families[108].

Hence if we consider the number of unregistered foundations, the total number must, at a cautious estimate, certainly be increased by 1,000 to 1,500, so we may assume that there exist roughly 20,000 foundations in Switzerland. This figure which, considering the size of the country, is extremely high, may partly be explained by the sound economic conditions which have existed for quite some time and were not affected by war with the result that great prosperity developed and large fortunes were made. From these conditions there emerged a widespread altruistic mentality which brought about the establishment of many foundations with humanitarian and ecclesiastical purposes. In addition, foundations with scientific and research tasks as well as foundations for the promotion of artistic and cultural interests were established. The individual inclinations and interests of the founders frequently found expression in the determination of more or less odd purposes. Finally, as has already been mentioned, the foundation was not infrequently used for the purpose of preserving and securing family estates[109].

Foundations with such purposes play a considerable part within the framework of the Swiss system of foundations even today. However, it is impossible to make any even remotely reliable statements as regards their assets. The total assets alone of the foundations which are subject to supervision by the Federal Government—338 at the moment—are estimated at approx. Sfrs. 350 million, this amount comprising only bank accounts and

---

[108] Cf. Gmür, Das schweizerische Zivilgesetzbuch verglichen mit dem deutschen Bürgerlichen Gesetzbuch, Bern 1965, pp. 93, 94.

[109] Mengiardi, Strukturprobleme des Gesellschaftsrechts in: Referate und Mitteilungen des Schweizerischen Juristenvereins, No. 1/1968, p. 25.

securities, but not real estate and certain movables such as artistic or scientific collections because a reasonable valuation of such assets is practically impossible. Instead of looking at the foundation's total assets a far more accurate picture can be formed by noting the expenditure effected for the fulfilment of the prescribed purposes, as, in addition to their permanent endowment a considerable number of foundations dispose of a steady flow of income which can be directly applied to this end. In 1968 185 foundations paid out Sfrs. 79 million directly to the beneficiaries, and 45 operating foundations expended a total of Sfrs. 167 million between them[110].

Among the foundations which are subject to supervision of the Federal Government and the foundations pursuing aims at the national level, but under Cantonal supervision the majority have assets amounting to between Sfrs. 1 and 4 million.

The appendix, written by Hans G. Wirz, Zurich, presents some of the larger foundations in terms of assets and/or expenditures. Many other major foundations—including those whose beneficial area is restricted to a single Canton—cannot be dealt with in this first survey.

Unfortunately no list yet exists of the foundations which come under the supervision of the Cantons and municipalities. It is estimated that the number involved may be in the region of between 2,000 to 3,000 foundations with total assets of approx. Sfrs. 1,000 million.

As regards purpose, it appears that most (probably 80%) of the foundations which are subject to supervision by the Federal Government devote themselves to scientific and research tasks involving for the most part narrowly defined, special fields (such as research in the field of corpuscular radiation technique or in the field of concrete and ferroconcrete construction). The majority of the other foundations serve charitable and/or cultural purposes. An almost diametrically opposite picture is presented by foundations whose scope of activity is limited to specific regions. Here, humanitarian and charitable tasks rank first by a wide margin, followed by cultural purposes in their widest sense. The proportion of foundations pursuing scientific tasks is a relatively modest one by comparison.

In spite of their considerable merits, the importance of the foundations dealt with above is today much smaller than that of the pension funds within the meaning of Art. 343 of the OR. Being privileged by tax law which exempts from taxation most of the welfare funds that have become legally independent, such funds have become an important institution in the economic process which can no longer be left out of consideration today[111]. In this

---

[110] Data provided by the Federal Department of the Interior.
[111] Cf. Wirz, Beaufsichtigung, p. 13 et ss. Mengiardi, op. cit., p. 25.

connection it is precisely the legal form of the foundation that is generally preferred to the co-operative society which, under Art. 343 of the OR is also admissible as an independent owner of welfare funds, because the foundation enables an enterprise to establish an organisation conforming entirely to its specific wishes and ideas[112]. Add to this, that on account of the supervision by the government, a number of Cantons will grant tax exemption only if the form of the foundation is selected. Apparently, the fiscal authorities concerned expect the supervisory authorities to ensure that the assets of the foundations are not used for other purposes than exclusively for the tax-privileged ones of welfare funds. In this connection an important part is played by the possibility—initially recognised by judicial practice[113] and later on also by the lawmakers in the former Art. 673 para. 2 of the OR—to effect the endowment of a pension fund solely by allocating a claim to the enterprise establishing the foundation[114], in which case the employee's contributions are to be set aside or appropriately secured.

This possibility enabled many enterprises, in particular those with relatively small liquid resources, to create welfare institutions without immediately withdrawing the requisite funds from the business. In this way a large increase in welfare institutions set up by enterprises was achieved. In some Cantons, however, supervisory provisions were issued under which security has to be lodged for the claims on the part of the enterprises. These measures were criticised quite rightly by different authors[115]. Other attempts to influence the investments of *Personalfürsorgestiftungen* in order to prevent abuses were made partly via the tax laws by making the granting of tax privilege dependent on the effective separation of the earmarked assets from those of the enterprise, or at least on the lodging of appropriate security[116]. The interests of the intended beneficiaries hardly seem to require such extensive protection as long as the supervision of foundations functions. If the founding enterprise goes bankrupt, the claims of the foundation which have arisen in connection with the dedication of assets are privileged.

The aforementioned supervisory and fiscal provisions have obviously not impeded the increasing spread of the *Personalfürsorgestiftungen* to any essential degree. According to a study by Wirz[117], their total number at the beginning

[112] Hindermann, Die Gründung von Personalfürsorgestiftungen, SAG 32, 1959, p. 34.
[113] BGE 51 II 465.
[114] Although Art. 343 *bis* of the OR which has now replaced Art. 675 of the OR has not taken over this provision, the possibility of a claim is—as far as we know—still undisputed.
[115] Cf. Bürgi, op. cit., Art. 673, Mar. No. 113 a.
[116] In detail thereon see Bürgi, op. cit., Art. 673 Mar. No. 113 a.
[117] H. G. Wirz, Die Personal-Wohlfahrtseinrichtungen der Schweizerischen Privat-

of 1953 was 6,551. He estimated that their assets then amounted to almost Sfrs. 2,600 million. Mengiardi[118] thinks that, in view of the development of private staff welfare within the last 15 years, it can be assumed that today more than one-half of all the registered foundations serve welfare purposes pursued by enterprises. Others who are familiar with the system of foundations believe that the estimated percentage of pension funds is still much too low; they estimate it at 66% or higher in relation to the total number of foundations. Indeed, such estimates do not seem to be exaggerated, if one discovers that, for example, 1,000 out of the 1,400 foundations registered in the Canton of Baselstadt serve staff welfare purposes (in 1953 the respective figure was 621). This result is confirmed if one consults the Swiss pension fund statistics (*Statistische Quellenwerke der Schweiz, No.423*) for 1966, according to which about 13,000 welfare funds set up under civil law were counted. Only 1% of them were estimated to be co-operative societies. The assets of the private welfare funds amounted, according to data supplied by the said statistics, to Sfrs. 13,000 million, this figure does not include the surrender value of group insurance policies.

With an annual net increase in assets of roughly 10%, the present total capital of pension funds should be well over Sfrs. 20,000 million. To this must be added the capital of the pension schemes run by the Federal Government, Cantons and municipalities as well as that of public and 'mixed' companies amounting to Sfrs. 10,000 million. In addition, group insurance policies have been issued in the amount of Sfrs. 10,000 million, which means that in Switzerland at present over and above the State run social insurance system (so-called first pillar of social security) about Sfrs. 40,000 million should be available for staff welfare (so-called second pillar). A comparison with the pension schemes in the US, the UK, Germany and other countries reveals that Switzerland can offer by far the greatest *per capita ratio*[119].

2. The Personalfürsorge-Gemeinschaftsstiftung (Joint Pension Fund)

The marked expansion of the staff welfare system in Switzerland led to the consideration as to how the operation of staff welfare could be facilitated, in particular, how even small and tiny enterprises could provide social welfare for their employees without being burdened with the founding and adminis-

wirtschaft—ihre Stellung im Steuerrecht und ihre Beaufsichtigung, Vol. B, Stäfa 1955 p. 17 et ss., 61.

[118] op. cit., p. 26.

[119] Wirz, in: Referate und Mitteilungen des Schweizerischen Juristenvereins, No. 4/1968, p. 698 et ss. (cited hereinafter as Wirz, SJZ).

trative expenses involved in establishing an independent foundation. The solution was found by establishing so-called *Gemeinschaftsstiftuugen* (joint funds). Within their framework employers may set up welfare funds for their employees which economically remain completely independent and whose assets may be used only for the performance of their own tasks. One of the most important joint foundations of this kind, the *Gemeinschaftsstiftung des Interkantonalen Verbandes für Gemeinschaftsfürsorge* (Joint Foundation of the Intercantonal Staff Welfare Federation) comprises, according to the Annual Report 1969 more than 250 pension and welfare funds of the most diverse nature, whose assets total more than Sfrs. 40 million.

3. The *Investmentstiftung für Personalvorsorge* (*Investment Fund For Staff Pensions*)

The growth of the pension funds has, to an increasing degree, also entailed property investment problems. The investment of the assets accumulated in staff welfare institutions has become more complicated, more time-wasting and thus more difficult. That is why the idea was born of establishing an institution for joint investment and administration—an idea designed primarily also for spreading the risk. This idea was realised in the beginning of 1967 by the establishment of the *Investmentkasse für Personalfürsorge* (Investment Fund For Staff Welfare), a special fund of the *Interkantonaler Verband für Personalfürsorge*.

The *Investmentkasse* makes it possible to invest assets of a pension fund in four separate and independent funds: Swiss bonds, foreign bonds, Swiss shares, foreign shares. At the end of 1969 roughly a 100 pension funds belong to the *Investmentkasse*, the total assets involved being in the amount of Sfrs. 12 million (mid-1970: Sfrs. 17 million). At the end of 1970 the assets invested with the Joint Foundation of the Intercantonal Staff Welfare Federation were transferred to a newly established foundation, called *Investmentstitfung für Personalvorsoge* (Investment Fund For Staff Pensions). It is to be expected that this new institution will experience a rapid expansion as numerous pension funds of all sizes are interested in joining it.

4. Special ways of using the foundation within the framework of staff welfare

Some staff welfare institutions have, through their method of endowment, gained quite a new, additional importance far exceeding the scope of staff welfare. For instead of, or supplemental to, being endowed with cash or with a claim against the founding enterprise, such foundation acquires interests therein; there ensues in this way an indirect participation of the staff in its own enterprise. This demonstrates ways of effectively resolving important, in many places even burning, social and economic problems. In 1964 a foundation was established by the firm I. R. Geigy, whose sole purpose was the participation of employees in the enterprise. The foundation subscribed, after a capital increase, to shares of the company worth Sfrs. 3 million and has the task of issuing them to the employees and also under certain circumstances of taking them back, and, furthermore, of depositing and administering them[120].

Foundations of this kind being special institutions for the participation of employees in their own enterprise appear to be an exemplary attempt to realise the idea of employees sharing in the control of an enterprise[121]. Although such foundations are as yet obviously not very widespread in this specific form, it appears that the model has good prospects[122].

5. *The foundation as the owner of interests in enterprises*

If a foundation acquires interests in an enterprise, it may, if it has an appropriate voting right, take part in the formation of intent within such enterprise (one-stock foundation). The most varied constructions are feasible depending on the strength of the position accorded to the foundation. Thus it may exercise an important influence already with a relatively small interest when it is a matter of adjusting conflicting interests between several companies or several groups of shareholders. The foundation may, however, even obtain a majority interest or even all titles to a share in the company and thus become an instrument of the management of the enterprise (holding foundation).

Foundations constituted in this particular form are already to be found occasionally in Switzerland, but, as distinct from the situation obtaining in Germany, the one-stock foundation or the foundation directly operating a business has hitherto hardly been considered the object of a special set of problems. In 1949 the *Bundesgericht* nullified a family trust established by a last will and testament as sole shareholder of a GmbH (limited liability company), but approved it after conversion into an ordinary foundation without expressing an opinion on the question as to whether it was admissible

---

[120] Cf. in detail thereon Vischer, Die Beteiligung der Betriebsangehörigen am Aktienkapital der Gesellschaft (Zur Mitarbeiterbeteiligung bei der J. R. Geigy AG, Basel), SAG 37, 1965, p. 1 et ss.

[121] Mengiardi, op. cit., pp. 214, 215.

[122] Mengiardi, op. cit., pp. 205, 215; Wirz, SJZ, p. 698 et ss.

for a foundation to be a shareholder of a GmbH[123]. The *Eidgenössische Amt für das Handelsregister* (Federal Commercial Register Office) on the other hand, decided in 1960 'with regret' that a foundation established for the purpose of operating a riding ring may be entered in the commercial register[124]. Gerhard[125] considers family foundations participating in the founder's enterprise and in this way acting as *entrepreneurs* to be inadmissible. Bär[126] expresses doubts in connection with the case decided by the *Bundesgericht* without, however, finally committing himself. The Federal Department of the Interior has recently assumed, but only with the greatest reservation, the supervision of a foundation which in time to come is to acquire, by way of inheritance, and to administer all the shares of a worldwide company domiciled in Zurich; it points out in particular that the *Bundesgericht* has not yet rendered any decision on the admissibility of such foundations.

Mengiardi[127] is the first to undertake a detailed and critical study of the nexus of related problems arising from foundations with commercial activities. In doing so he largely proceeds on the basis of the literature on this subject matter published in Germany. Mengiardi comes to the conclusion that the foundation as the owner of shares is a useful and attractive instrument for coping with important problems of the enterprise[128]. Although, he states, there is a likelihood of their being abused, this circumstance alone is not sufficient to withhold legal protection from such foundations. It is the duty of the lawmakers to take the necessary preventive measures.

6. *Arguments for a reform of the law relating to foundations*

Within the framework of the law relating to foundations, the lawmakers grant the individual the greatest possible freedom as regards the organisation of the foundation. Despite or even because of this fact, they have, in discussions about the foundation as an element in the organisation of enterprises, frequently been called upon to adjust the law relating to foundations to this extent to present conditions. Thus, for instance, Bürgi[129] demands a 'more effective, more liberal' (!) law relating to foundations. Primarily, however, it is only provisions for the protection against abuses that are demanded[130].

---

[123] BGE 75 II 81 et ss.

[124] VEB (Decisions of Swiss Federal Administrative Authorities), 1959/60, no. 43.

[125] Op. cit., p. 443.

[126] Aktuelle Fragen des Aktienrechts, ZSR 85 II, 1966.

[127] Op. cit., p. 204 et ss, in particular, p. 206 et ss.   [128] Op. cit., p. 214.

[129] Revisionsbedürftige Regelungen des schweizerischen Aktienrechts, SAG 38, 1966, p. 57 et ss.

[130] E. Wolf, Über die Verknüpfbarkeit einer Familien-Aktiengesellschaft mit einer Familienstiftung, SAG 37, 1965, pp. 225 et ss., 229; Mengiardi, op. cit., p. 215.

F

Mengiardi makes—probably also for the first time—more concrete statements[131].

In his view, what matters, first of all, is to make arrangements for internal
control and responsibility. The most important problem to be solved in this
connection is that of the balance of the forces inside the organisation of the
foundation. It involves, on the one hand, the question of responsibility in the
case of violations of the law, and, on the other hand, that of appropriate
provisions for the succession to posts in the highest organs of the foundation.

Here, the lawmakers themselves could create regulations, or they could,
with regard to specific points, just order the founder to establish such regulations.

In spite of such demands for a change or an extension of the law relating
to foundations, real efforts for a reform in this direction have hitherto not
been noticeable and are probably not urgent either. Hence, it can be stated
that one-stock foundations too may be established in any form as long as they
keep within the scope of what is legally and morally permitted.

IV. FOUNDATIONS SEEN FROM THE POINT OF VIEW OF TAX LAW

1. *The principles of the taxation of foundations*

Foundations with legal status are generally subject to the same taxation as
natural persons. This applies in principle both to the cantonal and to local
taxes; it generally applies to cases of non-recurrent taxes as much as to
recurrent taxation. Thus, on contributions at the time of establishment and on
future contributions, foundations must regularly pay the death duty or
donation tax which is nearly always levied by the Cantons. There are
exceptions to this rule only with regard to the Cantons of Obwalden,
Schwyz and Valais which have neither a death duty nor a donation tax.

The Cantons of Lucerne and Solothurn levy death duties but no donation
tax. Taxation may thus be avoided there by making contributions to a
foundation, while the founder is still alive.

If death duty is payable in the case of foundations established *mortis causa*,
it may be of importance whether such tax is levied as succession duty
(*Erbanfallsteuer*) as in practically all Cantons, or as estate tax or death duty
(*Nachlallsteuer*) as in the Cantons of Graubünden, Neufchâtel and Solothurn.
For the succession duty covers the individual portions or bequests separately
and in this way allows for consideration of special conditions, mostly of the
degree of relationship of the individual beneficiaries; this may have an effect

131 Op. cit., p. 215.

on private family foundations, namely if the degree of relationship between the founder and the intended beneficiaries determines the amount of the tax rate. The estate tax, on the other hand, burdens, without regard to the degree of relationship of the beneficiaries, the whole estate with a tax determined by the amount of the estate left.

Within the scope of the current taxation which is carried out by the Federal Government, the Cantons and as a rule also the local authorities, foundations generally have to pay income tax on the income from their assets and on the net profit realized by possibly existing business enterprises as well as, in addition thereto, property tax. In some Cantons (for instance Baselstadt, Fribourg, Glarus, Schwyz, Uri and Zug) only a progressive or proportional tax is levied on their assets. In addition, however, many Cantons levy special real estate, capital gains and other special taxes (for instance a hospital tax in Glarus).

2. Tax benefits and their prerequisites

Foundations which are beneficial to the community or charitable or which serve staff welfare purposes are granted considerable tax benefits, if not even exemption from all taxes[132].

The terms benefit to the community, charity and staff welfare are not defined anywhere in revenue law. However, the Order of the *Regierungsrat* (Governing Council) of the Canton of Bern relating to Deduction of Contributions made exclusively for Purposes beneficial to the Community from Cantonal Taxes and Taxes levied by the local authorities of 26th February 1965, states: 'Benefit to the community exists where the services of the donee institution are exclusively for the benefit of the community and are designed for the welfare of third persons to the exclusion of personal interests of the parties concerned[133].' In addition, some laws list examples of benefit to the community in which benefit to the community is sometimes considered a term comprising also charity[134]. Frequently, art and sciences are mentioned besides benefit to the community and charity[135].

---

[132] Wirz, Beaufsichtigung, p. 149 et ss., p. 4 et ss.

[133] No. 3, sent. 2 of the Order.

[134] Cf. e.g. Art. 16 no. 3 of the Wehrsteuerbeschluß (WStB—Defence Tax Act) as well as art. 6 para. 1 no. 5 of the Erbschaftsteuergesetz (Death Duty Act) of the Canton of Basel-Land.

[135] Cf. e.g. Art. 2 lit. b. of the Erbschaftsteuergesetz (Death Duty Act) of the Canton of Schaffhausen; art. 118 of the Gesetz über die direkten Steuern (Act relating to Direct Taxes) of the Canton of Appenzell- Außer-Rhoden; art. 2, lit. d. of the Gesetz über die Erbschaft-, Vermächtnis- und Schenkungsteuer (Act relating to the Death Duty, the Bequest and Donation Tax) of the Canton of St. Gallen.

As for the concept of the staff welfare, there are directives of the federal tax authorities[136] which, in regard to Cantonal taxes, are partly supplemented by special directives issued by the Cantonal Finance Departments. These directives consider as staff welfare for tax purposes the provision to the employee of security for old age, the care of the members of the employee's family in the event of his death, as well as aid in specific cases of distress, especially in the event of sickness, accident, disablement, unemployment or economic difficulties. Facilities for the immediate care of the employees during work breaks (such as canteens and restrooms), sanatoria and convalescent homes for needy employees as well as the establishment of homes for apprentices come within the scope of staff welfare[137]. The construction, for instance, of low-cost homes for employees, or of holiday homes or sports grounds does not come within this scope.

If a foundation serves purposes beneficial to the community in the sense stated above or staff welfare purposes within the meaning of the above-mentioned directives, the contributions to such a foundation are, under practically all cantonal acts relating to the death duty and the donation tax, exempt from death duty and donation tax. The Canton of Solothurn levies on contributions of claims a reduced succession duty of 1.5%[138]. In the Canton of Geneva the Governing Council may remit the death duty either wholly or in part[139].

Foundations serving purposes beneficial to the community or staff welfare purposes are also quite predominantly not subject to the current taxes. The Defence Tax (*Wehrsteuer*) as far as federal tax is concerned is always remitted[140]. Most of the Cantons and local authorities grant exemptions from income tax, while with regard to property, only half of it is taxed occasionally or a standard rate of 1.5% or 2% assessed (for instance in Aargau, Appenzell A.-Rh., Fribourg and Neufchâtel). On the other hand, most of the Cantons and their local authorities levy the special real estate taxes; frequently tax is payable on capital gains, in particular on profits realised from real estate. As an exception, some of the local authorities of the Canton of Graubünden

[136] Bundesblatt (Federal Gazette) 1947 III, p. 287; cf. Wirz, Beaufsichtigung, p. 4 et ss.

[137] Cf. Directives of the Finanzdirektion (Finance Department) of the Canton of Zurich relating to Exemption of Personalfürsorgestiftungen from taxes under sec. 16 lit. f. of the Steuergesetz (Tax Act) of 11 November 1958.

[138] Nos. 1 and 2 of the Order of the Regierungsrat (Governing Council) of 19th December 1919 relating to the Application of the reduced Death Duty in the Case of Bequests in Favour of Cantonal or general Swiss ecclesiastical or charitable Institutions or Institutions beneficial to the Community; sec. 2 of the Death Duty Act.

[139] Art. 6 para. 2 of the Death Duty Act.

[140] Art. 16 nos. 3, 4 *bis* of the WStB (Defence Tax Act).

which enjoy tax autonomy grant no exemption even from the income and property taxes.

Where tax privileges exist, such privileges are subject to strict conditions which, however, vary from one Canton to the other. Within the scope of the privilege based on benefit to the community, the foundation is as a rule required to serve exclusively those purposes which were, in its case, the grounds on which tax exemption was acquired. However, when considering the question of whether such purpose is present, liberal criteria are usually applied.

Pension funds are subject to especially strict requirements. Leaving aside differences in detail, these may be summed up as follows:

(a) The foundation must be a foundation with legal status subject to government supervision.

(b) The provisions of the charter or of such special by-laws as may possibly exist must ensure that all the funds once made available to the foundation are allocated exclusively, definitively and irrevocably to staff welfare. It is not permissible to link them with any other purposes. In the event of the liquidation of the foundation, its assets shall be utilised in accordance with the purpose of the foundation. Any surpluses must be allocated to purposes beneficial to the community.

(c) In some Cantons the assets of the foundation must be separated from the assets of the founding firm. They must be invested in such a way that the realisation of the purpose appears to be ensured in an optimal manner. Some Cantons demand that special security be furnished or refuse to grant the privilege if the foundation merely receives a claim against the founding enterprise.

(d) The funds of the foundation must indeed serve the purpose of staff welfare. A mere accumulation is not admissible. A certain running-in period may, however, be necessary, but one must be able to expect that the purpose of the foundation will be realised within a reasonable period of time.

(e) The circle of the intended beneficiaries must be confined to the employees and workers of the founding enterprise. The employer is in many Cantons not allowed to be among the beneficiaries. In the case of legal entities (stock corporations, partnerships limited by shares), some Cantons count even employees holding shares and executives among the staff if their main job comprises regular employment with the company and the welfare services rendered to them remain within the scope of the services available for the general benefit of the staff.

3. The treatment of contributions to tax-exempt foundations[141]

If a foundation in the sense of the foregoing statements serves purposes beneficial to the community or staff welfare purposes, important privileges generally accrue also to the founder or the founding firms, due to the fact that their contributions are deductible. Under Art. 22 para. 1 lit. f. of the WStB (Defence Tax Act) contributions of natural persons to a *Personalfürsorgestiftung* or to a foundation serving exclusively purposes beneficial to the community may be deducted from the taxable income 'if they are secured for such purposes in such a manner that any future use which is contrary to such purposes is excluded'.

Under Art. 49 para. 2 of the WStB this holds good also for the taxable net profit of legal entities. Similar provisions have been established also by certain Cantons and local authorities, though differing in details. As a rule, contributions to tax-privileged foundations are fully deductible also under these provisions.

In some Cantons, payments to pension funds are deductible, but not those to other institutions beneficial to the community, for instance in Basel-Land, Glarus, Graubünden, Lucerne and Ticino. In other Cantons contributions to foundations beneficial to the community are deductible if they reach a minimum sum ranging between Sfrs. 50 and 500 (Basel-Stadt, Appenzell A.-Rh., Valais; in Bern the upper limit is 5% of the net income or net profit). In some Cantons regular contributions to *Personalfürsorgestiftungen* may only be deducted up to the amount of 10 to 15% of the total payroll for wages and salaries (Appenzell I.-Rh., Bern, Ticino); contributions within the scope of the establishment of the foundation, however, are fully deductible, in Appenzell I.-Rh. only up to the amount of Sfrs. 20,000.

If payments to pension funds are deductible, this naturally holds good also for any contributions to be made by the employees. This is explicitly stated in the Tax Act of the Canton of Schaffhausen.

It should finally be mentioned that in Appenzell I.-Rh. property is exempt from property tax to the extent to which it is tied up with staff welfare purposes[142].

V. FOUNDATIONS WITHOUT LEGAL STATUS

1. The concept

As already mentioned before, there are no special provisions regulating the

---

[141] Wirz, Beaufsichtigung, p. 351 et ss., p. 4 et ss.
[142] Art. 5 lit. c. of the Tax Act.

foundation without legal status or—as it is sometimes called—the dependent foundation. Its characteristics are that assets are vested in a natural person or (mostly) in a legal entity for attaining a specific purpose and are separately administered by such person or entity. That is why one frequently meets the term *Zustiftung* (supplemental endowment) or *fiduziarische Stiftung* (fiduciary endowment).

2. The forms of foundations without legal status

The foundation without legal status may exist in different forms, and the legal classification and status differs depending on these forms. Thus the founder may make a donation or a bequest with the charge to use the contributed funds for a specific purpose[143]. Such a procedure comes into consideration especially where the purpose is not a perpetual one, for instance, where the contribution shall be passed on to any third parties in a specific manner or under specific conditions. It is also conceivable that the 'foundadation' is established in accordance with a commission[144], under which the commissioned person is obligated to administer and to use the contribution in the manner agreed upon. Finally, the 'founder' and the trustee may make a bilateral contract[145], under which the trustee promises a specific performance on his part (e.g. to construct a home for old people or to establish a library).

A donation entitles the donor ('founder') to revoke the foundation under certain conditions. The most prominent case in this respect is non-fulfilment of the charge[146].

If the fulfilment of the charge is in the public interest, the competent authority may request this after the decease of the donor[147]. In the event of a bequest anybody proving a legal interest has a claim to the fulfilment of the charge[148].

If a commission is involved, it may generally be cancelled by both sides[149]. A bilateral contract, however, cannot be cancelled.

If a contribution tied up with a specific purpose is made to a local authority it can be judged only in accordance with public law. The assets are in this case generally administered separately. The authority concerned issues special regulations regarding the manner of administration. These regulations may,

[143] Arts. 245 et ss. of the OR, 484, 482 of the ZGB.
[144] Art. 394 of the OR.
[145] Art. 19 of the OR.
[146] Art. 249 No. 3 of the OR.
[147] Art. 246 para. 2 of the OR.
[148] Art. 482 para. 1 of the ZGB.
[149] Art. 404 of the OR.

within the limits set by public law, consider also instructions given and charges imposed by the 'founder[150]'.

3. The importance of foundations without legal status

The importance in Switzerland of foundations without legal status is difficult to estimate, since they are not obliged to apply for registration and are certainly known to the general public only in exceptional cases. Thus they usually have a clandestine existence.

On the whole their importance is likely to be small compared with the foundations with legal status, since revenue law regularly makes privileged treatment dependent both on the determination of a purpose which is beneficial to the community and on the dedicated assets having a legal status of their own. This holds good both for the question of deductibility connected with the contribution on the part of the 'founder' and the donation tax or the death duty as well as for the current taxation of the beneficiary. Thus the deductibility usually presupposes that any use which is contrary to the purpose is excluded. This requirement is generally not met in the case of the mere contractual obligation within the system of foundations without legal status. Tax exemptions under the law relating to death duties and donations usually require that public or charitable institutions, i.e. institutions (*Anstalten*) or legal entities, are involved. Express exemption, however, is frequently granted those funds that are administered by public authorities. Thus for all practical purposes tax privileges come into consideration only in the case of *Zustiftungen* (supplemental endowments) to institutions beneficial to the community which already exist as legal entities and to public authorities.

VI. INSTITUTIONS RESEMBLING FOUNDATIONS

1. The Association (Verein)

The association is the most prominent among the institutions which are suitable for performing tasks similar to those of the foundations and which actually also perform such tasks. The lawmakers themselves consider the association a body devoting itself to a political, religious, scientific, artistic, charitable, social or other non-profit task[151]. Yet its function consisted originally in performing such tasks in the immediate personal interest of its members. Today, however, the association puts itself at the service also of a

[150] Egger, Personenrecht, Art. 80, Mar. No. 4.
[151] Art. 60 para. 1 of the ZGB.

smaller or larger section of the general public by aiming at the promotion of other people's physical, spiritual and economic welfare. It is especially in the cultural field that it frequently assumes in this connection such tasks as the respective local authorities including the State are actually obliged to perform but which, however, cannot be managed by them alone (such as schooling and education, training and sanitation[152].

Although the statements just made are far from constituting a comprehensive picture of the significance of the association in Switzerland, they may perhaps throw some light on its importance as an incumbent of tasks similar to those performed by foundations. Its advantage over the foundation lies, for one thing, in the simplified way of establishing it, for the other in its greater flexibility and adjustability. Its fiscal treatment resembles that of the foundations to the extent to which its tasks are to be considered as exclusively beneficial to the community. The question as to whether it is beneficial to the community is, in this connection, answered in the affirmative only if the general public or at least a not too narrow circle of persons is benefited.

An important example of an association whose tasks are similar to those performed by foundations is the League of the Red Cross Societies, the International Federation of the National Red Cross (in Islamic countries the Red Crescent or Red Lion and Sun) Societies having its headquarters in Geneva. The League represents its at present 110 member societies in international matters and supports as well as co-ordinates their activities both nationally and internationally in all fields of humanitarian aid granted under the sign of the Red Cross, the Red Crescent or the Red Lion and Sun. The costs of the Secretariat of the League are covered by the dues of the member societies.

The League has been subject to Swiss law since 1939, the date on which it set up its headquarters in Switzerland. Under an agreement made with the Swiss Government it is exempted from all direct taxes. As for indirect taxes, exemption can be obtained in specific cases under specific conditions. Naturally, the *Verein* cannot replace the foundation. There still remain many tasks which can be managed only by means of the foundation with legal status.

2. The co-operative society (Genossenschaft)

Tasks similar to those performed by foundations are—as already mentioned in another connection—sometimes assumed also by the co-operative society. It is, as regards its nature, related to the association in that it is a society of a

---

[152] Pestalozzi, Der Begriff des Idealen Vereins, Zurich 1952, p. 1 et s.

specific kind organised in a co-operative way, but differs from the association essentially by the fact that it aims principally at the promotion or safeguarding of specific economic interests of its members[153]. That is why it is used for tasks similar to those performed by foundations only where such tasks are of an economic nature, i.e. in the field of staff welfare. It is for this purpose that the lawmakers have specially provided for them in addition to the foundation[154].

However, even in this field, it does not attain the same importance as the foundation—quite probably for the reason that many cantonal tax acts privilege staff welfare institutions only when they have been constituted in the form of the foundation with legal status, but not when they are co-operative societies.

However, a clear development can be observed away from the form of the pension fund towards that of the co-operative society, a trend which is given added impetus by the prescription of the right of co-determination on the part of the beneficiaries, in proportion to the size of their contributions, together with a right to be kept informed[155]. This development is bound to continue within the overall framework of the expansion of the second pillar of the so-called 'three-pillar concept' of social security in Switzerland[156].

[153] Art. 828 of the OR.
[154] Art. 343 *bis* para. 1 of the OR.
[155] Art. 89 *bis* paras. 2 and 3 of the ZGB Wirz, SJZ, p. 689 et ss.
[156] State insurance—employer's insurance—personal insurance.

LITERATURE

Ackermann Der besondere Zweck der Stiftung unter spezieller Berücksichtigung des Zwecks der Familienstiftung, doctoral thesis, Fribourg, 1950.

är Aktuelle Fragen des Aktienrechts, ZSR 85 II, 1966.

Bürgi Kommentar zum schweizerischen Zivilgesetzbuch, Vol. 5, Obligationsrecht, Zurich 1947;
Revisionsbedürftige Regelungen des schweizerischen Aktienrechts, SAG 38, 1966.

Egger Kommentar zum schweizerischen Zivilgesetzbuch, Vol. I, Einleitung und Personenrecht, 2nd Ed., Zurich 1930; Das Familienrecht, 2nd Ed., Zurich 1933.

Gerhard Die Familienstiftung nach ZGB, ZSR 49, 1930.

Gmür Das schweizerische Zivilgesetzbuch verglichen mit dem deutschen Bürgerlichen Gesetzbuch, Bern 1965.

Hafter Kommentar zum schweizerischen Zivilgesetzbuch, Personenrecht, 2nd Ed., Bern 1919.

Helbling Autonome Pensionskasse oder Gruppenversicherung, Zurich 1962; Personalfürsorge, Bern 1964.

Hindermann Der Stiftungszweck, ZSR 47, 1928;
Die Gründung von Personalfürsorgestiftungen, SAG 32, 1959.

Mengiardi Strukturprobleme des Gesellschaftsrechts, in: Referate und Mitteilungen des schweizerischen Juristenvereins, No. I, 1968.

Müller Die Besteuerung der Familienstiftung, SJZ 28, 1931/32.

Pestalozzi Der Begriff des idealen Vereins, Zurich 1952.

Tuor Das schweizerische Zivilgesetzbuch, 8th Ed., Zurich 1968.

Vischer Die Beteiligung der Betriebsangehörigen am Aktienkapital der Gesellschaft (Zur Mitarbeiterbeteiligung bei der J. R. Geigy AG, Basel), SAG 37, 1965.

Wirz Die Personal-Wohlfahrtseinrichtungen der schweizerischen Privatwirtschaft— ihre Stellung im Steuerrecht und ihre Beaufsichtigung, Vol. B, Stäfa 1955; Vermögensanlage von Personalfürsorgestiftungen aus der Sicht der Aufsichtsbehörden, in: Personalfürsorge, Vol. 5/No. 3, May 1970.

Wolf. Über die Verknüpfbarkeit einer Familien-Aktiengesellschaft mit einer Familienstiftung, SAG 37, 1965.

Appendix: A Selection of Swiss Foundations

Hans G. Wirz

The Swiss Federal authorities maintain an unpublished list of the most important of the foundations falling under their direct supervision. On the other hand only a few Cantons have at their disposal for internal administrative purposes comprehensive records of the foundations coming within their own particular jurisdictions. In the Directory of European Foundations, published by the Giovanni Agnelli Foundation, Turin, in 1969, more detailed information is to be found—for the first time—about 34 Swiss foundations.

In Switzerland there is a serious lack of information about foundations and their activities. Consequently, it is a matter for considerable satisfaction that it has been possible to assemble the following data thanks to the ready co-operation of the Federal Department of the Interior and the spontaneous support of the foundations which were approached. It is hoped that this survey will serve to provide the necessary stimulus to bring about in the very near future the publication of a first handbook of Swiss charitable foundations.

In Switzerland there are no 'giant' foundations such as are to be found, for instance, in the United States[1] or the Federal Republic of Germany[2]. Nevertheless, when considered in relation to the total population, the number of Swiss foundations is markedly high. Swiss foundations can be sub-divided into the six main categories specified below. At the same time, however, it should be borne in mind that, side by side with the foundations proper, there are a host of institutions with the legal form of the association or of the co-operative society pursuing similar ends. To cite one example: The Schweizerische Gemeinnützige Gesellschaft (which came into existence in 1810 and acts as the central co-ordinator and promoter of charitable activities through-

---

[1] Rockefeller Foundation, Ford Foundation, Carnegie Corporation of New York.
[2] Stiftung Volkswagenwerk, Alfried Krupp von Bohlen und Halbach-Stiftung, Robert Bosch Stiftung GmbH, Carl-Zeiss-Stiftung, Fritz Thyssen Stiftung.

out the Confederation) is constituted as an association.

The foundations engaged in the advancement of the *Sciences and of Research* have seen a particularly marked growth in the course of the last few years. A peculiarly Swiss phenomenon are the foundations for the promotion of *Culture and the Arts*, as policy and action in this field fall outside the range of responsibilities assumed by the Federal Government.

Foundations play a relatively minor role in the field of *Development Aid*; next to the Federal Government, the most active body in this domain is the association HELVETAS, the Swiss Development Agency. Private efforts in regard to *Education and Assistance to Youth* and *Social Welfare* are a salient feature of Swiss life. Furthermore, a number of important *International Foundations* are registered in Switzerland. On the other hand, The Swiss Red Cross, the International Committee of the Red Cross (Comité International de la Croix-Rouge) and the League of Red Cross Societies, which brings together 110 national Red Cross Societies, are legally constituted as associations.

THE SCIENCES AND RESEARCH

The *Swiss National Fund for the Advancement of Scientific Research* (Schweizerischer Nationalfonds zur Förderung der wissenschaftlichen Forschung), Bern, was established in 1952 as a foundation under private law on the initiative of representatives of the major scientific societies (Swiss Society for the Natural Sciences, Swiss Society for the Arts and Humanities, Swiss Association of Lawyers, Swiss Society for Statistics and Economics). The Fund is, however, almost entirely financed by the Federal Government in the form of increasing annual subsidies. Up to and including the year 1969, the National Fund received moneys from this source totalling approximately 400 million Sfrs; for the year 1970 alone, the amount allocated was 70 million Sfrs. The application of these considerable means has had a steadily growing impact on the development of the sciences and research in Switzerland.

The *Werner Abegg Fund*, Zurich, provides the financial resources for the *Abegg Foundation* in Bern. The latter runs an institute for research in the arts with training centres for the conservation of fabrics and an art collection which is open to the general public during the summer months.

The *Ciba Foundation for Research in the Natural Sciences, Medicine and Technology* in Bâle, promotes training and research in the three aforementioned fields. It supports, in particular, schools and scientific institutes, research workers and students. The initial endowment ·and subsequent donations amounted to a total of 9.4 million Sfrs. The Foundation has so far been able to expend a total of 9.9 million Sfrs.

The *Geigy Jubilee Foundation*, Bâle, focuses on the educational advancement of Swiss university graduates and postgraduates and also provides support for research at universities and colleges of higher education, research institutes and clinics, particularly in the field of medicine and the natural sciences. The initial endowment and subsequent donations totalled 4.4 million Sfrs. Expenditure to date has exceeded 2.6 million Sfrs.

The *Green Meadow Foundation* (Stiftung im Grüene), Rüschlikon, which has for many years placed its landed property at Langhalden at the disposal of the general public as a recreation centre, is the umbrella organization for two institutes: the *Gottlieb Duttweiler Institute for Economic and Social Studies* functions as an international and interdisciplinary discussion and management training centre. Fifteen international study conferences and 30 management courses are held annually bringing together 300 teachers and 5,000 participants from 30 countries. The *Institute for Nutrition Research* conducts studies for the government authorities and private industry in regard to nutritional problems. At the end of 1969 the total assets amounted to 3,875,000 Sfrs. Expenditure over 1969 totalled 4,245,000 Sfrs., while conference and course registration fees brought in 2,284,000 Sfrs.

The *Hasler-Works Foundation*, Bern, promotes the development of communications and communication media in Switzerland. The Foundation is the main shareholder of the Hasler Holding Company, Bern. The funds which have been paid out since 1953 in the form of research contributions to technical universities, credit notes for the purchase of scientific equipment to technical colleges, and scholarships, total 10.7 million Sfrs.

The *Fritz Hoffmann-La Roche-Foundation for the Promotion of Scientific Cooperation in Switzerland*, Bâle, was set up in 1947 by the F. Hoffmann-La Roche Company at the national level. It seeks to foster team work in all fields of bio-medical research and related disciplines. Donations are made both to members of Swiss universities, research institutes, clinics and hospitals and to independent research workers, with the object of facilitating a concerted but many-sided approach to key issues in the field of medicine and the natural sciences. The Foundation utilises the subsidies and donations it receives on a year-to-year basis to finance the projects and requests submitted to it. Total expenditure over the last five years has amounted to approximately 1.5 million Sfrs.

The *Janggen-Pöhn-Foundation*, St. Gallen, enables highly gifted Swiss boys and girls to study for scientific and academic careers.

The *Nestlé Foundation*, Lausanne, is concerned with world food problems and finances scientific studies in the field of nutrition, physiology and agriculture. It has a capital of 20 million Sfrs. and has effected a total expenditure to date of 3 million Sfrs.

The object of the *Swiss Life Insurance and Annuities Office Jubilee Foundation for Public Health and Medical Research*, Zurich, established in 1957 to mark the 100th anniversary of this institution, is evident from its designation. Expenditure to date amounts to 1.2 million Sfrs.

The *Joh. Jacob Rieter Foundation*, Winterthur, was set up in 1963 by the Rieter Engineering Company to commemorate the 200th anniversary of the birth of their founder. The Foundation provides support for welfare, cultural, scientific and art institutions, priority being given to its immediate neighbourhood. However, support is also given to institutions in the Canton of Zurich and, in exceptional cases, in other parts of Switzerland. In 1970, to mark the firm's 175th anniversary celebrations, donations and grants in the amount of 3 million Sfrs. were paid out from the 8 million Sfrs. capital fund, the bulk of which was earmarked for support of education, training and research.

The purpose of the *Sandoz Foundation for the Promotion of Medical and Bio-Medical Sciences*, Bâle, is apparent from its designation. Grants are made for research outside the sphere of the research programme of the Company, at universities and hospitals. The Board of Trustees is predominantly composed of delegates from the 6 medical faculties of the Swiss universities. The initial endowment provided by the Sandoz Company in 1943 is supplemented annually (currently at the rate of 600,000 Sfrs. per year) according to the financial needs of the Foundation and the funds at present total about 2 million Sfrs. Over the last five years, the Foundation has disbursed 1.6 million Sfrs. in grants and subsidies.

CULTURE AND THE ARTS

The *Pro Helvetia Foundation*, Zurich, was established by the Federal Government after the Second World War in order to consolidate and ensure the continuation of an association which had already been in existence since 1939 for the purpose of preserving the Swiss cultural heritage, encouraging cultural activities and exchange within Switzerland and fostering cultural relations with other countries. The Foundation is financed from Federal funds on an annual basis, and the contribution for 1971 has been established at 5 million Sfrs. Since 1939 the total moneys expended amount to 35,725,000 Sfrs. Contrary to the situation obtaining in the majority of European countries, and in accordance with the provisions of the Swiss

Constitution, the power of decision in cultural matters is, in principle, in the hands of the individual Cantons.

The *Anniversary Foundation of the Union Bank of Switzerland*, Zurich, devotes its profits in the first instance to the promotion of the arts but it also makes funds available to individuals and institutions active in the cultural and scientific fields throughout the Confederation, whereby it attempts to ensure that an equitable distribution is made among the various language areas. The total assets amount to 10 million Sfrs., and 3.3 million Sfrs. have been paid out to date.

The *E.G. Bührle Foundation* (Art Collection), Zurich, established by the family of E.G. Bührle after his death, mainly comprises French 19th Century Impressionists together with some important works by Dutch, French, Italian and Spanish painters and a representative selection of mediaeval sculptures. The Collection is open to the general public and has been valued at almost 100 million Sfrs.

The *Gottfried Keller Foundation*, Bern, which came into being as a result of the donation made to the Swiss Confederation in 1890 by Mrs. Lydia Welti-Escher, purchases works of art of Swiss origin and places them in the safekeeping of Swiss museums and art galleries; wherever feasible, the works are returned to the places from which they originated. Furthermore, the Foundation tries to 'repatriate' Swiss works of art from abroad. The bulk of its property comprises, i.a., the former Benedictine Monastery St. Georgen at Stein-on-the-Rhine, the Segantini Paintings in St. Moritz, works by Niklaus Manuel, Hodler and Buchser as well as the carved chair-pews in the Monastery of St. Urban. The Foundations' total possessions comprise over 1000 paintings, sculptures, glass-paintings, lithographs, prints and etchings by important Swiss artists. With the revenues from the original endowment of 3 million Sfrs., the foundation has succeeded in assembling a collection worth well over 100 million Sfrs.

The *Kiefer-Hablitzel Foundation*, Bern, the gift of a successful Swiss couple living overseas, utilizes its annual proceeds to support representative Swiss cultural institutions and Swiss businessmen living overseas and wishing to return to Switzerland, and to provide scholarships for young Swiss musicians, painters and sculptors. The total assets amount to 9 million Sfrs. and expenditure to date 5 million Sfrs.

The *Oskar Reinhart Foundation*, Winterthur, which came into existence as a result of a gift made to the town of Winterthur by Dr.h.c. Oskar Reinhart, owns a collection of 500 paintings by Swiss, German and Austrian artists of the nineteenth century, of which the Swiss component constitutes the most comprehensive collection in existence of Swiss 19th Century paintings.

Dr. Reinhart donated his private collection at Römerholz to the Swiss Confederation. It comprises important works by the Old Masters and French painting from Poussin to Cézanne and constitutes one of the most important art collections in the world. It has been open to the general public since 1970. The total value of the two collections has been estimated at over 100 million Sfrs.

The *Swiss National Library Public Foundation* was established in 1920 and fosters the development and expansion of the library system for the spiritual, moral and professional advancement of the Swiss people, and thereby encourages the positive use of leisure. The Foundation has its administrative headquarters in Bern, six centres in different areas of the country, and operates mobile libraries. Its essential concern is to fill in the gaps which still exist in the library system in some parts of the country and to meet the growing need for information, further education and meaningful recreational pursuits.

DEVELOPMENT AID

The *Swiss Foundation for Technical Assistance*, Zurich, was established in 1959 and derives the bulk of its financial resources from contributions from Swiss private industry. It has a capital of 3 million Sfrs. and, by the end of the first decade of its existence, it had expended 13.5 million Sfrs. on projects in the field of vocational and professional training for industry and agriculture in India, Pakistan, Tunisia, Algeria, Nigeria, Dahomey, Peru and Costa Rica. In a few instances, projects are carried out in collaboration with the Office for Technical Co-operation of the Federal Government's Political Department, the central Federal agency for development aid.

EDUCATION AND ASSISTANCE TO YOUTH

The object of the *Pro Juventute Foundation*, established in Zurich in 1912, is to support and promote activities for the wellbeing of young people throughout Switzerland and also to play an active role itself in the field of assistance to youth and the protection of mothers. The main emphasis of the Foundation's work is on providing assistance of every kind to the mother and pre-school child, children of schoolgoing age and school leavers and on promoting the fruitful use of leisure. It runs a family holiday centre in Ticino and a holiday home for mothers in St. Moritz and provides the financial backbone for the *Pro Juventute High-Alpine Children's Sanatorium* in Davos. In addition it runs the urban recreation centres for the Zurich City

Council. Its main sources of income are the supplementary welfare charges which the Post Office levies on Pro Juventute postage stamps and on telegram forms, and from the sale of greeting cards. Additional income is derived from specially earmarked government contributions and from donations. The annual account for the year ended on 31st March 1970 showed an expenditure of approximately 14 million Sfrs. The balance sheet shows 21 million Sfrs. Since its establishment, the Foundation has disbursed a total amount of approximately 240 million Sfrs.

The *Pestalozzi Children's Village Foundation* runs a children's village in Trogen which takes in needy children from all countries of the world and brings them up in a climate of international understanding transcending national, religious and linguistic barriers. Up to the present day, more than 900 children have spent their childhood and youth in the village. The expenditure effected by the Foundation since its establishment in 1945 (construction and expansion of the village and providing for the children's everyday needs) amounts to 40 million Sfrs. The balance sheet for 1970 shows the amount of 4.5 million Sfrs. The Foundation receives no support from the State.

The *Pestalozzi World Foundation*, Zurich, promotes efforts designed to serve young people in keeping with ideas of Heinrich Pestalozzi. The main emphasis of its programme is currently on providing financial support for the further training of primary school teachers in developing countries. Total disbursements to date have amounted to over 1 million Sfrs.

SOCIAL WELFARE ACTIVITIES

The *Swiss Foundation for the Aged, Pro Senectute*, established in Zurich in 1917, is the largest welfare organisation working exclusively on behalf of the aged. As a specialized institution it includes within the scope of its interest all problems relating to old age. Beside making financial provision for needy old people, the most prominent feature of its work today is the marked extension of personal assistance (such as household and meal services, gymnastics for the elderly, organized holidays and excursions, old peoples' clubs, etc.) for all old people, together with the construction and expansion of a decentralized network of advisory and welfare units, also run by the Foundation. Since 1917 it has disbursed a total amount of 230 million Sfrs. The central office has assets totalling 2.7 million Sfrs. at its disposal.

The *Heberlein Foundation for the Promotion of Welfare Activities*, Wattwil, focuses on providing support for welfare work in the central part of Toggenburg (with particular emphasis on activities serving to improve the infrastructure), fostering social and cultural institutions and endeavours together with those serving education and training at the national and, in exceptional cases, the international level. The Foundation has assets totalling 1 million Sfrs.

The *Swiss National Appeal Foundation* (Stiftung Schweizerische National-spende), Bern, has as its object the provision of assistance to members of the Swiss armed forces and their families in need. It possesses assets of approximately 20 million Sfrs. and has effected disbursements totalling 61 million Sfrs. since its creation. After devoting itself primarily to private welfare work during the 1914–18 war, in 1919 the Foundation was transformed on the initiative of the military leadership, following a highly successful public appeal carried out during the previous year, into the central coordinating and financing agency for all efforts in this particular sector of social welfare. Even today, the Foundation makes a worthwhile contribution towards complementing the services of the public insurance system by taking care of the cases for which adequate provision is not available.

The *Volkart Foundation*, Winterthur, pursues social, educational, charitable and cultural aims. It promotes the development of public and private institutions active in the field of charity and social welfare, of schools universities and scientific activities, assists individuals and groups engaged in scientific work, as well as supporting cultural and artistic activity. Its geographical field of action covers Switzerland, India, Pakistan and Ceylon. Assets at the end of 1969 totalled 7,151,000 Sfrs. and disbursements to date 5.9 million Sfrs.

INTERNATIONAL FOUNDATIONS REGISTERED IN SWITZERLAND

The *International E. Balzan Prize Foundation* which possesses a total capital of 33 million Sfrs. provides the Balzan Foundation domiciled in Italy with the means it requires for the bestowal of the following prizes: for humanity, peace and brotherhood among the peoples of the world; for literature, the arts and humanities; for physics, mathematics, natural sciences and medicine. Prizes to a total value of 2.6 million Sfrs. have so far been awarded: for peace to the Nobel Foundation and Pope John XXIII, for music to Paul Hindemith, for biology to Karl von Frisch, for history to S. E. Morison, for mathematics to Professor A. Kolmogorov.

The beneficial area of the *International Foundation High-Alpine Research Station Jungfraujoch*, Bern, comprises the following countries: *Belgium*, represented by the National Fund for Scientific Research, Brussels; *Germany* represented by the Max-Planck Society for the Advancement of the Sciences, Munich; *France*, represented by the National Centre for Scientific Research,

Paris, and the University of Paris at the Sorbonne; The *United Kingdom*, represented by the Royal Society, London; *The Netherlands*, represented by the Royal Dutch Academy of Sciences, Amsterdam; *Austria*, represented by the Academy of Science, Vienna; *Switzerland*, represented by the Swiss Society for the Natural Sciences and the Jungfrau Transportation Company. The Foundation owns the High-Alpine Research Station Jungfraujoch (height 11,342 ft. above sea level) and rents the meteorological observatory on the Sphinx rock on the Jungfraujoch (11,713 ft. above sea level) as well as accommodation in the Gornergrat-Kulm Hotel (10,289 ft. above sea level). These stations are available to members for all scientific investigations which, for whatsoever reason, must be conducted at a great height or in an Alpine climate. The Foundation's assets total 1,012,000 Sfrs. and annual expenditure is at the rate of approximately 400,000 Sfrs.

The *Bernard van Leer Foundation* established by the Dutchman Bernard van Leer and registered in Lucerne is administered by a Board composed mainly of Dutch nationals supplemented by a Swiss Advisory Board. It concerns itself with the promotion of education and training of children and youth throughout the world, with particular emphasis on compensating for the deficits caused by social and cultural deprivation. Annual expenditure within Switzerland totals about 150,000 Sfrs. and expenditure in the other countries constituting its geographical field of action is very considerably in excess of this figure.

The *Foundation for Moral Re-Armament*, Lucerne, was founded in 1946 by Swiss citizens with the object of overcoming conflicts between nations, social classes and races by changing man and building up a just social order. The international conference centre is located in Caux and has so far received more than 150,000 participants from 118 countries. Expenditure over the last 10 years has amounted to 31 million Sfrs. and has been covered from private contributions (75% of the total coming from within Switzerland). In 1952 the pioneer of Moral Re-Armament, Dr. Frank Buchman, was decorated by the Governments of France and the Federal Republic of Germany for his efforts towards bringing about an effective reconciliation between nations. Subsequently, Moral Re-Armament played an influential role in the process of peaceful decolonisation and in development aid.

The *World Wildlife Fund*, Morges, established in 1961 is an international charitable organisation, dedicated to the protection of nature and natural resources on a world wide scale. It supports the establishment of a comprehensive, world-wide system of nature preservation (countryside, soil, water, fauna, flora), carries out publicity and propaganda campaigns and educational work, particularly among young people and, above all, raises funds for

Conservation projects. With regard to its projects it receives scientific and technical advice from the IUCN (International Union for Conservation of Nature and Natural Resources). Fund-raising and publicity are largely taken care of by the national subsidiaries established in many countries of the world. The Fund's assets total 3 million Sfrs. and grants to projects to date 25 million Sfrs.

International Foundation HUMANUM is one of the youngest international foundations with its seat in Switzerland. It was established on 24th September 1966 in Lugano and in May 1967 was placed under the supervisory office of the Federal Department of the Interior. The idea which inspired its creation was the offer of dialogue between the Church and the World made by the Fathers of Vatican Council II in the Constitution Gaudium et Spes. The Protestant World Council of Churches almost simultaneously took the decision to open up the Church (again) to the world. The purpose of the Foundation is to work towards the achievement of this goal by organising international and regional conferences, awarding prizes and promoting research and publications. The 1968 annual report indicates the amount secured from one-time or regular payments as 535,000 Sfrs.

Germany[*]

Ernst-Joachim Mestmäcker and Dieter Reuter

A. The Current Situation of Foundations in Germany

Since the beginning of the Industrial Age, foundations in Germany have on the whole participated in varying degrees in the economic growth of the country. Their evolution through the ages had made them into highly sophisticated organisations. This century has witnessed a break in the continuity of German foundations, as a result of two inflations, the rule of National Socialism and the division of Germany. The extent of the damage suffered by foundations and charitable endowments through the political and economic upheavals of recent decades is revealed by the fact that before the First World War there were approximately 100,000 foundations and trusts in the German Reich. Their assets were put at DM 3,800 million[1]. 90% of these foundations forfeited their assets and had to be wound up.

The moves to set up new foundations after 1948 were slow to gather momentum. The rapid expansion of government welfare and social security provision deprived the classical charitable foundations of the basis for their existence. In view of this state of affairs, the Federal and Land legislative authorities saw no point in renewing the antiquated and fragmented legal fundament on which foundations had hitherto been set up. For a long period of time, the basic political conditions for a generous promotion of foundations through tax privileges had simply not been present. The German tradition of regarding the promotion of the public weal as the exclusive domain of the State blinded people to the realisation that the very speed at which the State is pushing ahead in the historically most significant sectors for foun-

---

[*] Translated from the German.

[1] This estimate is largely based on figures given in M. Meyer's 'Statistik der Stiftungen im In- und Ausland', in: 'Jahrbücher für Nationalökonomie und Statistik', published in Jena in 1911—3rd series, Vol.42, p. 666 et ss. Compare also K. Neuhoff's '1000 Jahre Stiftungen in Deutschland', in: Das Parlament, p. 3 of no. 41 of 12th October 1968.

dation activity makes it absolutely necessary for socio-political reasons to supplement these efforts by private initiative.

We owe it above all to the major foundations set up after the Second World War, the Fritz Thyssen Foundation (1959) and the Volkswagenwerk Foundation (1961), that the general public again became aware of the special mission of and opportunities for private foundations. This impact gave rise to a widespread general and academic discussion about foundations and charitable endowments and to the creation of a number of important new foundations such as the *Robert Bosch Stiftung GmbH* and the *Alfried Krupp von Bohlen und Halbach-Stiftung*.

I. A SURVEY OF FOUNDATIONS IN GERMANY

It is difficult to quote precise figures in relation to the present state of foundations and charitable endowments in Germany because of the fragmentation of the law governing foundations and the absence of official foundation registers[2].

Nevertheless, various organisations interested in foundation matters are making good progress in their efforts to close this statistical gap[3]. Special mention should be made of the handbook published by the Stifterverband on *Deutsche Stiftungen für Wissenschaft, Bildung und Kultur* i.e. German Foundations for Science, Education and Culture[4].

There are about 4,000 legally independent foundations—excluding family foundations—in the Federal Republic of Germany. Of these 3,000 are foundations established under private law. The foundations established under public law are particularly numerous in Bavaria and in the Baden part of Baden-Württemberg. In the large majority of cases, these foundations under public law were also set up by private persons: their special feature is often merely the fact that they were transferred for administrative purposes to a public authority and when the Civil Code was introduced in 1900 they opted for the status of a foundation under public law[5].

[2] The one exception is Bavaria where the Bavarian Office of Statistics in Munich maintains a '*Verzeichnis der in Bayern bestehenden öffentlichen Stiftungen*', i.e. List of Public Foundations in Bavaria. This was brought up to date as of 1st October 1964. It should be added, however, that it does not include legally recognised foundations subject to the supervision of the Church.

[3] E.g. the *Arbeitsgemeinschaft Deutscher Stiftungen* (Association of German Foundations) in Augsburg, the *Wirtschaftspolitische Gesellschaft von 1947 (WIPOG)*, founded in Frankfurt in 1947, and the *Stifterverband für die Deutsche Wissenschaft* (Donor's Association for the Promotion of Sciences and Humanities in Germany) in Essen.

[4] Published in Baden-Baden in 1969 in the '*Schriftenreihe zum Stiftungswesen*', Vol. I.

[5] Cf. the 'Remarks on the actual situation of foundations in Germany', in Neuhoff—Vinken: *Deutsche Stiftungen für Wissenschaft, Bildung und Kultur, op. cit., p. XIV*.

Apart from foundations which possess legal status as such, a number of institutions similar in character to foundations but having a different status in law to the latter have been formed. This has been particularly the case in recent years. These substitute forms include the *eingetragener Verein (e.V.)*—i.e. registered association—and the *Gesellschaft mit beschränkter Haftung (GmbH)*—i.e. limited liability company. There are probably something like 500 such foundations in operation in Germany. They include notable institutions like the *Mahle Stiftung GmbH* and the *Robert Bosch Stiftung GmbH* (both in Stuttgart), the *Hochschul-Förderergesellschaften*—i.e. Societies of Friends of a University—who raise funds but also have substantial funds of their own as registered associations, the *Stifterverband für die Deutsche Wissenschaft e.V.* and similar organisations for the promotion of educational, cultural and scientific objects such as the *Studienstiftung des deutschen Volkes* (Fellowship Foundation of the German People set up in 1925), the *Friedrich-Ebert-Stiftung e.V.* and the *Konrad-Adenauer-Stiftung e.V. (1964)*.

There are special and virtually insuperable difficulties to face if one attempts to estimate the number of trust properties, endowments or dependent foundations (*unselbständige Stiftung*). With the exception of such foundations established under public law, they are not subject to supervision or any statutory requirement to be registered since German law only provides for foundations possessing legal personality under private law as *Stiftungen*. The administration of these foundations without legal status is often transferred to a public authority, a bank, a commercial enterprise, a university or one of the numerous cultural societies and this fact is only known to a small number of persons directly affected. Nonetheless, it may be assumed that the number of such juridically dependent foundations is at least as great as that of the independent ones and in fact probably exceeds it. No allowance has been made here for the innumerable very small foundations administered by the churches especially in South Germany: there are probably tens of thousands of them.

Only a rough estimate can be made of the market value of the assets held by foundations and trusts, including the substitute forms but excluding the purely private family foundations. The figure is roughly DM 15,000 mill. Difficulties of assessment are encountered from the very beginning because of the varying composition of foundation assets. The type of assets held—money, shares, loans, real estate, buildings, agricultural land and forests, commercial firms or art treasures—requires a varying system of evaluation.

Only about three quarters of overall foundation capital consists of assets which yield a profit. The relatively high percentage of agricultural land and forests, mainly owned by the foundations established under public law, together with the currently meagre disbursements effected by some of the more recently established major foundations mean that the average rate of interest in market value terms is only just over 2%.

In theory, one could thus compute an income on foundation capital of DM 200 mill to DM 250 mill. However, the actual revenue is considerably higher thanks to substantial subsidies from public authorities and additional funds provided by the founders, trade and industry and the general public.

A breakdown of foundation capital in terms of individual categories produces the following picture:

Foundations established under civil law	approx.	DM 8,000 mill.
Foundations established under public law	approx.	DM 4,000 mill.
Foundations without legal status	less than	DM 1,000 mill.
Substitute forms	approx.	DM 2,000 mill.
An estimated total of 300 Family Foundations	approx.	DM 5,000 mill.*

The order of magnitude of these foundations may be seen from the following important examples. The five biggest foundations set up under private law and representing total assets of about DM 4,900 mill. are:

Name	Date of Establishment	Capital (in DM mill.)	Donations and Allocations (1969) (in DM mill.)
1. Stiftung Volkswagenwerk, Hanover	1961	1,074[1]	93.1
2. Alfried Krupp von Bohlen und Halbach-Stiftung, Essen	1968	over 500[2]	.
3. Carl-Zeiss-Stiftung, Heidenheim	1889	201[3]	15
4. Fritz Thyssen Stiftung, Cologne	1959	200[4]	11.6
5. Stiftung FVS, Hamburg	1931	75[5]	3

* The latter capital is largely invested in the *Karg'sche Familienstiftung in Hamburg* (*Hertie Waren- und Kaufhaus GmbH, Berlin*), the *German Peter Klöckner-Familienstiftung in Duisburg* (*Klöckner & Co. K.G., Duisburg*) and the three foundations set up by the *Flick* concern (*Friedrich Flick K.G., Düsseldorf*).

The three largest foundations established under public law are probably:

Name	Year of Establishment	Size of Budget in 1967[1] (in DM mill.)
1. Preussischer Kulturbesitz, Berlin	1957	47.3[2]
2. Der allgemeine Hannoversche Klosterfonds, Hanover	1840[3]	14.4
3. Stiftung Julius-Spital, Würzburg	1576	13.8[4]

[1] A classification based on the size of the budget of a foundation set up under public law does not necessarily permit one to draw any conclusions about the magnitude of its assets. The budget figures are always particularly low if real estate is rented out as, for example, is the case in Hanover.

[2] Stems almost exclusively from public funds.

[3] In 1650 a separate administrative heading within the administration for the Crown Assets of Hanover was introduced to cover the assets of former monasteries and ecclesiastical foundations which were deprived of their former purpose during the Reformation. In 1818 a special body, the *Hannoversche Klosterkammer*, was set up to administer these assets. The independence of the foundation and the separation of State and foundation was guaranteed by the Hanoverian Constitutional Law of 6th August 1840.

[4] Excluding an extra-budgetary sum of approximately DM 3 mill.

[1] The equivalent of 32% of the shares in *Volkswagenwerk AG in Wolfsburg* ought to be added to the capital of the *Volkswagenwerk Stiftung* for purposes of comparison. These shares are held by the founders: the Federal Government and the Land of Lower Saxony. Pursuant to a usufruct, the dividends on these shares are paid to the foundation. In the event of their sale, the foundation has a claim to the proceeds of the sale. If these facts are taken into consideration and the evaluation of the shares is based on their price on the stock exchange at the beginning of February 1969, about DM 1,600 mill should be added to the foundation capital (which moreover, also contains undisclosed reserves). Its profit-yielding assets of almost DM 3,000 mill and its income of DM 123.9 mill in 1969 make the *Volkswagenwerk Foundation* the third largest foundation in the world, i.e. after the Ford Foundation and the Rockefeller Foundation.

[2] Stock capital of *Fried. Krupp GmbH*.

[3] Ledger values based on consolidated balance sheet.

[4] Stock exchange quotation of DM 105 mill shares of *August Thyssen-Hütte AG*.

[5] Ledger values.

Of the foundations without legal status constituted under civil law, particular importance attaches to the *Ziegler Fund* of DM 40 mill. established at the Max-Planck-Institute for Coal Research in Mülheim/Ruhr (1968). The largest foundation of this kind established under public law is almost certainly the *Zeppelin Stiftung* (1908) administered by the municipality of Friedrichshafen. It holds various shares worth nearly DM 40 mill. (ledger value)[6].

Of the foundations organised in other legal forms, special mention should be made of the *Robert Bosch Stiftung GmbH* which was set up in 1921 and whose capital resources were considerably increased in 1964 (shares with a ledger value of DM 258.97 mill.) and the *Mahle Stiftung GmbH* (shares with a ledger value of DM 60.9 mill.) established in 1964 whilst among the institutions which may no longer be regarded as foundations but which resemble foundations the outstanding example is the *Max-Planck-Gesellschaft zur Förderung der Wissenschaften e.V.* (Max Planck Society for the Promotion of Sciences) in Munich set up in 1911 as the *Kaiser Wilhelm Gesellschaft*. Although its assets only amount to DM 22.3 mill., its income in 1969, for example, was DM 321 mill., 95% of which stemmed from public budgetary sources.

It is scarcely possible to quote precise figures about the age of existing foundations in Germany. Nevertheless, it can be assumed on the basis of available information that about 35% of foundations established under private law were set up after the Second World War most of the remaining 65% were probably constituted prior to the First World War.

The oldest foundations in Germany may be designated as public institutions (*Anstalten*). A smoothly working welfare and education system was organised in the early and later Middle Ages with the help of such social and educational institutions which 'strictly speaking are not foundations in the legal sense of the term but juridically dependent institutions of other legal entities'[7]. The real estate vested in these foundations—land was often donated at a later date to cover recurring costs—has maintained its value over the centuries in some cases so that these bodies have been able to survive every political and economic convulsion. Toepke ascertained that the following foundations must be the oldest ones in Germany[8]:

1. Hospital Stiftung in Wemding, Bavaria (917)

[6] This foundation owes its existence to the spontaneous fund-raising campaign organized throughout Germany after the airship disaster of Echterdingen in 1908 in order to permit Count Zeppelin to continue his work on the construction of airships.

[7] H. Liermann: *Handbuch des Stiftungsrechts*, Vol. I—*Geschichte des Stiftungsrechts*, Tübingen 1963, pp. 78/79.

[8] U.-P. Toepke: *Staatsaufsicht über Stiftungen im deutschen und anglo-amerikanischen Recht*, Hamburg 1967, p. 262 et s.

2. St. Dominikus- und Blatternhaus-Stiftung in Kaufbeuren (1182)
3. Stiftung 'Hospital zum Heiligen Geist' in Frankfurt (1193)
4. St. Johannes-Bürgerspital-Stiftung in Passau (1206)
5. St. Katharinen-Spital in Regensburg (1226)
6. Paritätische Hospitals-Stiftung in Augsburg (1239)
7. Stiftung 'Kloster St. Johannes' in Hamburg (1246)

In comparison with earlier centuries, the geographical location of foundations has undergone certain changes. Whereas the main trading centres in South Germany or the Hanseatic towns in North Germany used to be the strongholds of charitable endowments, the main point of emphasis in recent times has been the industrial and trade conurbations, especially Hamburg, the Rhine-Ruhr and the Rhine-Main-Neckar regions.

II. THE ACTIVITIES OF FOUNDATIONS

The objects for which foundations were set up provide the best clue to their activities, and these objects can be grouped within various categories. The so-called 'classical' foundation purposes fall within the category of social assistance and welfare. In an analysis of the status and role of foundations in his book entitled *Stiftungen im gesellschaftlichen Prozess*[9], T. Schiller noted that the 'most striking feature to emerge from a study of the objects of foundations was the clear predominance of charitable purposes'. This group includes about two thirds of all independent foundations established under private law even though their share of capital is only just above 15%. One should add to this group those foundations set up by firms for the welfare of their staff. They probably number something in the region of 300. If one also adds their assets, the charity-cum-welfare foundations may be said to dispose of 20% of the capital held by foundations set up under private law.

The percentage of foundations established under public law which may be classified as eleemosynary foundations is even greater than that of private-law foundations. A subsidiary object in their case is the management and preservation of assets in the form of agricultural land or forests.

The remaining foundations were largely formed to promote education, culture and science[10]. Their share of the overall foundation capital is larger than average because the large foundations which have been recently set up all belong to this group. The more recent substitute forms and a few trusts

---

[9] Baden-Baden 1969, p. 128.
[10] Cf. the handbook published by the Stifterverband entitled *'Deutsche Stiftungen für Wissenschaft, Bildung und Kulter'*, *loco citato*.

(charitable endowments) may also be placed in this category. These foundations may be compared with the philanthropic foundations in the USA. Their historical precursors were the numerous school and scholarship foundations of the post-Reformation period and the large number of educational and vocational training foundations set up by the many patrons of the arts, sciences and humanities in the nineteenth century.

The large and medium sized foundations regard their task today primarily as developing initiatives of their own in science and education, trying out model or pilot projects and inspiring and promoting by their commitment those developments which could not be generated within the limits of the State's provision in the field of education and the sciences. The large German foundations constituted after 1945 have made a significant contribution towards the reforming of schools and universities as a result of their initiatives in the aforementioned fields.

The measures taken by the *Stiftung Volkswagenwerk* to remodel research and teaching have been especially noteworthy (the promotion of scientific co-operation and interdisciplinary research, studies on the opportunities for systematic correspondence courses, formation of an Institute for the Teaching of the Natural Sciences, introduction of a DM 75 mill. programme to overcome the shortage of mathematics and science teachers at grammar (high) schools, the first thorough-going measures to be adopted in Germany in the fields of molecular biology, biophysics and theoretical chemistry).

The main point of emphasis in the activities of the *Fritz Thyssen Stiftung* is the promotion of the arts and humanities and support for new entrants to the scientific professions. Programmes have been devised to provide special backing for research on the development of the arts and humanities (e.g. 'Research Project The 19th Century') and for supporting the work done by the Commission for Research on the Development of the Arts and Humanities in Eastern Europe. The 'Research Project East Africa' is devoted to the solution of current political problems there. In addition, there are research programmes for armament questions and international security, studies on the harmonisation of European law and the promotion of scientific projects within the framework of development aid.

The *Georg Michael Pfaff Memorial Foundation* in Kaiserslautern whose capital resources make it one of the smaller foundations, was formed to promote public education. It attempts to improve schools, to educate the individual to accept responsibility for and contribute towards the advancement of the society in which he lives, to activate youth welfare work and to grant scholarships with a view to improving school and vocational education.

The *Alfried Krupp von Bohlen und Halbach-Stiftung* in Essen which was founded in 1967 is still in the process of organisation. Unlike other big foundations, its aims embrace adult education, and the promotion of literature, music and the fine arts.

The fact that more and more foundations are being set up by the major groupings in our age such as the Churches, the trade unions, the political parties or the trade and industrial associations for their own purposes rather than by individuals exercises a substantial influence on the activities of foundations. Even the State resorts to the legal form of a foundation established under private law in order to farm out certain functions or it promotes such foundations from current budget moneys. These measures have been instrumental in producing a situation in which the legal form of foundation does not correspond to any precisely definable reality in modern society. Nevertheless, foundations remain the most important means of institutionalising and independently implementing the initiatives taken by private persons to promote public causes. The as yet unsolved problem is how to create the social and legal prerequisites for utilising the opportunities for widespread and varied foundation activity provided by the growth of the economy.

B. Foundation Law

I. THE CAUSES OF PROBLEMS IN FOUNDATION LAW

Any account of the legislation governing foundations in Germany is rendered difficult by the fact that such laws were only partly covered by the codification of civil law in 1900. Hence, Foundation Law is mainly Land Law. Although the *Länder* (States) which came into existence after 1945 have made frequent use of their legislative powers, the contents and trends of their legislation have not been uniform. This state of affairs in foundation legislation has also meant that little theoretical and academic consideration has been given to the subject. For this reason, the keen discussion in recent years on reforming foundation law and improving the general situation of foundations and charitable endowments can scarcely claim to rest on a firm legal fundament. One is faced by difficulties both in regard to the foundation as a legal form and to its function in relation to the State.

1. In his work on Foundation Law, D. Pleimes[11] considered the problems which arise from the designation of the foundation in the Civil Code as a legal form which, in principle, may be employed as and how the founder thinks fit. Unlike Anglo-Saxon law, the law in the Civil Code covering

[11] *Die Rechtsproblematik des Stiftungswesens*, 1938; *Weltliches Stiftungsrecht—Geschichte der Rechtsformen*, 1938; *Irrwege der Dogmatik im Stiftungsrecht*, 1954.

foundations does not govern the typical set of circumstances attending foundations—resulting as they do from historical and social evolution—whereby a private person dedicates all or some of his fortune to a public cause. On the contrary, it offers an instrument in law with whose aid assets tied to a specific purpose may attain an independent and permanent legal existence. A person who desires to settle money on an organisation is not committed to the legal form of a foundation and, by the same token, the choice of this legal form does not permit one to assume that a set of circumstances is present which can be said to constitute a foundation.

This concept has produced problems in two different ways: on the one hand, it has meant that the typical features of a foundation, i.e. a permanent dedication of assets to a prescribed purpose and an abiding observance of the founder's wishes, have only been taken into consideration in the Civil Code in respect of the legislation governing foundations, but not in that governing the substitute forms such as non-profit associations (*Vereine*) or private limited companies (*GmbH*), which are quite customary nowadays. In this respect, the rules contained in the Civil Code in regard to foundations are too limited in scope.

The other difficulty results from the major problem—which also exists outside of foundation law—of the degree to which legal forms should be employable to suit individual wishes or whims. The approach on which the Civil Code is based, namely that a free interplay of forces will in itself produce a just social and economic order, is nowadays also outdated in civil law. The enactors and administrators of the law are now taking a closer look at whether the prerequisites for the compatibility of individual liberty and the requirements of the law are present. This consideration has led to the question in foundation law whether and, if need be, to what extent the possible uses to which the foundation device can be put ought to be restricted.

2. Our currently valid foundation law is also marked by uncertainty about the relationship between foundations and State administration[12]. Even the materials on which the Civil Code is based contain two basically incompatible views. On the one hand, reference is made to the dangers of 'perpetuating the wishes of the founder' which have made it necessary in each case to obtain authorisation from the State for the projected foundation because of the impossibility of compiling a general list of purposes for which foundations may be set up[13]. This is obviously an expression of the reservations built into private law in regard to mortmain. On the other hand, the 'authori-

[12] Cf. Siebert—Schultze = v. Lasaulx, 10th Ed. Stuttgart, 1967, note before Art. 80 mar. No. 21.

[13] Protocol I, p. 588.

sation granted to a public foundation ought to be a decision which is as closely associated as possible with constitutional law'[13] and fall within the purview of competency of the Land legislature 'in view of the close connection between foundations and the public law of individual States' (Mot.I, p.321). The foundation law which is valid in former Prussian territories gives pointed expression to the constitutional attitudes behind these quotations in that it leaves the authorisation of benevolent institutions (i.e. in today's terminology, foundations operating an eleemosynary institution = *Anstaltsstiftungen*) to the discretion of the public authorities[14] whereas it raises a claim to the right to authorise family foundation[15]. Thus, Prussian law on foundation does not deem the need for State approval to be an instrument for averting the dangers ensuing from the 'perpetualisation of the founder's wishes' for, with the exception of the virtually insignificant possibility of dissolution by unanimous family resolution, the perpetualisation of the founder's wishes is precisely the same in a private family foundation as it is in a foundation organised to run an institution[16]. The decisive criterion is really the view that the State must exercise controls because and inasmuch as a foundation encroaches on the State's range of competence in its contributions to public welfare. This line of thought reflects the constitutional pattern which prevailed in the concept of the State from the age of enlightened absolutism to that of a constitutionally limited monarchy i.e. the advancement of the common weal is the business of the State alone. The latter can use its own discretion in determining the scope and limits of private intervention in this field.

The Bavarian legislation of foundations reveals another aim behind State participation in the affairs of foundations and charitable endowments i.e. the protection of foundations from abuse on the part of their executive bodies and from encroachments by third parties[17]. The State authority responsible for granting authorisation has the task of assessing whether each individual project for establishing a foundation can be deemed to justify the financial outlay which State 'protection' calls for[18].

These fundamental attitudes to the subject have a number of important legal consequences. The problems relating to eligibility for authorisation,

[14] ALR = General Civil Code for the Prussian States of 1794, 19 II Arts. 33, 34.
[15] ALR 4 II Art. 31.
[16] ALR 4 II Art. 39, which prohibited the dissolution of foundations or any substantial amendment of their statutes by decision of the family, was revoked in 1807. The discriminatory treatment in the granting of permission to family foundations and foundations operating an institution already existed before then.
[17] Cf. the heading of the second section of the Bavarian Law on Foundations.
[18] Vide Liermann, in: *Deutsches Stiftungswesen*, Tübingen 1968, p. 202.

H

State supervision, or the changing of aims can only be resolved in foundation law if the reasons for and implications of State participation in the domain of foundations and charitable endowments are clearly understood. A decision must also be reached *de lege lata* on the extent to which a democratic approach to foundation law free from State tutelage can be given free rein in the interpretation of laws which stem from another age.

II. THE DEFINITION OF FOUNDATIONS IN THE CIVIL CODE (BGB)

1. In keeping with its formal character as described at the beginning of this paper, a foundation is defined in the Civil Code as an independent legal entity which is created for the implementation of certain specified purposes and which does not comprise an association of individuals[19].

Pursuant to Art. 80 of the Civil Code, a foundation comes into being through a declaration of intent and the granting of State authorisation. The declaration of intent can be effected in the form of a legal act *inter vivos* or *mortis causa*. In each case, it involves as a rule a unilaterial declaration of intent which need not be communicated to other parties and which must indicate the founder's wish to have the foundation set up as an independent legal subject.[20] As we have already mentioned, the most important question in practice, i.e. the preconditions for authorisation, is determined by Land foundation law and not by the Civil Code.

In the main, the Civil Code describes the legal status of a foundation by references to Land Law. Art. 85 of the Civil Code states, for example, in regard to the constitution of foundations that the declaration of intent is the decisive element provided that Federal or Land Laws do not contain binding provisions to the contrary. Pursuant to Art. 86 of the Civil Code, the only contribution by Federal Law in this field is to establish the legal position of the Board of Directors and the foundation's liability *vis-à-vis* third parties. Moreover, the provisions in the Civil Code on the legal relationship between the foundation and the founder are no more than a fragmentary supplement to the law on associations. Art. 82 of the Civil Code imposes upon a founder the obligation to transfer the ownership of promised assets to a foundation set up *inter vivos* as soon as the requisite official authorisation has been

---

[19] Enneccerus—Nipperdey, *Allgemeiner Teil des Bürgerlichen Rechts*. Part I, 15th Ed., Tübingen 1959, Art. 117 para I.

[20] Enneccerus—Nipperdey, Art. 117 para I. By way of exception, the unilateral declaration of intent may be replaced by a contractual agreement. The establishment of the *Stiftung Volkswagenwerk* as a foundation in private law by a special Federal statute was a unique case.

accorded. In the view of most jurists, the founder's liability in respect of this debt is analogous to that obtaining in the case of a donation.[21]

In pursuance of Art. 84 of the Civil Code, a foundation which does not receive its authorisation until after the founder's death is deemed to have been created before his death as far as the transfer of assets is concerned. There are no special provisions governing the relationship between the foundation and the intended beneficiaries. The prevailing view is that, analogous to Art. 328 of the Civil Code, the intended beneficiaries have an enforceable claim in respect of the foundation's disbursements if the latter and the preconditions for their legal title are adequately set out in the statutes of the foundation. In the event of a default by the foundation, the beneficiaries only have one option open to them and that is to request action on the part of the foundation supervisory bodies—whose creation is provided for in nearly all Land legislation[22].

Finally, a foundation may be annulled or converted into another legal entity pursuant to Art. 87 of the Civil Code if it has become impossible to implement the purpose for which the foundation was set up or if the foundation represents a public hazard. When a foundation is converted into another legal entity, the fullest possible account must be taken of the founder's will.

2. This outline of foundation law contained in the Civil Code reveals the extent of prejudice in favour of providing controls at the level of Land legislation. To all intents and purposes, the Civil Code only has something to say about the characteristics of a foundation as a legal subject and the form of its participation in legal transactions, the formal preconditions for its creation, and the legal nature and certain legal consequences of foundation transactions[23]. In particular, questions pertaining to the cooperation and participation of State authorities are omitted and made subject to Land Law. Nevertheless, even the Land Laws on foundations or the relevant provisions in the Land Laws for the implementation of the Civil Code only provide an incomplete answer to the problems involved. This is true of permissible foundation purposes and foundation supervision.

[21] Art. 521 et ss. of the Civil Code: cf. Enneccerus—Nipperdey, Art. 118 para II; v. Staudinger-Coing, 11th Ed., Berlin 1957, note 4 to Art. 82; Palandt—Danckelmann, 28th Ed., Munich 1969, Art. 82, note 1; *Reichsgerichtsentscheidungen in Zivilsachen, RGZ*— Reich Supreme Court Judgments in Civil Cases, 54, 400.

[22] The exception is Bremen where there is no supervision of foundations. Cf. Toepke, p. 233; cf. also Enneccerus—Nipperdey, Art. 118 para. III; Supreme Court Decision— RG HHR—No. 1427 of 1931.

[23] Cf. Ballerstedt, in: Recording of the 44th Assembly of German Lawyers, Hanover 1962, Volume I (Opinion), Part 5, Tübingen 1962, p. 8.

III. THE PURPOSES FOR WHICH FOUNDATIONS MAY BE ESTABLISHED

The Foundation Law applicable throughout former Prussian territories limits its provisions to private family foundations and charitable institutions, i.e. foundations whose purpose it is to administer welfare institutions such as hospitals, orphanages, etc. No mention is made of principal fund foundations (*Hauptgeldstiftungen*), i.e. foundations which make grants to charity out of the profits derived from the assets they administer. Even as regards family foundations, the Prussian law does no more within the scope of its jurisdiction than dispel any doubts that may exist in regard to the preconditions for the authorisation of this type of foundation. Pursuant to Chap. 1 Art. 1 of the *Prussian AGBGB* (Law for the Implementation of the Civil Code) family foundations receive their authorization from the competent municipal Court. In accordance with Art. 31 of the ALR 4 II, a municipal Court *must* grant them permission if their statutes are set out in sufficiently clear and specific manner. On the other hand, ch. 4 of the *Prussian AVBGB* (Implementing Provisions in respect of the Civil Code) reserves the right of granting authorisation to charitable institutions to the King (nowadays a State body in compliance with the rules on competency issued by each Federal Land). Although such a decision does contain a legally binding element and authorisation may only be refused pursuant to Art. 34 of the ALR 19 II, if the implementation of the founder's wishes is impossible or harmful (a directive which nowadays could be enforced via the administrative Courts, if need be). All this is of little use in modern legal practice because the criteria by which the ALR assessed, for example, the harmfulness of a foundation belong to a past age with a totally different approach to constitutional and socio-political issues.

As we have already seen, the striking difference between the procedure for approving charitable foundations and that for approving family foundations—and in particular the more active participation by the State in the case of charitable foundations—typifies Prussian Foundation Law as the product of enlightened absolutism. Arts. 1, 7 and 8 of the ALR 19 II even go so far as to stipulate that foundations must fit in with the State's welfare programmes and that private initiatives in the foundation sector which compete with State plans are not admissible. Thus, the section in Art. 1 of the ALR 19 II entitled 'On Poor-houses and eleemosynary Foundations' sets out the principle at the very beginning that it 'is for the State to provide food and subsistence for those citizens who cannot earn their own livelihood and who cannot be given one by those persons who are obliged by law to do so'. Art. 7 prohibits incitement to 'pernicious idleness' and Art. 8 permits the

State to dissolve and expropriate foundations which 'set out to promote and support such detrimental inclinations'. In other words, the ALR postulates the exact opposite of the 'creative competition' which is viewed today as a foundation's prime objective. Hence, it is impossible to retain these standards of judgement.

The new foundation laws promulgated in Hamburg (1958) and Berlin (1960) desist from specifying positive prerequisites for the granting of authorisation and thus, in the final analysis, pose the same problem as the old foundation law applied through former Prussian territories[24].

The Bavarian Foundation Law (1954), which also served as a model for the foundation laws promulgated in 1966 by the Rhineland-Palatinate and Hesse, has quite a lot to say about the basic prerequisites for granting authorisation. Chap. 3 para. 1(2) of the Bavarian Foundation Law stipulates that a foundation ought to be approved if the aims it is pursuing are, in the main, of benefit to the community and, moreover, that it may only be approved if the lasting realisation of the aims of the foundation out of the profits accruing from the foundation's assets appears to be assured. Furthermore, Chap. 8 para. 2 prescribes the requisite contents of the statutes which, if need be, may be supplemented by the approving authority subject to the founder's permission if he is still alive.

A closer look at these regulations shows that they by no means eliminate the difficulties either. Certainly it is firmly established that no approval will be granted if the contents of the statutes are inadequate. Similarly, the stipulated requirement contained in Chap. 3 para. 1(2) of the Bavarian Law on foundations clearly states that authorisation may only be refused in atypical cases to a foundation pursuing purposes which are predominantly in the public interest[25]. However, no explicit explanation is given as to what constitutes a typical or an atypical case. The decisive criteria in this respect may only be deduced from the basic conception of the relationship between foundation and State which is revealed in the general attitudes contained in the Bavarian Law on Foundations.

Mention has already been made of the view taken in the Bavarian Foundation Law of the relationship between foundations and the State: it is recognised that foundations have an idealistic value of their own and, in particular, have played an important role in the history of culture and civili-

[24] Art. 6 of the Hamburg AGBGB, merely stipulates that the statutes must quote the name, official address, purpose, assets and administrative bodies. The approving authority may grant or withhold permission at its own discretion. Nothing is stated about the principles by which such discretion should be guided.

[25] Cf. Wolff, *Verwaltungsrecht I*, 7th Ed., Munich 1968, Art. 31 para. II(b) on the interpretation of stipulated requirements.

sation which makes them worthy of State protection. Accordingly, authorisation bears a direct relationship to the State's obligation to furnish care and protection, a requirement which is given detailed treatment in the second part of the law. The approving authority must ensure that only deserving undertakings are admitted.

The objections to such a standpoint are that State protection may be extended further than the characteristics of the foundation under private law would justify. An authorisation system which regards its task as singling out foundations worthy of State patronage may be tempted to assess the merits of any given case in the light of its own (i.e. the State's) point of view. If the prime task of foundations and trusts is to compete with the public authorities in promoting the public weal, such authorities should not be given the final word in approving or rejecting a concrete case.

Admittedly, the stipulated requirement in Chap. 3 para. 1(2) of the Bavarian Foundation Law exempts the bulk of foundations whose aims are largely of general public interest from the need to be evaluated by the approving authority. Nevertheless, a decision as to what constitutes general public interest contains a value-judgement about the aim which the foundation is pursuing. This also applies when an assessment is made as to whether a foundation's aims are predominantly of general public interest. On the other hand, both the South German foundation laws (in Bavaria, Rhineland-Palatinate and Hesse) and the North German foundation laws (Prussian Law, the Hamburg AGBGB and the Berlin Foundation Law) make allowance for the requirement that, in principle, any foundation aim should be permitted if its implementation does not contravene a prohibitory law or conflict with public morals[26] in that they all leave the granting of permission to the discretion of the approving authority.

The principle of admitting all foundation aims does not exclude objections to individual methods of making use of foundations. The distinguishing features of foundations as an organisational unit may make it appear undesirable to use them in certain circumstances. One characteristic of foundations is the tying of assets to the will of a founder and the theoretical perpetuity of this link. Such assets are not subject to the influence—an influence which reduces or divides power—inherent in the law of succession and in the law on the payment of death duties, which make their impact increasingly felt as one generation succeeds another. This leads to a problem, because in German law the foundation does not acquire legitimacy by virtue of its having 'charitable purpose' such as exists in Anglo-American law. This is

[26] Cf. Mestmäcker, in: *Verhandlungen des 44. Deutschen Juristentages*, Vol. II (Written Records), Part G, Tübingen 1964, p. 16.

revealed particularly clearly in the much-discussed foundations which run a business (*Stiftungsunternehmen*) and one-stock foundations. The prevailing view is that the granting of permission to such foundations is completely unproblematic[27]. The approving authorities act accordingly in practice. There are only a few cases of reference being made to possible economic disadvantages, which, however, are either left out of consideration because of the comparatively minor importance of foundations in terms of the national economy as a whole[28] or which the authorities are summoned to eliminate by enacting mandatory statute provisions[29].

The major foundations set up by private industry in recent years (e.g. *Robert Bosch Stiftung GmbH* or *Krupp-Stiftung*) have been marked by a willingness to enter into socio-political commitments coupled with the aim of guaranteeing the survival of the firm for as many generations as possible. The most significant motive is the wish to protect the enterprise from unsuitable heirs, from a fragmentation of the shareholding through inheritance or from the consequences of high death duties. In so far as the debilitating— i.e. power-depriving—influence of the law of succession and the provisions of death duty legislation is cancelled out in this way, there are certain reservations which must be made from the point of view of private law. However, the decisive factor governing the operational validity of private law is the requirement that the extent of private power remains confined to what may be deemed to constitute the indispensable minimum for economic reasons. Commercial law backs up this concern by obliging the owner of a company who chooses to constitute the latter as a capitalistic—i.e. corporate—legal entity (joint stock company—AG, limited liability company—GmbH) to renounce in large measure the possibility of ensuring that his own or his family's influence on the fate of the company remains paramount. This tends to provide an incentive for sticking to the 'person-related' form of business enterprise for as long as the conditions obtaining in regard to competition in the company's markets do not require that it assume the 'privileged' capitalistic form. If it is legally constituted in the form of a foundation, it is in a position to protect its endowment from the consequences of subsequent cases of succession and at the same time to guarantee that the founder and his family will maintain their influence 'for ever' over the said endow-

[27] Cf. Siebert—Schultze = v. Lasaulx, note before Art. 80, Mar. notes 43/48, with other authors.

[28] Cf. Neuhoff: *Die Bereitstellung von Unternehmenskapital für Stiftungen*, Cologne 1964, p. 63.

[29] Cf. Steuck: *Die Stiftung als Rechtsform für wirtschaftliche Unternehmen*. Berlin 1968, p. 98; Strickrodt: *Unternehmen unter frei gewählter Stiftungssatzung*, Baden-Baden/ Frankfurt 1956, pp. 34 et ss., 117.

ment. By building a foundation into an entrepreneurial structure, the owner thus escapes having to make a choice between two alternatives: immunity *vis-à-vis* subsequent cases of succession *or* the establishment of a lasting bond between the company and his own or his family's influence. There is a growing danger that this may result in a formation of concentrations of private power which is unnecessary from an economic point of view. Consequently, the earmarking of large bodies of assets for foundation purposes should, as far as possible, be regulated in such a way as to ensure that such foundations are debarred from exercising a determining influence on the fate of the company.

IV. THE SUPERVISION OF FOUNDATIONS

Although the Civil Code leaves State supervision of foundations to the Land legislators, a distinction should be drawn between the various kinds of stipulations contained in Land laws.

The Foundation Laws enacted in the former Prussian territories, for example, contain different provisions in line with the authorisation needed for family foundations and 'charitable (incl. ecclesiastical) institutions'. Whereas family foundations are not subject to any supervision, charitable institutions are liable to State supervision in pursuance of Art. 37 of ALR 19 II even if the deed establishing the foundation provided for supervision by another party. Under the terms of Art. 38 of ALR 19 II, the supreme State supervising bodies 'must ensure that such organisation will be run in accordance with the founder's directions, which have been tacitly or explicitly approved by the State'. Art. 39 of ALR 19 II grants such bodies the right of inspection and the power to rectify any abuses or shortcomings they may encounter. The arrangements for State supervision reveal the same trend in Prussian law, which we have already noted in connection with the authorisation of foundations, to intensify State influence the more intensively a foundation pursues aims serving the public interest.

The same trend crops up again in the new foundation laws passed in North Germany. Art. 8 para. 1 of the Hamburg AGBGB subjects foundations to State supervision, the extent of which is left to the discretion of the competent authority pursuant to Art. 2. The means of supervision are listed in Arts. 12 and 13 of the AGBGB. These state that the said authority has the right of inspecting premises and receiving information; furthermore the executive and administrative bodies of the foundation are obliged to give immediate notification of any changes in their structure and, if requested, to present their business and cash-books, files and other documents; they must also submit an annual statement of accounts, a statement of assets and liabilities and a progress report within three months subsequent to the conclusion of a business year; and, finally, they have to compile a list of foundation benefactions and their recipients.

Art. 14 para. 2 of the Hamburg AGBGB restricts the number of methods of supervision in the case of family foundations. If their assets do not devolve upon the Exchequer when they cease to exist, nor upon a juridical person incorporated under public law, nor upon some other charitable foundation and the founder has not made specific stipulations for a more intensive degree of supervision, the only duty of a foundation's executive and administrative bodies is to give due notification of changes in structure. The Berlin Law echoes this provision for State supervision and the two laws are, in part, textually identical.

In accordance with their different approach to the relationship between foundation and State, the more recent South German laws on foundations contain divergent stipulations on State supervision. An example of this is furnished by the Bavarian Foundation Law whose second section speaks of the requirement incumbent upon the State to furnish care and protection rather than of supervision. In concrete terms, the difference is that in addition to the inspection of premises and accounts envisaged in the Hamburg and Berlin legislation there are a number of legal transactions which are subject to authorisation (Chap.31 of the Bavarian Foundation Law; Art.34 of the Rhineland-Palatinate Foundation Law). The composition of this list of transactions is very reminiscent of the requirements in respect of the protection of minors pursuant to Arts.1821 and 1822 of the Civil Code. The same philosophy of affording care and protection may be traced in Art.38 of the Bavarian Foundation Law, Art. 45 of the Rhineland-Palatinate Foundation Law and Art.20 para. 4 of the Hessian Foundation Law which exclude ecclesiastical foundations from State care and protection. If the main reason for supervision is to protect the foundation, there is no need for the State to take action unless another party has not already provided such protection. The question remains whether in this connection as well as in the case of the granting of authorisation a way exists whereby *de lege lata* modern foundation philosophy may make its influence felt.

The partially stipulated limitation of supervision to checking the legality of a foundation's activities and their conformity to its statutes gives pointed expression to the determining legal principle[30]. As all laws leave the exercise

[30] Cf. Chap. 23 paras. 1(2) and 2 of the Bavarian Foundation Law; Art. 10 para. 1(2) of the Hessian Foundation Law; Art. 26 of the Rhineland-Palatinate Foundation Law; and Art. 7 para. 2 of the Berlin Foundation Law.

of supervision as a matter of individual discretion to the public authority in question, the long list of methods of supervision contained in various laws such as the Bavarian and Rhineland-Palatinate laws on foundations does not run counter to any such limitation of supervision. It would be incompatible with the function of foundations to implement independent schemes for the promotion of the common weal in addition to, and independently of, public authorities if such public authorities were given the right of judging the expediency of a foundation's conduct. Hence, the primary task facing the supervisory body is to organise the supervision in such a way that it can guarantee the legal functioning of a foundation in accordance with its statutes and thus vouch for the realisation of the founder's wishes. On the other hand, supervisory measures are considered to be inadmissible and therefore abusive of the above-mentioned discretionary powers if they are intended to induce a foundation to use its funds for State projects or forfeit its own programmes in consideration of competing State interests.

V. ALTERATION OF THE AIMS OF A FOUNDATION

The third problem to be largely settled by Land law is linked with a question which is of great significance in practice: what procedure should be adopted in the case of a change occurring in the circumstances which existed when a foundation was set up. Art. 87 para. 1 of the Civil Code states that the super-visory body may amend or annul a foundation's aim if it is becoming im-possible to fulfil it or if it represents a hazard to the common weal. However, Art.87 para. 1 of the Civil Code does not say what constitutes a hazard to the common weal. Moreover, the significance of this clause is impaired because it does not, in the prevailing view, set up a binding framework within which Land legislation could enact concrete provisions[31]. On the contrary, the Land legislators are empowered to extend the list of reasons given in Art.87 para.1 of the Civil Code for dissolution and extinguishment. Moreover, the relevant norms in the Land Foundation Laws do not furnish any real clarity on this subject either.

Art.41 of the ALR 19 II only differs from Art.87 in that the State must employ the assets and income of a charitable institution for another purpose as close as possible to the founder's wishes if the original purpose of the founda-tion has become impossible or harmful. Thus, the alternative of dissolving the foundation with the resultant devolution of the assets upon the heir named by the founder or successor designated in the statutes is excluded. The

---

[31] Cf. Ballerstedt, 44. *Deutscher Juristentag I*, p.11.

provisions of the Hamburg AGBGB and Berlin Foundation Law are some-what different. These affirm that the supervisory authority may amend the aims of a foundation subject to the conditions set out in Art.87 of the Civil Code or dissolve the foundation.[32]

Pursuant to Hamburg Law (Art.11 para. 1 of the AGBGB) the admissibility of changes in statutes within the ambit of the purpose for which the founda-tion was set up presupposes that they are necessary for reasons pertaining to the said purpose or that some other important reason is present. Moreover, the administrative bodies of a foundation may dispose of the foundation and its purpose subject to the approval of the supervisory authority if this appears to be desirable in the light of some major change in the relevant circumstances (a literal translation of Art.5 para.2(1) of the Berlin Foundation Law). Chap. 18 of the Bavarian Foundation Law refers to Arts.87 and 88 of the Civil Code. In the event of dissolution, Chap.20 of the Bavarian Foundation Law states that the successor in title shall, depending on the character of the foundation, either be the Exchequer, the competent territorial authority (e.g. Land or municipality) or the appropriate Church, all of whom are obliged to employ the assets in a manner which corresponds to the purpose for which the foundation was originally set up. The other Land Laws have substantially the same contents[33].

Hence, the question of the determining criteria arises in connection with the dissolution (and amalgamation) of foundations or with a change of their aims since the decision about the existence of a 'hazard to the common weal' and a choice between a change of aims and dissolution presupposes an evaluation. The answer links up with the considerations set out in the last section about the content and magnitude of State supervision. A supervisory authority must base its decisions on the valid laws and a foundation's statutes. The supreme guiding principle ought to be the implementation of the founder's wishes in accordance with the fresh set of circumstances.

VI. SUBSTITUTES IN CIVIL LAW FOR FOUNDATIONS

1. The main legal substitutes for foundations in practice are registered associations (*eingetragener Verein—e.V.*), non-registered associations and, to an

---

[32] Art. 9 Art 1(2) of the Hamburg AGBGB and Art.2, para. 1 (2) of the Berlin Foundation Law.

[33] Art. 9 para. 2 of the Hessian Foundation Law; Art. 23 para. 1 of the Rhineland-Palatinate Foundation Law; and Art. 23 of the Hessian Foundation Law; and Art. 25 of the Rhineland-Palatinate respectively.

increasing degree, limited liability (or private) companies (*Gesellschaft mit beschränkter Haftung—GmbH*). The reasons for resorting in this way to legal forms which are further removed from the set of circumstances out of which a foundation is born are many and varied. One important motive may be seen in the misgiving about leaving the authorisation and supervision of foundations largely to the discretion of the public authorities. Nor are there any economic disadvantages and in particular fiscal losses to be borne in selecting the form of an association or a limited liability company. The important criterion for tax purposes that a foundation must be of general benefit to the community is not exclusive in law to foundations[34].

2. The adjustment of institutions like associations and limited liability companies to accord with a founder's wishes and objectives involves a number of difficult tasks in connection with the drafting of legally sound contracts and they can only be solved on the basis of a far-reaching degree of freedom of arrangement in the legislation governing the setting up of such societies and companies. The problem is really how to guarantee the permanent inviolability of the founder's will against attacks from subsequent members of the association or company and the largely sacrosanct link between the assets of the association or company and the said will.

This leads in the first instance to the necessity in practice to exclude the possibility of effecting changes in statutes or at least in the aims of the association or company. Two methods are customary. On the one hand, the eligibility for membership of the association or company may be restricted to a category of persons who could be expected to observe the founder's wishes. As a rule, this is done by means of a clause in the articles of association that new members may be co-opted or that members or participants possess their membership rights in trust only and subject to the founder's wishes (e.g. *Robert Bosch Stiftung GmbH*). Furthermore, an amendment of the 'object of the foundation' or a dissolution of the 'foundation' may be made dependent on an objectively verifiable list of reasons for amendment or dissolution equally binding for all members. Finally, the right to sell or bequeath shares (particularly in the case of the limited liability company) and the setting aside of assets against the settlement of claims must be excluded as there may otherwise be a possibility that the 'assets of the foundation' will be lost. The prevailing view is in favour of recognising the legality of these provisions[35]. Objections to such legal forms are largely based on company law considerations and we need not discuss them at this point.

[34] Cf. Strickrodt, in: *Neue Juristische Wochenschrift*, p. 2085.
[35] Cf. Ballerstedt, op. cit., pp. 17/18; Strickrodt, *Neue Juristische Wochenschrift*, 1964, pp. 2086/2087.

VII. THE FOUNDATION WITHOUT LEGAL STATUS

1. A dependent foundation, endowment or trust (*unselbständige Stiftung*) is created when assets are transferred to an existing natural or juristic person subject to the proviso that they shall be administered by the recipient as a special capital separate from the recipient's other assets and used for a specific purpose[36]. Much in the same way as in the case of the substitute forms discussed in the last chapter, very little provision has been made for such foundations in law. The prevailing view is that, logically, they ought to be classified as institutes established under private law.

The opinion is also often voiced that such a foundation set up *inter vivos* should be regarded as a gift subject to a binding duty within the meaning of Art.525 et ss. of the Civil Code[37]. However, Liermann[38] quite rightly pointed out that the donation presupposed an advantage—however small—for the recipient. If, as is usual with trusts, the purpose for which they are set up involves the whole of the available assets and thus simply leaves the donee with administrative work to be done on behalf of a third party, one cannot speak indiscriminately of a gift[39].

Only in cases where the institution carrying responsibility for the foundation is a juridical person whose functions as stated in the statutes include the purpose for which the foundation was set up is there room for the acceptance of a gift. As a result, most jurists regard a foundation without legal status as a sort of 'subspecies' of trusteeships undertaken on behalf of a third party[40]. Subject to agreements to the contrary, the rights and duties of founders and the organisations responsible for the foundation should be governed by the regulations contained in Art.662 et ss. of the Civil Code. The question as to whether the intended beneficiaries enjoy their own claim to foundation benefits or not depends, as it does in the case of independent foundations, on the content of the declaration of intent. If a dependent foundation is set up *mortis causa*, this normally involves the appointment of an heir or a bequest in favour of the person or organisation responsible for the foundation subject to the proviso that the assets are to be used for the aim stated by the founder[41].

[36] Cf. Larenz, *Allgemeiner Teil des deutschen Bürgerlichen Rechts*, Munich 1967, Art. 17, p. 207.

[37] Cf. Enneccerus—Nipperdey, op. cit., Art. 117, para. I (1) and Larenz op. cit., Art. 17, p. 207.

[38] In: *Deutsches Stiftungswesen*, p. 236.

[39] Ballerstedt, op. cit. p. 15; Kuhn in *BGB-RGRK*, 11th Ed., Berlin 1959, Art. 516 note 4.

[40] Cf. Ballerstedt, op. cit.; Siebert—Schultz = v. Lasaulx, op. cit., note before Art. 80, Mar. No. 8 et ss.

[41] Cf. Ballerstedt, op. cit., p. 16. The appointment of heirs subject to the terms of a

The above-mentioned difficulties inherent in gifts subject to a binding duty do not arise in the event of the appointment of heirs and the bequeathing of property since the latter two cases are conceivable without the 'beneficiary' experiencing any advantages or even disadvantages.

2. From the point of view of the law, all these possible solutions contain significant weaknesses. In the first place, they neglect the essential feature of a foundation that the assets must be permanently earmarked for the fulfilment of the stated aims. There are no provisions in the valid law applicable to such mandates or enjoinments enabling an independent foundation to carry out the indispensable adjustment of its statutes and aims to accord with a new set of circumstances. The Reich Supreme Court rejected any supplementation to this effect by analogy with Art.87 of the Civil Code because foundations without legal status and foundations with legal personality are completely different in character. It is certainly correct to assume that the competency of the foundation authority envisaged in Art.87 of the Civil Code cannot be applied to such endowments or trusts. Such competency is a typical product of the mixture of public and private legislation which characterizes the present legal provision for independent foundations. It cannot be applied *de lege lata* to dependent foundations whose creation and administration are exclusively governed by private law.

However, it is another matter whether or not the essence of Art.87 is analogous and whether one could perhaps make allowance for the characteristic permanency of the two kinds of foundation by giving the body responsible for the foundation the right and the duty to amend the statutes of the foundation without legal status and if need be its aims, too. One should also bear in mind that such an obligation would normally correspond to the purpose of the trust agreement reached by the founder and the body responsible for the foundation upon the establishment of the dependent foundation, or to the stipulations and enjoinments decreed by the founder in his testament. Inasmuch as a dependent foundation has been set up by a legal act *mortis causa*, Art.2194 of the Civil Code provides that the founder's conditions must be fulfilled. Pursuant to this clause, the heir, the co-heir and the person who would immediately profit from the disappearance of the heir upon whom the conditions are incumbent, plus the competent public authority (in the unusual case that the conditions were imposed in the public interest) may voice the demand that the imposed conditions must be fulfilled. Such stipulations and conditions are supposed to include the amendments of statutes and aims which are indispensable for the permanency of the foundation, and

bequest is not suitable for foundation purposes because of time restrictions pursuant to Art. 2162 et ss. of the Civil Code (= 30 years.)

therefore the adjustment of the dependent foundation or trust to accord with changed circumstances is guaranteed under Art.2194 of the Civil Code. Where a foundation is established *inter vivos*, an analogous application of Art. 2194 of the Civil Code after the death of the founder is also possible in view of the similarity of interests at stake.

In the final analysis, this view is in line with the majority view held by authors who are in favour of an analogous application of Art.87 of the Civil Code to foundations without legal status[42].

On the other hand, it will probably be impossible *de lege lata* to eliminate another difficulty which many authors feel to be inherent in trusts and endowments, i.e. that the assets invested in such a foundation are legally assigned to the person or organisation responsible for the foundation. In principle, assets tied to a specific purpose belong, for the purposes of the law of contract, to the assets of the person who is technically the owner and therefore in the event of the enforcement of a judgement or in a case of bankruptcy such assets are placed at the disposal of his creditor. Most authors[43] today concede the settlor (or founder) the right of objection in respect of third persons pursuant to Art.771 of the Code of Civil Procedure (ZPO) *vis-à-vis* the enforcement of a judgment affecting the trust property and derived from a title adduced against the trustee. Equally, they concede the settlor a preferential claim under Art.43 of the Bankruptcy Ordinance (KO) in the event of bankruptcy.

Nevertheless, this is virtually no help at all for a typical dependent foundation. Neither the intended recipients nor any public institution are settlors in this sense of the word. Moreover, only the assets at hand when the trust was set up count as trust property—not the substitutes of a later date[44]. As changes in the composition of assets can hardly be avoided over the years, the special status of trust property for the purpose of enforcement of judgments and bankruptcy cases is largely of no significance for endowments or trusts.

What is unsatisfactory from the legal point of view is the fact that dependent foundations serving the public interest entrusted to private bodies who then carry responsibility for them are linked with the legal fate of the said bodies or of their own assets. A method ought to be found to secure a permanent basis for private initiative in this sector without necessarily

---

[42] Cf. Siebert—Schultz = v. Lasaulx, note before Art. 80, marginal no. 12; Liermann, in: *Deutsches Stiftungswesen*, p. 242 et ss.; Strickrodt: *Stiftungsrecht I*, Baden-Baden 1962, p. 7.

[43] Cf. Rosenberg: *Lehrbuch des deutschen Zivilprozessrechts*, 9th Edition, Munich 1961, Art. 185 para. III (3 c).

[44] Cf. RGZ, i.e. Reich Supreme Court Judgments in Civil Cases 153, p. 370.

giving foundations legal independence if only because of the whole concept of a foundation as an expression of private endeavour for the common weal. *Ballerstedt (op. cit. pp.* 51–52) mentioned such a method—which would be feasible *de lege ferenda.* His idea was that endowments and trusts and their assets ought to be entered into a new foundation register and then made public. The same would apply if there were any changes in the property held, with the result that irrespective of any changes in assets that might take place subsequent to the first capital donation, a foundation's assets would not be subject to seizure by the creditors of the body responsible for the foundation, the founder or the founder's heirs. Appropriately, *Ballerstedt* connects this (partial) independence of juridically dependent foundations with the demand for State supervision whose task it would be to prevent possible abuse—just as with foundations possessing legal personality.

VIII. FOUNDATIONS ESTABLISHED UNDER PUBLIC LAW

1. These foundations are very controversial, if only because of their essential distinguishing features. Inasmuch as Land Foundation Laws refer at all to foundations established under public law, they quite rightly start with a definition of what they understand by a foundation set up under public law rather than refer to a term whose meaning is taken for granted. Hence, Chap. 1 para. 2 of the Bavarian Foundation Law states that for the purpose of this law 'foundations established under public law' shall be understood as 'those which exclusively pursue public aims and which bear an organic relationship with the State, a local authority, an inter-communal authority or some other corporate entity or institution which renders the foundation itself a public organization'.

The views held by the Civil Code legislators were similar: they regarded the characteristic feature of a foundation established under private law as their origin in a transaction under private law unless their special character has adapted itself to the organic structure of the State or the Church in such a way as to classify it for this reason as falling under the category of foundations established under public law[45]. However, both the Bavarian Foundation Law and the Protocols in respect of the draft of the Civil Code are silent about what constitutes an adaption of a foundation to the organic structure of the State. The reason for this caution is that the classification of a juridical person as belonging to public law and therefore qualifying as an administrative unit cannot be decided in accordance with generally valid criteria; a positive

[45] Protocol I, p. 586.

decision can only be taken in each individual case by the competent Land.

For this reason, most authors[46] naturally expect a foundation established under public law to be set up by the State for a purpose connected with public administration or recognised by it as a public-law foundation. It should be added that once a public-law foundation has actually been established it is essentially as independent of the State as one constituted under private law. In particular, the characteristics laid down in the declaration of intent or in the act of instituting the foundation, i.e. aim, constitution, administration and employment of assets, are permanently withdrawn from the purview of the public authorities[47].

In their directory *Deutsche Stiftungen für Wissenschaft, Bildung und Kultur* (op. cit., p. XXXII), Neuhoff and Vinken point out that foundations established under public law need not necessarily be public institutions administered by State agencies to implement public tasks. 'On the contrary, there are quite a few of these foundations which, separated from the State, are pursuing charitable purposes under their own responsibility and financed by their own wealth.'

2. The legal status of public-law foundations differs from that of those established under private law in a few insignificant points only. As we have already noted, the main difference is to be found in the actual establishment of the foundation. Whereas a private-law foundation can only be set up by a juristic act, a public-law foundation can choose between a law, a juristic act or an administrative act, i.e. provided that the founder is a public authority. If the foundation is formed by a juristic act, or by an administrative act which does not involve the approving authority, it then requires authorisation from the public department responsible for foundations just as private-law foundations do[48].

For the rest, the only dissimilarity to private-law foundations lies in the arrangements governing the competency of the supervisory authorities. One example is Chap. 33 of the Bavarian Foundation Law, which states that in the case of state-administered foundations the powers of the supervisory authorities shall be replaced by the right of the foundation's senior authority to issue directives to it. However, the senior authority must obtain the permission of the competent approving authority in specially important cases.

---

[46] Cf. Wolff, *Verwaltungsrecht II*, 2nd Ed., Munich 1967, Art. 102 para. III (a) 2; Ebersbach, *Die Stiftung des öffentlichen Rechts*, Göttingen 1961, pp. 40/41.

[47] Cf. Wolff, Art. 102 para. I (a) 3, and the criticisms contained in Ebersbach, p. 30.

[48] Cf. Chap. 4 para. 1 of the Bavarian Foundation Law; Art. 10 of the Rhineland-Palatinate Foundation Law; Wolff, op. cit., Art. 103 para. I (a) 2.

I

IX. CHURCH FOUNDATIONS

The provisions in Federal Land Laws applicable to ecclesiastical foundations provide the clearest possible clue to the different constitutional origin of the various Foundation Laws. The foundation law in former Prussian territories contains no reference to the term 'Church foundation'. It subjects all charitable institutions to the same rules, regardless of whether they are ecclesiastical or secular. The more recent foundation laws promulgated by Hamburg and Berlin make no such distinction either.

The position is different with the latest legislation on foundations in South Germany. The Bavarian Foundation Law devotes a special section to Church foundations (Chaps. 36–40). Chap. 36 defines a Church foundation as it is understood in Bavarian law. It declares that Church foundations are foundations which are largely dedicated to the pursuit of the aims of the Roman Catholic, Lutheran and Reformed Churches provided that their statutes do not prescribe their administration by a State authority, a local authority or an inter-communal association. Chap.37 para.1 directs that Church foundations must request and receive permission provided that 'a lasting implementation of the aim of a foundation out of the profits on its assets appears to be ensured or is guaranteed by one of the Churches in question'. Pursuant to para. 2, Church foundations may only be converted or dissolved in agreement with the relevant Church. The requirement incumbent upon the State to afford care and protection is largely replaced by the same requirement in respect of the Church (Chap. 38 of the Bavarian Foundation Law). Chap. 40 of the Bavarian Foundation Law stipulates the application of Chaps. 36–39 *mutatis mutandis* to Jewish foundations and those of other religious groups if they are public-law corporations in Bavaria.

The Rhineland-Palatinate Foundation Law contains almost identical provisions (Arts. 41–46). Art. 41 classifies the following three groups as Church foundations—a more precise guide than in Bavarian Foundation Law, but also a more limiting one:

(a) local Church and benefice foundations,
(b) other foundations set up by the Church administration,
(c) foundations set up by other persons if the former are firmly integrated into the Church administration and organisation or if their aim is of such a nature that it can only be fulfilled in conjunction with the Church.

The degree of participation by the Church is in some respects greater than that envisaged by the Bavarian Law (cf. Arts. 42, 43 of the Rhineland-Palatinate Foundation Law).

Art. 20 of the Hessian Foundation Law is a summary of the Bavarian provisions. The only dissimilarity is the narrower definition of Church foundations—in agreement with Art. 41 of the Rhineland-Palatinate Foundation Law.

X. POSSIBLE REFORMS

1. Our account of current foundation law has underscored the imperfection and inadequacy of existing Federal and Land laws in solving the problems of foundations and above all the lack of allowance being made for a foundation's socio-political functions. Although a number of the questions at issue can be clarified by giving a wide interpretation to the valid law, legal safeguards can only be furnished by the promulgation of explicit laws. In addition, there are a number of requisite reforms which only the legislator can implement. An example would be the attainment of permanency for foundations without legal status.

The first proposals for a radical reform of foundation law came from Pleimes. In his history of law and dogma, he endeavoured to prove that the strict distinction drawn between foundations with juristic personality and without was dogmatically wrong and that the restriction of the Civil Code provisions to independent foundations had led to a neglect of other types of foundation, a development which has been detrimental to the whole concept of foundations. Pleimes repudiates the idea that a juridically independent foundation is the owner of the foundation property because the term 'ownership' does not embody an appropriate description of the legal status of a foundation's administrative and executive organs or of the beneficiaries. Instead of the discrimination between foundations possessing legal personality and those without, he suggested a differentiation in the legal provisions depending on whether the foundation effects financial payments to the beneficiaries out of the profits on assets (a *Hauptgeldstiftung*, i.e. principal fund foundation) or whether the foundation is used to operate institutions such as hospitals, schools, etc. (an *Anstaltsstiftung*).

The second initiative taken towards reforming foundations was in regard to foundations as a legal form for commercial undertakings. A good example of this is furnished by Strickrodt[49], whose three major works contain detailed proposals on organising such foundations. The reason for, and idealistic background to, these studies is a socio-political concern. Foundations ought to open up a path to overcome the social order of capitalism by offering an

[49] *'Die Stiftung als neue Unternehmensform'*, 1948; *'Unternehmen unter freigewählter Stiftungssatzung'*, 1956; and *'Probleme zur rechtlichen Struktur von Stiftungsunternehmen'*, 1960.

opportunity to talented but impecunious *entrepreneurs* to develop their capabilities.

2. The 44th Assembly of German Lawyers in Hanover in 1962 dealt with the reform of foundation law. The lawyers studied reports by Ballerstedt and Salzwedel and listened to a lecture delivered by Mestmäcker on the topic 'Should foundation law be reformed and standardized as Federal legislation and, if so, what ought to be its characteristic features'? Following the work done at this meeting and the submission of a report by the committee[50] appointed by the lawyers, a general consensus of opinion may now be said to exist on the following suggestions for reforms.

As the current view of the relationship between the State and society is that the advancement of the common weal is no longer exclusively the province of the State, the reason for the traditional link between foundations and the State no longer applies.

The realisation that private initiatives for the benefit of the whole community are possible independently of corresponding initiatives by the State and on an equal footing with them has led to a call for the incorporation of foundations into private law[51]. The competency of the Federal legislators in respect of civil law accorded under Chap.74 No.1 of the Constitution permits the State to provide a uniform act of rules for foundations at national level. Such standardisation would contribute to the lucidity and harmony of foundation law in the Federal Republic of Germany.

(a) Any future Federal foundation law ought to deal with the following subjects:

It should contain detailed provisions governing the organisational preconditions for the creation of an independent foundation. No clear decision has been reached as to whether this should also go hand in hand with a transition from the concessionary system hitherto applied to a system of authoritative rules for the creation of a foundation, i.e. the foundation comes into existence by observance of the legal requirements and registration. One argument in favour of retaining the present legal state of affairs is that the differences between a concessionary system and the system of authoritative rules loses much of its fundamental sharpness after the introduction of a complete system of protection in administrative law[52].

As we have already seen, the demand in practice for a precise definition in law of the preconditions for the establishment of foundations can be satisfied

---

[50] Cf. *Vorschläge zur Reform des Stiftungsrechts, Bericht der Studienkommission des Deutschen Juristentages*, Munich 1968, cited hereinafter as Report of the Committee.

[51] Report of the Committee, p. 14.

[52] Ballerstedt, op. cit., p. 41.

by the introduction of an obligation—which is perfectly in keeping with a modern constitutional State—to obtain permission from a public authority. Be that as it may, the concessionary system is an extraneous element in private law, irrespective of whether it is tied to certain obligations or not. Preference should in fact be given to the system of authoritative rules because legitimate restrictions in the freedom to set up foundations are only conceivable on the basis of and within the framework of private law. This would then bring foundations in line with other institutes of private law, such as joint stock companies (AG) and limited liability companies (GmbH)[53].

Instead of the present requirements for State permission, it has been suggested that the constitutive precondition for setting up a foundation ought to be entry into a new foundation register. This would be operated centrally for a fairly large area by a specified municipal Court[54]. The judge in charge of the register would examine the given preconditions for entry and reach his decision in accordance with the principles of voluntary jurisdiction. At the same time, the introduction of a foundation register would also promote the attempt to improve the present imperfect arrangements for public information about foundations. The facts which should be made subject to compulsory information would be: name, registered office, aim(s), date of establishment, duration, administrative bodies and status as a non-profit organisation for tax purposes[55].

(b) As is already partly the case in some of the latest Land foundation laws, State supervision would be of a general nature and explicitly limited to the control of the legality of the operations conducted by the foundation's board of directors and their conformity with the statutes. The concept of a rivalry of ideas between foundations and the public authorities excludes any State supervision of the expediency of a foundation's work. In practice, the most successful means of supervising foundations has proved to be the requirement for the board of directors to submit their accounts and present annual reports.

A great deal of controversy still attaches to the question of whether the supervision of a foundation ought to change from public administration to voluntary jurisdiction. The supporters of such a move claim that voluntary jurisdiction means greater willingness and ability to really limit the supervision to examination of conformity with the law and the statutes[56]. The disadvantage would be the abolition or considerable reduction of the advisory

---

[53] Report of the Committee, p. 20.
[54] Report of the Committee, pp. 23/24.
[55] Report of the Committee, p. 30.
[56] Mestmäcker, op. cit., p. 85.

work of the supervisory authority, which has meanwhile assumed large proportions[57].

(c) Inasmuch as foundations owning business or major participations in them were permitted in pursuance of para. 17 of the Law on Joint-stock Companies (*Aktiengesetz*), they would have to conform to special rules[58]. As from a certain size, they would have to set up an obligatory control organ: its legal status could, for example, be similar to that of the supervisory board of a limited liability company[59]. Furthermore, there should be a requirement to submit accounts: the magnitude of the foundation would determine to what degree this has to be done.

(d) The discriminatory legal treatment of public foundations and private family foundations, particularly under the foundation law valid in the former Prussian territories, ought to be abandoned. No agreement has been reached on whether the duration of family foundations ought to be subject to a time-limit (30 years) corresponding to the time limit for obligations set up by the testator on obligations in respect of his estate (Arts. 2044, 2109, 2162 (3) and 2210 of the Civil Code).

(e) In principle, Church foundations ought to be liable to normal foundation rules just like family foundations. An exception would be considered for foundation supervision which some lawyers advocate should be implemented by ecclesiastic rather than by State agencies. However, most jurists reject the idea of special provisions for Church foundations[60].

(f) Another suggestion is that the permanency of foundations without legal status pursuing charitable purposes should enjoy greater protection than hitherto. The idea is that they should be entered into a second part of the envisaged foundation register. Furthermore, their legal fate would be largely independent of the assets held by the person or organisation responsible for the foundation and the founder or his heirs. Upon registration, these foundations would then also be subject to foundation supervision.

C. Fiscal Treatment of Foundations

Whether plans to set up a foundation can be carried through or not depends in large measure on tax considerations. The basic principle obtaining in this connection is that foundations do not have an exceptional status in respect of

[57] Vide Toepke, op. cit., pp. 250/251.
[58] Report of the Committee, p. 49.
[59] Report of the Committee, p. 41.
[60] Cf. Report of the Committee, p. 55.

taxation. Special provisions only come into consideration if and insofar as foundations pursue purposes serving the general interest.

I. TAX LIABILITY IN RESPECT OF THE ESTABLISHMENT OF FOUNDATIONS

Gifts or donations to a foundation which already exists or which still has to be set up can give rise to tax liability on the part both of the donor (founder) and the foundation itself.

The founder is normally liable to tax if—as often happens in practice—he transfers property from his business assets to a foundation. The real value of such property is usually considerably in excess of its ledger value. When such property is disengaged from the invested capital, the reserves which this difference comprises come to the surface and are made subject to income tax or—if the founder is a company—to corporation tax.

As regards the foundation's liability, the contribution, which constitutes a gratuitous transaction, is subject to inheritance or gift tax, depending on whether a disposition *mortis causa* or *inter vivos* is involved[61]. The consequences of both kinds of tax are the same in that they normally scoop off up to 50% of the donated value. This very drastic taxation is based on the special character of the inheritance or gift tax, namely that of assessing the rate of taxation in accordance with the relationship obtaining between the founder and the recipient[62].

Contributions to a foundation are not viewed as being made in favour of a specific person but as the earmarking of assets for a special purpose. As such they fall, in principle, within the highest tax bracket obtaining in respect of payments to outsiders. An exception is made in the case of family foundations in respect of which the taxation of the original endowment (not assets added later to the endowment) is based on the relationship existing between the founder and the farthest removed of the intended beneficiaries as specified in the foundation's statutes[63].

In practice, however, this arrangement generally works out less advantageously than might at first appear to be the case as fiscal jurisdiction stipulates that the determining question in this connection is not who is the beneficiary at the time of the foundation's establishment but who can subsequently assume this status.

Important exceptions to the principles outlined above come into play if the foundation under consideration is charitable. In the first place, the recently

[61] Cf. Arts. 2 and 3 *ErbStG* (Inheritance Tax Act).
[62] Art. 10 para. 1 *ErbStG*.
[63] Art. 10 para. 2 *ErbStG*.

(1969) enacted regulation contained in Art. 6 para. 1 No. 4 EStG (Income Tax Act) enables property forming a part of business assets to be withdrawn at its ledger value if it is to be applied for the promotion of activities in the field of the sciences, arts and humanities or of education and professional training at all levels. If this is the case, the considerable tax burden is lifted—albeit only in respect of part of the full range of possible foundation objectives—which would otherwise be imposed on the founder in respect of the reserves thrown up by the removal of assets from his invested capital.

In addition to this, the founder may, up to a specified ceiling, deduct the contribution from his taxable income[64]. The ceiling for tax deductibility is normally 5% of total annual income or—in the cases of companies—2% of total turnover plus payroll for the calendar year. Where the advancement of purposes in the field of the arts, sciences and humanities or of civic nature is involved a maximum of 10% of the donor's total annual income is tax deductible. Finally contributions to charitable foundations are exempted from inheritance or gift tax[65].

The conditions governing tax deductibility are laid down in details in Arts. 17–19 of the 'Steueranpassungsgesetz' of 16th October 1934 (in the 13th July 1961 version) as well as in the implementation ordinance relating thereto, the so-called Charity Decree (Gemeinnützigkeitsverordnung—GemVO) of 24th December 1953. The following purposes are specified therein as being subject to preferential tax treatment:
— advancement of the common weal (charity in the broader sense);
— support of needy persons (charity in the more traditional and narrower sense);
— promotion of religious corporations under public law (ecclesiastical purposes).

In order to benefit from tax concessions such a purpose must be pursued constantly, exclusively and directly; this is checked on the basis both of the foundation's statutes and its actual operation. Over and above this the statutes must contain a provision to the effect that, in the event of obsolescence or disappearance of the purpose pursued hitherto or of the dissolution of the foundation, at the very least, the assets which have accrued (i.e. the increase) since the foundation's establishment will continue to be applied to tax-privileged objectives[66].

---

[64] Cf. Arts. 10(b) EstG and 11 No. 5 KStG (Corporation Tax Act).

[65] Cf. Arts. 18 para. 1 no. 19(b) and 20 ErbStG.

[66] This limitation to the assets which have accrued since the foundation's establishment and not to the total assets made over to it was introduced in 1969 by virtue of a modification of the Charity Decree (Gemeinnützigkeitsverordnung).

In assessing whether a given foundation qualifies for preferential tax treatment, the fiscal and legal authorities generally apply very strict criteria which
—as Strickrodt[67] puts it—not infrequently amount to giving 'philanthropic
activity a quite distinct bias'. This attitude is in complete contradiction with
the concept of charitable foundations as social forces which through the
initiation and development of their own projects and programmes, should
play an independent role alongside the State in the common concern to serve
the general interest. In the interests of encouraging foundations to operate
freely and efficaciously, these criteria should instead be broad and liberal.

The legislature could already give a green light in this direction by extending the scope of tax deductibility both in respect of the field covered (removal of the restrictions confining preferential treatment to only a few
charitable objectives) and in respect of the maximum permitted (raising the
ceiling of tax deductibility) in order to provide a stronger incentive for
private commitment to the service of the community. After all, in a free
society preferment should, in any case, be given to private initiative to the
extent that it can carry out tasks of communal benefit as effectively as
Government. There should be no doubt as to the fact that the possibilities in
this field are by no means exhausted[68].

II. TAXATION OF FOUNDATION ACTIVITIES

Pursuant to Art.1 No. 5 Corporation Tax Act (KStG), foundations are in
principle subject to corporation tax. The rate of tax amounts to 49%.
Expenditure incurred by a foundation in relation to the tasks prescribed by its
statutes does not generally lower its taxable income, unless it covers internal
expenses within a business enterprise maintained by the foundation. Furthermore, the foundation is liable in respect of property tax. Trade tax applies
insofar as the foundation conducts a trade or business.

Exceptional provision comes into play for charitable foundations—just as in
the case of tax treatment in respect of the foundation's establishment—in

[67] Cf. *Stiftungsrecht—Geltende Vorschriften und rechtspolitische Vorschläge*, Baden-Baden
1962, VII 1(b), p. 6.

[68] Unfortunately these ideas have not prevailed in parliamentary circles or with the
tax authorities. For example, in the summer of 1970 the draft report for the Revenue
Code (*Abgabenordnung—AO*) was published as the first reform law within the framework
of the 'great tax reform'. The new Revenue Code will, with effect from 1974, replace
the old regulations dating from 1919 and will also contain the provisions of the *Steueranpassungsgesetz* and the Charity Decree. To judge from its substance no far-reaching
changes or even alleviation measures in relation to the legislation governing charity are
proposed.

regard to recurrent taxation: corporation tax, trade tax, real estate tax and property tax are completely waived; turnover tax (value added tax) is reduced by half (5.5%). As these privileges would give the foundation an unfair advantage over other enterprises in the field of economic competition, they are cut down if and to the extent that a *per se* tax-preferred foundation running a business enterprise engages in market activities. Consequently the foundation is fully liable to tax in spite of its fulfilment of charitable tasks. Practice indicates that the fiscal authorities and tribunals do not consider that major shareholdings in a business company prejudices tax privilege, provided that it only comprises a form of administering the foundation's assets. However, tax liability is also incurred in this instance if the foundation—in particular if it has a majority or even 100% controlling interest—exercises an entrepreneurial influence. On the other hand so called 'purpose-fulfilling' enterprises such as old people's homes, kindergartens, museums, and theatres are not liable to tax. All charitable foundations are placed under the supervision of the competent revenue office for tax purposes (cf. Arts.16 and 17 Charity Decree).

III. TAXING FOUNDATION BENEFICIARIES

Beneficiaries may be liable for both gift and income tax in respect of foundation payments. Recurring payments are subject to income tax, one-time payments which are not made in line with the foundation's statutes are subject to gift tax. On the other hand one-time payments effected in accordance with the statutes are tax exempt. Liability for income tax does not apply because such revenue does not fall into the definitive enumeration of different forms of income contained in the Income Tax Act. The gift tax presupposes that an act of generosity on the part of the giver is involved; this is not deemed to be the case if the foundation's statutes impose an obligation to make payment to the beneficiaries.

LITERATURE

Bächstädt, Peter Die unselbständige Stiftung des Privatrechts, Göttingen 1966.
David, Walter Die Carl-Zeiss-Stiftung—Ihre Vergangenheit und ihre gegenwärtige rechtliche Lage, Heidenheim 1954.
Ebersbach, Harry Die Stiftung des öffentlichen Rechts, Göttingen 1961.
Fischer, Gerhard Die Staatsaufsicht über die öffentlichen Stiftungen unter Ausschluss der Kultusstiftungen nach dem bayerischen Stiftungsgesetz vom 26.11.1954.
Goerdeler Reinhard Die Stiftung als Rechtsform für wirtschaftliche Unternehmungen, Heidelberg 1948.
Kersten, Eduard Stiftung und Handelsgesellschaft. Ein Beitrag zur Unternehmensstiftung und ihre Erscheinungsform, in: Festschrift für den 45. Deutschen Juristentag 1964.
Liermann, Hans Handbuch des Stiftungsrechts, I. Band: Geschichte des Stiftungsrechts, Tübingen 1963.
Neuhoff, Klaus Die Bereitstellung von Unternehmenskapital für Stiftungen, Cologne 1964.
Pavel, Uwe Eignet sich die Stiftung für den Betrieb erwerbswirtschaftlicher Unternehmen? Bad Homburg v.d.H. 1967.
Plagemann, Jochen Die Stiftung als Unternehmensform, Marburg, 1950.
Pleimes Dieter Die Rechtsproblematik des Stiftungswesens, Weimar 1938.
Pleimes, Dieter Weltliches Stiftungsrecht—Geschichte der Rechtsformen, Weimar 1938.
Pleimes, Dieter Irrwege der Dogmatik im Stiftungsrecht, Münster/Cologne 1954.
Rosenkranz, Olaf Die Stiftung als Unternehmensform, Cologne 1957.
Schiller, Theo Stiftungen im gesellschaftlichen Prozess, No. 2 of the 'Schriftenreihe zum Stiftungswesen', Baden-Baden 1969.
Steuck, Heinz-Ludwig Die Stiftung als Rechtsform für wirtschaftliche Unternehmen, Berlin 1968.
Strickrodt, Georg Die Stiftung als neue Unternehmensform, Brunswick/Berlin/Hamburg/Kiel 1951.
Strickrodt, Georg Unternehmen unter frei gewählter Stiftungssatzung, Baden-Baden/Frankfurt 1956.
Strickrodt, Georg Probleme zur rechtlichen Struktur von Stiftungsunternehmen, Baden-Baden 1960.
Strickrodt, Georg Stiftungsrecht (Loose-leaf collection), Baden-Baden 1963.
Toepke, Utz-Peter Die Staatsaufsicht über Stiftungen im deutschen und anglo-amerikanischen Recht, Hamburg 1967.
Troeger, Helmut Die Carl-Zeiss-Stiftung im Lichte der Wettbewerbsordnung, Mayence 1954.
Voll-Voll Kommentar zum Bayer. Stiftungsgesetz, Munich 1962.

Bericht der Studienkommision des Deutschen Juristentages Vorschläge zur Reform des Stiftungsrechts, Munich 1968.
Deutsche Stiftungen für Wissenschaft, Bildung und Kultur edited by Klaus Neuhoff und Horst Vinken, No. 1 of the 'Schriftenreihe zum Stiftungswesen, Baden-Baden, 1969.
Deutsches Stiftungswesen 1948–1966 Wissenschaft und Praxis, Tübingen 1968.
Soll das Stiftungsrecht bundesgesetzlich vereinheitlicht und reformiert werden, gegebenenfalls mit welchen Grundzügen? Verhandlungen des 44. Deutschen Juristentages Hannover 1962, Kurt Ballerstedt—Jürgen Salzwedel, Vol. I (Gutachten) 5. Teil, Tübingen 1962; Ernst-Joachim Mestmäcker, Vol. II (Sitzungsberichte) Part G, Tübingen, 1964.

Denmark*

Klaus Neuhoff

INTRODUCTION

Most European countries appear to have taken little interest in the problems connected with foundations and charitable endowments until the beginning of the 1960s. Hence, it is hardly surprising that, generally speaking, arrangements for keeping the general public informed about foundations are woefully inadequate. This is also true of Denmark.

However, reports on a number of exemplary institutions and attempts to compile national monographs reveal that certain countries in Europe have made greater efforts than others in this field.

Strangely enough, a downward trend is discernible as one moves from North to South. A few introductory remarks may help to explain the reason for this.

Before private persons and enterprises can be inspired to make a worthwhile and lasting contribution to public welfare, a number of pre-conditions have to be simultaneously present. The availability of large or medium-sized fortunes is an indispensable prerequisite for the creation of foundations which may be expected to have a significant impact. In the age of economic and political liberalism, there was nothing to thwart the amassing of such substantial sums of money. The possessors of these large fortunes were often inspired in their good deeds by a somewhat harsh 'protestant' code of ethics in regard to work. On the other hand, they were not indifferent to their responsibility for the social conditions of their time. They considered themselves to be the standard bearers and trustees of certain ideals and they carried out their good works in accordance with these ideals. Public opinion was quite prepared to accept their view that private enterprise should take precedence over government measures, and to accord its achievements full recognition. In other words, all that the State was expected to do was to ensure political stability at home and abroad and provide a certain number of legal safeguards.

* Translated from the German.

The questions relating to the law of succession and to tax legislation, the ascendancy of public virtues over private ones, and the fairly democratic, albeit not pluralistic, attitude adopted by some of the most prominent citizens of the country constituted further determining factors.

These conditions tended to be present in North European countries and, to a lesser extent, in some Central European States, rather than in the South. The best indication of this is to be found in the existence in such countries of a large number of foundations and charitable endowments.

THE DEVELOPMENT OF FOUNDATIONS IN DENMARK

The first foundations in Denmark probably emerged in much the same way as in other European countries. The advent of Christianity in about the year 828 also introduced Denmark to the ideas and institutions of the Church of Rome. The first foundations were thus probably established in the classical manner, i.e., private fortunes were bequeathed to the Church or its institutions[1]. Unlike most other countries, however, no laws were passed in Denmark against 'mortmain' to try to counteract the economic effects of the accumulation by the Church of wealth and property over a period of centuries[2].

As a result, foundations and other charitable endowments in Denmark were able to flourish free from external influences. Nor did the acceptance of the Reformation in the year 1536 significantly change the situation. It is quite probable that the increased use made of the possibility of royal confirmation of such arrangements *piis causis*, subsequent to the establishment of a hereditary monarchy in 1660 in the reign of Frederik III gave an added stimulus to the willingness to donate for charitable purposes because it offered greater legal safeguards. The royal family and the aristocracy took the lead with exemplary endowments[3].

It is not surprising to learn that an eleven-volume 'Handbook of Danish Foundations'[4] was able to list 2,500 foundations and legacies, including 50 from pre-Reformation days[5].

[1] Cf. Ernst Andersen: Legater og Stiftelser, pp. 125–26, Copenhagen, 1962.

[2] Cf. Ernst Kauffmann: Erhvervsdrivende Selvejende Institutioner, 2nd Ed., p. 77, Copenhagen, 1968.

[3] The best-known foundations of this age are the '*Herlufsholm*' School set up by Admiral Herluf Trolle and Mrs. Brigitte Gøye near Nœstved, Zealand, in 1565, and Christian IV's '*Regensen*', the Collegium Regium at Copenhagen University, which dates back to 1569.

[4] Hans de Hofman: Samlinger af publique og private Stiftelser, Fundationer og Gavebreve, som forfindes udi Danmark og Norge, I–XI, 1755–1780.

[5] Compared with the thriving profusion of foundations in the medieval trading towns

The introduction of freedom of trade in 1857 was a further incentive to provide endowments. From that year onwards, it was possible to set up donor-related companies under foundation control (*erhvervsdrivende selvejende institutioner*)[6]. But this happened at a time when donors in Denmark were having fresh thoughts about foundations and reorganising their activities in this field.

The starting-point of modern charitable endowments in Denmark may well have been the ideas propounded by Nicolaus Frederik Severin Grundtvig (1783–1872), the reformer of Danish education, the restorer of Danish national feeling and the great model for young aspiring Danes[7]. His political and educational work—he set up the first Folk High Schools, promoted further education for adults, advocated and systematically organised vocational training—helped the little country, which had been dozing peacefully outside the main course of world events, to become a modern State within a short period of time.

As a result, the big Danish foundations were given a clear-cut mission to promote education, science, culture and—a novelty in the history of foundations and charitable endowments—trade and industry.

THE PREREQUISITES FOR SETTING UP FOUNDATIONS AND CHARITABLE ENDOWMENTS

Prior to the early 1950s, the Danish Governments scarcely had sufficient funds for basic research over and above the financing of colleges, museums and scientific libraries and thus it was left to private enterprise to close the substantial gaps that existed in this sector. And this was more or less fully taken care of by commercial firms and a number of large foundations, especially the *Carlsberg fondet*. 'For a long time this could be regarded as a fairly adequate means of supplementing the sums allocated from public funds[8].'

in such countries as Germany or England, this may not seem to be a particularly substantial total. Nevertheless, one should bear in mind the inferior economic position of Denmark's largely agricultural economy and, in connection with the political tension in the Baltic, the consequences of the Swedish siege of Copenhagen in 1658 and the great fire there in 1728. The Danish capital was, and still is, the focal point of foundations and endowments in Denmark.

[6] Cf. E. Kauffman, p. 84.

[7] Cf. R. Schairer: Weiterbildung—Der Neue Weg, Bonn, 1965, available as a duplicated manuscript, p. 28.

[8] Det Danske Selskab (publisher): Major Danish Foundations for the Support of Science and Art, Copenhagen, 1955, p. 4.

However, the situation changed radically in about 1950. The funds provided by private persons or firms to promote learning and research which were not earmarked for any specific purpose were simply not sufficient. 'The reasons for this are the general rise in prices, the steadily growing need for costly equipment for scientific research, and the fact that virtually all branches of science are undergoing rapid development which has opened the way to an increasing number of possible objects of research to which Danish contributions could only be sparing owing to the shortage of funds[9].'

In view of these facts, energetic action was taken. In 1948, for example, the capital of the *Rask-Ørsted-Fondet*[10], which the Government had set up in 1919, was increased from 5 mill. kr. to 8 mill. kr. In 1954, a further 2 mill. kr. were added. This meant that the available funds increased by an annual sum of 250,000 kr. to 500,000 kr[11].

A further step towards increasing the State's participation in the subsidising of the arts and sciences was taken in 1952 when the State General Scientific Foundation (*Statens Almindelige Videnskabsfond*) was established. An annual sum of 2 mill. kr. was allocated in the budget to this foundation (1965 = 6 mill. kr). Unlike the *Carlsbergfondet*, the largest private foundation with scientific interests, its programme includes the promotion of applied agriculture and therapeutical medicine.

Mention should also be made at this stage of the establishment of the Youth Education Fund (*Ungdommens uddannelsesfond*) in 1952. At that time, an annual total of 1.5 mill. kr. of public funds was being allocated for scholarships and student loans (ratio = 62:38) via this foundation.

During the 1960s, further Government measures were taken to support education and culture, science and research. The most important events were the setting up of a State Foundation for Technology and Science (*Statens Teknisk-videnskabelige Fond*) in 1960, a closer integration of the Danish Fellowship Fund (*Dansk Studiefond*)—which was established in 1913 and which grants loans to students—within the general programme for the furtherance of higher education (1965/66 = 971,000 kr.) and a considerable increase in the contributions to the Youth Education Fund (1962/63 = 63 mill. kr. and 1965/66 = 113 mill. kr.).

[9] Det Danske Selskab, pp. 18–19.

[10] This foundation was named after the philologist Rasmus Kristian Rask (1787–1832) and the physicist Hans Christian Ørsted (1777–1851). The aim of the foundation is, as its subtitle 'Danmarks internationale videnskabelige fond' indicates, to support the arts and sciences in Denmark in conjunction with international research, e.g. the publication in other languages of academic books, support for scientific expeditions with Danish participants, invitations to foreign scholars and subsidised study trips for Danish scholars.

[11] In recent years, the foundation has spent an average of 1.8 mill. kr. per year.

The recent past has been characterized by efforts to re-organise the whole field of academic studies throughout the country. Apart from the technological sciences—e.g. the Academy of the Technological Sciences (*Akademiet for de tekniske Videnskaber*) founded in 1937 and the Research Council set up in 1946—the Danish system of co-ordinating scientific endeavours was characterised by systematic de-centralisation of various public and private institutions[12]. This finally led to a fragmentation of effort and money. However, a law was enacted on 31st May 1968 (No. 206, *Lov om forskningsråd*), and an implementing ordinance promulgated on 13th June 1968 (No. 242) to enable Denmark to adopt the usual device of a central Research Council. This council is subdivided into five departments. In future, it will carry out certain of the functions at present undertaken by the existing public foundations or integrate them within the organisational set-up of the council. The major change for these foundations will be that they will develop their own programmes. Instead of waiting for the more or less fortuitous suggestions brought to their attention by applications for grants they will concentrate on certain priority programmes.

This is, by and large, the framework within which foundations have carried out their work in Denmark. Mention should also be made of the publicly financed Cultural Trust (*Den kulturelle fond*) set up in 1935, and the State Foundation for the Fine Arts (*Statens kunstfond*). The latter organisation was founded in 1964 and it disposes of a yearly budget of 4.2 mill. kr.

Thus, private foundations in Denmark now face stronger competition from public ones in view of the Government's greater interest in a field which was formerly largely left to private enterprise.

The reaction of founders and foundations to these various measures seemed in the first instance, to be a movement away from the furtherance of pure science in favour of applied industrial research and the granting of a larger number of scholarships. During the second stage, i.e. since the early 1960s, this trend has been even more marked. In line with the greater emphasis on the granting of public scholarships, preference is now given to the construction of student hostels. Nothing can yet be stated, however, about what effect the reorganisation of the scientific programme which was undertaken by the State in 1968 will have on the individual programmes of the larger foundations. It is probable that the tendency on the part of some foundations since the early 1930s to promote the interests of Danish industry will grow[13].

12 Cf. Det Danske Selskab, p. 3.
13 Cf. Det Danske Selskab, p. 21, and Fr. Vinding Kruse: Das Eigentumsrecht, Berlin/ Leipzig, 1931, p. 609.

K

THE LEGAL BASIS OF FOUNDATIONS IN DENMARK

In order to enable the reader to understand the laws governing the establishment of foundations in Denmark, it is appropriate to begin with a few introductory remarks about legislation in general in this country. In the first place it should be pointed out that, unlike most Continental countries, Denmark has no codified laws like the *Code Civile* or the *German Civil Code*[14]. Instead, there are a number of different laws which only cover certain specific fields[15].

Precedents do not play the important rôle which they do in the Anglo-Saxon administration of justice. The judges concentrate on each particular case without indulging in any fundamental consideration of the ways in which their jurisdiction might affect possible future cases. The underlying idea behind this is that old legislation should not be allowed to impede the progress of modern law[16].

Jurisprudence has a special part to play in this sytem, namely to provide stimulus, leadership and advice in respect of existing laws, but at the same time to act critically and constructively when considering issues which have hitherto not been brought before the Courts[17].

As the Danish laws on the establishment of foundations are not codified and are thus common law, these last two features of juridical theory have attained a certain degree of importance for the growth of law in this field.

It is thus possible to trace a constant, albeit not comprehensive, interest on the part of Danish lawyers in the problems involved in the establishment of foundations over a period of almost two centuries[18].

Furthermore, a certain amount of marginal attention has been paid to the questions which arise in connection with the laws governing foundations in various standard works on company law, law of persons, proprietary rights and the law of succession.

[14] Cf. The Danish Committee on Comparative Law: Danish and Norwegian Law, Copenhagen, 1963, p. 15.

[15] Cf. Fr. Vinding Kruse: A Nordic Draft Code, Copenhagen, 1963, p. XIII, and The Danish Committee on Comparative Law, p. 68.

[16] Cf. The Danish Committee on Comparative Law, pp. 15, 23, and 27.

[17] Ibid., pp. 29, 32, and 34.

[18] Cf. Philomusus (Rasmus Fleischer?): Om Stiftelser, Copenhagen, 1771; Anders Sandøe Ørsted: Om Regieringens Ret til at ophœve eller forandre Stiftelser, som private Mœnd have oprettet, in: Eunomia I, p. 1–38, Copenhagen, 1815 (reprinted in: Privat-retlige Skrifter, Anden Afdeling, Copenhagen, 1930); R. Th. Oppermann: Den danske Rets Bestemmelser om Stiftelser, Copenhagen, 1860; J. H. Olivarius: Stiftelser, Copenhagen, 1910; E. Andersen loc. cit., and the first (Copenhagen 1963) and second editions of the work of E. Kauffmann on commercial foundations.

The most important of the early publications, and one which had a major impact on the future course of legislation, was Ørsted's lecture in 1801 on 'The Government's Right to Terminate or Alter Private Foundations'. (Incidentally, Ørsted was a brother of the famous physicist of the same name.) The most noteworthy of recent works on special aspects of this subject are perhaps the various editions of Vinding Kruse's *Ejendomsretten*[19] of which both a German and an English translation have been issued[20].

Equal importance, especially in regard to the laws on foundations, may be attached to the fact that Danish law has largely been able to escape the influence of Roman law. This is due to the codification of laws carried out in 1683 during the reign of Christian V, largely in the form of a compilation of their various sources (*Danske Lov*).

In Danish, a foundation is known as a 'self-owning institution' (*selvejende institution*). In everyday language, however, the old expressions *legat, stiftelse, fond* or *fondet* are still most commonly used[21]. Other designations such as *Fideicommis* (entailed estate), *Kollegium* (board), *Institut* (institute) and *Laboratorium* (laboratory) etc. are rare and, much as with the names of firms, provide no clue as to the legal form of the institution.

The expression *selvejende institution* dates back to the beginning of this century and, in fact, it originated in canon law. In former times, a few Churches were known as *selvejende kirker* or *kirker, der ejer sig selv*. This appreciation of the independence and autonomy of certain organisations was first extended to foundations running a charitable institution (*Anstaltsstiftung*); this was hardly surprising in view of the analogy between such institutions and the Church[22]. Nevertheless, one should bear in mind that the question of the juridical personality of the foundation is not at issue here since this problem has always been resolved in common law by deciding that foundations are juridical persons[23]. This custom probably dates back to Denmark's Catholic days. Even at that time, there were probably independent foundations functioning under the aegis of the Church and subject to the provisions of the *corpus iuris canonici*. There is no evidence, however, that there used to be any independent foundations outside of the Church[24].

[19] I–III, 3rd Ed., Copenhagen, 1951.
[20] Das Eigentumsrecht; The Right of Property, Oxford, 1939.
[21] About 90% of the foundations in Denmark use the word 'legat' in their names.
[22] Cf. Kauffmann, pp. 19–24.
[23] E. Andersen, p. 126, noted that 'it has long been accepted in Danish law that a foundation which has a special administration, special rights and special duties can be constituted by a testament or declaration of trust and that no permission or recognition on the part of the authorities is needed for the creation of such a legal entity'.
[24] Ibid., p. 96.

Common law—and this includes the legal provisions governing the Danish foundations—grew as a result of constant use over long periods of time and man's conviction that he acts justly. Under certain circumstances, common law can even overrule statute law. On the other hand, it is an established practice that the Courts can disallow such provisions if they have unjust consequences[25].

In Denmark, *selvejende institution* is understood as property or capital which has been allocated for a specific purpose, which is treated as a legal entity and which is only subject to self-administration. The characteristic feature is the non-existence of members in that there are no proprietors of the assets of such institutions in the traditional sense of the word[26]. Although the rule is that the organisation should pursue objectives beneficial to the general public, it is not a qualifying characteristic for the acquisition of legal capacity.

It is only in a text-book[27] and in tax legislation that a differentiation is made in the light of the above-quoted definition between *selvejende institution* and foundations and legacies as a special form of self-owning institution.

Apart from the written or unwritten rules about foundations, there are a number of subsidiary legal sources, habitual practices stemming from every-day administration and, in the case of certain foundations (business enter-prises under foundation control and welfare institutions), analogous cases stemming from other legal or organisational entities which may be taken into consideration[28].

In other words, the Danish laws on foundations are very liberal indeed, and are only limited by statute law and *bonos mores*. Moreover, the super-vision of foundations is also implemented in a liberal manner. Accordingly foundations in Denmark are to be found in a large number of forms.

THE ESTABLISHMENT OF FOUNDATIONS

In Denmark, a foundation can be set up by a disposition *mortis causa* or *inter vivos*; this can be done by individuals or by several natural persons, or even by juridical persons. In order to establish a foundation, it is necessary to first determine its objectives and its organisational structure (including a board of trustees). If this intention is clearly expressed, there is no need for such provisions to be formulated in writing, although this is almost always done as

---

[25] Cf. The Danish Committee on Comparative Law, p. 40.
[26] Cf. at this juncture the various definitions collected by E. Kauffmann, p. 18 and pp. 49–51.
[27] Cf. Bernhard Gomard: Aktieselskabsret, Copenhagen, 1966, p. 11.
[28] Cf. E. Kauffmann, p. 369.

a precaution. The dedication of the assets is not absolutely essential[29]. Thus, neither an official permit nor entry in a register are required for a foundation to acquire legal capacity.

This freedom accorded to individual founders seems incredible by the standards of nearly any other country in Europe. One would imagine that, in practice, there would be a chaotic mixture of foundations or at least a large amount of litigation. However, this is not the case in Denmark.

This is due to the fact that the overwhelming majority of foundations are known to the competent supervisory authorities despite the absence of any special regulations about keeping the general public informed. According to one observer in the Ministry of Justice, most foundations are set up by means of a testament. And when a testament is submitted to a notary public[30], this is noted in a Register of Wills[31].

Hence, the weakness of the Danish system as regards access to information about all existing foundations for supervisory purposes, is that the ready availability of such information in respect of a small number of foundations set up by a testament and an increasing number (especially in recent years) of foundations *inter vivos* is more or less a matter of chance.

A founder is not necessarily bound by his declaration of intent, which is valid in other respects. Not until he undertakes concrete steps e.g. by stating the aim of the foundation, installing an *ad hoc* guardian or appointing an executive board (apart from himself), is he obliged to carry out the promised performance[32].

It is interesting to note in connection with rights of succession that the Danish law of succession is characterised by a certain lack of testamentary freedom. This is due to the fact that it took a long time for testamentary bequests to be recognised under Germanic law. According to the latter, the surviving spouses and children of a founder must first obtain at least their legal portion (up to one half of the bequest). On the other hand, an administrator of the estate may be named or a trustee appointed to manage the legal portion of the assets for one generation[33].

However, since the promulgation of Law No.139 on 1st May 1954 (Law on the Conversion of Family Entails into Free Property), it is prohibited to set up entailed estates[34]. The reason for the prohibition is the 'all too obvious

[29] Cf. E. Kauffmann, pp. 216–17 and p. 219.

[30] Less use is made of the possibility of signing the will in the presence of neutral witnesses.

[31] Cf. The Danish Committee on Comparative Law, pp. 63–64.

[32] Cf. E. Kauffmann, pp. 220–21.

[33] Cf. The Danish Committee on Comparative Law, pp. 59–62.

[34] According to the law, this is capital or property which is meant to be bequeathed

intention of evading the payment of death duties[35]'. Notwithstanding 'family foundations set up for the granting of scholarships etc. are customary and in many cases they enjoy the special protection of the State'[36].

SUBSTITUTE FORMS AND FOUNDATIONS WITHOUT LEGAL PERSONALITY

In view of the extremely liberal basic trend in the Danish legislation on foundations, it is not surprising that founders scarcely find it necessary to substitute corporate forms of organisation for foundations.

However, foundations without legal personality (endowments or trusts) do exist, and quite a lot of use is made of them in practice, principally in the case of smaller donations to non-profit organisations.

Despite the fact that most foundations are associated with a different institution (i.e. administration for a third party), they have a separate existence in law. Andersen[37] calls this a terminological inaccuracy which can only be explained by the fact that the 'classical' form of the foundation and its legal consequences and implications have been forgotten.

Such a trust comes into being when assets are transferred to a juridical person without the founder having expressly declared his intention of establishing a foundation with a separate existence in law or if one of the essential characteristics of an independent foundation is lacking. Andersen (p.128) thinks that the danger in this is that the recipient of such assets and the concomitant duties may simply terminate such a foundation by subsequently altering its aims, for instance at a time when nobody can any longer recall what the duties comprised.

ROYAL CONFIRMATION

The institution of royal confirmation has been incorporated in the law on foundations from the law of succession. The functions of such royal approval of the statutes of a foundation are to provide legal safeguards, facilitate proper supervision, to bring influence to bear in the event of a modification of the foundation's aims, and to encourage a certain measure of publicity about foundations[38].

within a certain family in such a way that, upon the founder's death, it will devolve upon a number of as yet unborn persons in pursuance of a special order of succession.

[35] Cf. Olaf Rosenkranz: Die Stiftung als Unternehmungsform, Diss. Cologne University, 1957, p. 83.

[36] Ibid., p. 83.

[37] Cf. E. Andersen, p. 128.

[38] Since 18th August 1923, the names of foundations which have received royal

These various functions will be discussed in detail in connection with another matter. It should be pointed out, however, that there is no obligation to apply for royal confirmation and not every foundation enjoys this privilege.

The granting of royal assent is, in the first place, a guarantee that the statutes of a foundation accord with certain working principles jointly established by the Ministries concerned. Moreover, only those foundations are granted royal confirmation 'whose aims are recognised as deserving of encouragement'[39]. If there is a lack of public interest in the activities of a foundation or the extent of public influence on such activities is too limited, the competent Ministries may decline to accept a kind of part responsibility by granting royal confirmation. For this reason, there exist a number of family foundations and foundations established for certain purposes which do not possess confirmed statutes[40].

Nevertheless, it can be said in general that the terms 'deserving of encouragement' and 'public interest' are given a liberal interpretation.

The royal confirmation is granted by the Ministry which, in the light of the stated aims of the foundation, is deemed to be competent. The Ministry of Justice is the responsible authority for family foundations, foundations established for the care of animals, and for foundations which are difficult to classify.

SUPERVISION OF FOUNDATIONS AND ALTERATION OF PURPOSE

As a result of the granting of royal confirmation, 'a foundation is placed under direct public supervision, particularly in regard to the maintenance of the assets'[41].

This means:

1. The safeguarding of the assets through registration certified by a Court.
2. The right to request the submission of an annual report.
3. The checking of cash holdings and assets by an auditor appointed by the supervisory authority.
4. The authority, either ex-officio or pursuant to a private complaint—and there is no specific delimitation of the category of persons entitled to

---

confirmation as well as the aim of the foundation, the date of the confirmation, the name of the responsible Ministry and the supervisory body are published in the Ministry Gazette—'Ministerialtidende'.

[39] Cf. O. Rosenkranz, p. 83.
[40] Cf. E. Andersen, p. 129.
[41] Cf. Fr. Vinding Kruse: Das Eigentumsrecht, p. 613.

prosecute i.e. the right of prosecution is not restricted solely to the intended beneficiaries—to put a stop to conduct which is contrary to the statutes, or to call for conformity with the statutes and, in case of refusal, to take the matter to Court.

5. The establishment or approval of the salaries paid to members of the foundation's administration.
6. The appointment, if necessary, of a new administration; and
7. The imposition of an obligation upon the administration of the foundation to seek the supervisory authority's advice in cases of doubt[42].

A distinction is made in the supervision of foundations whose statutes have not been confirmed between 'public' and 'non-public' aims. The latter are defined as purely personal or family-related aims.

In the case of foundations with public aims, the supervisory body (i.e. the Ministry which regards itself as competent) has the right, but not the duty, to intervene in pursuance of the criteria set out under 4 or to implement the measures listed under 5 and 6[43]. However, this can, obviously, only occur if the competent authorities are aware of the existence of the foundations in question.

In the case of foundations with non-public aims, the supervisory authority has neither the right nor the duty under the existing legislation to intervene, not even by taking Court action. The exception to this is infringements of the law which could form the subject of public censure. Kauffmann has remarked that this is an unsatisfactory state of affairs[44].

It should be stated at this point, however, that all foundations have to observe the provisions of the laws in regard to commercial, fiscal and hygienic matters, etc. If they are disregarded, this does not lead to any action on the part of the foundation's supervisory body, but instead on the part of the competent authority.

The problems involved in changing the purpose of a foundation (*permutationsret*) have been described in a relatively large number of Danish publications. Andersen's study, for example, is described in the sub-title as having been written 'with special consideration of the drafting and amendment of statutes'. This detailed examination of special aspects of foundation legislation can be ascribed to the lack of legal provisions and the resultant need for the development of a right of permutation in everyday administrative practice[45].

---

[42] Vide E. Kauffmann, pp. 338–9.
[43] Ibid., pp. 339–40.
[44] Cf. E. Kauffmann, p. 342.
[45] Cf. E. Kauffmann, p. 346.

A close study of the permutation law reveals that the Danish legislation
on foundations is inspired by the founder's wishes as the most decisive factor
in any foundation. Hence, 'it is essential that the State should observe the
testator's declared wishes in spirit and letter insofar as possible and for as
long as possible'[46].

The competent Ministry, in co-operation with the Ministry of Justice, is
the responsible body for approving a change in the statutes of foundations
which have royal confirmation. In the case of foundations without royal
confirmation, the right of permutation rests with the Ministry of Justice
pursuant to Art. 69 of the Law on Succession (Law No. 215 of 31st May
1963). The administrative practice with foundations that were not set up
for a public purpose is that an alteration of that purpose by the board of
trustees of the foundation does not have to be approved by the supervisory
authority. Nonetheless, the Courts exercise a certain measure of control
(subject to an application by the beneficiary)[47].

The precondition for any change in the aims of a foundation or other
basic statutory provisions is either the impossibility of, or a major and increasing difficulty in fulfilling stated aims or in carrying out the foundation's
tasks. The alteration itself must approximate as closely as possible to the
founder's original intentions.

In line with the development of property law from an individual and
liberal one to a law with a collective and social touch[48], a number of authors
have recently been invoking aspects of our modern society and calling for
greater freedom in the alteration of 'outmoded' statutory provisions[49].

A Government Ordinance (No. 330) which was promulgated on 16th
September 1966 contained certain guiding principles for the administration
of foundation assets. However, it does not apply to the initial endowment of
a foundation or to assets tied to certain statutory provisions. The idea behind
this ordinance is probably more to avert speculation with foundation funds.
Moreover, foundation administrators are not allowed to engage in self-
dealing practices.

This ordinance laid down three criteria for the investment of a foundation's
assets:

1. the assets may be invested in specified bonds;
2. they may be invested in mortgage bonds (up to 70% of their value for
   tax purposes);

46 Cf. Fr. Vinding Kruse: Das Eigentumsrecht, p. 610.
47 Cf. E. Andersen, p. 130.
48 Cf. The Danish Committee on Comparative Law, p. 69.
49 Cf. E. Kauffmann, p. 356.

3. up to one third can be invested in (officially quoted) shares.

ENDEAVOURS TOWARDS CODIFICATION OR REFORMS

To all intents and purposes, no attempt has been made to bring about a codification of the legal provisions. Neither the administrative authorities nor the foundation experts have pushed ahead with such endeavours. An indication that this is indeed the case can be found in a joint Nordic Civil Code called for by Kruse and then virtually written by that author on his own as the basis for further deliberations[50]. Chap.9 of this book deals with legal status and capacity to act which, after listing various organisations in para. 100, Kruse also wishes to award to foundations. However, he did not go on to expand his ideas on foundation law in this connection.

Nor are there any serious attempts—by whatever means this can be done in the case of unwritten law—to bring about reforms. Although criticism has been voiced about certain aspects of valid legislation or the unsatisfactory nature of certain states of affairs, no real reform movement has emerged. The author of the present study was told at the Ministry of Justice that the present system was working in practice and there was no need for any change. The relatively small number of Court cases appears to support this viewpoint.

The criticisms voiced and the first steps towards a possible reform are more or less all enumerated in Kauffmann's book[51]. In keeping with the basic approach adopted by this author, the main focus is, however, on the financial aspect of foundations. Narrowing down the field even further, Kauffmann noted a certain need for a law on private, profit-making self-owning institutions (business enterprises under foundation control).

TAX LAWS

The generosity of the Danish foundation laws *vis-à-vis* donors and foundations is also reflected, though of course with certain limitations, in the tax laws governing foundations. This is a further demonstration of the esteem in which the nation holds the foundation and the possibilities it offers. The Danish tax legislator, who in other respects is not exactly diffident, was for a long time extremely chary about taking away certain privileges from founders and placing foundations on more or less the same footing as similar organisations.

[50] Fr. Vinding Kruse: A Nordic Draft Code, p. XIII.
[51] pp. 369–73.

However, the large number of foundations established in the last few years in particular, encouraged as they were by the situation described above, have brought about a decisive change. Equal treatment in regard to taxation plays a not inconsiderable rôle in this development.

Many authors on fiscal influences affecting the establishment of foundations have adhered to the traditional method of studying the tax relief enjoyed by a founder when he establishes or expands a foundation and, on the other hand, the tax burden or relief in respect of the foundation itself.

In Denmark, too, the State gives recognition to the efforts of its citizens to take the initiative and make a contribution to the general weal. It recompenses this 'lessening of the State's financial burden'[52] by granting non-profit organisations exemption from the payment of taxes and by making donations to such organisations tax deductible.

The minimum amount which may be donated to an organisation recognised as non-profit making[53] is 50 kr. (almost £3 or $7). Proceeding from the assumption that smaller amounts ought to be borne by the donor in the first instance, the authorities have stipulated that tax deductibility does not come into play until an amount of over 100 kr. has been given. Up to an annual total of 1,000 kr. can be deducted from one's income.

At first sight, this legal position does not seem particularly promising. However, in Denmark the opportunity also exists to deduct amounts of any magnitude from one's annual income if a binding obligation for a period of at least 10 years (e.g. for payments to certain persons or as financial support of institutions) has been entered into. This possibility for the founder of providing funds for his foundation during his lifetime from his income is of particular importance.

Moreover, the legal position in this field has been fluid since a recent Court decision. The Court held that a period of ten years was too long a time for the founder to undertake a binding obligation. It is quite possible that it will in future be reduced to perhaps five years[54].

The Law (*Ligningslov*), as amended in Ordinance 491 of 19th December 1967 in Art. 8 A, para. 2 and Art. 14, paras. 2–5, names three conditions for this kind of obligation, known in the United Kingdom as a covenant:

1. a legal obligation must have been entered into;
2. either sums of an unspecified magnitude (but expressed as a percentage

---

[52] Cf. Fr. Vinding Kruse: Das Eigentumsrecht, p. 150.

[53] A circular issued by the Ministry of Finance on 19th January 1968, on the basis of Art. 8 A of the Tax Assessment Law (ligningslov) lists approximately 800 such organisations which ask the public for donations.

[54] This information was supplied by the Danish Ministry of Finance.

of one's yearly income) must normally be pledged for a period of not less than ten years or fixed sums of money for an indefinite period (in principle, for the lifetime of the donor or the recipient); and
3. only paid-up sums may be deducted.

Deductibility in connection with such long-term obligations is not restricted to non-profit making organisations. However, the support given to close relatives cannot be deducted from one's taxes in this way.

Joint-stock companies cannot deduct single donations from their taxes. Nevertheless, they too may enter into a long-term obligation to give evidence of their 'corporate responsibility' *vis-à-vis* the common weal. But it is essential that there be a large number of beneficiaries and the organisation to whom the donation is made must be recognised as a charitable one. The subsidies paid by enterprises into their own staff relief and welfare funds can be deducted as operating expenditure.

In the case of death duties (inheritance taxes), the tax rate on testamentary bequests is 30% irrespective of the magnitude of the donation pursuant to Art. 2 of the Law on Death Duties (*Lov om afgift af arv og gave*—Law No. 138 of 29th April 1957 and Ordinance No. 63 of 9th March 1964). However, Art. 3 empowers the Ministry of Finance to reduce this figure to 10% if the donation is earmarked for public institutions, associations, societies or foundations. Foundations or legacies where the members of a certain family are the main beneficiaries for more than two generations are not regarded as charitable. These provisions are not only applied to existing foundations, but also to such as have yet to be erected pursuant to a testament[55].

There is no tax on gifts in Denmark to correct pre-inheritance transactions. Notwithstanding, this cannot be taken to mean—as George Nebolsine implies in his 'Fiscal Aspect of Foundations and of Charitable Donations in European Countries'[56]—that donations *inter vivos* may, in all circumstances, be transferred free of tax, to an organisation which has been recognised as non-profit making. If these donations take the form of shares or landed property, they have for some time now been subject to the payment of a special income tax of 30% of the added value. This represents the difference between the market value at the time of acquisition by the founder and the market value when the donation is made.

Contrary to the provisions on taxation in some other countries, the Danish tax legislation does not contain any definite stipulation that charitable organisations are subject to tax. The problem of taxing non-profit organisations is

---

[55] Cf. Kauffmann, p. 99.
[56] Available as a duplicated typescript, Amsterdam, 1963, p. 55 and p. IV.

solved by means of the provisions of the Corporation Income Tax Law (Law No. 255 of 11th June 1960—*Lov om indkomstbeskatning af aktieselskaber*) as amended by the Ordinance of 3rd January 1968. Art. 1, para. 1, No. 6 states that associations, foundations, corporations or self-owning institutions are only liable to pay tax inasmuch as they engage in commercial activities. Art. 3, paras. 2 to 4, contain other exceptions to the liability to pay taxes.

This states that the Minister of Finance can waive the taxes payable by a non-profit organisation on income from commercial activities to the extent that this income is used to implement the aims set out in the statutes[57]. In a case where there is an income which does not stem from commercial activities in addition to income which does accrue from such activities, the former is regarded from the beginning as being spent *in toto* on charitable purposes. Disbursements to ensure that such purposes are fulfilled are regarded as deductible expenditure. However, it is a precondition that such amounts (reserves) must be separated from the working assets and that the administration of the foundation undertake not to use these funds for the commercial side of the organisation. The reserves have to be shown separately in the annual report to the tax authorities. A sum of money re-invested in the enterprise is subject to a supplementary tax payment of 25% over and above the current rate of taxation. Nonetheless, the Ministry of Finance can waive payment of the tax in full or in part if the given circumstances warrant this.

There is a provision in Art. 1, para. 3 that income derived from commercial activities not pursued by an association, corporation, foundation, legacy or self-owning institution but to which such an organisation has a claim, shall also be regarded as income stemming from commercial activities. Owing to the lack of precise instructions about controlling interests etc., the current philosophy and everyday practice on the part of the taxation departments is that this rule is not applicable to dividends on shares and interest on bonds[58].

The rate of assessment for corporations and equated types of enterprise is 36% with effect from 1968/69. When the tax is computed, half of the taxable income, but at most a sum of money amounting to 2.5% of the paid-up capital stock in terms of its nominal value, is deductible from the said income for the purpose of arriving at liability to tax. The rate for foundations and similar organisations is 34% because there is no possibility of deducting an allowance due to the lack of any statutory provisions about the capital stock.

[57] However, it has been customary since 1940 that the Ministry of Finance does not grant this exemption if the foundation or organisation is engaged in commercial activities which compete with firms having another legal form. Cf. Kauffmann, p. 92.

[58] Cf. Kauffman, p. 94.

Prior to a transitional arrangement with varying tax rates created by the Law of 1960, the tax paid by joint-stock companies amounted to 44%. The latter were, however, allowed to deduct an allowance amounting to half of the taxes payable. Foundations and similar organisations used to be liable to pay a 6% tax rate. If one includes the fixed surtax and the supplementary municipal rates, this meant that their level of assessment was normally not more than 12%. This tax was then waived if the profit made by the organisation or foundation in question was used in full for charitable ends.

This highly liberal approach to corporation taxation in the years prior to 1960 is probably one of the reasons why a relatively large number of firms in Denmark adopted the legal form of a self-owning institution and that enterprises were transferred to numerous existing non-profit organisations[59].

Under the existing law, neither corporations nor self-owning institutions attract property tax. The various attempts which have been made to levy a 0.5% property tax on the industrial assets of foundations have so far not met with any success[60].

As regards the tax on land and buildings, the Ministry of Finance can exempt the landed property owned by non-profit organisations from the tax pursuant to Art. 50 of Ordinance No. 305 of 1st August 1960 (*Lov om vurdering og beskatning til staten af faste ejendome*).

Organisations and institutions which have been recognised as non-profit making are still subject to the supervision of the tax authorities and they must submit annual reports. An organisation qualifies as non-profit making if its statutes and actual activities are likely to be of benefit to the community as a whole. The requirement of being in the public interest is fulfilled by the existence of a fairly large number of beneficiaries. As a precaution against the activities being discontinued, there must be a provision in the statutes that the assets will continue to be used for charitable ends. Apart from securing the assets which provide the income, the proceeds from gainful activities must only be used for the organisation's non-profit work.

In the conclusions he reached on the situation of non-profit organisations under the Danish tax law, Nebolsine[61] was perfectly right to point out that

---

[59] It should be emphasised, however, that this provision did not cause the tax legislator any undue difficulties because the Danish corporation income tax was not developed, as it was in other countries, into a pillar of the fiscal system in order to safeguard the earning powers of business enterprises. In the years 1965/66, for example, it only yielded 7.3% (953,784,000 kr.) of the income from taxes and levies. The foundations and other societies accounted for only 2.5% of this sum (23,428,000 kr.). The main point of emphasis in Danish tax legislation is on turnover tax and excise duties and on personal income tax.

[60] E. Kauffmann, p. 99.

[61] Cf. p. 56.

the tax incentives for occasional donations by individuals or firms are small but that the generosity shown in the case of long-term pledges is much greater than the relief granted in other countries.

We are also in agreement with Kauffmann's view[62] that there are no provisions in Danish tax law which exclude the establishment or running of a concern in the legal form *selvejende institution*, or which render its practical administration more difficult, even considering the fact that the formerly privileged position of self-owning institutions now seems to have been substantially modified. The view is even expressed that the administration of controlling interests by a foundation or the running of a business by a foundation enjoy somewhat more favourable tax treatment both during the establishment and the existence of such organisations.

THE PRESENT SITUATION AND ROLE OF FOUNDATIONS

This relatively favourable attitude towards foundations on the part of the tax legislator may, however, have been partly deliberate since the encouragement it gives to private persons to divest themselves of their assets leads to 'a new intermediate form between private property and public property... which includes all kinds of joint property which are in the interest of the common weal but whose economy is independent of the State'[63]. As the assets of foundations are no longer closely connected, as used to be the tradition, with a private property-owner and 'important social tasks' are fulfilled for the benefit of the whole community, 'the total assets of foundations are in reality an important part of the nation's social investment'[64].

In view of the existing legal position, it is difficult to indicate the approximate size of this common property in Denmark. In spite of the fact that the authorities know about most of the existing foundations, there is no central agency which deals with the whole range of questions pertaining to these organisations.

There are a number of handbooks and guides on this subject and they probably contain a full list of the most representative foundations[65]. In 1966 the Danish Student Council published the 8th edition of a reference book which enumerates about 300 scholarship foundations[66]. In addition, there are

[62] Cf. pp. 102–3.
[63] Cf. Fr. Vinding Kruse: Das Eigentumsrecht, p. 150.
[64] Ibid., p. 609.
[65] E.g. pp. 985–98 of the Kongelig Dansk Hof og Statskalender 1968 which list 100 of the largest foundations. Vide also p. 741, pp. 874–81 and pp. 917–20.
[66] Danske Studerendes Fœllersråd: Legathåndbog (Legater, Studielån, Kollegier), Copenhagen, 1966.

approximately 200 endowed scholarships at the University of Copenhagen. However, the author has found the most important source of information to be a 'Guide to Legacies'[67]. The 12th. edition of this standard work published in 1964 and reprinted in 1966 named 2,258 institutions which may be approached for financial aid. A sample test of the listed organisations showed that 7% could not be considered as foundations (i.e. they were societies, associations, etc.). This leaves a total of 2,000. If one adds the foundations since set up and foundations covered by the 'Handbook on Legacies,' the number then rises to 2,400. The author assumes that there are a further 600 foundations in the form of theatres, museums, libraries, schools, research institutions[68], miscellaneous enterprises, hostels, social welfare amenities, pension funds, saving banks[69], harbour facilities[70], universities, churches and newspapers[71]. If one appends certain amenities in the social, cultural or economic sectors, one arrives at a nice round number of approximately 3,000 foundations in Denmark.

On the other hand, Anderson[72] computed that there are many more than that. His view was that in the year 1962 or thereabouts there were 'hardly any fewer than 10,000' independent foundations. This huge number of foundations, each with its own organisational set-up appeared to Andersen to be in 'a frequently very inexpedient form and often inconvenient for future developments'. He proposed instead endowment funds and the employment of the foundation's capital by a non-profit organisation whose structure would largely be that of a corporation, or an even greater measure

[67] Carl Flyge: Vejviser for Legatsøgende, Copenhagen, 1966.

[68] Vide E. Kauffmann, pp. 31-2 on free research institutes and the foundation institutes attached to the Academy for the Technical Sciences.

[69] Since 1919, the only permissible legal form for savings banks has been the 'self-owning savings bank'.

[70] Pursuant to Law No. 109 of 29th April 1913, the commercial harbour of Copenhagen is administered as a foundation under its own harbour administration whilst other harbours are run as State or municipal enterprises or as joint-stock companies.

[71] The independent newspaper 'Information' (circulation approximately 20,000) which originated in the Resistance Movement was operated as a foundation in order to maintain its independence. Towards the end of 1968, it got into financial difficulties and had to be converted into a joint-stock company. Finally in May 1970, a generous offer by the principal shareholder enabled the 105 employees to acquire two thirds of the shares in their company at a quotation of only 10.

In addition to this then typical case of a 'daily newspaper foundation', a number of publishing-houses operate as foundations: some of these enterprises publish special literature without any great interest in achieving a profit. Examples are: the architects' publishing-house (Arkitektens Forlag); the lawyers' publishing-house (Juristforbundets Forlag); and the dentists' publishing-house (Odontologisk Forlag) in Aarhus.

[72] Cf. p. 126.

of association with an existing organisation (which has hitherto in any case been customary and frequent). This would be done in the form of certain stipulations governing the use of a foundation's revenue. In practice, this means the creation of corporation assets with conditions about how the revenue may be employed.

In view of this complex pattern in the field of foundations, it is of course very difficult to say much about their capital and the dividends paid. Nevertheless, an attempt will be made. The author feels he is justified in so doing because his studies on foundations in various countries have led him to believe that there are certain regular patterns to be detected in this field. For example, by far the largest proportion of foundation funds in any given country are often administered by the five, ten or twenty largest foundations there. However, their share of the overall grants is not uniform. This stems from the fact that these large foundations were often established quite recently and they are still subject to certain stipulations laid down by the founder's family or the enterprise in which the foundation's assets are invested. Hence, 90% of foundations are not of great importance as regards the magnitude of their capital or their income. Moreover, in many cases they cannot be considered as 'modern' foundations in regard to the purpose for which they were set up. The majority are characterised by their social functions or the support given to certain organisations or institutions and they are not particularly selective in their choice.

All this is more or less equally true of Denmark. We have listed below the ten largest foundations in the country. As these foundations often do not give any exact statistics about their work, the attempt had to be made to estimate the market value of their assets invested in equities by means of their current stock exchange quotations or the yield or stock exchange prices of comparable competitors in the economic life of the nation. The important thing is not to name a precise figure, but to gain an approximate idea of the order of magnitude of the biggest foundations (see p. 154).

A great stir was caused in 1967 when the shares of the firm Tjœreborg A/S were transferred to a foundation called the *Tjœreborg Fond*. The general public felt that the founder of the biggest travel organisation in Scandinavia (with his own fleet of aircraft), E. Krogager, a vicar from Tjœreborg in Jutland, had made this move for tax reasons. However, the firm denied this, and stressed that the Danish laws on the tax privileges granted for the purchase of ships and aircraft (the writing-off of items before they are entered in the balance sheet, and the creation of reserves for capital investment) and for the implementation of transactions with other countries were so generous that it was not at all necessary to obtain possible advantages by thus linking

L

Foundation	Capital (estimates in millions of kr.)	Date of Establishment	Founder
Carlsberg-fondet, Copenhagen[1]	500[2]	1876	J. Chr. Jacobsen and his son C. Jacobsen as co-founder
Skibsreder A. P. Møllers og Hustru Chastine McKinney Møllers Fond til almene Formål, Copenhagen	300	1953	A. P. Møller
Egmont H. Petersens Fond, Copenhagen[1]	150	1920	Heirs (wife and 5 children) to E. H. Petersen, a printer who died in 1914
Thomas B. Thriges Fond, Odense[1]	50	1934	Th. B. Thrige and wife
Det Classenske Fideicommis, Copenhagen[3]	50	1792	Major-General J. F. Classen
Otto Mønsteds Fond, Copenhagen[1]	40	1934	O. Mønsted (died in 1916) and his wife (died in 1933)
Nordisk Insulin- laboratorium/Nordisk Insulinfond, Gentofte (and 6 associated foundations)[1]	over 30	1924	H. C. Hagedorn, A. Kongsted and A. Krogh
Louisiana Fonden, Humlebœk[4]	30[5]	1954	K. W. Jensen
Tuborgfondet, Copenhagen	25	1931	A/S De forenede Bryggerier
Knud Højgaards Fond, Copenhagen	21	1955	K. Højgaard

[1] In connection with the origin, purpose and economic function of these foundations, the following work of the author is of relevance: Die Bereitstellung von Unternehmenskapital für Stiftungen—Stiftungsunternehmen und unternehmensbezogene Stiftungen, Cologne University, 1964, pp. 223–40. (The provision of industrial assets for foundations—Business enterprises under foundation control.)

[2] In May 1970, reports appeared in the press to the effect that, in view of the competitive situation which would result from Denmark's prospective accession to the E.E.C., the two largest Danish breweries, Carlsberg and the United Breweries Ltd. (better known under the name of its beer, Tuborg) wished to effect a merger. The Carlsberg Foundation would incorporate its enterprises within Tuborg, and receive 50% of the latter's capital stock (which had been increased to 171 mill. kr.) plus 16 mill. in cash. The current market price of Tuborg shares on the Copenhagen Stock Exchange is 230 (compared with nearly 430 at the end of 1969). Thus, in line with the present (August

a firm to a foundation. They said that in this particular case the foundation had been set up in order to guarantee the continuity of the firm.

When the question of Tjœreborg Fond's attribution of assets is finally decided, this organisation will probably rank amongst the five biggest foundations in Denmark. This would mean that the 10 or 11 largest foundations set up by private donors would be administering a capital of over 1,200 mill. kr. These 10 foundations have spent 25 mill. kr. on donations or programmes of their own (i.e. excluding administrative costs). Their revenue has probably amounted to over 45 mill. kr. and they have spent the difference between these two sums of money on administrative costs and the safeguarding of their capital (accumulation).

There are a further 20 foundations which administer a foundation capital of about 10 to 20 mill. kr. That makes a total of roughly 250 mill. kr.

The group of foundations with a capital of between 1 and 10 mill. kr. is probably well represented. The records of 25 foundations show that they have an average capital of 4 mill. kr. per foundation. All in all, one can assume that there are some 150 foundations of this order of magnitude (this also comprises most of the business enterprises under foundation control and foundations with a majority holding in smaller joint-stock companies, and charitable institutions). Their capital might well amount to over 250 mill. kr.

The difficulty in estimating the assets of the other foundations is to arrive at a fairly reliable average figure. Two orders of magnitude stand out. At various universities and colleges in Copenhagen, for example, there are

---

1970) state of affairs—which, however, is not very representative in view of the worldwide slump on the stock-markets—the value of Carlsberg's working funds in stock-exchange terms is about 220 mill. kr. This price seems to have been somewhat depressed (for example the shares of another brewery cost 330) because the envisaged rationalisation measures have caused a certain amount of worry amongst employees about the future of their jobs. The long-term value of these shareholdings is probably 300 mill. kr. or more. To this figure should be added the substantial non-commercial assets of the company, including (in September 1968) securities with a book-value of over 110 mill. kr. If one deducted the firm's liabilities, there was at the end of September 1968 a balance-sheet volume of approximately 375 mill. kr. This normally corresponds to the book-values of a foundation. In the case of Carlsberg, foundation liabilities amounting to nearly 28 mill. kr. should also be deducted so that the book-value of the foundation's assets on the basis of the balance-sheet alone is about 350 mill. kr.

[3] Designated by E. Kauffmann (p.38) as probably being the oldest (agricultural) enterprise under foundation control in Denmark.

[4] There was a very instructive article by G. Joppe called *Das dänische Museum am Meer* (The Danish Museum by the Sea) in the *Frankfurter Allgemeine Zeitung*, No.59, of 9th March 1968, about the foundation and the museum it runs.

[5] This figure is perhaps too high.

approximately 500 legacies and research funds[73] worth 40 mill. kr.[74] to administer. This means that the average is 80,000 kr. per foundation. If one subtracts 200 smaller scholarship foundations, one arrives at an average foundation capital of 127,000 kr[75]. This tallies with the computations in the *Vejviser* in respect of 30 foundations. Their figure was 135,000 kr.

If one assumes that half of the foundations quoted in the *Vejviser* are of that order of magnitude, the total is approximately 160 mill. kr. The remainder i.e. over 9,000 foundations in 1968 probably dispose of an average of 10 to 15,000 kr. The total is thus over 100 mill. kr.

If one adds up these individual amounts, one arrives at a grand total of over 1,960 mill. kr. so that the capital and property in foundations set up by private patrons and philanthropists are worth roughly 2,000 mill. kr. This excludes foundations run by the public authorities and foundations whose programmes are regularly supported by the public authorities or the big social groups[76].

This figure of 2,000 mill. kr. in itself does not say much about a nation's philanthropic works as invested in foundations. It would perhaps be useful to compare the wealth tied up in foundations with that of the whole nation. Unfortunately, no figures are available for Denmark. As a rough estimate, one can, however, take the gross national product, whatever arguments there may be against this. In Denmark, the wealth of the foundations is 2.6% of the gross national product (1967). The corresponding figures for the USA and the Federal Republic of Germany are 2.9% (1965) and approximately 1.6%. The assets of Danish foundations are 58 dollars per head of population, 105 dollars in the USA and approximately 33.5 dollars in the

[73] Cf. Hof og Statskalender, p. 741.

[74] As a foundation's assets held by public authorities are usually invested in public loans, this figure quoted on 31st March 1967, probably represents the current market value.

[75] Cf. Legathåndbog, p. 11.

[76] This phenomenon which one might well term the 'socialization' of foundations and charitable endowments and which has also been observed in other countries, has been particularly in evidence in Denmark during the last two decades. The public authorities, the two sides of industry or some other social group have set up foundations which— in the case of state-run organisations, for example—are not given full administrative powers (the enterprise known as *Det Danske Selskab*, for instance, calls itself by the misleading name of 'company': however, its function is cultural exchanges with other countries and its budget is mainly furnished by the public authorities). These 'public' foundations are usually given an independent administration. Sometimes they are even given the right of co-option. Financial dependence, however, is the reverse of the ideal of a truly independent foundation with a wide measure of freedom of action. Nonetheless, the trend toward delegating tasks, the deconcentration and the adjustment to the way of life in a pluralistic society is unmistakable and welcome.

Federal Republic of Germany. The assumption that Denmark is keen on foundations is thus confirmed by these figures.

Fr. Vinding Kruse[77] estimated in his book on property law that at the end of the 1920s the foundations in Denmark had capital and property worth 230 mill. kr. This means that their wealth increased eightfold in approximately 40 years in spite of the collapse of the currency and the inflation which Denmark was not spared. Even if one takes into account the rise in the price-index from 100 to 360[78], this still means that the capital and property of Danish foundations have roughly trebled by the addition of new foundations during that period.

The inflation problem seems to be carefully studied by present-day founders. This may be partly due to the fact, however, that there have been decisive changes in the pattern of investment by private foundations. After all, the only wealth one can put into a foundation is what one has either inherited or earned.

Kauffmann[79] thinks a distinction can be made between the following periods in the history of foundations in that the wealth given to foundations assumed different forms in each of them:

1. Up to the middle of the nineteenth century, the preferred form was a bequest of landed property.

2. From 1845 to 1914, the majority of foundations were given monetary claims (mortgage debentures, government loans). The stable political and economic situation was a guarantee of the stability of such investments. The State encouraged this trend by laying down stipulations that publicly administered assets must be invested in 'gilt-edged' securities.

3. As a result of the ending of the liability to make payment in gold by the National Bank in the year 1914 and the rapid depreciation of currency caused by the First World War, the foundations started to receive more and more assets which had been hedged against inflation. These were usually investments in industrials in the widest sense of the word.

ONE-STOCK FOUNDATIONS

Particular importance has attached in recent years to the 'one-stock foundations' in Denmark i.e. both forms thereof, the foundation with a majority holding in a joint-stock company and the business enterprise under foundation control.

[77] Das Eigentumsrecht, p. 610.
[78] Cf. E. Kauffmann, p. 154.
[79] Pp. 150–8.

It is interesting to note in connection with foundations linked with firms on the basis of a dual organisation, foundation joint stock company, that a foundation cannot become the sole shareholder in a firm. Pursuant to Art. 9, para. 2, and Art. 59 of the Law on Shares (as amended by Ordinance 313 of 28th August 1952), there must be three shareholders. This has given rise to such organisations as the *Otto Mønsteds Fond* where the foundation administers 6,998,000 kr. of the total capital stock of 7 mill. kr. or the University of Aarhus, itself a foundation, where the associated but independent *Aarhus Universitets Forskningsfond* owns nearly all the shares of A/S Cheminova and where the rector and pro-rector (vice-chancellor) act as custodians and hold two shares in trust.

The second kind of one-stock foundation, i.e. the business enterprise under foundation control, may be divided into two types. Either the enterprise and the foundation form a single unit (the narrower definition of the term) or the enterprise virtually only acts as a source of revenue for the foundation to finance its other, non-commercial activities. Examples of this latter fairly uncommon type are the Carlsberg foundation (before the proposed merger) where the profits from the brewery provide the funds for grants as well as for the foundation's own research programme, *Skagens Museum* where the revenue from *Brøendums Hotel* serves to maintain the institution, and *Nordisk Insulinlaboratorium* where the profits on the manufacture of insulin are used to finance a scholarship programme and, most important of all, to support the research hospital for metabolic illnesses (*Niels Steensens Spital*).

According to Kauffmann[80], an '*erhvervsdrivende selvejende institution*' is characterised by three things:
1. The active employment by the foundation's administration of the foundation's assets for commercial gain;
2. the regular assumption of obligations in connection with these business transactions; and
3. the investment of the assets in 'real' securities.

The general reasons cited for the emergence of a relatively large number of one-stock foundations in Denmark are[81]:
1. The wish to maintain the value of the foundation's capital;
2. the wish to guarantee the cohesion of the enterprise for a fairly long period of time;
3. the wish to stabilize the capital situation within the enterprise;
4. the wish to maintain the continuity of the firm's management;
5. the wish to keep an enterprise under family control; and finally

[80] Cf. p. 36.
[81] Vide Kauffmann, pp. 149–84.

6. the possibility of obtaining personal advantages when a foundation is set up.

For a certain time, this included a number of tax advantages.

The advantages listed under 2. and 4. were of great importance for the larger and medium-sized foundations and enterprises. This is often clearly in evidence in the text of the statutes.

In his critical appraisal of the problem of foundations in business life, Kauffmann comes to the conclusion that foundations in particular can have an inhibiting effect on the dynamism of economic life and can render it more static.

An illustration of this was the case of the *Thomas B. Thriges Fond* in Odense —though the details were not ascertainable in full. In the year 1964, the Thrige combine employed 6,000 persons in its various enterprises, including 3,500 in the foundation's works. The manufacturing programme included the construction of heavy machines, electric motors and ships' equipment. The aims of the foundation in connection with the commercial enterprises were to maintain and continue the undertakings at a high technical level and to employ the profits for the greatest benefit of Denmark's science, industry and trade[82]. There were two decisive factors which caused the concern's economic difficulties. In the first place, the narrowness of the Danish market and the keen competition from abroad did not admit the existence of two enterprises of this size (*Thrige and Titan A/S*). Then again, the management of the firm probably did not pay enough attention to the founder's instructions about aiming at a particularly high technical level in the enterprise. The result was a permanent obsolescence of the production programme. Not being a joint-stock company, *Thrige* did not have to concern itself with the quotation of shares on the stock exchange or to pay dividends to the shareholders. Moreover if need be, it could draw on the reserves from previous years. The firm was able to postpone the commercial consequences which would as a rule have rapidly ensued from such a situation for a considerable period of time. The general economic crisis finally led in December 1965 to the amalgamation of *Thrige* and *Titan* into *Thrige-Titan A/S*. Fortunately, the statutes did not make it difficult to implement a merger or conversion. On the contrary, they even included a provision about such a future contingency[83]. Such elasticity in the statutes and the greater measure of adaptability to changed conditions partly cancels out the argument that the capital of business enterprises connected with foundations has a potentially retarding effect on the dynamism of economic life.

[82] Cf. K. Neuhoff, pp. 230–1.
[83] Cf. K. Neuhoff, pp. 132–3.

AIMS OF FOUNDATIONS

A study of the various aims of foundations reveals that they are of a decidedly practical character. Less importance has attached in recent years to those foundations whose aims are purely in the realm of welfare. Nevertheless, it is surprising in a country that is marked by a predilection for welfare that social foundations are still set up or that no more use is made of the possibility of changing the purpose of a foundation i.e. by modernizing obsolescent functions. However, inasmuch as institutions of a social character are still set up, this criticism of the founders is probably not justifiable.

Foundations have always been noted for the efforts they have made to promote higher education. The objectives of scholarship grants are probably closest in character to public welfare and could perhaps be regarded as a first step towards superseding the older foundation traditions. A handbook of legacies issued by the Danish Students Council[84] estimated that foundation scholarships accounted for 3% to 4% of the total of available funds.[85] This in turn means 4.5 mill. kr. It is interesting to note that there are no charges for university studies in Denmark.

The foundations have also discovered that there is a serious shortage of accommodation for students. The concentration of the Government, the business world and the arts and sciences in the country's capital has caused the price of housing to rise sharply. The foundations have attempted to ease the situation. Of the 32 colleges in Copenhagen, eight are foundations, five are owned by a foundation, six belong to the university and the other thirteen are private property. Thus, 68% or approximately 1,825 of all the rooms and all the 238 apartments belong to foundations. These provide accommodation for 8% of the total number of Copenhagen students[86].

Of the 14 colleges at the University of Aarhus, five are foundations, one is owned by a foundation and the remaining eight are owned by the Students' Council. The foundations provide accommodation for approximately 1,200 students i.e. over 14% of all those studying in Aarhus.

This change in the pattern of the purposes for which foundations are established has been evident since the end of the 1920s and the beginning of the 1930s[87]. In his book *Ejendomsretten*, Vinding Kruse[88] lists some of the

[84] Cf. A. Nygaard Andersen, Forord, p. 3.

[85] Pursuant to the provisions on scholarships endowed by public foundations, this figure would represent 1,000 scholarships (approximately 2.7% of all—37,000—students in 1966/67) or 6.7% of all students who receive public support (= 40% of the overall total).

[86] Cf. Legathåndbog pp. 70–6.

[87] Cf. Det Danske Selskab, p. 21.   [88] Cf. Das Eigentumsrecht, p. 609.

aims of foundations in addition to the classical objectives: the furtherance of industry and the crafts, the training of young people and the publication of works on this subject, the promotion of agriculture, forestry, maritime shipping and fisheries, and maintaining the continuity of enterprises. 'These foundations, with all the differences they display, have certain common features: they render assistance to students in trade and technology, they support correspondence schools with grants for special purposes, and they help to further scientific research of interest to Danish trade and industry. It is this last feature which distinguishes the industrial foundations and gives them a place in the industrial life of modern Denmark as necessary complements to the assistance given by public authorities and the Carlsberg Foundation to the education system and the basic science.'[89]

This is not surprising since the founders were usually industrialists and knew from their business experience where additional funds were urgently required. The only astonishing feature was the consistency with which they parted with their property and capital.

It was above all the reluctance and the half-hearted efforts by the State in the provision of funds for science and education that touched off this process. The government's expenditure on research between the years 1953/54 and 1966/67 rose from 65 mill. kr. to 550 mill. kr.; but in relation to overall government expenditure or the gross national product this only amounted to an increase from 1.6% to 3.5% and 0.2% to 0.7% respectively[90]. The result is that research and development in Denmark only account for just under 1% of the gross national product.

Hence, it was incumbent upon private founders and foundations to implement complementary and counterbalancing functions since public funds were largely disbursed on basic research whose usefulness for the economy of a country is not felt for some considerable time.

It is particularly amongst the large number of one-stock foundations that these factors play an important part. As a result of withholding part of the total profits, the enterprise is furnished with funds to invest in research or development or with which to expand. This permanent safeguarding of the real assets is of particular significance in a country where firms have a relatively small ratio of capital resources of their own. Moreover, the money spent by the foundations (e.g. on agricultural research, shipping research and sometimes on more concrete business matters) benefits the whole economy of the country in one form or another within the shortest possible space of time.

This attitude of the leading men in the country's economy is also evidenced

---

[89] Det Danske Selskab, p. 21.
[90] Cf. Forskningens Fœllesudvalg: Årsberetning 1965–6, Copenhagen 1966, pp. 92–3.

by the fact that even fairly large concerns with a wide range of shareholders endow foundations. An instance of this was the firm *A/S De Forenede Bryggerier* who set up *Tuborgfondet* in 1931 on the 40th anniversary of the founding of the firm and furnished it with a capital of 1 mill. kr. in the form of shares in the firm[91]. In addition, the foundation receives an annual sum of 600,000 kr. from the firm.

Other examples of such foundations are *Dansk Esso Fond, Det Danske Trælastkompagnis Jubilæumslegat, Det Forenede Dampskibs-Selskabs Jubilæumsfond, LK-Fond* (*Laur. Knudsen A/S*), etc.

A number of foundations have been set up to promote art and culture. Frequently, they are associated with appropriate organisations and institutions. However, where an institution is clothed in the form of a foundation, as for example in the case of museums, music academies, theatres, libraries, etc., it requires national or municipal support[92]. About 30% of the 70 larger museums are foundations[93] and it may be assumed that most of them need subsidising. Prominent exceptions are the *Louisiana Fonden* (which had 193,160 visitors in 1967 and is thus one of the most popular museums in the country) and the *Hjerl Hedes* open-air museum of Jutland which belongs to the *Hjerl Fonden* (set up in 1915).

Amongst the cultural foundations, the *Sonning Fonden* (established in 1949) at Copenhagen University enjoys a particularly good reputation. Every year, this foundation awards the Sonning Prize (100,000 kr. up to 1967 and 140,000 kr. from 1968) for meritorious efforts in the cause of European culture. Various European universities have the right to propose winners. The prize-holders include W. Churchill (1950), A. Schweitzer (1959), B. Russell (1960), K. Barth (1963), W. A. Visser't Hooft (1967), A. Koestler (1968), and H. Laxness from Iceland (1969).

An example of a cultural foundation in the widest sense of the word is the foundation established by the great American philanthropist Andrew Carnegie in 1912: *Carnegies Belønningsfond for Heltemod i Danmark* (capital = 1.6 mill. kr.). This is one of the Carnegie Hero Funds which also exist in other countries: the purpose is to honour especially brave deeds performed in everyday life. The policy of the Danish foundation's administration seems to be above all to distinguish young people in order to encourage public service and responsibility amongst the youth of Denmark.

---

[91] Admittedly, this was also inspired by the publicity impact achieved by their great rivals, Carlsberg, when they established a major non-profit foundation linked with the company.

[92] This also applies to schools and research institutes.

[93] Cf. the enumeration in the Hof og Statskalender, pp. 874–81.

There is a whole range of foundations in the field of tuition and education e.g. private grammar (high) schools, secondary schools, seminars, council schools, domestic science schools, evening classes, polytechnics, commercial schools and adult education colleges (folk high schools).

This kind of private school has to fulfil certain conditions to attain State recognition of its tuition. In many cases, the only way to ensure the continued existence of private schools has been for them to be converted into foundations since the State then bears 90% of the regular costs and also undertakes investments[94]. Where a private school is converted into a foundation, the State grants loans in order to acquire buildings and real estate from former owners[95].

In his book on adult education colleges, a Danish invention, Fridlev Skrubbeltrang[96] states that 'the law promulgated in 1942 probably helped to maintain the total number (69 in 1965/66—author's note) of existing colleges and speeded up the conversion of individual properties into foundations, which is characteristic of the last 30 to 35 years'. The oldest foundation of this kind is the school in Askov, which was made into a self-owning institution in 1898.

Of the institutions of higher education, the University of Aarhus (in pursuance of Law No. 73 of 7th March 1952, set up through private and municipal initiative in 1921) and the Copenhagen and Aarhus Colleges of Commerce (Law 193 of 26th May 1965) are foundations[97].

We should like to conclude our remarks on foundations in Denmark with a reference to an example of initiative in the field of foundations taken in June 1968 which is certainly very unusual by modern standards. Kraks Legat in Copenhagen, Denmark's leading publishers of business directories, address books and export manuals, whose foundation purpose is the continuity of the firm and its *Vejviser* and the employment of the profit 'for the service of Danish trade and industry' (in the words of the statutes), earmarked 60,000 kr. from the profits for 1967 for this very purpose. If Mohammed does not come to the mountain, the mountain must go to Mohammed. This might be the interpretation one could proffer when the foundation management's final decision in respect of this sum was publicly rewarded[98].

94 Cf. Aksel Nellemann: Schools and Education in Denmark, Copenhagen, 1964, p. 145.
95 Ibid., p. 138.   96 Cf. Die Volkshochschule, Copenhagen, p. 194.
97 On the other hand, the University of Copenhagen, which was set up in 1478, was converted into a State institution by a royal decree of 5th October 1936, as was the new University of Odense by Law No. 190 of 4th June 1964, The same is true of all the other universities and colleges in Copenhagen. Cf. E. Kauffmann, p. 469.
98 Cf. Berlingske Tidende of 22nd June 1968, p. 22.

LITERATURE

Andersen, Ernst Legater og Stiftelser, Copenhagen 1962.
Flyge, Carl Vejviser for Legatsøgende, Copenhagen 1966.
Gomard Bernhard Aktieselskabsret, Copenhagen 1966.
Hofmann, Hans de Samlinger af publique og private Stiftelser, Fundationer og Gavebreve, som forfindes udi Danmark og Norge, I–XI, 1755–1780.
Joppe, G. Das dänische Museum am Meer, in: Frankfurter Allgemeine Zeitung, No. 59, 9th March 1968.
Kauffmann, Ernst Erhvervsdrivende Selvjende Institutioner, 2nd Ed., Copenhagen 1968.
Nebolsine, George Fiscal Aspects of Foundations and of Charitable Donations in European Countries, Amsterdam 1963.
Nellemann, Aksel Schools and Education in Denmark, Copenhagen 1964.
Neuhoff, Klaus Die Bereitstellung von Unternehmenskapital für Stiftungen (Stiftungsunternehmen und unternehmensbezogene Stiftungen), Cologne 1964.
Olivarius, J. H. Stiftelser, Copenhagen 1910.
Oppermann, R. Th. Den danske Rets Bestemmelser om Stiftelser, Copenhagen 1860.
Ørsted, Anders Sandøe: Om Regjeringens Ret til at ophæve eller forandre Stiftelser, som private Mænd have oprettet, in: Eunomia I, p. 1–38, Copenhagen 1815 (Reprint in: Privatrechtliche Skrifter, Anden Afdeling, Copenhagen 1930).
Philomusus (Rasmus Fleischer?) Om Stiftelser, Copenhagen 1771.
Rosenkranz, Olaf Die Stiftung als Unternehmungsform, Cologne 1957.
Schairer, R. Weiterbildung—Der neue Weg, Bonn 1965.
Skrubbeltrang, Fridlev Die Volkshochschule, Copenhagen.
Vinding Kruse, Fr. Das Eigentumsrecht, Berlin/Leipzig 1931; The Right of Property, Oxford 1939; A Nordic Draft Code, Copenhagen 1963.

The Danish Committee on Comparative Law Danish and Norwegian Law, Copenhagen 1963.
Det Danske Selskab Major Danish Foundations for the Support of Science and Art, Copenhagen, 1955.
Danske Studerendes Fællesråd Legathåndbog (Legater, Studielån, Kollegier), Copenhagen 1966.
Forskningens Fællesudvalg Årsberetning 1965–6, Copenhagen 1966.
Kongelig Dansk Hof- og Statskalender 1968 pp. 985–98, 741, 874–81, and 914 et ss.

Spain[*]

Staff Members of the Fundación Juan March

I. CONCEPT AND CHARACTERISTICS

Foundations in Spain are juristic persons created by private will to meet physical or intellectual needs without financial gain; they are provided with an endowment for the realisation of their objects and are bound to operate in accordance with the norms laid down by the founder at the time of their creation.

1. Foundations are juristic persons and as such, from the time of their constitution, have full juristic identity and are legally empowered to exercise their rights and fulfil their obligations, and are entitled to acquire and possess assets of all kinds and to contract and cancel out their liabilities.

2. Foundations are endowed with a patrimony for the execution of a charitable or educational purpose. The endowment comprises the gift or bequest which the founder has allocated for the aforementioned purpose, specifying the amount and the sources of revenue, the aims to be fulfilled, and, in general terms, the criteria by which the foundation shall be governed.

3. Foundations are created with a specific purpose: to provide for physical or intellectual needs without financial gain, meaning, conclusively, that foundations shall apply such assets or monies at their disposal to a charitable or educational end.

II. LEGAL REGIME

1. *Constitution*

Two phases must be clearly distinguished in the process of constitution or emergence of foundations as legal entities.

(a) Manifestation of the founder's will

The first rule of all foundations is that the founder's will constitutes the law of

[*] Translated from the Spanish.

the foundation. At all times, therefore, the will of the founder must be respected. The directorship or governing board of the foundation will devolve upon the persons designated by the founder, the revenues derived from the foundation's assets shall be used in accordance with the specifications set forth in the statutes, etc. The regulations laid down by the public authorities have only a supplementary function and can only be applied if they do not contradict the founder's will as clearly expressed in the foundation's statutes.

The founder's will can be manifested by an act *inter vivos* or *mortis causa*: in the former case by public or private deed, not requiring special qualifications unless the gift includes real property or royalties in which case it is indispensable that an official deed be issued; in the latter case, the founder manifests his will through his testament.

(b) State recognition

Once the expressed will of the founder is manifested, it has to be submitted for the approval of the State which, through the corresponding Ministry and after careful consideration of the deed of foundation, proceeds to its classification and accords full validity to the statutes. Through the classification is determined the Ministry which will be responsible for the control and supervision of the foundation.

2. *Categories*

(a) According to their origin foundations are

Public: created by the State, province or municipality or with the intervention of a public company with a non-voluntary contribution indispensable to the maintenance of the foundation;

Private: created and endowed by private individuals. A foundation which is partly subsidised by the State, province or municipality will remain a private foundation provided the contribution is voluntary and not indispensable to the existence of the foundation.

(b) According to objectives foundations are

Charitable: those which fulfil general charitable aims or provide material assistance (sickness, food, clothing, housing, etc.). Their control and supervision falls under the Ministry of the Interior;

Charitable—educational: their purpose is to provide for intellectual needs (education, teaching, teaching and advancement of the sciences, arts and humanities). Their supervision falls under the Ministry of Education and Science;

Mixed (dual-purpose): those which have a capital endowment administered by a single and indivisible board of trustees and pursue parallel but distinct and independent aims; one of material assistance and the other of an educational character. Their control falls under the Ministry of the Interior;

Agricultural: for the promotion of research and training in agriculture and animal husbandry and under the supervision of the Ministry of Agriculture;

Industrial: created by virtue of an agreement between a firm and its employees for the latter's benefit, and supervised by the Ministry of Labour.

3. *Operational norms*

As already indicated, the will of the founder constitutes the law of the foundation, the said will having to be respected at all times, the legal norms only being applied in its absence. It is, therefore, for the founder to designate the person or persons who will legally represent the foundation and administer its funds, determine the utilisation of these funds, the tasks to be discharged, the functions of trustees or administrators, etc.

(a) The foundation's patrimony

It comprises the capital and/or property bestowed by the founder and that which may be subsequently acquired by the foundation through gifts, inheritances, legacies, bargain and sale, or such other means as are established in law.

In Spain foundations may be established with any kind of capital, property, real estate, or goods and chattels and are free to own, acquire and/or transfer the same.

Foundations, in the past, had to invest their capital in non-transferable Government bonds. Subsequently, the law was made more flexible and it was declared legal for foundations to invest their capital in securities which did not necessarily have to be converted into bonds, but which had to be regarded as non-transferable foundation property.

Finally, and that is the situation at present, the will of the founder is absolutely respected. The founder is free to empower the administrators of the foundation to invest, transfer and/or freely dispose of the foundation's assets in order to best realise the philanthropic aims pursued. The clause binding administrators not to transfer real estate forming part of the foundation's assets has also been rendered non-effective; administrators are, at present, entirely free to invest, use and deposit the foundation's capital, being only bound to keep and maintain it in an appropriate manner and in the name of the foundation at any establishment serving such purpose.

(b) Administration and representation

The administration of the foundation devolves upon the person or persons designated by the founder who is entitled to exercise this function himself during his lifetime.

Unless the founder has himself set certain limitations, the administrators or trustees are fully entitled, in order to serve the foundation's purposes, to administer the foundation's property as if belonging to them.

Broadly speaking and except for explicit limitations, the trustees are free to administer, invest and dispose of the foundation's capital and can buy, sell, donate, transfer, mortgage and redeem real estate for the price they may deem suitable without need for public auctions; buy, sell, donate, transfer and pledge any kind of securities and goods and chattels which they can deposit and redeem at will; obtain annuities, borrow money, contract loans, reclaim and concede any rights, etc. (cited by way of example and not limiting).

The representation of the foundation devolves upon the physical or juristic persons designated by the founder who can employ agents to negotiate with State, provincial or municipal offices in any transaction, claim or investigation related to the foundation's property.

In all cases, the offices of the representative and of the administrator of the foundation are in the nature of a trust—honorary and non-remunerative—the administrators only being allowed to deduct amounts considered as a reward or as administrative expenses but never as a fixed or permanent remuneration. In no case can the administrator have shares in the capital of the foundation or own part of the foundation's property.

(c) Supervisory or controlling agencies

Bearing in mind that a foundation pursues the satisfaction of collective needs, it is clear that the State has a right to intervene to exercise control over foundations through the State agencies on which the foundation's control devolves, this function being conditioned to the limitations established by the founder.

The main task of the supervisory agencies is to ensure that the will of the founder is carried out and to protect the foundation's administrators in the exercise of their rights with a view to guaranteeing the effective operation of the foundation, but, under no circumstance, can the supervisory agencies overrule the founder's will, altering the purpose, means, organisation or policies stipulated in the foundation's statutes.

Except in the case of the founder having made provision to the contrary, the supervisory agencies can assume the right to dismiss administrators who do not possess the necessary qualifications, to accord authorisation to settle cases in Court, to mortgage or sell real estate, and can demand submission of financial statements and evidence of due execution of the foundation's tasks and responsibilities.

(d) Auditing and submission of accounts

The founder determines the book-keeping procedures to be followed by the foundation. Only in cases where the founder has not made provision for the financial administration of the foundation will the rules laid down by the public authorities come into play.

In principle the foundation's administrators or lawful representatives are bound to submit accounts to the supervisory agencies in accordance with the norms established for that purpose. Nevertheless, and in keeping with the principle that the founder's will is the law of the foundation, the administrators may be exempted from this obligation if the founder has expressly stipulated that the realisation of his will shall be left to the discretion and good faith of the trustee or administrator. In such case, the trustee or administrator is only bound to solemnly declare that the said tasks and responsibilities have been fulfilled in a lawful and moral manner. In other words, in order that the trustees shall be exempted from the obligation to submit accounts to the supervisory agencies, the founder must have clearly and explicitly expressed his will to that effect.

However, the fact that the trustees or administrators are exempt from submitting accounts, only declaring solemnly the proper discharge of their duties, should not be interpreted as meaning that the supervisory agencies cannot demand evidence that the foundation's aims are being fulfilled should this be considered necessary.

(e) Foundations' privileges

The State is interested in encouraging and promoting the establishment of private foundations by, on the one hand, intervening through the supervisory agencies and, on the other hand, protecting their creation and development by granting certain privileges.

Apart from fiscal privileges which will be discussed under the heading *Fiscal regime*, the protection of foundations is evidenced by:

M

Proceedings before Courts of law. Foundations have a right to State aid in all juridical or administrative matters, whether they appear as claimant or defendant, and are not obliged to pay lawyers' or solicitors' fees, or to pay fees to secretaries and officers of the Courts. Moreover, only paper with the letterhead of the Court is used for all written statements and communications.

The defence of foundations in Court devolves upon the lawyers designated by the founder or, in the absence of such provision, upon the Charity Solicitors chosen from amongst renowned lawyers by the Ministry of the Interior.

Protection of foundations' property. The property of foundations cannot be subjected to juridical pressure, therefore, no Court or authority is entitled to issue writs of execution or appropriation orders against the property or income of foundations.

In the case of a foundation pronounced guilty in Court, the sentence will be executed in a similar way to that exercised in sentences against the State, it being incumbent on the supervisory agencies to determine the form in which the sentence against the foundation will be carried out.

III. FISCAL REGIME

1. *In the constitution of foundations*

It has already been indicated that foundations can be created either by an act *inter vivos* or *mortis causa* and, in both cases, foundations are endowed with an initial patrimony which can be a gift, legacy or inheritance.

In each case, the constitution of foundations is exempted from taxes, in general, and exempted from transferred capital and juridical act deeds taxes, in particular, the latter being in Spain the tax on transference and acquisition of real and personal property.

To claim this privilege it is essential that the office of trustee or lawful representative of the foundation should be a non-remunerative appointment.

Once granted, the constitutional act or deed must be submitted to the offices of the Ministry of Finance which will accord tax exemption provided the foundation meets with the necessary prerequisites and will inform the relevant Ministry of the foundation's statutes and the assets intended for its creation. The Ministry will then approve and classify the new foundation and will exercise the supervisory functions.

2. *During the operational life of the foundation*

(a) Local real estate tax

Foundations enjoy total and permanent exemption from paying rates on the buildings in their possession designed to serve a general or local charitable purpose as long as they do not derive an income from such properties.

(b) Corporation income tax

Foundations do not come under the same legal status as corporations, therefore, they are exempt from the income tax which applies to corporations.

In conclusion, they are not compelled to declare their profits nor do they pay any taxes on them.

(c) Tax of juristic persons' property

The juristic persons' tax in Spain is a substitute for the inheritance tax and charges at the yearly rate of 0.5% the capital of foundations and other juristic persons provided that the said capital is not susceptible to hereditary transfer, either directly or through bonds or shares representing the same.

Nevertheless, foundations may be exempted from this tax provided that the appointments of trustee or lawful representative be non-remunerative. To claim exemption from this tax application must be made to the offices of the Ministry of Finance, submitting the foundation's deeds, the order of approval or classification and a statement of the properties which comprise the foundation's patrimony.

(d) Tax on transfer of assets and juristic deeds and general tax on inheritance

Acquisition of liquid assets and real estate realised during the operational life of already established foundations are exempted from capital transfer tax and juristic deeds tax (if the acquisition is transacted by an act *inter vivos*) and inheritance tax (if the acquisition is transacted through gift, inheritance or legacy), provided the appointment of trustee or representative be non-remunerative. To obtain this exemption from the offices of the Ministry of Finance it is essential that the foundation should already have been classified by the relevant Ministry.

(e) Local excise duties

Over and above the privileges granted by the State's fiscal regime, foundations enjoy considerable advantages in provincial and municipal taxation being exempt, for instance, from municipal tax on the increased land value in cases where the land is permanently dedicated to welfare or educational purposes.

(f) Other taxes

Foundations' revenues such as interest, dividends, and other returns derived from shares, bonds and other securities owned by a foundation are liable to capital gains tax, although the responsibility to declare and retain the tax amount falls on the person or organisation paying the benefit to the foundation so that the foundation receives the interest or liquid dividend after tax deduction.

Finally, employees working with foundations are liable to normal taxation having to pay personal income tax. The responsibility for declaring and retaining this tax falls on the foundations.

3. *Other fiscal encouragements*

With the purpose of promoting the creation and development of foundations, physical or juristic persons appropriating any sums of money for welfare or educational purposes are granted certain fiscal advantages in respect of income taxes.

(a) Income tax

With regard to this tax, to determine the basis of taxation, the amounts donated to charitable or educational foundations are deducted from gross annual income if satisfactory evidence has been furnished to the Government's supervisory agencies that the sums in question have directly and permanently been applied to the charitable purposes for which they were appropriated.

(b) Corporation income tax

In the same way, with regard to corporation income tax, to determine the basis of taxation, deduction is made of the amounts donated to third parties for teaching or research purposes. Application for this exemption must be submitted to the Ministry of Finance which will grant or refuse the claim after consideration of the relevant data.

4. *Fees on rendered accounts*

It has already been indicated that, except for the cases in which the founder himself has expressed his will to the contrary, the administrators of a foundation must render an annual account of their administration. These accounts must be submitted to the Provincial Charitable Boards who have a right to exact, as auditing charges, 1% of the annual revenue of the foundation concerned including the *honoraria* which the trustees may receive for administrative services, amounts deducted for administrative costs or even the annuities devolving on the foundation if the trustees give their services voluntarily or no administrative charges were deducted.

The Provincial Boards can reduce the estimated 1% auditing charge or not exact it at all should they deem this appropriate and have sufficient resources to cover their services.

The said percentage is applied to the ordinary income and interest deriving from the foundation's assets, any occasional or extraordinary revenues being exempted from the charge (e.g. added value in the sale of stocks).

Finally, in the case of a founder having relieved the trustees or administrators of the responsibility to render accounts, stating that his will be carried out according to their own conscience, it is clear that no auditing is to be exercised, therefore, no amount can be charged as auditing tax.

IV. NUMBER AND ACTIVITIES OF SPANISH FOUNDATIONS

It is extremely difficult to specify the exact number of Spanish foundations as there are so many small foundations attached to various Ministries[1].

There are three foundations with a capital equal to or exceeding one thousand mill. pesetas (1,000,000,000 ptas.): *Fundación Juan March, Fundación Barrie de la Maza*, and *Fundación Aristrain*. The three have been constituted as dual-purpose foundations and, as such, are under the supervision of the Ministry of the Interior, their objectives being simultaneously both charitable and educational.

[1] The big catholic welfare organization *CARITAS ESPAÑOLA* commissioned a 'Plan for Social Development, Assistance and Welfare' (Plan C.C.B.—Christian Distribution of Wealth) to be followed by the Catholic Church which was published in 1964 (Plan C.C.B.—*Recursos para un plan de promoción social, asistencia social y beneficencia*, Edit. EURAMERICA). The study contains in its para. 6 (pp. 397–406) a detailed analysis of Spanish charitable foundations and quotes (as of 1963) a figure of 4,425 foundations (as against 9,600 in 1913). The nominal value of their assets is reported to amount to over 3,324 mill pesetas (about $48.2 mill or almost £20 mill). 2,981 foundations are under the supervision of the Ministry of the Interior, 1,437 foundations are supervised by the Ministry of Education and 7 by the Ministry of Agriculture. Of the total, 727 foundations are classified as being religious, 117 serve socio-economic aims, 1,435 aim at the relief of poverty ('in favour of the poor'), 725 care for the sick, 1,560 foundations serve educational ends and 811 foundations were set up to pay welfare subsidies and pensions (adds up to more than 4,425 due to the multi-purpose nature of a number of foundations). The Editors.

The *Barrie de la Maza* and *Aristrain* foundations are of recent creation and it would be premature to write about their activities.

The *Fundación Juan March* (founded in 1955), in accordance with its statutes, has for its objective the non-profit satisfaction of physical and intellectual needs. This wide objective comprises:

the creation and maintenance of prizes for culture and merit;

provision for registration fees, certificates, scholarships, or maintenance grants for needy students;

to provide teaching material, to encourage the education and training of workers and, more generally, to support moral, professional and educational training;

to promote culture and scientific research and to intensify scientific, cultural and artistic relations between Spain and other countries;

to create, maintain or assist institutions catering for the welfare of needy persons;

to award prizes for works on religion, philosophy, medicine, surgery, law, the exact, physio-chemical and natural sciences, political and social sciences and economics, literature, history, arts, philanthropy, and social co-operation.

In order to achieve its social objective, the *Fundación Juan March* offers annually:

1. *Research grants*

Grants to Spanish persons who undertake to carry out, within a period of two years, research into any of the following subjects:

Industrial Technology
Mathematics
Physical Sciences
Chemistry
Applied Natural Sciences
Medicine
Law
Economics
History

2. *Fellowships*

To Spanish persons who undertake to produce within one year a working paper on one of the aforementioned subjects.

3. *Grants for literature and the fine arts*

The objective of these grants is to encourage and assist the activities of Spanish persons of proven dedication and ability who devote themselves to literature and the fine arts. A jury selected from amongst outstanding personalities in the country for each subject, awards the scholarships and grants. The selection of jury members devolves on the council of the *Fundación Juan March*, and the highest organisations, both public and private, connected with each of the subjects for which financial assistance is sought.

4. Independently from the aforementioned forms of assistance, the council of the *Fundación Juan March*, if deemed appropriate, studies and considers applications for financial assistance for

homes and orphanages
hospitals and health centres
training schools for workers
works of a socio-religious character
educational organisations, conferences, and seminars
works of a social, cultural, artistic, religious, research or pedagogical character
any other objective of educational or philanthropic character.

France[*]

Michel Pomey

Preliminary Definitions

The term *fondation* (foundation) is commonly used in France in a number of senses covering quite a variety of *de jure* and *de facto* situations.

In principle, however, there ought to be no doubt about its meaning. In French law, the term foundation can only be used, strictly speaking, to designate private non-profit organisations of benefit to the community which are juristic persons established pursuant to the valid French legislation governing foundations. In other words, they must be in possession of a special authorisation from the Government which recognises their character of being in the public interest, i.e. the rough equivalent of 'charitable status', (*d'utilité publique*) and approves their statutes.

In practice, however, this term does not enjoy any protection in law and it is frequently applied—albeit wrongly—to certain private organisations which are admittedly non-profit making, but which are not recognised as having charitable status (mere associations), or even as not possessing a legal personality distinct from that of their actual creators (*de facto* bodies). Nor should one forget to mention private bodies pursuing material gain in some form or other and unscrupulous enough, in certain cases, to flaunt this prestigious title.

It should, furthermore, be borne in mind that the term foundation in its strictest sense, does not cover all private charitable bodies, but only some of them, i.e. those set up in strict conformity with the French law on foundations, an account of which will now be given.

Under the circumstances, if one wished to include under the heading of foundation every private establishment of a philanthropic character, i.e. those serving 'unselfish' aims, one would have to list not only foundations in the strict sense of the term but also other institutions serving the common

[*] Translated from the French.

weal: associations officially recognised as such as well as those which simply make a declaration to the effect that they are associations (*associations simplement declarées*).

I. FOUNDATIONS WITH LEGAL PERSONALITY

In the precise meaning of the word, a foundation in possession of legal personality, and therefore of the capacity to contract, is simply an institution which has been conceived and organised as such by its founder and given explicit non-profit status by the Government in the form of a decree issued by the State Council (*Conseil d'Etat*). The latter recognises a foundation's statutes if they conform with certain standard models which it has established.

In keeping with the administrative provisions enacted by the State Council, foundations are classified:

—as institutions set up by private initiative from a capital endowment, also of private origin, earmarked to provide for the said institution's financial needs (theoretically in perpetuity) by means of the income derived therefrom;

—as institutions administered by their own board of directors whose members are in part appointed by the founder, in part designated by the public authorities by virtue of their personal aptitudes or their official functions, and, in part, co-opted by the other members.

Unlike associations, these foundations have no members as such and consequently no annual general meeting: they are confined to their board of directors which may, in turn, appoint committees and experts to assist them in the discharge of their duties and responsibilities.

They receive no membership subscriptions and their income from outside sources is thus confined to the gifts and legacies (in the form of capital) which they may be authorised to accept as well as the various public or private subsidies which may be accorded them.

Such foundations are subjected to a certain amount of administrative supervision (prior approval of: gifts and legacies, transfer of property or rights, mortgages, loans, standing orders) plus various controls (the annual report, the budget and the accounts must be forwarded to the foundation's competent administrative authority which may, moreover, have the institution inspected).

Finally, in the case of abuse of the statutes, the administrative authority may order the foundation's dissolution and liquidation by asking the State Council to issue a decree withdrawing its status as a charitable institution.

In principle, foundations may only spend the income they derive from their capital. Until recently, the latter had to be invested in public bonds and registered securities and in such real estate as was directly necessary for the attainment of their charitable purpose—and not in profit-making real estate or negotiable securities of any kind. However, this latter restriction has just been lifted by the State Council in regard to foundations proper.

They may only carry out activities which are in conformity with their statutory aims i.e. invariably of a charitable nature. In particular, they are not allowed to participate in industrial or commercial activities which are foreign to such aims. Nor may they distribute any profits to their founders or promoters.

As for charitable organisations set up not as foundations but as associations, they may like any other freely created association apply for official Government recognition as an *établissement d'utilité publique* (i.e. an organisation serving the public interest), a status which is conferred by a State Council decree.

The Government then instructs them to draw up their statutes in conformity with certain standard models which have also been established by the State Council for such associations. Their standing regulations are very similar to those described above for foundations. Above all, they qualify to receive gifts and legacies although, in each case, they require permission from their administrative authority. However, in contrast to foundations, 'recognised' associations—like any other association—have paying members as well as a general meeting of such members who nominate and supervise the board of directors.

Finally, charitable bodies may simply be set up in the form of 'mere associations' (simple associations) pursuant to the Law of 1st July 1901 on associations. In this case, they can be established in complete freedom, especially as far as their statutes, organisation and operation are concerned, with the sole exception of the requirement that a Court of Law must confirm that they are really charitable (non-commercial). Nevertheless, if they wish to acquire a legal personality and thus the capacity to act as such, they must notify the general public to this effect by submitting a declaration to their administrative authority together with a copy of their statutes and a list of their leading members.

Yet even in a case like this, the 'mere association' enjoys fewer rights than a recognised non-profit association. Above all, they are not allowed to accept gifts or legacies unless the objects they pursue are exclusively those of beneficence and assistance (Law of 14th January 1933). They may, however, accept public subsidies, and also private subsidies provided that they first obtain from the administrative authorities the special authorisation to this end, which has hitherto been reserved to bodies engaging in activities of scientific interest.

II. FOUNDATIONS WITHOUT LEGAL PERSONALITY

As we have indicated above, foundations and recognised non-profit associations enjoy almost total freedom as legal persons within the confines of the conditions and limits established in their statutes. As for mere associations, they also enjoy legal personality, but are subject to narrower limitations.

The only charitable bodies which exist without legal personality are those set up either as mere *de facto* organisations or as 'undeclared' associations. Such bodies, however, cannot be deemed to constitute foundations.

III. ANALOGOUS INSTITUTIONS

There are no other forms which charitable or benevolent bodies may take other than those cited above. Nevertheless, there are certain organisations such as the trade societies and associations and their centres for scientific and technological research, and the mutual aid societies, etc., which have a number of features in common with the aforementioned charitable bodies: they do to a certain extent serve the public interest. They cannot, on the other hand, be said to pursue really 'unselfish' aims in view of the fact that their *raison d'être* is to operate for the benefit not of the public as a whole but for their own members.

These various bodies are governed by special legislation and provisions and cannot really be described as charitable bodies, and certainly not as foundations.

IV. COMMERCIAL ENTERPRISES IN THE FORM OF FOUNDATIONS

In France, any activities carried on with the aim of securing a profit to be shared amongst a number of people may only be pursued either by private individuals or within the legal framework of civil law or commercial law companies. Such aims could not be pursued by a foundation or by any other kind of charitable body ('recognised' and 'declared'—or 'mere'—associations).

Although charitable bodies may not seek to distribute profits amongst their beneficiaries, this does not mean that they are not allowed to engage in profit-making activities, and, in particular, in activities of a commercial nature, provided that such activities are compatible with their charitable object, are necessary for its realisation, and are solely of a subsidiary nature.

V. LEGISLATION GOVERNING FOUNDATIONS

Foundations, recognised and mere associations are private bodies governed by private law and, therefore, subject to the common law jurisdiction of Civil Courts. The latter have exclusive competence to deal with disputes that may arise, for example, with third parties, beneficiaries, members or staff, etc. On the other hand, as regards their relations with the State any litigation in which the latter is implicated falls under the jurisdiction of the administrative tribunals (Courts of first instance, and the State Council in its capacity of the Court of Appeal and Supreme Court).

This would particularly apply in the case of litigation questioning a decree issued by the State Council which granted or withdrew recognition of charitable status, or of an administrative provision approving or rejecting a decision relating to areas directly subject to official supervision (e.g. acceptance of a gift or legacy).

Naturally, in any such cases heard before an administrative Court, questions which come exclusively within the purview of civil law (for example, matters concerning testaments and inheritances) may have to be referred by these Courts to a Civil Judge for a preliminary hearing.

VI. THE TAXATION OF FOUNDATIONS

Foundations and, in part, other charitable institutions enjoy a number of tax advantages in France. We shall take a look at their fiscal situation, firstly from the point of view of the foundation itself and then from the point of view of its benefactors.

It should be pointed out straightaway that there are no fiscal provisions in France which are solely applicable to foundations as such, or even to foundations and recognised charitable associations. They are thus subject to the same general rules which apply to all non-profit bodies.

The fiscal situation of foundations proper

First of all, a brief outline will be given of the tax on gifts, the tax on profits, the turnover tax, and the other taxes.

1. The tax on gifts

Endowment

In theory, tax exemption is granted—as it is to all other associations—in respect of movable effects whilst a reduced rate of 1.60% is levied on real estate.

Gifts and legacies

In their capacity as charitable bodies, foundations are entitled to receive gifts and legacies subject in each case to administrative authorisation. The same is true of recognised associations, though not of 'mere associations'. In principle such gifts *inter vivos* or *mortis causa* are liable to the tax paid on the gratuitous transfer of ownership (*droits de mutation à titre gratuit*). In the case of non-profit organisations i.e. including foundations, however, these taxes are usually reduced or even waived. Thus, after making provision for a reduction in tax in Arts. 781 and 782, the *Code Général des Impôts* currently grants complete exemption from tax, by virtue of Art. 1231, in respect of gifts and legacies in the form of:

— works of art, monuments or other objects of a historic character and books, printed documents or manuscripts earmarked for display in a public collection;

— sums of money or real estate if these gifts are earmarked for the purchase and preservation of the above-mentioned works of art, monuments, etc.;

— gifts and legacies earmarked for work of a beneficial, non-profit character, whether scientific or even cultural or artistic, provided that, in the latter case, the relevant work and/or donee body has obtained prior approval from the Minister of Finance;

— gifts and legacies granted to charitable bodies active in the field of free higher or popular education which are subsidised by the State, or in the field of poor relief, provided that, in the latter instance, the beneficent character of the body in question is recognised in the administrative act authorising acceptance.

2. *Tax on profits*

General tax on income (company tax)

In its capacity as a charitable institution—duly recognised as such by the decree which brought it into existence—and, therefore not pursuing 'selfish' ends (even to the extent of excluding any distribution of profits to interested parties), a foundation—which may indeed, as already indicated, make and even seek to make a profit—is not liable to company tax in respect of the totality of its income and the overall profit which may be derived therefrom; nor it is liable to the industrial and commercial gains tax (*BIC i.e. bénéfices commercials et industriels*)—(*Art. 206 of the Code Général des Impôts—C.G.I.*). However, it may well be liable to taxation in respect of some of its income.

Taxes on certain types of income

Pursuant to para.5 of Art. 206, a foundation, even if it is not subject to company tax, is nevertheless liable to the said tax in respect of the income it derives from:
— the letting or occupation of premises or landed property;
— the running of farming or forestry enterprises;
— movable assets (if not already taxed at source).

In these three cases, the tax is not levied at the full rate but at the reduced rate of 24% (Art. 219), or at least insofar as and to the extent that these various revenues are not inextricably linked with a main or subsidiary activity of a commercial nature, which would be subject to taxation at the full rate. *A priori*, this ought not to be the case with a foundation provided, of course, that its objects, actual activities and the way in which it is run are duly checked.

This principle, which is self-evident and is, moreover, applied in the jurisdiction of the administrative Courts, has finally been confirmed (at least indirectly) by the provision contained in Art. 208 of the C.G.I.

By virtue of this article, institutions of a social or charitable character are exempt from company tax pursuant to Art. 206 para.1 in respect of profits stemming from their profit-making activities insofar as these activities are exempt from turnover tax as provided for in Arts. 271–44 and 1575–2–36. As will be seen below, the said provisions are applicable to foundations.

3. *Turnover tax (T.V.A.)*

In accordance with Art. 8 para. 1 No. 9 of the Law of 6th January 1966, the transactions of non-profit undertakings are exempt from turnover or value added tax (*taxe sur la valeur ajoutée*). Hence, this applies to foundations, which are of a social or charitable character:

(a) either when the remuneration attaching to these transactions does not correspond to the cost of the services rendered and the resources of the bodies concerned are made up by contributions from public or private charity;

(b) or when the prices charged have been endorsed by the public authorities, the conduct of business is of an 'unselfish' nature, and analogous transactions have not been generally engaged in by enterprises which are subject to the tax.

In regard to the implementation of the above-mentioned para. (b), decree No. 67–731 of 30th August 1967 is very precise in its description of those elements which characterise the management of non-profit undertakings.

Even though it is limited in its objective, this provision is applicable to all bodies which claim exemption, and hence this includes foundations. In order to benefit from this provision, they must satisfy the criteria laid down by the decree and carry out activities which fulfil either one of the conditions contained in paras. (a) or (b) of Art.8 para.1 No.9 referred to above.

This being said, it should be pointed out that the decree of 30th August 1967 recapitulates the provisions of Art.1 of decree 66–737 of 30th September 1966 and specifies in detail the arrangements for granting exemption which were envisaged by former legislation (Art. 29 of Ordinance No. 58–1372 of 29th December 1958; Art. 271–44 and 1575–2–36 of the C.G.I.) in favour of organisations of a social or charitable character, and that Art. 2 of the latter decree relates to transactions identical to those defined in paras. (a) and (b) of Art. 8 para.1 No. 9.

It follows that the exemption which foundations of a social or charitable character could enjoy in the past is still valid in analogous circumstances since the entry into force of the law of 6th January 1966. The replacement of the concept of 'institution' or 'body' (*oeuvre*) by that of 'undertaking' (*organisme*), does not alter the field of application for the said exemption.

As for foundations which are particularly concerned with the provision of institutionalised care for the sick and disabled they continue to benefit from the exemptions which were specifically devised for them under the provisions of Art. 271–31 of the C.G.I. amended by those of Art. 55 of the Finance Law for 1966.

4. *Other taxes*

(a) Trade tax (*patente*)

In conformity with administrative jurisprudence, foundations are in principle exempt from the payment of trade tax in the same circumstances as those obtaining for exemption from turnover tax and income tax.

(b) Entertainment tax

If they stage entertainments, foundations may—according to their making use of such events—benefit from the preferential treatment envisaged in Arts. 1561 and 1562 of the C.G.I.

(c) Miscellaneous taxes

Finally, in the case of all the taxes which only take account of the existence of persons, things or acts, foundations as juristic persons are governed by common law and are thus not subject to any special preferential treatment. This applies, for instance, in regard to:

— the taxes on tenants (rent tax, municipal taxes, on billiard tables, pianos, registration of interest rates);
— the real estate taxes (land taxes—but allowing, of course, for the exemptions provided for under common law);
— the tax on employers (1% on accommodation, 5% on wages for Social Security, etc. but not the apprenticeship tax which is tied to the tax on industrial and commercial gains);
— the stamp and registration tax.

As for the tax charged on the transfer of ownership effected for gain, foundations enjoy a reduced rate of 4.20% (2.80% + 1.40%) if real estate is acquired which is necessary for the accomplishment of objects relating to assistance, welfare or health.

VII. THE TAX TREATMENT OF FOUNDATION BENEFACTORS

In addition to gifts and bequests of capital (which make the beneficiary liable to the tax on the transfer of ownership indicated above), foundations are permitted to receive from private persons or companies cash payments deducted from the latter's income.

In the case of private individuals, i.e. anyone other than a business or company, who are thereby exempt from the company tax, Art. 238 of the C.G.I. allows deduction of up to 0.5% of the taxable income on payments made to charitable undertakings or bodies pursuing educational, scientific, social or family objects, and, therefore, to foundations in particular. No special authorisation is required in this connection.

As for business and companies, which are subject to the tax on commercial and industrial gains or to company tax, a deduction is admissible of up to 0.1% of turnover for charitable payments of the same order as specified above (Art. 238 *bis*), and of up to an additional 0.2% for payments to bodies, in particular to foundations, engaging in scientific or technological research and especially approved by the Minister of Finance (Art. 238 *bis* A), albeit for a limited period of time (see lists of permits at the B.O.C.D.: Ordinances of 15th January 1964, 2nd February 1965 and 21st December 1965).

VIII. THE CURRENT SITUATION OF FOUNDATIONS

It is not easy to describe the current *de facto* position of French foundations

N

because so little is known about them. There is in fact no directory or list of foundations and other charitable bodies comparable with, for example, the Foundation Directory in the USA.

Admittedly, the Ministry of the Interior is drawing up a list—complete with name, address, special characteristics, etc.—but only for his own use. He has not yet given the general public access to it[1]. Similarly, the decrees issued by the State Council which grant recognition to foundations as charitable bodies and approve their statutes are only published in the Official Gazette (*Journal Officiel*) in the form of extracts which, notably, exclude the statutes. Nor are foundations very forthcoming about their activities, finances and organisation, or about their founders and directors. Only in exceptional cases do they publish annual reports.

Moreover, there are not a great number of foundations in France—unlike associations which are legion—and they are not very affluent. The result is that, although satisfactory legal provision has been made for them, they have never formed the subject of a fundamental law similar to the 1901 Law on Associations. All in all, they hardly ever attract the attention of the public or of specialists, not even legal experts.

When one adds that many authentic foundations do not designate themselves as such, whereas other organisations which are not, strictly speaking, foundations avail themselves of this prestigious name, and that charitable institutions of such importance as the Red Cross, Catholic Aid, the *Institut de France* or the *Collège de France* do not belong to the category of foundations, it is understandable that so little is known about foundations in France and that their value is not duly appreciated. Hence, it is well worth while to attempt to give a brief account of their number, importance, activities and organisation.

[1] However, this list was published at the beginning of 1970 (Ministère de l'Interieur: Fondations, Journaux Officiels No. 1351, Paris 1970). It is preceded by remarks on the development of foundations and charitable endowments, the legal status of foundations and the appropriate provisions of civil and fiscal law. The list concludes with the full text of a State notification of permission and a model set of articles of association (statutes). The list itself enumerates 259 foundations, which were established between 1666 and 1969.

In addition, in the summer of 1971 a 'Directory of Charitable Foundations in France' (FONDATIONS reconnues d'utilité publique en France) was published by Jean-Jaques Soulis. This handbook covers about 240 foundations, classified according to their fields of interest (cultural foundations, educational foundations, research foundations, health foundations, and relief foundations), and reports about the foundation's aims, its organisational structure, its financial resources, its history, gives a biography of the founder and the president, and finally, lists the names and functions of the members of the Board of Directors. (The Editors)

1. *The number and the significance of French foundations*

According to a recent census conducted by the Ministry of the Interior, it is estimated that there are about 250 foundations in France. Although not many new ones are set up, recent years have nevertheless witnessed the successive creation of a certain number which have attracted attention: *Maison des Sciences de l'Homme, Fondation Royaumont, Fondation Maeght, Fondation pour la Recherche Médicale Française, Maison de la Chasse et de la Nature, Fondation Nationale pour la Gerontologie, Fondation Nationale pour l'Enseignement de la Gestion des Entreprises, Fondation Le Corbusier* and, quite recently, the *Fondation de France*. In addition, there are plans for many more. In other words, the current situation seems to be marked by a revival of interest.

On the other hand, it is very rare for foundations to be wound up: even when they run out of assets they vegetate for a long time before disappearing.

Most of the 250 existing foundations are of rather limited importance and impact. The reason is that the day is long past when private fortunes in France were, on their own and whatever the circumstances, large enough to secure for foundations a future safe from economic and financial crises, and those which would still be in a position to do so receive hardly any encouragement from the public authorities in general and the Inland Revenue in particular. Furthermore, the initial capital of most of the older foundations has virtually melted away because of monetary depreciation.

By and large, French foundations have not been successful either in bringing in new men and new ideas and in initiating new activities. Be that as it may, some of them are nevertheless active institutions which have achieved great fame, even if it is not always realised that they are in fact foundations. Their number includes for example: the *Société Philanthropique* (established in 1780), *Fondation Thiers, Institut Pasteur* and *Musée Social* (now = *CEDIAS*) —all three of them being founded in the 1890s— the *Singer-Polignac* and *Rothschild* foundations, *Maison de la Chimie*, the *Orphelins d'Auteuil*, etc., and, of course, the *Fondation Nationale des Sciences Politiques* which was established in 1945 so that the former *Ecole libre des sciences politiques* could be nationalised but at the same time preserve a part of its status in private law.

Almost all foundations were set up on the initiative of private individuals and their families. There are virtually no examples in France of foundations established, promoted and financed by business firms. Moreover, the latter are obliged by law to entrust their social security schemes to the so-called *comités d'entreprises*.

As there is no legal equivalent in France to the charitable trusts in Anglo-

Saxon countries, there have been no examples of collective foundations like the community trusts in the USA until the very recent creation of the *Fondation de France*. Nonetheless, a certain number of foundations have been established on the initiative of the public authorities, generally for the purpose of running in co-operation with the interested parties, social service schemes or certain semi-public facilities for teaching, studies and research.

As the relevant information is not available to the public, it is impossible to estimate the financial strength of French foundations either in regard to their assets or their expenditure. The truth would seem to be that, with few exceptions, their financial power is on a very modest scale both individually and collectively. Their importance in relation to the overall national budget is minimal just as it is in relation to that of French charitable activity as a whole which is still largely in the hands of private persons and religious institutions.

2. *The activities of French foundations*

Until the recent creation of the *Fondation de France*, there was no example in this country of a general-purpose foundation. Generally speaking, foundations have a more or less narrowly defined object or set of objectives which fall within various sectors of general public interest, and particularly within those comprising the traditional domain of charitable activity, for example:

Assistance and beneficence

Asylums, old peoples homes, homes for the blind, the deaf-and-dumb and sick children (*Fondation Anne de Gaulle*) orphanages (*Orphelins d'Auteuil*), and various others (*Rothschild, Furtado-Heine, Cognacq-Jay, Société Philanthropique* etc.).

Health

Fondation médicale franco-américaine du Mont-Valérien (*Hôpital Foch*), *Hôpital américain, Sanatorium des étudiants, Fondation Curie*, the regional centres for the fight against cancer, *Hôpital des Jockeys de Maisons-Laffitte*, etc.

Social welfare and similar amenities

The *Enfants du Métro, Fondation Louis Lépine* (*Préfecture de Police*), *Fondation d'Aguesseau* (Ministry of Justice), *Cité Universitaire Internationale, Fondation Deutsch de la Meurthe, Office du Tourisme Universitaire*, etc.

Research

Academic—*Fondation Thiers, Fondation Singer-Polignac, Institut de Synthèse,*

Comité de l'Encyclopédie Française, Fondation Teilhard de Chardin, etc.

Medical—*Institut Pasteur, Fondation Calmettes, Institut Gustave Roussy, Centre de recherches chirurgicales Poincaré à* Strasbourg, *Fondation pour la recherche médicale Française, Fondation nationale de Gérontologie.*

Scientific or technological—*Institut de paléontologie, Institut d'optique, Bureau d'études géologiques et minières, Centre scientifique et technique du batiment, Maison de la Chimie,* etc.

Social sciences and humanities—*CEDIAS—Musée Social, Centre français de droit comparé, Institut d'aménagement et d'urbanisme de la région parisienne, Maison des sciences de l'homme, Fondation Royaumont (Gouin-Lang) pour le progrès des sciences de l'homme,* etc.

Teaching—*Fondation Nationale des sciences politiques, Institut catholique de Lille, Ecoles d'art américaines de Fontainbleau, Fondation Nationale pour l'Enseignement de la gestion des Entreprises,* plus the above-mentioned research institutions, etc.

Memorials, museums and other collections—*Fondation Clemenceau, Fondation de Chambrun-La Fayette—mémorial de l'escadrille La Fayette, Institut néerlandais, Musée Cognacq-Jay, Maison de la Chasse et de la Nature, Fondation Le Corbusier.*

Arts and culture—*Fondation Laurent Vibert à* Lourmarin, *Cité Internationale des Arts, Fondation Royaumont, Fondation Maeght à* St. Paul de Vence, etc.

International activities—*Centre international de l'enfance, Cité Internationale des arts, Bourses Zellidja,* etc.

It will be seen that recent foundations have departed from the traditional sectors of assistance, welfare and public health, etc., which are increasingly becoming the direct responsibility of the State, and they are turning towards fresh tasks such as medical research, the social sciences or international relations even in cases where, like, for instance, the *Royaumont* and *Maeght* foundations, they are also committed to more classical, artistic and cultural pursuits.

3. Organisation and operation of foundations

Without reconsidering in detail the internal workings of foundations, it should be pointed out that, as regards their organisation, they are administered by a board of directors (*conseil d'administration*) composed of honorary members who, on the one hand, represent either the founder and his family or the public authorities and, on the other, are chosen from among outsiders who are often prominent public figures. However, it is fairly rare to find businessmen, lawyers or even financial experts amongst them. Moreover, their management is entirely disinterested and has no connection with the business world. The staff is usually kept to a minimum and it is only the most important foundations which have people working for them on a full-time basis, and, in particular, call on outside specialists for expert advice, generally on a voluntary, non-remunerative, basis.

As regards their financial affairs, foundations rely in principle on the income they derive from their capital which originates in the gift originally made by the founder, or in exceptional cases, in a public subscription (*Institut Pasteur, Maison de la Chimie*) together with any gifts and legacies which may subsequently have come their way.

This capital takes the form of immovable assets, generally real estate needed for the proper functioning of the institution—or sometimes, albeit rarely, leasehold property—or transferable securities.

They may also enjoy income obtained from the exploitation of their assets if this is a legitimate by-product of the pursuit of their charitable purpose. Examples are admission charges for historic monuments or museums; daily rates for hospital care and even reimbursement of social security payments in relation thereto; the proceeds of the sale of vaccines in the case of the *Institut Pasteur* or of artistic documents in the case of the *Fondation Maeght*, etc.

As for regular payments from individuals or firms, they are still on an extremely modest scale within the framework of the current provision for tax deductibility in respect of income or profits. These advantages are often not used at all by firms either because they seem too slight to be really of interest or because there is a lack of information about the possibilities of charitable giving, or because the spirit of charitable giving is not sufficiently developed, or simply because profit margins are too small. Mention should nevertheless be made of the recently constituted *Fondation pour la recherche médicale française* which mounted a particularly active campaign and managed to collect more than 4 mill. francs in 1965–6. Two thirds of this sum came from firms or public institutions.

The same applies to public subsidies, unless the foundation is closely associated with a public service (social work carried out by a given ministry, *Fondation Nationale des sciences politiques, Institut d'aménagement et d'urbanisme de la région parisienne*). In the future, however, foundations pursuing objects of scientific interest should have a greater share of public funds at their disposal for research purposes as should those active in the field of health and of social and cultural activity.

As regards their expenditure, their running costs are normally modest and the foundations distribute the funds available to them in the form of payments and subsidies of various kinds or in the form of in-house activities. Sometimes both forms of support are given.

IX. THE ATTITUDE AND PRACTICE ADOPTED BY GOVERNMENT AND GOVERNMENT ADMINISTRATION *vis-à-vis* FOUNDATIONS

Traditionally, foundations in France have always been regarded with a certain amount of suspicion by Government. Their precipitate growth prior to 1789 was in fact accompanied by a number of abuses and this led the Revolution to suppress all of them. The indictment covered *mortmain*, the position of foundations as intermediary institutions between the State and the people, the vanity of the founders, etc.

Moreover, the French State has always considered it its prerogative to make due provision, through its public services, for all areas of general public need and interest: schools, universities, hospitals, museums, etc. The result is that the charitable, or philanthropic, sector (i.e. including the foundations) has never really developed very much—with few exceptions such as the *Institut Pasteur*—all the more so as private fortunes have been on the decrease. However, the principles of concerted economic action, decentralisation and participation have stimulated renewed interest in their favour in recent times and over the last few years the Government has officially accorded charitable status to a number of foundations.

It should also be stressed that, in everyday practice, foundations and associations enjoy almost total liberty of action, free from any inopportune interference on the part of the administrative authorities, in spite of the fact that, by virtue of their recognised charitable status, they are subject to administrative supervision. Such intervention only in fact occurs on the occasion of the creation or dissolution of the foundation (award or withdrawal of charitable status) as well as on the occasion of additions to *mortmain* property (authorisation of gifts and legacies).

X. MOVES TOWARDS REFORMING FOUNDATION LAW

Current studies and research seem to point in the following directions:
— an increase in fiscal advantages, especially in favour of private foundation benefactors;

— the creation of collective foundations either of a 'mixed' character—i.e. linking both the private and public sectors—or in the form of trusteeships —i.e. general-purpose foundations empowered to gather in funds and redistribute them in the same fashion as the 'Community Trusts' in the USA. This is particularly true of the *Fondation de France*, which was recently set up by a group of public and private financial institutions.

XI. THE FUTURE OF FOUNDATIONS IN FRANCE

In conclusion, it may be stated (although this presupposes an improvement in their fiscal status) that French foundations will develop in three directions in future.

Firstly, it may be assumed that despite the reduction in large private fortunes, a number of the traditional type of foundations will be set up. They will owe their existence exclusively to the initiative of a private person and to the funds forthcoming either during his lifetime or upon his decease from the whole or part of his fortune and will generally have a limited objective determined by the founder in accordance with his special wishes and the resources at his disposal.

Such initiative may obviously only be encouraged if it involves an object which is of irrefutable and lasting public interest and at the same time backed by sufficient financial support to guarantee both initially and in the face of all eventualities that it will survive and develop in a normal manner.

If these preconditions are lacking, it would be better to discourage initiatives which, though generous, are too hazardous, and instead to invite the persons concerned to join forces with similar ventures which are either already in existence or planned for the future.

That is why it would appear appropriate to maintain the requirement in regard to the establishment of a foundation that the State Council must issue a decree recognising the foundation as a viable charitable organisation.

In the normal way, such foundations ought essentially to be able to live on their own resources (income from their capital endowment or from the profitable activities permitted by their statutes) without excluding, but only as a subsidiary source, occasional outside contributions (public subsidies or, rather, private donations given either direct or via organisations of the 'trust' type which we shall be describing at a later stage). However, as the latter source of money is of an unpredictable character, it can only play a supple-mentary role and could provide the necessary minimum financial basis needed to ensure the viability of the foundation. As a result, even though it would be desirable to accord their outside benefactors the benefit of a reduction in the tax on income and profits, they would above all need to be exempted themselves from any tax on their own assets and activities.

In the second place, there is likely to develop a new type of foundation of a mixed character, closely combining both private and public initiative and finance and conceived not so much as a private, initial endowment permanently earmarked for a special purpose but a living body operated by a flexible and collective management to fulfil a mission of general public interest, necessary in its own right, at every stage of its existence.

In regard to foundations of this type, such backing on the part of the public sector will constitute, *a priori*, a guarantee that they are of general public interest and thus augur well for the future. This would not be sufficient, however, to assure a sound financial basis.

In view of the collective, rather than individual, character of the venture, the requisite financial basis ought normally to be assured by public and private contributions from outside.

As regards private funding, this will only be forthcoming if exemption from the tax on income and profits is accorded to contributors, i.e. to private persons in particular and not just to firms. Fiscal reform to this end is thus the essential prerequisite for the development of this type of foundation.

As regards public funding, and even if it turns out that the public authorities take an interest in the venture, give it their backing and take concrete action towards bringing the foundation into being, it would not be enough to just count on mere promises of financial assistance from this quarter in view of the unpredictability of political and budgetary developments. If such funding is necessary and envisaged, it ought to be guaranteed in advance by binding commitments in due and proper form drawn up by financial experts.

Mixed foundations of this kind could be set up, without involving undue duplication of effort in the various sectors of general public interest, either with a highly specialised object such as the fight against cancer or the advancement of music or with a fairly broad objective such as medical research or the advancement of culture, broken down into subdivisions (cancer, heart diseases, music, plastic arts, etc.).

The third thing which would have to be done to close the principal gap on the current French scene would be to take the charitable trusts in Anglo-Saxon countries and, in particular, the community trusts in the USA as a model and, allowing, of course, for the essential modifications, to bring about the establishment of an entirely new type of foundation. The aim of the latter would not be to intervene directly in any particular charitable scheme, but to support all of them by collecting private gifts from private persons or firms in the form of capital or income and to regroup the latter into large units without overriding the individual wishes and preferences of the donors and to administer them efficiently, principally by investing in as secure and profitable a way as possible. It would then redistribute the profits and even the capital gains and some of the capital for the purpose designated by the benefactors in favour of various organisations serving the public interest, especially other charitable institutions which they would support financially on a large scale instead of competing with them. Moreover, it would be easy to build in the appropriate controls and guarantees.

Such trusts, which would have to operate above all with outside support in the form of capital or contributions, are obviously only feasible if given the above-mentioned fiscal advantages for the benefit of their contributors as well as in respect of the income they derive from the management of the funds with which they have been entrusted.

In order to be able to collect such funds on a sufficiently broad basis— according to the law of large numbers—it would be necessary for these foundations to be able to satisfy the countless wishes of potential donors and thus to pursue not a specialised purpose but a general one which could accommodate any charitable scheme and to be subdivided into specialised sections for the distribution of funds. By virtue of their dual, i.e. financial and charitable role, these foundations ought undoubtedly to emulate the example of the Charitable Trusts: they should on the one hand be set up in close co-operation with financial bodies which can offer every guarantee and, on the other hand, to have a distribution committee which is largely accessible to outside persons.

This is the case with the *Fondation de France*, whose recent creation was thus an event of considerable importance.

LITERATURE

Brichet, Robert Etablissements d'intérêt public: fondations, in: Répertoire Dalloz administratif.

Canet, Louis Le régime des Fondations en France, in: Livre Jubilaire du Conseil d'Etat 1949, Sirey, 1952.

Chassagnade Belmin, Paul Fondation, in: Encyclopédie Dalloz—Droit Civil.

L'Huillier, Jean Etablissements d'utilité publique, in: Répertoire Dalloz administratif.

Ozanam, Charles Associations, Syndicats et Fondations, Sirey, 1964.

Pomey, Michel Le Mécénat et les Fondations. Notes et Etudes Documentaires. La Documentation Francaise, Paris 1966;
Les Fondations en France et aux Etats-Unis, published by Fondation Royaumont, Paris 1967;
Des institutions d'avenir: les Fondations, in: revue 'Promotions', 3 trimestre, Paris 1968.

Sauvel, Tony Les fondations, leurs origines, leur évolution, in: Revue de Droit Public, 1954.

Soulis, Jean-Jaques Fondations reconnues d'utilité publique en France. Les Éditions du Vieux-Logis S.A., Clichy-sous-Bois, 1971.

Fondation de France Décret du 9 janvier 1969, Journal Officiel du 15/1, p. 500.

Journaux Officiels Associations—Fondations (textes législatifs et réglementaires, fonctionnement, modèles de statuts), Paris 1966.

Journaux Officiels Fondations, Paris 1970.

Rapports préparatoires à la Société d'Etudes Législatives Paris 1937, Sirey.

Semaine internationale du Droit, 1937 (III) (see especially the paper of Pierre de Font Reaulx).

England and Wales

Christopher P. Hill

Introduction and General Observations

1. The word 'foundation' has no precise significance in English law, and in common parlance varies in meaning. It tends to connote a permanent charitable institution supported by income from property rather than by subscriptions or collections. In a stricter sense it implies that the institution was 'founded' by a single large donation of property, only the income from which is to be used for the charitable purpose prescribed by the 'founder'. It would be mistaken however to suppose that all institutions in Great Britain with a charitable endowment are entitled 'foundations' or now possess great wealth, although collectively they represent a great part of the charitable effort of the country. Moreover, in modern times it has become the practice not to restrict the power of the charity trustees (the persons conducting the charity) to spend capital, and to rely instead on their observance of the general intention of the donor that the benefits should continue indefinitely. Some 'foundations' therefore have no permanent endowment in the legal sense.

2. The most important distinction in this field of English law is between 'charities' and other undertakings. The term 'charity' includes a great range of philanthropic institutions, with widely varying objects. Those which are 'charities' enjoy a number of constitutional and fiscal privileges, including protection by the Crown in the interests of the community; those which are not, are treated as purely private undertakings. It is of primary importance for an understanding of the English system, to appreciate that the Crown has for centuries undertaken in substance, to secure that private property devoted to public charitable purposes shall be used only for the purpose prescribed by the donor, and enforces this obligation for ever, subject to modifications to meet changing circumstances. The system therefore favours the accumulation of property by a viable charitable institution; and many charities of varying origin have now consequently grown to positions of great wealth

and widespread benefaction; many others, of course, have failed to survive.
3. Institutions are 'charities' if they are established for 'charitable' purposes
only, in the sense in which 'charitable' is interpreted by the Courts; they are
not charities if they are established for purposes which are not 'charitable' or
are not exclusively 'charitable'. The form of the institution is of little
importance; each, whether established as a trust by deed or will, as a corporation by Royal Charter or Act of Parliament, as a registered company, or as an
unincorporated association, is subject to the particular code of law applicable
to that class of institution, whether charitable or not. All 'charities' however
are treated alike, in that the law of trusts is applied to the persons administering the charity property; they are regarded as trustees holding the property
for the benefit of the community, and liable to account for it to the Courts.
4. Much of the work that in other countries is carried on by 'foundations' of
comparatively recent origin, is here performed by charities of other kinds,
for instance associations incorporated by Royal Charter, such as the Royal
Society, which in the course of years have developed some of the characteristics mentioned above by the accumulation of many benefactions, particularly legacies, from many sources. The fact is that the growth of charitable
institutions in this country has continued without interruption for 400 years
and their origins can be traced back for a further four centuries. As a result
of this process of development, such institutions today display an enormous
variety of form, wealth, and purpose, and their funds are usually derived
from more than one source. It would be wrong therefore to assume that any
sharply differentiated class of 'foundation' can be distinguished unless the
term is given an arbitrary definition. In order to make the position intelli-
gible, it is necessary to give a brief account of the unique English law of
charity.
5. First, however, it is perhaps worth pointing out that the difference between
English and American usage of the term has a historical basis. A typical
USA 'foundation' comes into existence by the gift of large blocks of shares
in a commercial enterprise in the modern world of well-developed civiliza-
tion and communications. This has only become possible as a result of the
invention of the joint stock company, and can only occur when the economic
system allows and the economic situation favours the accumulation of great
surpluses of wealth in the hands of individuals. In this country, likewise, the
founders of some modern commercial empires have used their assets to
create large charitable foundations e.g. the Nuffield Foundation, the Wolfson
Foundation, the Wellcome Trust. But, here, the period of economic
expansion when in proportion to the population, the greatest amount of
private wealth was devoted to public charitable purposes, occurred three

centuries ago, when the main transmissible form of wealth was land, and communications and public services remained undeveloped. It was in those times that, in quite different circumstances, very many English charities were 'founded'; and the variety of their development since that time has imparted to the English meaning of the term 'foundation' a latitude which American usage probably does not yet admit.

6. As the researches of Professor W. K. Jordan have shown (see e.g. 'Philanthropy in England, 1480–1660', Allen & Unwin, 1962), during that period the public welfare services of this island were shaped by an enormous outpouring of wealth (comparable to that now proceeding in the USA) by an intelligent class of merchants inspired by a clear and common vision of the society they wished to see, in the fields of education, of care for the young, the poor, the sick and the aged, and of religion. There was a strong tendency to localise the benefits to the inhabitants of some particular area with which the donor was connected; and since the unit of local administration at the time was the parish or the borough, the great majority, numerically, of English charities with a permanent endowment were thus limited to such area. They might have been, and in many cases were, denominated 'foundations'; and they have survived as the precursors, and often the basis, of modern welfare services, but characteristically remain localised, even though the process of modernisation may have greatly enlarged the original area of benefit.

7. The value of the endowments of such charities has often varied capriciously, however; where they consisted of rents or similar fixed charges, the fall in the value of money may have reduced them to minimal proportions, whereas if they comprised freeholds of land, the increase in value of e.g. some fields in what was the village, but is now the City of Westminster, may have produced a wholly unexpected increase in the benefits available. It is part of the history of the law of charity that machinery has been set up to ensure that such increases are applied to the best effect connected with the original intention of the 'founder'. This may be a convenient point to mention the important reforms carried out by the Charities Act 1960, which recognised the principle of co-operation between statutory and voluntary social services as equal partners in the modern Welfare State, and provided up-to-date machinery, including a classified central register of charities, to enable charity resources to be used to the best effect in today's changing social conditions, under the tutelage of a body of Charity Commissioners.

8. Enough has perhaps been said to explain why no exact parallel to the USA concept of 'foundations' would be valid in the English scene, and their functional counterparts may be encountered in any of the numerous varieties

of charitable institution known to English law. Indeed it is probable that most examples will resemble USA 'foundations' in some respects but not in others. As an example, the Royal Foundation of Saint Katherine, Ratcliffe, in East London was established by Queen Matilda in 1148 as a religious house and hospitalry where the sick could be cared for and strangers lodged. After centuries of vicissitudes in meeting changing needs, it now provides, in its present premises near the original site, a small religious community, the borough local authority and voluntary services' centre for old people's welfare, a residential education centre for lectures, conferences, training courses for management, clergy, social workers and the like, and outward-looking services for the social and for the religious needs of the area. Again, the Royal Society (the 'Royal Society of London for Improving Natural Knowledge' to give its full title) originated in informal meetings of scientists and interested amateurs from 1645 onwards, reached the state of a formal society in 1660, and was incorporated by Royal Charters of 1662 and 1663. In the course of three hundred years it has accumulated very large charitable trust funds and is now recognised as the national centre of knowledge of the natural sciences.

9. These examples illustrate classes of old 'foundations' which make no grants, or make grants in addition to carrying on other work. On the other hand, the creation of new charities goes on apace, and a fair proportion of them are new grant-making trusts, large and small. The number of separate 'charities' is enormous, and probably exceeds 250,000. It is estimated that about 500 new charities are registered every year, and a few, but not many, go out of existence. A large proportion of these are comprised under the heads of 'the advancement of religion' and 'the advancement of education' and include the endowment of churches, schools, universities, missionary societies and very many other bodies. The type of 'foundation' contemplated in this study would usually fall into the classes of charities with wide general purposes, or those for 'the relief of distress' and 'other purposes beneficial to the public'—the remaining heads of the traditional four-fold classification of English charity.   (See also Editors' Note on page 222)

10. The great majority, numerically, of 'charities' as has been explained, are local charities restricted to a defined geographical area; but the Central Register of Charities maintained for public inspection by the Charity Commissioners includes over 10,000 classified as 'general'. The 'Directory of Grant-Making Trusts' second compilation published in 1971 by the Charities Aid Fund of the National Council of Social Service, contains particulars of nearly 1,700 charitable trusts which make grants to charities; a high proportion of these have been established in the last ten years. In the discussion of

'Activities of foundations' in s. XI below, it has seldom been possible to do more than mention one or two representatives in each class of the very wide range of important charitable institutions. Complete information may be obtained by consulting the classified indexes at the Central Register of Charities, St. Albans House, 57 Haymarket, London, S.W.1 (or Curzon Street House, W.1 for the section maintained by the Department of Education and Science).

11. This paper discusses only the law of England and Wales, and does not deal with the Scottish or Irish systems. These parts of the United Kingdom have had a very different religious and social history and their economic systems did not favour the accumulation of wealth. Consequently, they are much poorer in local charities, and comparatively few general charities have been founded for their sole benefit. The law of Scotland regarding property differs from that of the rest of the United Kingdom and recognises a class of 'public trusts' but not 'charity'; but the few 'foundations' domiciled in Scotland do not differ noticeably from those in England. There is a National Trust for Scotland that is the counterpart of the National Trust for Places of Historic Interest or Natural Beauty; and Scottish learned societies corresponding to the English, and Scottish religious and educational foundations, pursue their parallel course. But the Carnegie (United Kingdom) Trust, though domiciled in Scotland, benefits the whole of the United Kingdom; in the same way the Pilgrim Trust, though its headquarters are in London, operates throughout Great Britain. The law of England and Wales is one and the same system, and that of Northern Ireland is based upon it, though administered by a separate Government and Courts. There is no Scottish Charities Act and no Central Register of Scottish foundations, though Northern Ireland legislation now follows the plan of the English Charities Act. For income tax relief purposes, the definition of charity in English law is applied to Scotland and Northern Ireland; and appeals lie from the Courts of those countries to the House of Lords, so that in this report the application of law is uniform.

The English law of charity

12. The law of charity is concerned with private property devoted to public purposes; it is based on the concept of 'trust' that permeates the English law of property and deals with it by an interlocking system of constitutional law, statute law, and judge-made law in the form of the principles of equity laid down and developed by the Courts over the centuries.

13. The law of trusts is concerned with the position of trustees, that is,

o

persons holding property entrusted to them by another for the benefit of a third party. The third party, or beneficiary, is entitled to apply to the Courts to compel the trustee to carry out the trust impressed on the property by the donor. No trust will be recognised as valid unless both the conditions of the gift and the beneficiaries can be ascertained with sufficient precision to enable the Court to enforce it.

14. A trustee bears a heavy responsibility, and is liable to make good from his private fortune any loss to the beneficiary occasioned by his misconduct or negligence or departure from the terms of the trust, though the Court will usually excuse him for a mistake made in good faith. It is however a settled principle of law that a trustee must not personally profit from his trust: and if he does so, even in good faith, he can be compelled by the Court to pay such profits over to the beneficiary.

15. The above description relates to a 'private' trust. In the case of a charitable trust, the same principles apply, but the distinctive feature is that the beneficiary is not any identifiable person, but the community, or a sufficient class of the community. No private person is therefore, able to sue for the due execution of the trust. The remedy provided by the British Constitution in this situation is based on the Royal Prerogative; the Sovereign is the protector of those classes who are unable to protect their property themselves e.g. minors, lunatics, and charities, and, as *parens patriae*, acting through the principal Law Officer of the Crown, the Attorney-General will take steps, if necessary, to bring a charity trustee before the Court for the enforcement of the trust or the recovery of charity property for the benefit of the community.

16. For centuries it has been public policy to encourage the gift of private property for purposes of the public welfare. No State permission is required before doing so; and donors are enabled to prescribe the particular purpose for which they intend their property to be used (subject to certain limitations to be described later), and the Courts undertake to enforce the trust so declared for ever. Since the donor after he is dead would be unable to take any steps to enforce his intentions, the privilege of enforcement at the suit of the Attorney-General is an extremely valuable and important one.

17. From this constitutional position flow other important privileges of charities. A trust of property for charity will endure for ever, unless it is expressly limited in time; English law however will not permit property to be tied up in any other way for any period exceeding what is known as 'the perpetuity period'—roughly, just under 100 years. Further, by a constitutional convention, the Government of the day will not tax the income of charities, since this would amount to applying part of the income to public purposes chosen by itself, not by the donor; and for the same reason various

other fiscal advantages are enjoyed by charities. So, too, the Government traditionally does not legislate to alter the purposes declared by charitable donors, or to alter the extent of the field of charitable purposes, since this is the province of the Courts in dealing with private property. Indeed, the Courts exercise the most important jurisdiction of altering the terms of a charitable trust so as to enable the intention of the donor to be carried out when circumstances have altered so as to make it impracticable or ineffective to do so in the way he originally prescribed; in the case of a private trust, the trust would become void in such circumstances, and the property would revert to the donor or his heirs.

Charitable purposes in English law

18. The value of the fiscal and other privileges of charities in English Law have often made it important to obtain a judicial decision whether the purpose of a gift of property is charitable or not. These decisions are embodied in a corpus of case law developed over the last three centuries. There is no simple answer to the question 'what is charitable in English law'? Charity has never been exhaustively defined. The truth is that charity is an elastic notion; and the Courts have sought to preserve the traditional spirit of charity and to adapt it to the developing social needs of a living and changing society. As new social needs come into existence with changes in society, so new endeavours have been made by private benefactors to meet those needs; and generally speaking, the Courts, by extending analogy upon analogy, from cases already decided, have been disposed to regard gifts for such new purposes, when intended to confer a definite and altruistic benefit upon the community, as included in the charitable field. It is true that this indefinite situation leads sometimes to considerable uncertainty as to the status of a trust; but in recent years machinery has been provided whereby a quasi-judicial decision whether or not a proposed gift would be charitable may be obtained quickly and without cost.

19. Certain essential conditions must in all cases be satisfied. In the first place, the purpose of the trust must be beneficial to the community or to a sufficient part of the community. If, as in the case of associations, benefits will accrue partly to the members and partly to the community, it may be a matter of some difficulty to decide whether the prevailing intention was benefit to private individuals, or the community; and it is mainly in relation to such cases that the need for judicial decisions has arisen in recent years. The Court alone is empowered to decide whether or not a purpose is beneficial to the community; the opinion of the donor will not suffice. Thus the prevention of

experiments on animals (commonly known as anti-vivisection) was recently held not to be charitable since it did not contain the requisite element of public benefit.

20. Second, the purpose of the gift must be within the spirit of the list of examples of charity recognised by the Statute of Charitable Uses 1601 (now repealed). This list of charitable purposes followed no observable plan; and the interpretation of what is within its spirit leaves much to the discretion of the judge. Charities have been roughly classified under the heads of the advancement of religion, the advancement of education, the relief of poverty and other purposes beneficial to the community not falling under any of the preceding heads. There has been a tendency to regard the fourth class, bearing in mind the statute of 1601, as comprising mainly but not exclusively public services such as public works.

21. Third, as mentioned above, the Court reserves to itself the power to determine what is beneficial to the community. It does not suffice that a donor considers e.g. anti-vivisection to be beneficial to the public. As a corollary, the Court will not accept as charitable a purpose that can only be achieved by legislation, since only Parliament is empowered to decide whether a change in the law is for the public benefit. Fourth, the purpose must be expressed with sufficient clarity for the trustees to know whether they are carrying it out and for the Court to compel them to do so if they do not; thus such general words as 'the promotion of international friendship' or 'peace' have been held by the Courts not to constitute a charitable purpose, since private trustees cannot know whether they are carrying out the trust, and indeed international relations, peace and war are the province of Governments, not of private individuals.

22. The Charities Act 1960, in sections 4 and 5, provided for the first time machinery to secure an impartial and authoritative legal decision quickly and without charge regarding the charitable status of an institution. The Charity Commissioners for England and Wales (and the Department of Education and Science as regards educational and certain other trusts) were required to set up a public register of charities and to enter therein every charity holding a minimum amount of charity property (apart from certain classes of charity provided for in other ways). An institution entered in the register is conclusively presumed to be a charity unless and until it is removed from the register; objections to its inclusion may be made to the Commissioners and an appeal lies from their decision to the High Court. In practice these arrangements have been found to work well; the decisions of the Commissioners have made themselves generally respected and it is rare for objections to be lodged and virtually unknown for appeals to be made to the Court.

Forms of Charity

23. The concept of trusteeship has now been extended to all persons having the general control and administration of a charity, whatever its form (Sec. 46 Charities Act, 1960). A 'charity' for this purpose is defined as any 'institution', corporate or not, which is established for charitable purposes only and is subject to the control of the High Court in the exercise of the Court's jurisdiction with respect to charities (Sec. 45 id.); 'institution' includes 'any trust or undertaking'. The essential feature of a charitable 'foundation' in English Law is thus that its property is charity property and the persons administering it are charity trustees; the form of its constitution is less important.

24. The requirement in the definition of 'charity' that the 'undertaking' should be within the jurisdiction of the High Court, means, first, that the charity property is property held by private people, not public property held by a public authority. It is of course quite common for public services to be carried on for purposes that are also 'charitable', e.g. the relief of poverty. Charities are carried on with private property which is applied according to the intentions of the donor, while public services are carried on by funds derived by taxation from the public and can be administered by a local authority or the Crown. The limitation by jurisdiction also limits the powers of the Court to institutions of which either the property or the trustees are within the limits of the Court's territorial jurisdiction, in accordance with the generally accepted application of municipal law.

25. A 'charity' may thus be broadly described as an institution of some kind with some private property, which the holders are bound, and can be compelled by the Court, to use for one or more of a certain class of public purposes specified in the 'trust instrument'. The 'trust instrument' is the document which constitutes the charity; it is usually in legal form e.g. a deed of gift or a will, a conveyance of land, the memorandum and articles of association of a Company registered under the Companies Act 1948, the rules of an unincorporated association, a 'scheme' made by the Court or the Commissioners, a public or private act of Parliament, a Royal Charter, or Royal Letters Patent. We may perhaps distinguish between three broad forms of constitution

(a) strict trusts i.e. wills, deeds, conveyances, declarations of trust, similar to those used for establishing private trusts or property for the benefit of named individuals;

(b) corporations i.e. artificial persons created to carry out charitable purposes by procedures under the Companies Act or by Royal Charter, or by other acts of State; and

(c) societies i.e. private persons who band together for common purposes, but are not incorporated.

26. In some cases the 'trust instrument' may be informal like the terms of a public appeal or a letter from an individual making the gift. In others there may be no trust instrument; for example there may be no surviving record of the ancient gift that established the charity, the existence of a building fund to enlarge a church may be based merely on a general agreement among the worshippers to establish such a fund from their offerings, or the trust may have been created merely by the spoken words of the person making the gift. The trust so created is no less binding on the trustees who hold the property; but naturally as time passes, its exact terms become more difficult to recall or ascertain. The Central Register of Charities is designed to remedy this situation, since even in such cases, the purpose of the trust will, if the charity is registered, be recorded authoritatively in the register entry.

27. After these introductory explanations, we may turn to a discussion of the eleven questions brought up at the Berlin Conference of November 1964. As will be seen, their application to the English system of law is at times awkward, but it is hoped that the replies bring out the points on which information is desired.

I. FOUNDATIONS WITH LEGAL STATUS

28. As explained in the introduction, a distinction between charities with and without a legal status is not readily made in English law. All 'charities', whether registered in the Central Register of Charities or not, and whatever the form of their constitution, are recognised as legal entities, subject to the charity jurisdiction of the High Court and the protection of the Crown on behalf of the nation. Perhaps the most meaningful distinction would be made between charities of which the trustees are incorporated in some way, and those of which the charity trustees are individuals, capable only of suing and being sued in their private capacity.

29. Incorporation, i.e. the creation of an artificial legal personage to act for certain specified purposes, has many advantages; since such a personage never dies, for instance, the property vested in it never changes hands. In feudal times, the grant of Royal Charters, the only means of creating legal incorporation, was jealously guarded, and Royal licences to hold land *in mortmain* were required. Since the dissolution of the monasteries and the reassignment of their lands under Henry VIII 'ecclesiastical corporations'

now survive in law only as a part of the machinery of the Established Church of England. The principal chartered 'civil corporations' surviving from mediaeval times, are now the councils of municipal boroughs, the Livery Companies of the City of London, and the ancient universities, all of which carried out some part of the functions of Government; and since these bodies had perpetual existence, it was natural that a person wishing to found a perpetual charity should appoint as trustee a corporation with which he was connected. Owing to the confusion liable to arise between the administration of public funds and charity funds by the same body, the Municipal Corporations Acts, 1835–83, removed borough councils from the trusteeship of the borough charities, and empowered them to appoint individuals as trustees instead. The governmental powers of Livery Companies and universities are now minimal, and they continue as trustees of very large charitable funds.

30. In Tudor times, it became a practice to establish 'charitable corporations' by Royal Charter or even by legislation (e.g. the Hospitals for the Poor Acts, 1572–97). These were typically groups of persons associated for some common charitable purpose and supported by the charitable endowment of the corporation. The surviving examples are mainly the Colleges of Oxford and Cambridge, whose charitable purpose is the education of their members, and certain types of 'hospital' or almshouse, of which the corporators were the master and the inmates, whose poverty was relieved by the endowment. Owing to the obvious abuses open to bodies of trustees who are also the recipients of the charity benefits, the original constitutions of such foundations have been much reformed over the centuries.

31. As the feudal relationship between sovereign and liegeman faded from English institutions, the political objections to incorporation diminished; and from the seventeenth century, it has been frequent for important charities to be incorporated by an Act of State. Sometimes this has taken the form of Letters Patent issued by the Crown, sometimes Public or Private Act of Parliament, sometimes, and most usually in recent years, by Royal Charter.

32. A Royal Charter for a charity is nowadays regarded as honorific; its grant implies a recognition by the Crown of the worth of the cause, and by the Sovereign of the worth of the promoters, and careful enquiry is invariably made before one is issued. Letters Patent are a less formal device, for similar purposes, now seldom resorted to. During the eighteenth and early nineteenth centuries, it seems often to have been a matter of accident whether incorporation was obtained by Public or Private Act of Parliament; under more modern Parliamentary practice, a Public Act would be appropriate only in a matter arousing widespread public interest, and probably requiring some

form of regulation for which the Court has insufficient power. A Private Bill can be presented by any person, but is a relatively costly procedure; it is usual for modern universities to obtain Private Acts governing their proceedings and powers, as well as incorporation by Royal Charter. Charities established in any of these ways normally require an Act of State of some kind for their dissolution.

33. Two main forms of incorporation on private initiative may be encountered. Charity trustees may be incorporated by an order of the Charity Commissioners under the Charitable Trustees Incorporation Act 1872; the effect of this is however merely to establish a body with perpetual succession for the purpose of holding charity property, and as this is now more easily and simply effected by vesting the property in the Official Custodian for Charities, this Act is seldom resorted to. A far more frequent mode of incorporation is registration as a company under the Companies Act. Any body of persons can register a company for any lawful purpose, and can bring it to an end by the simple procedures provided. The code of company legislation regulates the relations between the members of a company, and between them and the public. It is designed primarily for those who pool their funds with the intention of making a profit; there is some awkwardness in its application to non-profit-making companies, and a risk of confusion between the company's own funds, contributed by the share-holders, guarantors, or others for the general purposes of the company, and those contributed for special purposes by the public, which the company holds as trustee. Since there would be no effective remedy against a company with little or no funds of its own, should it misuse trust property, the creation of companies whose purpose is to act as corporate trustees is regulated by the Lord Chancellor.

II. FOUNDATIONS WITHOUT LEGAL STATUS (I.E. UNINCORPORATED)

34. The type of charity established by one large donation of a wealthy individual, however, rarely takes an incorporated form. Like many other smaller gifts, it is usually constituted by a trust deed, in which the founder himself specifies the property, the purpose for which it is to be applied, the persons responsible for carrying it out, and the mode of execution; in the case of a large undertaking such as the Wellcome Trust established by will, these instructions may be long and detailed. No official permission is required, and no Act of State is necessary to bring it into force; but as with other charitable trusts, the trust can be changed or brought to an end only by the Court or the Charity Commissioners. If the trustees are involved in legal

proceedings, they sue or are sued in their personal capacities. The great majority of small charities are of this type.

35. The unincorporated association is another kind of 'unofficial' charity. There is no bar on any persons joining together to pool their resources for a common lawful purpose and agreeing upon whatever terms of association they please; if the objects are charitable and beneficial to the public, it will acquire the character of a charity. A village sports club, for example, if open to all the inhabitants, is usually charitable; but a tennis club limited to elected members is not. Charities of this kind are commonly supported by subscriptions and collections, and if their operations and resources become extensive enough to justify the appellation of 'foundation' (such as the Spastics Society), it is usually convenient to establish a trust fund, or seek incorporation. If the original terms of association expressly enable them to do so, the members may alter its purposes or bring it to an end; in other cases, a scheme of the Charity Commissioners is required. The funds contributed by the members for their common charitable purposes are held on trust by the officers of the society for this purpose, and the law of charity deals with them as charity trustees and the funds as charity property.

III. OTHER LEGAL ENTITIES

36. It is not easy to think of any form of comparable undertaking that does not fall into one of the classes considered under I and II. In so far as they do not, it can only be, in the main, because they are not charities. This may be because

(a) the purposes are not charitable at law, or not exclusively charitable,
(b) the benefits accrue to identifiable individuals rather than to the public,
(c) the property is not private, but provided by Government, or it is not administered in pursuance of trusts impressed on it, but according to the policies of local or central Government.

Examples of (a) are the Gulbenkian Foundation and the United Nations Association, which have purposes that are mainly charitable but include some that have been held by the Court not to be charitable. In (b) are to be found Friendly Societies providing mutual sickness benefits for members, certain scientific societies where the increase of knowledge and other benefits appear limited to members, and research institutions established by commercial firms for their own advantage. The distinction between charitable and non-charitable institutions in these categories sometimes turns on niceties of drafting of the trust instrument. Many institutions, again, in class (c) are administered for purposes that are charitable, but as a function of Government and not as a trust of private property, e.g. Chelsea Hospital, the Nature Conservancy, the Medical Research Council, and certain Agricultural Research Stations.

The City Livery Companies

37. No account of the charitable system of the country would be complete without reference to the Livery Companies of the City of London. These are not themselves charities; originally they were mediaeval guilds for the regulation of the trades and crafts of the City. Some, such as the Goldsmiths' Company and the Fishmongers' Company still exercise powers recognised by law, e.g. marking the standard of gold and silver articles or regulating the fish-market. The majority however, have become mainly social organisations which themselves use their very substantial corporate funds largely for charitable purposes, and usually also administer numerous charities founded by former members. Their concern with education is widespread; several maintain large schools of national repute; thus the Mercers' Company are governors of St. Paul's School, and the Merchant Taylors Company of the Merchant Taylors Schools, Northwood and Crosby. Nearly all the companies, major and minor, still concerned with crafts, e.g. the Blacksmiths', Farriers', Carpenters', Weavers', Salters' and Goldsmiths' Companies provide institutes, schools (e.g. the Building Craft Training School, the Salters' Institute of Industrial Chemistry) and in some cases, the funds available are so large that they have been extended to assist many other classes of charity, such as libraries, museums, art exhibitions, recreation grounds, and prizes or grants for technical education and advanced research in their special fields of interest. There are indeed few charitable purposes that have not at one time or another received support from one or other of the twelve great Companies. The Lord Mayor of London is in close contact with the Companies and with the Corporation of the City. While he is not in any sense the director of their benefactions, he occupies a position of unparalleled influence in calling upon the vast wealth of the City for charitable causes; and it is customary for him to take the lead in making a great appeal for a new foundation for national purposes (e.g. the John F. Kennedy Memorial Fund) which in modern times occurs every few years.

IV. ECONOMIC ENTERPRISE UNDER THE GUISE OF FOUNDATIONS

38. It is the essence of the English law of trusts that no trustee may personally profit from his trust. This is strictly enforced, and applies to a charitable trust

in the same way as to any other. If its property is used for any purpose other than the charity purpose, the Attorney-General on behalf of the Crown may apply to the Court to remove the trustees and appoint others, and to recover from them any profits derived from the charity property. It follows that no charitable foundation may use the endowment for the private profit of the trustees, shareholders, or any other individuals; and grave consequences would follow in the civil law, if not in the criminal law also, for any trustee guilty of so gross a breach of trust. The Court moreover has power to pursue into other hands and recover the charity property and any profits derived from it, and to set aside any dealings in it that appear prejudicial to the charity.

39. It is sometimes found that individuals conducting a charity, particularly if it is incorporated, attempt to enrich themselves by authorising the payment of excessive remuneration or expenses as officers, the provision of benefits such as accommodation and a car, or the use for private profit of laboratories or other facilities belonging to the charity. The Charity Commissioners have full power to investigate abuses of this kind, and may take emergency action to protect the charity property by suspending or removing the trustees and freezing the bank account or other assets, preparatory to an application by the Attorney-General to the Court.

40. How far, however, may charity trustees engage in trading with the charity property for the benefit of the foundation? This is a question of some difficulty. In the first place, unless the trust instrument expressly authorises them to do so, trustees are not permitted to put the charity capital at risk, and are restricted in their investment to the securities defined in the Trustee Investment Act 1961. If the charity capital consists of land, however, the trustees must be presumed to have power of management and improvement, in the same way as any other land owner. The use of capital, or the raising of loans by charity trustees, however, for this purpose is strictly regulated by law; in general, land development transactions require the consent of the Charity Commissioners.

41. The trust instrument, however, is sometimes deliberately drafted so as to enable the trustees to carry on business. The question may then arise whether the powers so conferred on the trustees are to be interpreted as objects of the undertaking. If so, conducting a business is not generally a charitable purpose in law; so that the whole undertaking might cease to be exclusively charitable and to enjoy the fiscal benefits of charity; it would become an ordinary commercial undertaking.

42. On the other hand, the nature of the charity may require that trading of some sort must be undertaken. The Income Tax Act 1952 Sec. 448 (1) (c)

illustrates the accepted principle in such circumstances. Relief from income tax on trading profits of charities will be given only when 'the trade is exercised in the course of the actual carrying out of a primary purpose of the charity' e.g. in running a civic theatre, or 'mainly . . . by the beneficiaries' e.g. where a charity for retraining disabled persons and re-settling them in society supports itself by sales of their products. But printing and selling Christmas cards in aid of the charity funds is an ordinary commercial enterprise and not inherent in the nature of the charity: and profits are therefore taxable. It has been found best to incorporate a trading company separately to carry on the Christmas card business, which can then covenant to pay its profits to the charity and thus avoid corporation and income tax.

43. Broadly speaking, the fundamental principle that the income from charity property belongs to the community, and the machinery for its enforcement in this country, effectively prevent commercial enterprises passing under the guise of 'foundations' in order to obtain the fiscal benefits of charitable status. Where the income is derived from blocks of shares which comprise the whole capital of a commercial enterprise, the trustees may find themselves as the only possible directors of the company; but even so, the two undertakings are normally carefully kept separate in law, as in the case of the Wellcome Foundation and the Wellcome Trust.

V. JURISDICTION REGARDING FOUNDATIONS

44. All charities, as has been explained, are subject to the charity jurisdiction of the High Court, which is an inherent, non-statutory power based on the principles of equity and is exercised by the Chancery Division at first instance. The object of this jurisdiction is to secure the due execution of the intention of the founder, modifying if need be, the details of his expressed wishes in order to meet changed conditions which he could not be expected to foresee. The Court may change the trustees and vest the property in other persons if it sees fit, and may make what is called a 'scheme' of administration to alter the detailed provisions of the trust instrument. If the objects of the charity are altered, this will be done in accordance with what is known as the cy-pres principle, that is, as nearly as possible to the original expressed purpose. There is a right of appeal from the Chancery Division to the Court of Appeal, and from the Court of Appeal to the House of Lords. Since most of the adjustments of charity administration are non-contentious, the Charity Commissioners are empowered by the Charities Act 1960 (Sec. 18) to exercise the powers of the High Court in such cases in order to save legal costs.

45. This jurisdiction is exercisable only on the application of the trustees, or the Attorney-General, or of certain other persons in the case of small local charities. The Court will not hear 'strangers' i.e. persons unconnected with the charity: their proper course is to persuade the Attorney-General to act or to permit them to institute proceedings in his name as 'relators'. In order to prevent charity money being spent on costs unnecessarily, the trustees are not permitted to apply to the Court on matters which can be dealt with free of charge by the Charity Commissioners, except with the leave of the Commissioners or a judge of the High Court. Charities are thus protected, and indeed prevented, from incurring legal costs unnecessarily in charity proceedings.

46. Not all trust instruments, however, fall within the jurisdiction of the High Court. The Court has no authority, for instance, to alter an Act of Parliament or a Royal Charter issued by the Sovereign. In these cases, however, special provisions of the Charities Act empower the Charity Commissioners to prepare 'schemes', which are made effective by statutory instruments laid before Parliament, or after an appropriate Order-in-Council, respectively.

47. The machinery of registration and inspection of charity accounts by the Charity Commissioners, established by the Charities Act, 1960, coupled with their searching powers of enquiry, are intended to provide a systematic examination of charity affairs with a view to reports being made to the Attorney-General if charity proceedings appear necessary. In practice, the supervisory machinery limits both the likelihood and the possibility of abuse, so that Court proceedings are rarely required.

48. Trustees are required by law to apply to the Charity Commissioners for a scheme altering the terms of the trust instrument when the circumstances require it. If they refuse unreasonably to do so, the Commissioners may request the Home Secretary to refer the case to them: and if he does so, they may proceed to make a scheme in the same way as if the trustees had applied. This new jurisdiction conferred by the Charities Act 1960, Sec. 18, has not yet been used.

49. Sec. 3 of the Charities Act establishes an Official Custodian for Charities, as an officer of the Charity Commissioners in whose name charity land and securities can be placed voluntarily by the trustees and donors, or compulsorily by the Court. He has the functions of a custodian trustee as defined under Sec. 4 of the Public Trustee Act 1906.

50. The Charity Commissioners, besides exercising the scheme-making power of the High Court, may also authorise a particular transaction in charity property under Sec. 23 of the Charities Act, unless it is expressly

prohibited by the trust instrument. Generally speaking, the first step of foundation trustees wishing to take any action or pursue any course not clearly within the powers conferred by the trust instrument, should be to approach the Charity Commissioners for a temporary or permanent variation.

51. The Department of Education and Science exercises the Charity Commission functions under the Charities Act in relation to certain classes of educational and recreational charities with which that Department is administratively concerned. Although the Secretary of State for this department is a Minister responsible to Parliament, he has a dual capacity as Charity Commissioner in which he deals also with charitable trusts and is responsible to the Court. In practice this occasions little difficulty; indeed it results from the special powers exercised by the department under the Endowed School Acts, 1869–1948, over certain classes of educational foundation, which are not subject to review by the Courts.

VI. FISCAL PROVISIONS REGARDING FOUNDATIONS

52. Charities have always enjoyed relief from income tax, since otherwise the Government would in effect be diverting income from the public purpose selected by the founder to purposes of their own choice. Much use is now made of covenants to pay annual subscriptions for a period of seven years or more: this device is treated as transferring income from the donor to the charity, and the charity being exempt from tax, is enabled to recover the income tax already paid by the donor on the amount of his subscription.

53. Charities are also exempt from the capital gains tax and corporation tax imposed by the Finance Act 1965, and can recover selective employment tax paid in respect of their staff.

54. Charities are also entitled to mandatory relief of 50% from rates on premises used and occupied for the charity purposes, and the rating authority has discretion to grant exemption up to a further 50%, under the Rating and Valuation Act 1961.

55. They also enjoy certain preferential rates of stamp duty on documents effecting the disposal of property.

56. No fiscal benefit however accrues to the donor of gifts to charity—indeed, if the gift consists of securities, he is liable to pay any capital gains tax due at the moment of transfer. This also applies to gifts of land, subject to a class of exceptions not easy to state with certainty. A tendency is observable since the Finance Act 1965 for foundations to be established not by gifts of blocks of shares but by seven-year covenants to pay subscriptions,

sometimes very large, from the profits of a company; such subscriptions are deducted as business expenses before calculation of corporation tax.

VII. LEGAL SITUATION OF FOUNDATIONS

57. The main features of the system of charity law have been described in the introduction and Sec. V. To recapitulate, it consists of three elements:

(a) Customary or constitutional law relating to the exercise of the Royal Prerogative for the protection of charities.

(b) Judge-made law, comprising the principles of equity established by the Chancery Division over the centuries, its special charity jurisdiction, and the corpus of case law derived from decided cases.

(c) Statute law. The principle statutes are:

The Trustee Act 1925
The Charities Act 1960
The Trustee Investment Act 1961

A general account of the system is given in non-technical language in 'A Guide for Charity Trustees'—see Sec. IX; the legal text-books mentioned deal in greater detail with limited aspects of the subject.

VIII. POLICY AND PRACTICE OF GOVERNMENT AND DEPARTMENTS IN RELATION TO FOUNDATIONS

58. As already noted, it has been settled policy for centuries past to encourage, by the grant of various privileges, the devotion of private property to public purposes; and the privilege of perpetuity, in particular, gave a quality of permanence to charitable foundations which have moulded the modern social welfare services.

59. Accordingly, in 1948, when the benefits provided by the post-war social legislation began to overtake the traditional objects and charities, the questions began to be asked, 'What is to be done with charity property in these conditions? Should it be confiscated by Government and applied in relief of rates and taxes (as indeed happened to hospital property under the National Health Service Act 1946)? Or should charity trustees continue to administer it strictly in accordance with their trusts, regardless of changed conditions around them?' A committee under the Chairmanship of Lord Nathan was appointed by the Prime Minister in 1950 to report on the changes in law and practice necessary to enable the maximum benefit to the community to be derived from charitable trusts. The findings of this committee, which reported in 1952, were acted upon by the Government (subject to certain modifications noted in a White Paper in 1955—see Sec.

IX) and formed the basis of the settlement recognised in the monumental Charities Act, 1960.

60. In substance, the Nathan Committee pointed out that there is virtually no service which cannot be provided under its discretionary powers by some local or central Government authority, but that many public services could not be carried on without the help of charities or voluntary workers. They recommended therefore that charity property should continue to be held by charity trustees and administered by them in accordance with the intentions of the donor; in other words, it should continue to be trust property not public property. The trustees should have regard to changing social circumstances and the benefit provided by other charities and services operating in the same field—in other words, the activities and operations of voluntary and statutory service should be co-ordinated; and—as the debate on the Charities Bill made clear—that this should be done on a basis of equal partnership, not of subordination. The Committee added that while trustees need not withdraw from a public service (e.g. education) in which their resources were already committed, it was the peculiar function of charities to pioneer. This conception was based on the pre-war practice of some of the great 'foundations', like the Carnegie (United Kingdom) Trust, or the City Parochial Foundation. A grant, usually after consultation with the appropriate department of Government, might be made for an experimental local service over a period of say 5 years. If it was not a success, it would then be dropped; if it proved itself, however, the foundation would not support it indefinitely but would expect the Government to take it up and make it general by legislation.

61. Whereas, immediately after 1948, some officers of newly-established statutory welfare services appeared to have the impression that there was no further need for charitable aid, this attitude is now rarely to be met with; and co-operation between statutory and voluntary agencies is steadily making progress. In some fields, e.g. the welfare of the blind, integration is virtually complete; in others, there is still room for much improvement. For pioneer experiment, a Government department will often turn to a charitable foundation to finance a speculative venture on the fringe of its interest, as for example, when the Wolfson Foundation, partly at the instance of the Home Office, provided an Institute of Criminology at Cambridge University.

62. The policy of the Charities Act having been laid down by Parliament in 1960, it was left to the Charity Commissioners to bring the Act into operation and implement it. The Charity Commissioners are a small Government department deliberately insulated from ministerial pressure, and charged to act solely in the interest of charities and secure the execution of the inten-

tions of the founder according to law. They approach their tasks as the friends and advisers of trustees, to help them to carry out their trusts to the best advantage and avoid legal difficulties. They exercise the administrative powers of the High Court in non-contentious cases. Their services are free to trustees; and it has been said that they represent the State's contribution to charity by way of paid management. They present an annual report on their proceedings to the Home Secretary, who lays it before Parliament; it can be debated, but in practice this occurs very rarely. A fuller discussion of their powers and functions, of the relations between charities and central and local authorities and of the topics touched on above will be found in 'A Guide for Charity Trustees' (see Sec. IX below).

63. In the early 1950s, under the Labour Government, the Minister for Education exercised his powers under the Endowed Schools Act to amalgamate all the local school charities of Hertfordshire into the Hertfordshire Educational Foundation, a grant-making body administered in the main through the local education authority. This experiment proved so unpopular, and indeed contrary to the principles of the Nathan Report, that it has not been repeated.

64. The new forms of taxation imposed by the Finance Act 1965, and the Selective Employment Tax were, when first published, regarded as prejudicial to charity income; and organised representations on behalf of charity to the Government were successful in securing relief. The National Council of Social Service has become increasingly recognised by all classes of charity, including the 'great trusts', as the guardian of their interests and their spokesman *vis-à-vis* the Government. Generally speaking, it appears to be the wish of the Government to maintain the existing fiscal position of charities.

65. The united political strength of charities is very great, and no Government would wish to be labelled 'anti-charity'. The constituency of every Member of Parliament contains numerous charities of impeccable purposes, and commanding much public esteem and support. Legislative proposals likely to damage their interests would call forth a storm of popular protest; and it is noteworthy that in modern times no legislation of this kind has passed the House of Commons in face of the opposition of organised charity.

66. So far as the role and administration of charities are concerned, therefore, both official and charity opinion appears to regard the Charities Act 1960 as disposing of most outstanding issues. Its operation has barely advanced beyond its initial stages, and may in due course give rise to proposals for its amendment, but has not yet done so. The Charity Commissioners in their annual reports laid before Parliament publish comments on the progress made and the situations encountered.

P

IX. BIBLIOGRAPHY AND DOCUMENTATION OF CHARITIES

67. The 'Annual Charities Digest' published by the Family Welfare Association, contains much detailed information about individual charities; and more general information about voluntary and statutory organisations active in the field of social welfare can be obtained from 'A Guide to Voluntary Service' (H.M. Stationery Office) ,'Voluntary Social Services' (National Council of Social Service), and 'A Guide to the Social Services' (Family Welfare Association). The 'Directory of Grant-Making Trusts' published by the Charities Aid Fund of the National Council of Social Service, is mentioned in paragraph 10.

68. 'A Guide for Charity Trustees', C. P. Hill (Faber, 1966) gives an up-to-date account in non-technical language of the general system of charity law and practice as it now is since the coming into force of the Charities Act, 1960, on which the fullest legal commentary is 'Nathan on the Charities Act, 1960' (Butterworth, 1962).

69. Other publications on the position of charity are:
'Voluntary Action', Lord Beveridge (1948).
'Philanthropy in England, 1480–1660', W. K. Jordan (Geo. Allen and Unwin, 1962).
'Report of the Committee on the law and practice relating to Charitable Trusts' (H.M.S.O. 1952 Cmd. 8710).
White Paper: 'Government Policy on Charitable Trusts in England and Wales' (H.M.S.O. 1955 Cmd. 9538).
'Annual Reports of the Charity Commissioners', 1960 onwards (H.M.S.O.).

70. Other legal textbooks include:
'Tudor on Charities' (6th ed., 1967).
'The Charities Act, 1960' (with notes), Spencer G. Maurice (1960).
'The Modern Law of Charities', Prof. G. W. Keeton (Pitman, 1962).
'Halsbury's Laws of England', 3rd ed. with supplement, Vol. 4. Sec. V. 'Charities'.

71. Information about some foundation activities is given in annual or periodical reports published from the Carnegie United Kingdom Trust, Nuffield Foundation, Pilgrim Trust, Leverhulme Trust, and some other foundations. Many, however, prefer not to publish reports: their accounts are however available for public inspection in the Central Register of Charities. 'Welfare in Trust', a history of the Carnegie United Kingdom Trust from 1913–63, was published by the Trust in 1964.

X. MOVEMENTS FOR LAW REFORM REGARDING CHARITIES

72. The comprehensive Charities Act 1960 was at once the culmination of twelve years' deliberation and negotiation regarding the role of charities in the modern Welfare State, and a complete revision of the whole of the unreformed statute law regarding charities, dating back to Tudor times, and in one case to Edward I.

73. The present settlement of their position (see Sec. VIII) is regarded as satisfactory by the charity world and, it is hoped, will endure as a firm foundation for future development. Politically, while the Labour Party traditionally favours governmental rather than private activity, both parties welcomed the Charities Bill and recognise the indispensable part played by charities in the services of the community. Some members of the Party during its tenure of office were however known to be pressing for legislation to reduce the privileges of charity.

74. Proposals are sometimes made by party politicians, for the sake of the fiscal advantages enjoyed by charities, to bring into the field of charity institutions of which they happen to approve (such as the United Nations Association) which are not charitable at law, or to exclude from it charitable institutions which they dislike (such as the public schools). This would involve altering the present position, in which it is for the Court to decide whether or not the purpose of a trust or undertaking is charitable, and substituting a statutory definition. The question of creating a statutory definition of charity was discussed during the passing of the Charities Act. The resulting difficulties and uncertainty about existing trusts of property and the *corpus* of case-law were recognised as being alarming; and no Government is likely to embark on alteration of this law in this respect unless an overwhelming case can be made for it. It is moreover apparent that if one Government were to alter the definition to benefit organisations of which it approves, another could equally extend or reverse the process for its own ends; and this in turn would impair the traditional right of the private person to devote his property, before or after death, to whatever cause he pleases. Governments are generally well content to leave doubtful cases to the impartial arbitrament of the Courts, and avoid exposing themselves to political pressure by opening the way to legislative interference with the definition of charity.

XI. ACTIVITIES OF FOUNDATIONS

75. As already indicated, the enquiry of the Legal Committee of the Berlin Conference presumably is not, in the main, directed to the very large number

of charities for the advancement of religion, of education, or for the direct relief of poverty. In other charitable fields, the advancement of science and art and the provision of public services, it is hard to think of any purpose that has not at one time or another been supported by one charity or another. 76. Some of the largest foundations have adopted a policy of concentrating their resources for a period of say, 5 years at a time, on some particular section of the charitable field, within their trust instrument, and then on another for the next quinquennium. The operations of the Carnegie United Kingdom Trust as described in their Annual Report for 1966, illustrate the working of this principle and the great range of the enterprises to which grants were made, e.g. the assistance of adult amateur groups in drama and music, a school in decor for amateur producers and stage designers, the development of musical activities in youth clubs and among handicapped children, commissioning a choral operetta for festival performance, assistance to week-end painting groups, and art classes on merchant ships, assistance for museums (in this quinquennium directed to (a) the commissioning of expert reports on museums (b) grants for the development of small museums (c) travel grants for museum curators and (d) a contribution towards the cost of the Museums Association's educational services, including e.g. the training of taxidermists), quinquennial grants to Councils of Social Service, buildings for community use in New Towns and Redevelopment Areas, aid to the Special After-Care Trust for ex-prisoners, projects for the welfare of the handicapped, especially children, support for the National Council for the Single Woman and her Dependants (which provides practical service such as emergency help in crisis, holiday relief, etc., and undertakes research as a basis for practical action), a number of youth club improvements and new facilities, buildings for visitors to National Parks, Field Studies centres for Naturalists, courses for amateurs run by the British Astronomical Association and the Royal Meteorological Society, and an experimental three-year project in a rural county for a community to improve its countryside.

77. It would be an enormous task to detail or even to classify roughly the great number of enterprises, large or small, in the field of community services and the arts financed by or undertaken by charities of widely varying purpose and resources (see Sec. IX). Societies for the preservation and restoration of ancient buildings, and the £2,000,000 'Neptune' fund for the preservation of the coast line established by the National Trust are instances of the widespread movement for maintaining town and country amenities.

78. In the field of the advancement of science, first among the institutions carrying on scientific research of all kinds are the universities. The ancient universities of Oxford and Cambridge are composed of a number of colleges,

each of which is a charitable foundation incorporated by Royal Charter, with a considerable endowment for its maintenance. The majority of these are over 300 years old, and though like the modern universities are now extensively assisted by Government grants, the Oxford and Cambridge Colleges' foundation endowments still defray about half their expenditure. The universities themselves though not 'founded' by an individual's endowment have, over the centuries, accumulated large trust funds both for their general purposes and for prescribed objects, many of them for the support of research. Modern universities are established on the same pattern of charitable foundations incorporated by Royal Charter. They are seldom constituted by a number of separate colleges, or possessed of large endowments, but provide ample facilities for research of all kinds.

79. Another important class of institution supporting or carrying on scientific research includes the numerous learned, scientific and professional societies, such as the Royal Society, the Industrial Society, and the Institute of Mechanical Engineers, which are treated as charities because of the increase of knowledge made available to the community as a result of their activities.

80. Medical research is now an extremely active branch of charity work carried on largely in the teaching hospitals founded by individuals (e.g. Guy's Hospital, London) or by public subscription. They were made part of the National Health Service in 1948 and supported by Government funds, yet retain control of their endowments for research and education. The Medical Research Council is a Government organisation which maintains a number of research units and subsidises other projects. Besides these, there are a large number of voluntary bodies, financed by endowment, grants, or collections, which support or carry on research in particular pathologies (e.g. the British Heart Foundation), particular forms of handicap (e.g. the Royal National Institute for the Blind) or more generally (e.g. the Wellcome Trust). King Edward's Hospital Fund for London not only provides comfort and amenities for patients in National Health Service hospitals in Greater London, but also carries out research into their home living conditions and the best forms of hospital equipment. A co-ordinated survey of medical research programmes is much needed.

81. The care of animals has a particularly strong charitable appeal in Britain. The Royal Society for the Prevention of Cruelty to Animals, for instance, has an endowment income of £100,000 per annum, and a subscription income twice as large, and in a recent year (1966) received over £750,000 in legacies. The Wildfowl Trust is internationally known for its research unit for the study and conservationof wild ducks, geese and swans, and there is of course a British National Appeal for the World Wildlife Fund.

82. It is impossible to embark in this paper upon a catalogue or directory of large charities and their activities, but from the legal aspect two points should be noted that apply to all charities. First, a charity may not use its funds for any purpose except those laid down in the trust instrument; otherwise the trustees will be in breach of trust and can be compelled to make good from their own pockets any money wrongly expended. Second, if a grant is made by a charity to another organisation, that organisation must itself be a charity; otherwise the first charity would be spending its funds for purposes that were not charitable or not exclusively charitable: and not only would the trustees be in breach of trust (for which the Court might excuse them) but tax relief on the charity's income would be forfeited in so far as it was not applied for charitable purposes, and this the Inland Revenue have not power to excuse.

EDITORS' NOTE

According to the *Report of the Charity Commissioners for England and Wales for the year 1970*, at the end of 1970 nearly 77,000 charities were registered by the Commissioners to which some 25,000 educational charities registered by the Department of Education and Science must be added. But the Commissioners also remark that a large number of religious charities are not obliged to register.

Italy*

Alberto Predieri

1. In the history of modern Italian society, much less importance has been attached to private foundations than in other countries, especially the Anglo-Saxon ones. For a long time, charity and welfare were the exclusive concern of the Catholic Church, and donations, bequests and foundations were solely governed by Canon Law.

The traditions of the private institutions, universities and academies had diminished and prior to the realisation of Italian unity, these bodies had become an essential part of the small absolute States. When the politically divided peninsula was finally unified for the purpose of self-defence as a result of the belief in liberal culture and the interests of the governing class, the Italian State adopted and maintained an attitude of distrust and opposition towards all the intermediate bodies including foundations and associations. Its attitude was determined by three basic factors.

(a) Firstly, it was hostile towards the Catholic Church (and by the same token towards the foundations which depended on it directly or indirectly). This hostility had been well represented amongst the lay traditions of Tuscany and the Duchies of Parma and Modena before the unification of the country, and this had been strengthened under Napoleonic rule since the Church was closely connected with the Papal State, which was an obstacle to Italian political unification.

(b) Secondly, it harboured an aversion towards associations of any kind, especially of workers, but also cultural ones. Any institution which stood between the State and the citizen was looked upon with disfavour if not with outright hostility by the liberal political class which defended its power and its medium, the unitary State.

(c) Thirdly (and this was a typically Italian phenomenon), the State felt the need for caution towards any organisation which could be suspected of local patriotism of a chauvinistic nature.

* Translated from the Italian.

For all these reasons, any kind of autonomy appeared as a crack in the foundations of the State through which *l'ancien régime*, the power of the old municipalities or the Papal State and the Catholic Church could regain the upper hand, and reverse the current of events in Italian society.

The secularisation or laicisation of schools, welfare and cultural institutions and the unification of the laws on education and schooling represented one of the most sustained efforts on the part of the politically inspired class of the *Risorgimento* in the pursuit of their aims. The concomitant disadvantage was their hostility towards the social activities, which were flourishing elsewhere and a rigid control by the State on all these types of activities (welfare institutions, donations to help those in need, the education of the poor, administration of hospitals, the administration of universities and so on). This control discouraged autonomy and it ensured that the institutions produced by spontaneous efforts on the part of the citizens were integrated into the State fabric and given subordinate status and that the French pattern of legislation governing foundations and private associations was adopted. It did not prove too difficult to fit into this pattern in view of the common experiences and the cultural influence.

The Constitution did not recognise any right of association (or the right to set up foundations). The Civil Code, which enjoys particular prestige and significance in a liberal State, had no provisions, either on associations or foundations. One law (issued by the Piedmontese Monarchy in 1850, and, like other legislation, retained by the Italian Kingdom) made the purchase of real estate by juridical persons subject to Government authorisation so as to avoid the forming of *mortmain*, i.e. the concentration of economic power (then considered as landed wealth) in entities not owned by the State and pursuing non-commercial social aims. A later law, No. 6972 of 17th July 1890 brought about the administrative recognition of charitable institutions including foundations. This law, still in force today, defines a public institution as any charitable institution and any juridical person that *in toto* or in part pursues the aim of giving assistance to the poor, to provide for their education and their moral and economic improvement.

The system of recognition set out in this law was followed by others, and the administrative practice applied to non-profit juridical persons (i.e. foundations and associations) was patterned on them. In fact, by 1882 commercial firms did not need the administrative concession of legal personality since registration with a Court was enough. On the other hand, foundations and associations could not become entities which could enter into legal relations: in the case of foundations, they could not even exist if recognition had not been granted by Government authority. The system of recognising their legal personality by administrative concession and successive controls, which were maintained during the Fascist era, was included in the 1942 Civil Code, which is still in force. In the meantime, Italian society and the structure of its institutions have radically changed; the old hostility towards the Catholic and union organisations has long since disappeared; the harsh laws which regulated the former were frequently replaced by beneficent ones following the signing of the Concordat with the Holy See.

Today the Italian State is an openly and largely pluralistic State (Art. 2 of the Constitution). For this reason, there is a gap between social reality and the institutional set-up on the one hand, and the rules of ordinary legislation on the other. This is underscored by the increase in the significance of foundations.

2. In Italian law, the term 'foundation' had a precise meaning in private law (leaving aside public law foundations or religious foundations). A foundation is a type of juridical person, different from either associations or corporations, and recognised as such by administrative concession. To set up a foundation, it is necessary for some of the founders' property to be detached from the estate; this is given as a gift or via a will, and it constitutes the foundation's assets. It has its own special purpose or aim, both of them essential for its constitution. At the request of the parties concerned, the estate becomes a subject of law (by a process of personification, i.e. by the granting of legal personality).

The recognition of legal personality depends on the assessment made by the public authorities, to whom one has to submit documentary evidence of the aim or aims of the organisation and the adequacy of the funds for attaining them. Recognition is granted in the form of a decree signed by the President of the Republic, subject to the advice of the Council of State, or, in a few cases, a decree signed by the President of the Region, and in some other instances by the Prefect.

Once it is recognised, a foundation is subject to the supervision of the public authorities.

It cannot purchase real estate, accept donations or inheritances without Government authorisation. The Government controls and supervises the administration of foundations; it appoints and replaces administrators when the provisions set out in the declaration of intent cannot be carried out; it overrides decisions, which are contrary to statutory rules, to the declaration of intent, to public order or to *bonos mores*; it can disband the administrators and appoint a special Commissioner delegated by the Government to supervise the foundation if the administrators do not act in accordance with the statutes or with law (Art. 26 of the Civil Code). The Government can also arrange for the co-ordination of the activities of more than one foundation, or the unification of their administrations, honouring, when possible, the founder's intention. It can also declare the foundation extinct, when its aim has been fully attained or become impossible or of little use, or if the funds are no longer sufficient. Moreover it can transform it, keeping as closely as possible to the founder's intentions. In the case of extinction of the foundation, the funds are liquidated by persons appointed by the President of the Court in the city where the foundation has its seat, unless the statutes stipulate otherwise, but in any case under supervision and by means of some kind of auction.

The juridical person's estate which is left after the liquidation has been carried out is distributed in accordance with the provisions of the statutes. If the latter do not contain any provisions on this particular point, the Government takes necessary measures.

3. The controls on foundations set up for welfare and charitable purposes are even stricter as they are considered public, and come under the supervision of the Ministry for Internal Affairs.

A number of cases of incompatibility of office have been defined in respect of the administrators of these foundations, e.g. if they hold certain public appointments, or if they are related to each other. The rules of procedure for the deliberations of the boards of directors (majority votes, preparation of minutes, etc.) are governed by legislation which lists situations where acts are void. Certain deliberations have to be approved by the Government authority to be considered effective. The foundations set up for welfare and charitable aims must submit a provisional budget and a final balance sheet; any amounts which exceed the ordinary needs have to be deposited at a bank chosen by the Government. The customary standards and rules of auditing in public authorities are applied to the administration of assets, for example, public auctions, sales or leases.

The responsibility of the administrators is also governed by the established practice of accountancy and auditing.

Whenever an administration fails to comply with the law or the statutes of the foundation, or whenever it prejudices the latter's interests, it can be dissolved by the Prefect. He may, at any time, direct that inspections and investigations be carried out and replace the administrators who do not abide by instructions by a special representative; he can also ask to see the copies of any meetings which may have been held.

4. As we noted before, the recognition of juridical personality is an essential prerequisite before a foundation can be set up. According to Italian civil law, juridical persons may be foundations, associations or companies (in

USA = Corporations). The latter are set up to make profit, or, in most cases, for entrepreneurial purposes; they are granted their juridical personality in other ways, i.e. without any administrative concessions. Italian law does not recognise non-profit companies. While US foundations may also be corporations (in UK = Companies) provided they are non-profit making, foundations have a different type of legal personality to such corporations. Associations differ from foundations in that, in the former, the patrimonial element may be lacking (the patrimony, if it exists, is an instrument but not a constituent element of juridical personality), whereas the personal element must exist. In practice, some associations, mostly with cultural aims, resemble cultural foundations, especially operating foundations. In this paper, however, we have confined ourselves to the more usual kind of foundations. The civil law also contains provisions pertaining to associations which have not applied for legal personality. These organisations are not subject to the above-mentioned controls, which are the same for both foundations and associations which possess legal personality.

'Non-recognised' associations, i.e. which have not been granted legal personality, are both numerous and important in Italy: one need only think of all the political parties, the labour unions or all the entrepreneurial associations who do not wish to apply for legal personality so as not to be subject to supervision (and this also often happens in the case of cultural associations, even though one should add that both for the latter as well as for foundations, the controls are not at all as systematic and oppressive in practice as one might think after reading the civil law). On the other hand, the law does not provide for any foundations without legal personality. However, there are bodies which call themselves foundations, but which have not been granted legal personality (i.e. *de facto* foundations). There is no obligation to use the word 'foundation', and the term does not enjoy any legal protection. Hence, there are recognised foundations which are not called foundations, and there are *de facto* bodies which call themselves foundations.

5. The foundations (i.e. the recognised ones) enjoy some tax relief.

As regards the taxes on capital, business and wages (*imposta di ricchezza mobile*), Art. 84 of the unified law provides for exemption in the case of subsidies paid by the State or by other public organisations purely as charity, as well as for amounts granted as bonuses to employees, and those donated by anyone for the same reason to legally recognised organisations, institutions or associations, up to 5% of declared income when the donation is clearly earmarked for the promotion of education, social work, religion, or welfare; this is also the case with the interest on loans made by firms and banks to the regions, provinces, communes, charitable institutions and other public organisations, and with the payments made as scholarships. As regards registration and mortgage taxes (*tasse di registro e ipotecarie*), Art. 1 of the Royal Decree of 9th April, 1925, No. 380, exempts all donations from these taxes (even if they are onerous as long as the onus might possibly rest on the aim for which they are made) to provinces, communes and other corporate bodies or institutes, even if they are foreign (Law of 10th February 1903, No. 59), whether already in existence or yet to be founded, when the specific aim of the donation is to further welfare, schooling or education (as well as religion, according to the Law of 27th May 1929, No. 810 and Royal Decree of 28th February 1930, No. 289). The exemption from mortgage taxes, already provided for in the above mentioned decree, was reaffirmed in Art. 13 of the tariff (annex C) in the Law of 25th June 1943, No. 140, which sets out the provisions governing public bodies recognised as juridical persons or associations or foundations possessing legal personality, founded or to be founded, when the specific aim of the donation is to promote welfare, education or religious purposes.

As regards income tax, Art. 1 of the Law of 18th December 1962, No. 1717, exempts '. . . the donations made to bodies or institutions with religious, charitable, welfare, cultural, educational or hygienic aims or which were set up to advance the public weal, as well as the donations made by the same bodies to institutions, hospital services supported by public bodies, or public assistance . . .'.

The exemption depends pursuant to Art. 12 of RDL of 3rd June 1943, No. 452, on the non-existence of 'any *quid pro quo*, even if indirect, or of any kind of insurance between the said bodies and the patient or inmate'. The tax on company share dividends does not apply to foundations which have charitable, educational, instructional or scientific aims. Foundations which wish to enjoy the exemption must submit to auditing by the tax authorities.

Other provisions, though of less importance, concern the advertisement tax (*imposta di publicita*), the road fund tax (*tasse di circolazione*—for lorries and motor-boats exclusively used by hospitals or humanitarian institutions for the transportation of patients in need of medical or surgical care); the manufacturing tax (*imposta di fabbricazione*—reduced rate for the petrol used by the ambulances of charitable and first-aid institutions in the transportation of the sick and the wounded); and the excise duties (for example on drinks purchased cheaply and distributed free to the poor by public charitable institutions and by other legitimately founded corporate bodies). Other special privileges have been granted to a number of foundations by law; for example the contracts of the National Museum for Science and Technology in Milan and the '*Acropoli Alpina*' are governed by the same special fiscal provisions as those of documents of State. The *Gustavo Enrico Hermnann Foundation* and the *Vittoriale degli Italiani Foundation* are exempt from any registration and mortgage tax; the latter body is also exempt from the payment of tax on capital, business and wages; the *Villa Serbelloni Centre* (which is sponsored by the Rockefeller Foundation) at Bellagio enjoys special rights; the *Gerolamo Gaslini* has the same privileges as those of the charitable foundations, although it is not subject to the Law of 17th July 1890.

6. It is not known how many foundations there are in Italy. The information, which might be available at the appropriate Ministries, is not published (except for the Ministry of Education which publishes a list of those foundations, academies and associations which are subject to its supervision), and no research or collation has been done in this field. One might make a rather arbitrary estimate and quote a figure of one thousand recognised foundations, to which should be added at least three hundred *de facto* foundations[1]. Generally, they are foundations set up under a modest bequest for the distribution of prizes and scholarships; but sometimes, there are *de facto* foundations whose activities are not limited to awarding prizes and which are prominent and prestigious organisations—for instance, the *Calamandrei Foundation* or the *Carlo Erba Foundation*.

During recent years, there has been a trend towards increasing the number and significance of foundations, especially the cultural ones.

The proof of this has been the setting up of a series of foundations, some of them of striking financial magnitude by Italian standards even if they are much smaller than their North American counterparts and which are to be found among the group of operating foundations or general purpose foundations.

The different types of Italian foundations i.e. in regard to their aims and activities, as well as their origin (e.g. family foundations, foundations tied to an enterprise, etc.) are not dissimilar to those in other countries. Four groups may be distinguished, though hybrid forms are also encountered.

(a) Foundations whose sole function consists in awarding grants. This group may be subdivided into two types:

(i) Foundations which distribute prizes, scholarships, subsidies etc. to beneficiaries chosen by the foundation or by a body defined in the statutes. These foundations may have cultural purposes: for instance the ones set up at the *Accademia dei Lincei* (*Feltrinelli Foundation*, *Donegani Foundation*, *Stanislao Cannizzaro Prize Foundation*, *Angelo Livio and Jacopo Novaro Foundation*,

[1] However, a preliminary result of a recent survey being undertaken by the Giovanni Agnelli Foundation for the publication of an Italian foundation directory comes up with a figure as high as about 2,000. (The Editors)

Guiseppe Borga Foundation, F.S. Nitti Foundation, Battisti Grassi Foundation, Luigi d'Amato Foundation, Giovanna Jucci Foundation, Guido Lenghi Foundation, Pasolini dall'Onda Foundation); those constituted at the Academy of Sciences in Turin, the *Crusca* in Florence; in State offices (e.g. the *Marchi Foundation* at the Florence Superintendent's Office for Monuments); at the State General Auditing office; at the universities (quite numerous, but small in size); the military academies; associations of various kinds (for instance, the foundation for scholarships distributed by the *Cavalieri del Lavoro Federation*). Some foundations are altogether distinct from other bodies and are not linked in any way (*Marco Besso Foundation, Marzotto Prize Foundation*). In other cases the foundations have charitable aims (for example the *Crespi, Pirelli, Guiseppina Saragat Foundations*, the two *Piaggio Foundations*, the first *Agnelli Foundation*) whilst some serve mixed purposes.

(ii) Foundations which give grants and which are institutionally tied to a body or organisation to which the foundation bears a similar relationship to that of a holding *vis-à-vis* an enterprise (for instance the *Toniolo Foundation* which finances Milan's Catholic University; the *Carlo Maurilio Lerici Foundation*, which finances the Italian Cultural Institute in Stockholm; the *Guilio Gori Foundation* which finances and directs the *Piccola Città Pestalozzi* in Florence, which is a public school governed by a convention between the Ministry of Education and the said Foundation; the Foundation for Social Sciences of Genoa which finances the Institute for Social Sciences; the *Gaslini Foundation* which finances the *Giannina Gaslini Institute* for abandoned children).

(b) Foundations set up for the enjoyment of a certain endowment (for example the *Croce Foundation* which runs the *Benedetto Croce Library*, and whose aim is its conservation and enjoyment by scholars or the Museum of Sciences and Technology Foundation in Milan).

(c) Operating or general purpose foundations which carry out varied and continuous activities, directed under the statutes to pursue aims chosen and classified by the administrators and which embrace a multitude of duties and types of action (granting subsidies, contributions, funds, promotion and organisation of research, studies, meetings, etc.; sometimes, direct participation in research, cultural and social services, publications, etc.). This kind of foundation presupposes a substantial bequest. The major foundations which have been recently set up belong to this group:

the *Cini Foundation* (set up in 1951),
the *Olivetti Foundation* (1962),
the *Agnelli Foundation* (1966),
the *Rui Foundation* (1959—assistance to foreign students).

These foundations have either cultural or social, or mixed aims (for example the *Cini Foundation* has cultural and social goals, and the *Humanitarian Society* known also as *P. M. Loria Foundation*, which has long-standing traditions pursues educational, social and cultural ends).

These foundations are similar to the operating foundations which have either charitable (for instance the *Pro Juventute Foundation*) or hygienic aims (e.g. the International Radiography Centre for free medical assistance to seamen); or conduct scientific research (Laboratory for the Study of Complex Polymers and Plastic Materials at the Chemistry Institute of Turin University; the Laboratory for Research on Plastic Material Foundation at the Polytechnic of Milan; the Foundation for Study of Administration).

The operating foundations, especially the major ones, often act through branches which may have different organisational structures and may be permanent or not. For example, the *Cini Foundation* comprises three centres: 'Maritime affairs', 'Arts and Crafts', 'Culture and Civilisation'. The latter centre functions either direct or through the agency of St. George Cultural School, a foundation subdivided into four institutes dealing with the history of art, the history of society and the State, *belles-lettres*, music and theatre, and the study of relations between Venice and the East respectively. The Olivetti Foundation acts either direct or in its sponsorship of the International Affairs Institute, or it promotes COSPOS (Committee for Political and Social Sciences) set up on its own initiative together with the New York Social Science Research Council.

The Italian foundations are rather diffident about furnishing data on their activities and, in general, they do not publish reports or balance-sheets. Their assets are unknown, and only very approximate estimates of a few of them can be supplied.

7. We have mentioned the process by which Italian foundations were set up —mostly in the cultural field. This had led to a request for modification of the currently valid legislation so as to bring it in line with constitutional principles and to rationalise tax relief (for instance if donations to foundations are tax-free, the donation itself is subtracted, to a very small degree, from the donor's income; though dividends are tax-free, this is not the case for capital gains of shares subject to the tax on capital, business and wages).

Hence, truly efficient fiscal controls ought to be instituted. Proposals of this kind were presented at the meeting held in Rome in 1966 by the *Cini* and *Olivetti Foundations* and the Italian Cultural Institute (see bibliography). These suggestions were partly incorporated in a Bill presented by Deputy Flavio Orlandi, and now being discussed by the Chamber of Deputies.

The new legislation should favour the development of foundations and avoid some of the inconvenience revealed by the experience of other countries. The foundations in Italy will be able to carry out important functions, though they will never attain preeminence over the State whose work, especially in the fields of welfare, education and scientific research, cannot be curtailed. The foundations should, however, be strengthened by means of decisive structural reforms.

The rôle played by private organisations in Italy cannot rival, either quantitatively or qualitatively, that of the State and public authorities (as indeed it cannot in the United States and Great Britain for that matter). A pluralistic society does not necessarily imply quantitative identity between each group or equality between the private and public spheres of influence. In cultural promotion and education, as well as in economic affairs (and technological research is the link between these fields of activity), there are some sectors where private enterprise is predominant, others where the Government and public authorities enjoy ascendancy and some where private and public influence are equal.

The magnitude and importance of these sectors vary from branch to branch, mostly as a result of action by the public authorities who, under an efficient form of Government, have to coordinate private and State activities, the extent and substance of which are determined in advance by the two sides themselves.

It is obvious that the area of polarisation will be different for each branch: pure and applied scientific research will be different to that of primary education or welfare, just as the polarisation of research in anthropology and the social sciences is different to that in physics, chemistry and biology. In general, private enterprise cannot replace the rôle of the public authorities in those spheres where they exist side by side; it can only complement and round it off (and this is particularly the case with education). In their complementary function, private organisations do have some advantages over public institutions, especially the traditional ones, such as agility in the broadening and changing of activities, in the evaluation of situations or the distribution of funds, in the assumption of responsibilities and risks in their work, in the establishment of links or the co-ordination of functions especially in the international area. This suppleness and skill are all the more useful when there is a need to introduce new methods and to renew the techniques of organised cultural work and scientific research as in present-day Italy where all structural forms of organisation and administration will have to be reshaped.

LITERATURE

Recent Italian literature on the activities and social rôle of the foundations has been sparse. Mention should be made of *Funzioni e finalità delle fondazioni culturali*, which recorded the proceedings of the international meeting promoted by the Istituto Accademico di Roma, the Giorgio Cini Foundation and the Adriano Olivetti Foundation, held in Rome on 12th/14th May 1966. This was published in Rome in 1967 and includes a general report by Eugenio Montale, a discussion between V. Branca, S. Cotta, M. Fichera, G. Negri and E. Zolla, on legal problems:

Galateria, L. La disciplina giuridica della Fondazioni culturali in Italia.
Berliri, A. Problemi fiscali delle fondazioni in Italia.
Dus, A. Il trattamento fiscale delle fondazioni nella legislazione italiana.
Predieri, A. Proposta per una nuova disciplina legislativa delle fondazioni e degli istituti culturali privati in Italia.
Rescigno, P. Recenti indirizzi legislativi in materia di Fondazioni in Germania.
Aurisicchio, G. Verso una tipologia delle fondazioni italiane.

This meeting made a big impact in Italian culture, as it attracted the attention of public opinion and gave rise to discussions, most of them legal ones.

The literature on the legal aspects of foundations is vast. Among the most recent papers, to which we would also refer the reader for further bibliographical data are:

Predieri, A. Sull'ammodernamento della disciplina delle fondazioni e istituzioni culturali di diritto privato, in: Rivista trimestrale di diritto e procedura civile, 1969.
Rescigno, P. Fondazione (dir. civ.), in: Enciclopedia del diritto, XII, Milano, Giuffrè, 1968, p. 790 et ss.
Rescigno, P. Fondazione e impresa, in: Rivista delle Società, 1968, p. 812 et ss.
Corti Fondazione e impresa, in: Rivista di diritto civile, 1968, p. 1 et ss.

There has been a lack of new studies on private foundations set up for charitable aims (though one can refer to the items 'assistenza', in: 'Enciclopedia del diritto', Milan, Guiffrè, Vol. III, and 'beneficienza e assistenza', in: 'Nuovissiomo Digesto Italiano', Turin, Utet, Vol. II, p. 305, which also provide more bibliographical data).

Netherlands

Frits W. Hondius

ACKNOWLEDGEMENTS

In the Netherlands, a foundation is an important legal institution as well as being of great sociological importance. All the scholars and lawyers whom the author approached for advice or information took a keen interest in the project. The author wishes to express his particular indebtedness to Mr. J. Th. A. M. Duynstee, a barrister of Arnhem, for his critical review of the manuscript. Advice was also given by Professor J. M. Polak of Wageningen Agricultural University and by Professors R. Feenstra and J. Th. de Smidt of the Law Faculty of Leyden University. The author's brother, Mr. E. H. Hondius of the same Faculty, made a number of suggestions on English legal terminology.

The Ministries of Justice, Finance and Education and Sciences at The Hague also furnished information on administrative and judicial practice.

Some interesting data on Church foundations were contributed by Professor J. J. Loeff at the Secretariat of the Roman Catholic Church in the Netherlands, 's-Hertogenbosch, and by Mr. J. A. Ebbinge Wubben, General Synod of the Netherlands Reformed Church, The Hague.

The author gained further insight into the practice of foundations as a result of his interviews with the administrators of several foundations.

The above acknowledgements do not release the author from his responsibility for this paper and the shortcomings it almost certainly contains.

I. INTRODUCTION

The rôle of foundations in Dutch society

The important rôle which foundations play in Dutch public life is indicated both by their number and by the variety of activities which they cover. In 1968, the total number of officially registered foundations was put at well over 26,000 (1st January 1970: 28,500). To this should be added an unknown multitude of non-registered foundations, Church foundations, scholarships and pension funds.

The evolution of Dutch foundations has been determined by two historical circumstances. Firstly, the social and moral climate in the Netherlands favours private initiative in the promotion of communal interests. The religious and political history of the country has exerted a significant influence on this development.

In the nineteenth century, a political doctrine of 'subsidiarity' evolved, stressing the full legal equality of private and public structures. In Dutch society today, State organs and voluntary organisations alternate and intertwine like the two halves of a zip-fastener. In the intermediate zone between State and society, foundations have a particular function to perform. They are not only the channels through which private funds and private initiative are made available for the common weal, but also the channels through which the State feeds funds and knowledge back into the private sector.

The second factor which helped the development of Dutch foundations has been the very liberal legal provisions. Dutch law is content with a bare minimum of conditions for the establishment and existence of foundations. The range of purposes for which foundations can be set up is virtually unlimited.

In several ways, the concept of a foundation in the Netherlands covers a wider range of organisations than in other countries. In international terminology, a 'foundation' is defined as 'an instrument for the contribution of private wealth to a public purpose'. The essence of such an organisation is its financial means. The assets of a foundation are constituted as an independent legal entity or as a dependent fund held in trust, which makes funds available through its own programme of operations (operating foundation) or to projects of other organisations or persons (grant-making foundation). Most Dutch foundations, however, are identified solely by their activities, not by their property. They do not own capital endowments of any importance. Many of the large foundations operate on annual budgets which are much larger than their capital, and some have hardly any capital at all.

The modern Dutch foundation is basically a form of organisation, which is protected but not restricted by law, easy to found and easy to manage. From the traditional field of charity, foundations have broadened their scope and now embrace a wide range of other fields. Here lies a fundamental difference to foundations in other countries. Dutch foundations are not necessarily set up for charitable purposes. The Dutch foundation system has its specific advantages and defects. It is well suited to the social mobility and structural complexity of our time. But the foundation concept may also be exploited as a legal smokescreen. The foundation in modern Dutch law provides a legal framework for almost any kind of organised activity, be it an agricultural exhibition, a radio corporation or a vocational school. Foundation status is a simple formula for acquiring legal identity and legal capacity and for exempting founders and trustees from personal liability. Moreover, Dutch foundations are not encumbered by some of the limitations inherent in other Dutch forms of corporation such as limited duration, external control over decision-making or the requirement of a public concession.

To sum up, the term foundation is applied in the Netherlands to practically[1] all projects for which it is employed in other countries, but also to numerous projects which have little or nothing to do with charity.

A general classification of foundations

Broadly speaking, Dutch foundations can be divided into five main categories, according to their aims and structure:
(a) *'Classical' foundations* of the traditional type. These are endowed with private funds and devoted to charitable purposes. Foundations of this kind, are, for instance, the *Prins Bernhard Fonds* (promotion of culture), the *NOVIB Foundation* (private development aid) and the *Koningin Wilhelmina Fonds* (fight against cancer). Some of them implement their own projects, others restrict their activities to rendering financial support to the work of other organisations or persons, and/or to fund-raising. Many classical foundations are indicated as 'fund' (*fonds*). Well known examples are the *'universiteitsfondsen'* and *'hogeschoolfondsen'*, foundations which mobilize private support for the universities.
A separate category should be allocated to the ancient scholarship foundations, which were founded before the Napoleonic era. These foundations retained a separate status under Dutch law. Moreover, there are a number of bursaries and funds which have not attained full foun-

---

[1] One notable exception is that the largest grant-giving body in the field of scientific research, an organisation entitled ZWO, is constituted not as a foundation but as a public body *sui generis*. Another exception in contrast with English law is that a body constituted as an association can never at the same time be a foundation.

dation status (i.e. legal personality and an independent board), but have been constituted as dependent trust funds.

(b) *'Institutional' foundations.* Many foundations in the social, educational and religious sphere are composed of a single institution or complex of institutions. Their purpose is restricted to a narrowly defined object which is usually tied in real estate property: a school, a museum, a hospital, a nature monument, etc.

(c) *'Organisational' foundations.* This category, by far the largest of all, includes foundations which serve as the legal embodiment of community projects or group interests. In contradistinction to the two previous types, neither property nor permanence nor charitable aims are essential. Foundations can be set up for purposes which do not require funds, for example a mutual consultation organ. The purpose may be ephemeral, such as the organisation of a jubilee. It may be idealistic, such as the propagation of a certain religion, or mundane, such as promotion of the consumption of ice-cream. The original concept of 'charitable purpose' has been replaced in the course of time by the absolutely neutral criterion of 'a certain purpose'.

(d) *Church foundations.* Along with a number of ancient vicarage funds, these foundations lead an existence which is separate from ordinary foundations. Historically, this is explained by the separation between Church and State, but the distinction has lost much of its meaning today. In 1963, an optional clause was introduced into the Dutch Foundations Act making it possible for ecclesiastical foundations to obtain the status of ordinary foundations.

(e) *Pension and insurance funds.* Owing to their special character—social benefits for a restricted number of beneficiaries—these foundations have also been given separate status under Dutch law.

Foundation research

Given the important place of foundations in Dutch community life and the thoroughness with which the Dutch keep records of everything under the sun worth recording, one would expect much data on foundations to be available. This is not the case, however.

In the past, insufficient quantitive and qualitative research was done in this field. A report drawn up by Professor J. M. Polak in 1963 was a first attempt at stock-taking by random sample. We shall be discussing this report later on. Some catalogues and inventories have been compiled for specific purposes (for example, a list of foundations giving grants for scientific research). Qualitative research has been mainly restricted to historical treatises and to analyses of the legal structure of foundations. More research ought to be done on the political and sociological aspects of foundations.

II. GENERAL DEVELOPMENT OF DUTCH FOUNDATION LAW

Art. 1 of the Foundations Act of the Netherlands (*Wet op Stichtingen*) of 31st May 1956 defines a foundation (*stichting*) as 'a legal person, created by statute which has no members and which aims at realising a definite purpose with the aid of assets earmarked for that purpose'.

This rather colourless formula is the result of a long and peculiar history. The vast properties held by the Churches, monasteries, and Church offices of early Christianity can be regarded as predecessors of modern foundations. To supplement these institutions, the Church encouraged the establishment of secular endowments for charitable purposes.

Some of the controversies on modern foundations, such as the questions of legal personality, ownership, control and demarcation of spheres of influence between the State and society are as old as foundations themselves.

The institutions of the early Christian world received their crude legal shape from canon law which was based on post-classical Roman law. The Reformation and the gaining of national independence (sixteenth and seventeenth centuries) not only permitted the Netherlands to continue the ecclesiastical foundations, but also fostered the emergence of new secular foundations mainly in the field of social welfare. The foundation law of this period was part of Roman-Dutch law.

It should be noted that the trial of strength which took place throughout European history between secular rulers and the Church on the question of control of communal property was also waged in the Netherlands. Strong political régimes attempted to curb the wealth and immunities of the Church, and to restrict or supervise *mortmain* property. One would expect that the Reformation would have tipped the scales in favour of secular power in the Netherlands, but precisely because Dutch independence was a victory for individualism and against centralisation and absolutism, the legal climate remained favourable to the continued independence of separate legal complexes, such as foundations.

Neither the French Revolution, nor the process of centralisation and codification of law, set in motion by Napoleon, affected the foundations. The French Code Civil, introduced in 1811, and its Dutch counterpart, the *Burgerlijk Wetboek* of 1838, did not contain a single rule on foundations as they were completely alien to the French system. For nearly one and a half centuries after the 1814 Constitution had proclaimed the principle of codification, foundation law continued to develop exclusively on the basis of custom and case law.

The absence of any legal provisions on foundations had some important consequences. While other forms of corporate bodies in the Netherlands could exist only *propter legem*, foundations flourished *praeter legem*. The law of foundations was moulded by the concrete interpretations laid down by the notaries public. Moreover, judicial precedent carried more prestige in this field than was usually the case with civil law. In addition, the term 'foundation' was redefined to cover new purposes during the successive phases of social development.

The evolution of Dutch foundations in the nineteenth century mainly took place in the field of private charity. This period witnessed the shaping of different forms of legal personality, corresponding with the social, economic and political processes of the Europe of the Industrial Revolution. Apart from the impact on the Dutch scene of the debate between German scholars on the true nature of juridical personality, the interest in foundations in the Netherlands concentrated on questions pertaining to property and on various aspects of legal capacity.

In the twentieth century, there was an accelerated development. Emphasis shifted from property to organisation. The criterion of property, since time immemorial an essential feature of foundations, was watered down to a point of relative importance. Foundations were discovered to be a convenient instrument for giving organisational structure and legal personality to any social purpose, whether in the private or public sphere, or halfway between the two. The absence of statute law and of any form of State concession fostered this development. Since the 1930s, the Netherlands have experienced a veritable boom in foundations.

It lasted until 1956 when a minimum number of rules on foundations were laid down by act of parliament, the Foundations Act (*Wet op Stichtingen*). The main effect of this act was to provide a system of registration, making their basic data available to the public. The new Register of Foundations made it possible to obtain an overall survey of foundations, albeit by no means a complete survey. Even so, the harvest was substantial. By the end of 1969 28,500 foundations had been registered and new registrations were being filed at an average of 20 per day.

The inventory remained incomplete, primarily because registration is not obligatory so that there are still an unknown number of non-registered foundations. Secondly, the data which the register contains are far from complete. Thirdly, certain categories of foundations have been explicitly excluded from the terms of the Foundations Act.

III. ANCIENT LAW[2]

Canon law extended to the Christian Church the post-classical Roman law concepts of corporation. Originally, Church institutions showed a certain dichotomy, reflecting in their organisation as they did traits which were characteristic both of 'associations' and of 'foundations'. The Church was the community (*universitas personarum*) of the congregation. But it was also a divine institution, founded by Christ and ruled by the laws of the Holy Script. It was this second trait which prevailed in the organisation of individual Churches. As from the second century, Churches were organised hierarchically. The faithful were in the position of beneficiaries, not of owners, or rulers, of the Church.

As regards ownership, the usual view was that the general Church belonged to God or to Christ, while separate Church properties were donated or bequeathed to local saints.

In addition to the basic property of the Churches and monasteries separate properties were set aside for the purpose of divine worship or of charity. Donations made by private persons for the latter purpose, the *piae causae*, can be considered as prototype foundations.

Joubert considers the critical element in the development of foundations to have been the evolution of the notion of legal personality and, in this connection, calls Archbishop Moyse of Ravenna (twelfth century) the 'father of foundations'. Feenstra opposes both theses. First of all, if anybody deserves this name, then it is Pope Innocent IV, who was the first one to use the word *persona* for a legal person. Secondly, independent legal existence is not the proper historical criterion for the study of foundations. Feenstra points to the existence of a second type of foundation, the dependent foundation (*Treuhand* or Trust) which derived from classical Roman Law. This institution consisted of a donation to a natural person or group of persons together with instructions as to its use. This form was especially appropriate for those secular foundations which consisted of a sum (*Hauptgeldstiftung*) which, or the proceeds of which, were to be distributed for a certain purpose (e.g. alms or the ransom for prisoners). In the Middle Ages, the formula *fundare* emerged as the technical term for the establishment of a distinct property. A characteristic of these properties was that beneficiaries (e.g. the poor, the orphans) had no direct claim. As a rule, the *piae causae* were established without any licence by the secular authorities. The Church hierarchy supervised the administration of the Churches and the separate endowments

---

[2] The facts on which this chapter is based have been borrowed in the main from the works of De Blecourt, Coopmans, Feenstra, Joubert and Van Tricht, see *Literature*.

and charitable foundations. The *oeconomus* (administrator of Church property) was responsible to the *episcopus* (master of the Church).

In the Middle Ages, the dual authority of ecclesiastical and secular power was reflected in the existence of different kinds of legal entities and jurisdictions. In the Netherlands, the secular entities (*universitates*), were viewed as associations or persons who were subject to the wordly ruler. They were defined in terms of their size—such as the neighbourhood (*buurschap*), manor (*ambacht*)—or their function—such as the guild (*gilde*). The estates serving ecclesiastical or charitable purposes (*venerabiles domus vel loci*) were viewed as Church property and remained under ecclesiastical supervision.

While in general, the demarcation line between temporal and spiritual powers was well observed, there was animosity in the sphere of property. The great wealth of the Churches, abbeys and monasteries—often reinforced by fiscal and judiciary immunities—was beyond the reach of secular authorities. Some rulers (e.g. Charlemagne) limited or forbad the acquisition of property by the Church. Others placed their property under the final supervision of the ruler. The Church resisted these measures and in periods of weak secular power attempted to recover its privileged position.

A peculiar counterpart of the Church properties, exempted from secular jurisdiction and subject to canon law, were the Churches and endowments founded by medieval lords on their own estates, subject to their own jurisdiction (*Eigenkirchenrecht*), and generally exempted from ecclesiastical supervision.

The distinction between properties under religious and those under secular power accounts, according to Feenstra, for the difference between independent and dependent (trust) foundations.

With the rise of Nation-States, secular authority asserted itself convincingly against the Church. In the Netherlands, Emperor Charles V vigorously imposed the rule—in his proclamations of 1518 and 1520—that the donation of property to Churches, monasteries and charitable institutions or the setting up of property for the latter's use required the consent of the lord of the land.

During the Reformation, the Dutch provinces and cities seized control over the Church and its property. The struggle for independence in the Netherlands was a combined war against the Catholic Church and against the usurpation of power by central authority. Political power was jealously divided between the provinces, the cities, rural lords, and various public corporations. This development fostered the existence of many separate legal entities, including foundations. Their status varied. In many instances, their relationship to a family or a public body resembled that of a trust.

Part of the property of the Catholic Church was reconverted for Protestant use; other parts were secularised. Church buildings and estates (*fabricae ecclesiae*) served henceforth for Reformed Church services and the housing of Reformed Church ministers, school teachers, scholarships or for aiding the poor. Some buildings were changed, for example, into plague infirmaries or hospitals.

The monasteries declined, although their existence as distinct groups of buildings was not directly challenged. A number of them were utilised for different purposes, as, for example, in Gelderland the *juffrouwstiften* (institutions to support spinsters of noble birth).

The collegiate Churches of Utrecht, known as *kapittels*, survived the Reformation and some of them were changed into foundations for the support of certain families. A similar fate befell many vicarage properties (*vicarieën*) which became family trusts or scholarship funds. The presbyteries (*pastorieën*) and vergers' funds (*kosterijen*) were administered either by Church officials subject to the supervision of local or provincial authorities, or directly by the latter authorities. To this end, offices for the supervision of clerical estates (*kantoren van geestelijke goederen*) were set up. Not infrequently, Church properties were merged in the course of time with public property.

After the Reformation, too, religious charitable institutions, such as the 'Holy Spirit foundations' (*Heilige Geestfundaties*) for the poor, and the 'Houses of God' (*Godshuizen*), were established. The distinction between religious and secular charitable institutions lost its importance. They were all independent foundations, autonomous in their management and policy, but subject to supervision by local or provincial authorities.

The great prosperity of the Netherlands under the Republic was evident by the large number of new charitable donations: alms houses, orphanages, *hofjes* (social welfare settlements), etc. Many of the foundations thus established enjoyed privileges, such as the right of a hospital to inherit from its inmates. These privileges were sometimes confirmed by octroi, sometimes acknowledged as a natural right which did not seem to need confirmation. Foundations were created by private citizens as well as by public authorities. (Joubert cites the example of a silk spinning shop for poor girls, established by magistrates of Amsterdam in 1682.)

No permission by the authorities was required for the establishment of foundations by private persons. Nor did their existence depend on hard and fast legal rules. The most usual vehicle was a person's last will and testament. Generally, the founder(s), the property, the beneficiaries (the poor, the old, etc.) and the administrators (usually four *regenten*) were clearly identified, but the legal ownership of the foundation remained somewhat vague.

The term *stichting* first made its appearance as a separate concept in Roman-Dutch law, towards the end of the sixteenth century. Originally, it referred to the act of establishing a building or institution. Later, it came to mean the institution itself. During the later period of Roman-Dutch law, the word *stichting* was used particularly to denote a charitable institution, also known as a *fundatie* or *fondatie*. The precise meaning was gradually shaped by the lawyers. While there was a consensus about the act of establishment, the designation of a purpose of some permanence and the earmarking of assets for a certain purpose, there was no general rule about the minimum size of such assets.

IV. NINETEENTH-CENTURY LAW

The foundations were affected in certain details, but not in principle, by the chain of events touched off by the French Revolution. The Republic of the United Netherlands was superseded by the Batavian Republic (1795), later the Kingdom of Holland (1806), to be incorporated into the Empire of Napoleon (1810). In 1813 the Netherlands regained their independence as a unitary Kingdom which until 1830 also comprised Belgium.

The codification of the law was one of the many innovations of the new era, but the foundation law was neither codified nor abolished. In French civil law, which had been applicable in the Netherlands since 1st March 1811, the phenomenon of private foundations was unknown. For this reason, the Dutch foundations were affected only inasfar as they were incompatible with specific French laws. An example was the decree of 15th November 1811, by which all educational and scholarship funds were incorporated into the property of the Imperial University.

After the end of French domination, there was a controversy among Dutch lawyers, between those who wanted to revert to the legal system of the old Republic and those who wanted to retain the benefits of the French system. The draft civil code of 1820, prepared by Joan Melchior Kemper, attempted to offer a compromise. It proposed acknowledging foundations *expressis verbis* as institutions of Dutch law, but subject to the proviso that no foundation should exist unless recognised by the central authority (the King). The draft was an effort to codify genuine Dutch law, instead of adapting the Napoleonic Code to Dutch conditions. The 24th Section of Book One, entitled 'On Corporations, Associated Bodies and Foundations, regarded as Persons' was the first attempt to codify the legislation governing Dutch foundations. It fell through, however, as a result of the objections raised by the Belgians, who preferred a French Code Civil with minor adjustments.

The Dutch Civil Code (*Burgerlijk Wetboek*), entered into force on 1st October 1838 (though in the Province of Limburg not until 1st January 1842), is still valid today, even if it is admittedly gradually being replaced by a new code[3]. The 10th Title of Book III of the Code dealt with juridical persons (*zedelijke lichamen*), but unlike the draft of 1820, this comprised only corporations of persons, not foundations.

The idea prevailed in the nineteenth century that a legal person had to be defined by law in order to exist. The corporations of persons in private law were gradually made subject to legal provisions which were enacted to complement the Civil Code. Associations (*verenigingen*) were regulated by the Act of 22nd April 1855 (*Staatsblad* No. 32), which had, undoubtedly, been inspired by events in other parts of Europe in 1848, the year of the revolutions. The main rule was that no association should have legal personality unless by Royal consent or unless authorised by law. Some problems arose with regard to corporations in the commercial or semi-commercial sphere. In the latter field, there were mutual insurance companies (*onderlinge verzekerings of waarborgmaatschappijen*) and cooperative societies (*coöperatieve verenigingen*). Their aims could not be considered sufficiently idealistic—a generally accepted qualification for associations—nor sufficiently profit-making for them to come under company law. An Act of 14th September 1866 (*Staatsblad* No. 123) gave the mutual insurance companies a separate status under Art. 14 of the 1855 Act and under Art. 1691 of the Civil Code. Cooperative societies were governed by an Act of 17th November 1876 (*Staatsblad* No. 227) replaced by the Act of 28th May 1925 (*Staatsblad* No. 204).

As regards the various forms of commercial companies—shipowners (*rederij*), partnership (*maatschap*), firm (*vennootschap onder firma*), limited partnership (*commanditaire vennootschap*), limited company (*naamloze vennootschap*), abbreviated as NV—there was little doubt about their juristic identity. The major issue was, firstly, the question of risks and responsibilities and secondly, to what extent juristic personality could be desirable in addition to, or instead of, the personal liability of business partners. Commercial companies were regulated in general by the Commercial Code (*Wetboek van Koophandel*) of 4th July 1837 (*Staatsblad* No. 51). In the case of the NV a special Act was adopted on 2nd July 1928 (*Staatsblad* No. 216). This amended the Commercial Code. Prior to the establishment of a NV, the founders must obtain a statement of 'no objection' by the Minister of Justice.

Church societies (*kerkgenootschappen*) were covered by an Act of 10th

---

[3] See J. Dainow, 'Civil Code Revision in the Netherlands' in *Lousiana Law Review* (1957), p. 273.

September 1853 (*Staatsblad* No. 102). These societies were, for this reason, deemed to be exempt from the provisions of the Act on Associations of 1855. The State exercises a very limited degree of supervision over the public actions of the Churches. This supervision aims at avoiding a clash of interests between the numerous Churches.

The foundation proper remained the only legal person untouched by direct legislation. While the aforementioned forms of corporations existed *propter legem*, the foundations existed *praeter legem*. The fact that they legally existed at all was proved by indirect references such as in Art. 4, para. 2 of the Poor Law (*Armenwet*) of 28th June 1854. This Act also acknowledged that a foundation (an institution of private law) could be established by a public body, e.g. a municipality. The Poor Law (which was replaced by a new Act in 1912) referred only to Church and charitable foundations. The question remained whether other foundations could still be established since the Civil Code was silent on them. This question was answered positively by a judgment of the *Hoge Raad* (Supreme Court of the Netherlands) on 30th June 1882 (the *Jan de Koningfonds* case).

The question of the legitimate existence of foundations thus decided, attention shifted to their usefulness. Objections were of two sorts. The first was the old grievance that foundations accumulated *mortmain* property. The second objection, voiced in 1873 by Professor S. J. Fockema Andreae, held somewhat dogmatically that members of the board of a foundation would be less motivated or diligent than the members of the board of an association.

In the absence of general rules on foundations[4], the former were regulated in the main by the interpretations of the notaries public and of the Courts of justice. A number of criteria evolved from these practical interpretations. A fully-fledged foundation had to fulfil three essential conditions: the existence of assets, a purpose and an organisation. A proforma prerequisite (though not an absolute condition) was the existence of written evidence.

Although, historically, the existence of property was essential for the setting-up of a foundation, this requirement gradually lost much of its importance. Some scholars even did not deem it necessary for property to be set aside for a special purpose in order to launch a foundation. A judgment by a Kanton judge of Amsterdam of 2nd August 1934 that the existence of a

---

[4] Occasional references to foundations were contained in the Higher Education Act of 1876 (Art. 170), the Poor Act of 1854 and 1912 (Art. 5), the Trade Register Act of 1918 (Art. 11), the Trade Name Act of 1921 (Art. 4) the Civil Code (Art. 946), the Civil Procedure Code (Art. 242 and 324), the Housing Act of 1901 (Art. 52) and the Agricultural Labourers Act of 1918 (Art. 6).

foundation required the '...lasting earmarking of property for a certain, more or less major purpose...' was quashed by the District Court of Amsterdam (*Amsterdamsche Aardappelen- en Groenencentrale* case). Another Kanton judge of Amsterdam ruled, on 19th October 1934, that property worth f 100,- was sufficient since no minimum was set by the law. Though the practice of setting aside a certain amount of money still existed as a formal requirement, it degenerated into a meaningless ritual.

It was generally advocated that the purpose of a foundation should be idealistic. Traditionally, this meant a purpose in the field of charity, science or arts. But in the twentieth century, jurists were bound to take cognisance of the increasing use made of foundations for other ends. The concept of 'idealistic' was gradually replaced by the criterion of 'non-commercial'. Again, this was interpreted with considerable latitude. A foundation established for the purpose of administering shares for shareholders or for advancing the interests of shareholders of a certain company was thought to be quite in order. Moreover, foundations that made a profit for the purpose of financing a noble cause were perfectly acceptable.

In the case of foundations whose aims had become obsolete, an Act of 1st May 1925 (*Staatsblad* No. 174) enabled the *Hoge Raad* to slightly change the purpose of the institution provided that forty years had elapsed since the death of the founder.

Case law on the organisation of foundations limited itself to the question of how and by whom the board (which sometimes even consisted of one person!) was appointed, how vacancies were filled and what the board's terms of reference were. In practice, the boards of foundations were very powerful. They could exceed their powers, or fail to do anything at all. There was hardly any power which could exercise control over them.

Special problems arose with regard to the establishment of foundations by last will[5]. In contrast to Roman-Dutch law and Napoleonic law, the Dutch Civil Code of 1838 left open the possibility of creating foundations by testament, and thus reverted to the rules of classical Roman Law. While French Law held that a testament is an act by which a person disposes of his estate after his death, Art. 922 of the Dutch Civil Code held that a testament is an act by which a person lays down what he wishes to happen after his death (...*eene acte over hetgeen iemand wil dat na zijn dood zal geschieden*...).

Should a foundation established by a testament be regarded as an 'heir'? This question was of some importance in view of the application of the Succession Act. Since Art. 946 of the Civil Code provides that an heir must exist at the moment of the death of the testator, it should be determined

[5] Cf. the case of the Städelsches Kunstinstitut in Frankfurt, Germany, 1816.

whether the foundation created by a testament could receive a legacy or the entire estate under the same testament. Originally a *Hoge Raad* decision of 30th June 1882, held that a foundation created by a testament is an heir, but in three judgments rendered in the years 1894-6 (the first judgment on 2nd February 1894) the *Hoge Raad* reversed its opinion. In 1907 the Law on Estate Duties was changed in order to circumvent the new situation created by the judgment of the *Hoge Raad*: the new Act considered a foundation created by a testament to be an 'heir'. However, the Succession Act contained a provision on a reduced scale of duties if the legal person who was to enjoy the inheritance could prove that it 'was mainly promoting a general charitable purpose, and principally active as a charitable institution whose main aim was care for the sick or handicapped' (Art. 80).

An interesting series of lawsuits on the legislation governing charitable foundations established by testament took place in the years 1923 to 1928. The cause was a charitable foundation called *Pape-Fonds* which had been set up by a wealthy gentleman who died in May 1922, and who had transferred his entire assets into a charitable fund, in order '. . . to render financial aid where the board may deem it expedient'.

Apart from an unsuccessful lawsuit by the frustrated heirs, the board of the foundation and the Netherlands' Treasury fought each other for several years in Court over the question whether the foundation had been improperly taxed on death duties and the estate duty on gifts.

V. DUTCH FOUNDATIONS TODAY

Until the first decades of the twentieth century, the traditional foundation was a privately donated fund which was set up to finance a social purpose defined in its statutes.

In the 1920s and 1930s, the basic importance of foundations as legal persons shifted from capital to activity. The foundation was discovered as a useful legal instrument for circumventing legal obstacles or outwitting the legislator. There were some notorious cases of foundations created, for example, in order to obviate the provisions of the Stamp Duty Act of 1917 or to incorporate a body which could not obtain recognition as an association. Moreover, government organs at all levels, but particularly at local level, started to make use of foundations as institutions of private law which were able to execute tasks which are covered by public law.

In his book *Osmose* published in 1930, Professor G. A. Van Poelje was the first to call attention to the phenomenon of cross-fertilisation between public administration and private management.

The Government made increasing use of institutions of private law to fulfil their public functions. The oldest and most prominent example was government participation in commercial companies. This started in the nineteenth century, particularly in the field of public utilities. For some time, it was a matter of discussion whether the government was in this case acting on an equal footing with other parties in private law, or with preferential status. It was generally agreed that there was no justification for special treatment.

Van Poelje cites as an early example of a public foundation (*overheids-stichtingen*) a foundation established by the city of Rotterdam in 1918 for the administration of municipal houses, or an inter-municipal water-works established in 1923. In the 1920s, the city council of The Hague set up foundations for the central administration of municipal housing, for the management of public baths, the education of sick children and the adminis-tration of sports and playgrounds. The central Government made use of foundations, *inter alia*, in the Crisis Agricultural Act of 1933 which set up agricultural agencies in the form of foundations.

The most usual reason for the establishment of public foundations was that the Government, like private persons, either wished to profit from the absence, or flexibility of rules, or to collaborate on an equal footing with private parties. Van Poelje cites an example to show this case. The city of Amsterdam entrusted the management of its school gardens to a foundation, whereas in the city of The Hague the same task was entirely the responsibility of local government and carried out by a municipal service. The explanation is that in Amsterdam, school gardens were originally looked after by private associations.

The use which the Government made of foundations sometimes led to complicated relationships. For example, in 1950 the Government founded, and has ever since subsidised, an independent organisation for the advance-ment of pure research (*Nederlandse Organisatie voor Zuiver Wetenschappelijk Onderzoek*), a legal person *sui generis*, created by law; this organisation, in turn, created and is still subsidising a private foundation for fundamental research of matter.

By 1959, there were in the strict sense of the word 876 public foundations in the Netherlands; 234 of them were set up by the central Government, 96 by provincial Governments and the other 546 foundations by the municipal authorities. By public foundation in the proper sense, we understand (a) foundations established by a Government organ or by a Government organ together with private bodies or persons. In a wider sense, public foundations are also: (b) foundations in which the Government has a say or (c) foundations

R

entrusted by the Government with a public function. In addition to foundations set up by Government departments, the legal form of a foundation is sometimes also chosen by business enterprises incorporated under public law (*publiekrechtelijke bedrijfslichamen*[6]).

Van Poelje confirmed that, in some cases, governmental authorities have made use of a foundation in order to fill gaps in the law or to circumvent the law. Thus, for some time, foundations have been used for the promotion of the interests of several municipalities, because the law provided no other means for doing so. Some provinces used foundations to obtain more influence in the cities than they were allowed under public law.

In almost all public foundations, the major part of their financial needs are met by annual Government grants and the size and interest of the 'capital endowment' is of marginal importance only. It is not uncommon for a public foundation with an annual budget of more than a million guilders to have a capital of one hundred guilders.

VI. THE FOUNDATIONS ACT

History of the Act

The Bill for an Act to regulate foundations was presented by Royal Message of 29th April 1954 to the Second Chamber of the States-General of the Netherlands[7].

The accompanying Explanatory Memorandum (*Memorie van Toelichting*) by the Minister of Justice recalled that a previous Bill, submitted to Parliament on 2nd April 1937 had been withdrawn on 5th May 1948 because it had met with considerable opposition and, at the time, it was deemed more appropriate to await the rules to be laid down on this subject by the draft for the new Dutch Civil Code.

However, on account of the untimely death of Professor E. M. Meijers who had been commissioned in 1947 to draft the Code, the new Code took a long time to emerge. It is to be regretted for many reasons that he did not live to finish his work. His treatment of foundations would probably have resulted in a brief and concise codification. The Ministry of Justice, which took over the task, produced a draft law which bore the imprint of the civil servants' concern with detail. The drafters stated that there were pressing

---

[6] J. Groenendaal, 'Het gebruik van stichtingen door publiekrechtelijke bedrijfslichamen', in: Sociaal-Economische Wetgeving, Afd. Nederland (1961), p. 169 ff.

[7] Wettelijke regeling inzake stichtingen, Zitting 1953-4, Nr. 3463, Handelingen Tweede Kamer der Staten-General.

reasons for not delaying a foundations act much longer. Foundations were occupying a more and more prominent position in public life, even though they were not governed by the provisions of any single law or even a by-law. Thus, the Explanatory Memorandum remarked, '...mismanagement or waste can take place unnoticed, the board may favour itself unduly. Often, nobody is entitled to oppose this. Since it is not known what foundations exist and who are members of the board, it is even very difficult to discover embezzlement.'

The drafters considered codification desirable, both in order to reaffirm customary law and jurisprudence and to provide consistent and adequate legal rules for foundations where common law and case law had failed so far.

As regards the question of property, the memorandum pointed out that jurisprudence formally supported the idea that no foundation can be established unless it has some assets, but that in reality this criterion had been reduced to a mere formality. The draft law took an intermediate position by not making the absence of funds a cause for nullity but by providing the possibility for the Court to dissolve a foundation if there was no guarantee that the foundation would acquire the necessary means for its operations.

On a second issue, the Bill was more outspoken: it categorically rejected the use of a foundation for commercial purposes.

One extremely delicate aspect of the Bill was the treatment of public foundations and the practice of national, provincial and in particular local authorities undertaking certain activities not in the form of an institution incorporated under public law, but as a foundation.

The Bill referred to the general principle laid down in Arts. 228 h and 234 of the Municipalities Act, namely that participation by Government departments in organisations incorporated under private law (such as foundations, limited companies, associations, etc.) is only permissible if this legal form is indispensable in view of the nature of the subject matter. This provision would serve as a check upon the excessive use by municipalities of foundations.

The Minister of Justice, L. A. Donker, felt that there were cases where the State could legitimately participate in foundations, for example as a mixed form involving cooperation with natural persons. Since the present Bill was meant to cover foundations which were general institutions incorporated under private law, the Minister proposed to exempt from its jurisdiction all public foundations. A similar exception was made for those foundations which were charged by law to perform certain public tasks, for example foundations set up to control the quality of agricultural export products. Another category which the Minister of Justice wished to exclude from the

Bill were the Church foundations (*kerkelijke stichtingen*) and charitable institutions (*instellingen van weldadigheid*), as well as pension and savings funds (*pensioen en spaarfondsen*).

The Bill emphasised that public control over foundations should be restricted to rectifying abuses and that it was not intended to introduce preventive control.

On 10th June 1955 the Committee for Justice in the Second Chamber submitted its report on the Bill. It examined a number of basic questions:

1st. Should foundations be regulated by separate law or by the new Civil Code? The general opinion was that there was no objection against a separate law, if it accorded with the general principles set out in the new Civil Code.

2nd. Should the legislator intervene in any disputes involving legal doctrine? The Minister was of the opinion that a law could forestall abuses and provide greater legal security.

3rd. Should foundations be permitted to develop into more than one direction? In particular, the question was posed as to whether a foundation might be used if its main purpose was co-operation between persons or the making of profit. Since co-operation between persons could best be implemented by an association (*vereniging*), which had to fulfil stricter requirements for recognition than a foundation (namely a statement of Royal assent on the statutes and validity for 30 years only), the granting of permission to establish a foundation for this purpose would in fact be tantamount to providing a legal loophole.

A borderline case were those foundations created by the holders of preferred shares in limited companies in order to administer their shares. Were these real foundations or companies in disguise? As the purpose of such foundations was deemed not to be the making of a profit but the control of power and the forestalling of any surprises at the shareholders' meeting, the Minister considered them as a case covered by the provisions of the present law.

4th. Should a foundation have an initial capital? There was a general feeling that the possession of initial capital was not essential for the foundation. Even if the foundation has limited means, this may not prevent it from getting more funds later on. The Minister, therefore, omitted from the draft the requirement that the possession of capital would be of 'more than incidental importance'.

5th. Is profit-making at variance with the basic character of foundations? The original draft contained the condition that foundations should have a purpose which did not consist in the making of a profit. It was objected that this was confounding the ends with the means. It would be all right for the foundation to make profit as long as this was to be used for an idealistic purpose. Moreover, it was felt that the form of a foundation was admissible for an organisation which, without being directly engaged in commerce, was promoting the commercial interests of a group of persons. 'Non-commercial purpose' was, therefore, deleted from the draft and replaced by '...definite purpose ...'.

6th. Elimination of abuses or preventive control (concession)? Some members of the Committee questioned the appropriateness of the system of negative controls. This could lead to the anomalous situation where a foundation, created in clear violation of the requirements laid down by the law, would nevertheless exist legally until a Court would intervene. From the point of view of the foundations, the possibility of intervention by the Court would loom over them like the sword of Damocles.

The main arguments against preventive control were, first of all, that a proposal to this effect would meet with great political resistance, and secondly that it would necessitate a very detailed description of the criteria for foundations, since otherwise preventive control could lead to arbitrariness.

7th. Why judicial rather than administrative supervision? In his reply to the Committee, the Minister stressed that the Act aimed at reducing Government control over foundations to a minimum. Supervision by administrative organs would involve an evaluation of the policy of foundations. This would be contrary to the Dutch system, which ensures the board of a foundation freedom in its policy-making. Only clear cut cases of violation of the law or of mismanagement should be redressed or stopped by the judge.

8th. Public foundations (*overheidsstichtingen*). There was no enthusiasm in the Committee for the Government's proposal to keep public foundations outside the jurisdiction of this Act. This would enable the State to use the services of an institution incorporated under private law without subjecting it to the rules of private law.

In connection with the preparatory work done by the Second Chamber, the Minister changed some parts of the draft law by means of amending bills (*Nota's van Wijzigingen*), dated 10th June 1955, and 26th October 1955.

The debate on the Bill took place in the meetings held by the Second Chamber from 25th to 28th October 1955. In the discussion, some members pointed out the danger inherent in the fact that foundations would remain outside the direct supervision of the State, and thus of the democratic control of the people and that, on the other hand, the ruling that foundations must not have any members excluded the interested parties from having a say in their administration. This would tend to concentrate power in the hands of a few. They contrasted the 'dictatorial' character of foundations with the 'democratic' character of associations. The Minister of Justice observed that the prohibition that a foundation could have members which resulted in the absence of a control system such as that applied to associations, would be offset by judicial control.

It was stressed that the endowment was of no consequence and that the precondition that a foundation must possess capital was a 'leftover from old times'. The example was cited of a foundation performing the rôle of an advisory body. In this case, the possession of capital was irrelevant for the existence of the foundation.

One member gave a succinct explanation '. . .foundations have become so popular that not only is the local telephone book packed with the numbers of foundations, but also each of us is connected in some way with at least half a dozen. . .because, Mr. Chairman, there is a need to be able to act, administer and combine quickly, cheaply and simply'.

A warning was voiced against making things too easy or setting up foundations as a refuge for limited companies (for example, in order to evade tax) and associations (to escape democratic control). It was argued that the flexibility of a foundation was one of its charms and this fact, demonstrated by its efflorescence in everyday life, should compensate for the lack of clarity about what exactly constituted a foundation.

The Communist fraction of the Second Chamber opposed the exemption of Church foundations from the Act.

In his reply to the Chamber, the Minister of Justice once again outlined the guidelines of the Bill. Firstly, to obtain clarity about the nature of a foundation. Secondly, to prevent abuses such as the creation, in the form of a foundation, of a legal person seeking to avoid the legal controls existing for associations or limited companies. In order to curb the spread of further abuses, the Minister was not willing to delay the Bill until the enactment of the new Civil Code. The Minister clarified the relationship between the assets and the aims of a foundation. The Bill did not require that every foundation should, at the moment of its creation, possess a certain initial capital. At the moment of its creation or some time afterwards, a foundation should have or be able to acquire such property as would be adequate for the realisation of its aims. One delegate cited the example of a foundation created for the preservation and study of ancient papyri. The papyri were donated to the foundation after its creation and constituted its entire (and perfectly adequate) assets.

An important function of the Bill was to provide protection for the public by a clearer definition of foundations. For this reason, the Bill directed that the word 'foundation' (*stichting*) must be part of the name, a rule comparable to the rules contained in laws on limited companies and cooperative societies.

In order to meet some of the objections raised by members of the Chamber, the Minister agreed to amend the Bill on certain points. One change concerned the rule about not having any members. This prohibition was mitigated by a new provision that the right of persons to fill vacancies in the board of the foundation would not be construed as a right of 'membership' of the foundation.

As regards para. 3 of Art. 1, the Minister clarified the difference between 'idealistic' and 'social'. Some authors ascribe to 'idealistic' a more restricted meaning in the sense of religious, scientific and cultural purposes. 'Social' is a characteristic of modern times.

The Minister assured the Chamber that the Registrar of the central register would adopt a 'passive' attitude when accepting the registrations of new foundations. The only exception to this rule was that the Registrar would be enjoined to draw the attention of the public prosecutor to facts which might give rise to an intervention from the latter's side.

The Chamber was unanimous in its opposition to the exception clause for public foundations proposed by the Minister. They were afraid that public foundations would become a State within the State. The State should not run with the hare and hunt with the hounds to obtain the advantages of institutions incorporated under private law but avoid some of the rules which otherwise govern them. As this issue jeopardized the whole Bill the Minister proposed, and the Chamber accepted, that within five years the Government would come forward with a final solution. This was to be prepared by a State commission.

On 28th October 1955, the Second Chamber adopted the Bill with 55 to 12 votes. It was forwarded to the First Chamber, whose Committee of Rapporteurs published its comments on 15th February 1956. The Government replied with a Memorandum and the Bill was discussed in the Chamber on 23rd and 29th May 1956. This time, the Minister of Justice was Professor J. C. van Oven, Minister Donker having died in the meantime.

In their report and the subsequent discussion, members of the Chamber pointed out that the practice of setting aside symbolical sums of f 30,- or f 100,- made a mockery of the requirement that a foundation should have some assets. Would it not be better to withdraw this requirement, based as it was on dogma rather than on the exigencies of common usage?

The problem of the extent to which it was necessary to replace common law by State law was also discussed. The learned and eloquent Senator, Professor I. A. Diepenhorst noted that foundations had always been 'outside of the law'. But far from eliminating foundations, this status of outlawry had hastened the rapid multiplication of foundations.

The need to define a foundation by law was recognised by all but it was not until 1937 before a first (and unsuccessful) attempt was made. The belated action was all the more surprising as foundations have been an institution recognised by Dutch law since time immemorial.

The peroration of Professor Diepenhorst's speech reflected the mood of the House:

> 'Mr. Chairman! This Bill will be supported by myself and by my political friends. But let me now conclude with the following remarks. Some years ago, people were complaining that foundations were threatening to become the "naked show-window dummy whom all clothes will fit". Now, our foundations are not only properly dressed, so that they are no longer naked, but the dress has also been carefully fashioned. The law has not given them a pompous robe. The prescribed fashion line is characterized by its clear cut and simplicity.'

In his final comment on the Bill, Minister van Oven cited an example which he read in the newspaper as a striking illustration why foundations should finally be codified. A number of flat-dwellers had been of the opinion that they had been forced to pay too much rent. They set up a foundation to reclaim what had been paid in excess. This was a typical example of something for which a foundation should *not* be used. They should have reclaimed their money under Art. 1395 of the Civil Code.

On 29th May 1956, the Act was adopted (in Dutch: *Wet op Stichtingen*[8]). It took effect as from 1st January 1957. Article 29 provisionally exempted public foundations from its jurisdiction.

Main provisions of the Act

The introduction of the Act did not fundamentally affect foundations. It confirmed rather than restricted their position. The Act brought more logic

---

[8] It was emphasised that it was not called 'Wet op *de* Stichtingen' (Act on *the* Foundations), since that would seem to imply that all foundations were covered by the Act which was not the case.

into the general system and staked more clearly the boundaries between foundations, associations and commercial enterprises. Art. 1 of the Act prohibits foundations from having members, or making payments to persons, except for idealistic or social purposes. In practice, however, foundations have continued to have members (a notable culprit being the European Cultural Foundation), particularly with a view to fund-raising.

The Foundations Act contains two sets of rules. The first set deals with registration, the second with judicial supervision. The main object of the Act is not to interfere with the establishment or functioning of foundations, but rather to make them more accessible from outside and to provide for corrective action if this is desirable within their own terms of reference.

Foundations are created *inter vivos* by notarial deed, or *mortis causa* by last will and testament. The deed of establishment (declaration of intent) must contain the statutes and mention the name of the foundation, its aims, and a description of the procedure for the appointment of members of the board (Art. 3).

The board of a newly founded foundation should have it entered into the Public Central Register of Foundations, together with the full name and domicile of the founder(s) and the members of the board. Moreover, a certified copy of the statutes must be deposited. Similar registration and deposit takes place in the case of any change of officers or amendment of the statutes.

A decree dated 18th October 1957 entrusted the Department of Justice at The Hague with the administration of the Register and laid down detailed rules for the registration, deposit and issue of copies and abstracts. Anyone may consult the contents of the Register free of charge and is entitled to obtain copies and abstracts upon payment of a fee (Art. 9). Every registered foundation has its own case-file and serial number.

The registration system has ended the seclusion in which many foundations had hitherto been wrapped. It does not affect their freedom and independence. Registration serves to prove the existence of a foundation *vis-à-vis* third parties, but it is not a condition governing the validity of the foundation as such, nor is it compulsory. The Dutch registration system is passive and relies on self-registration by the foundations. While the Registrar may keep track of unregistered foundations which come to his attention, no attempt is made to induce such foundations to register. It is estimated that the foundations registered so far represent perhaps two thirds of the total number of existing foundations. In cases of incomplete or incorrect entries, corrective action may be taken only by a District Court, not by the Registrar. It should further be noted that the Register records the existence, not the activities or financial operations of foundations. There is no obligation for foundations to report to the Registrar.

The powers of supervision and redress in respect of foundations are exercised by the judiciary by virtue of Arts. 9–23 of the Act. Their main purpose is to ensure the proper functioning of foundations within their terms of reference. In this respect, the supervision system in the Netherlands is fundamentally different from other countries where the creation and activity of foundations is subject to considerations of public policy. The Dutch judiciary seldom uses its powers of intervention on its own initiative. Usually, they are set in motion as a result of an internal problem within a foundation.

The competence of the District Court (*Arrondissementsrechtbank*) includes the power to dissolve a foundation (a) if it has members, (b) if its purpose is to make payments to founders, members of the board or other persons (except for idealistic or social purposes), (c) if the aims of the foundation have been fulfilled or can no longer be attained, or (d) if the property of the foundation is utterly inadequate for the attainment of its goals and it is equally improbable that sufficient property will be acquired within the foreseeable future.

Courts may dismiss members of the board for violating the statutes or for mismanagement. Should unaltered maintenance of the statutes result in consequences which could not have reasonably been foreseen when the foundation was established and should the statutes fail to provide for redress, or should those who are competent to rectify the situation fail to do so, the District Court may amend the statutes, deviating as little as possible from their original terms. A decision by the District Court may also be invoked for filling vacancies on the board of a foundation if no provision to that effect can be made on the basis of the statutes. Finally, in case of doubts about the *bona fide* application of the Act or the statutes or about the proper conduct of the administration, the public prosecutor is competent to request information from the board. If necessary, the President of the District Court may issue an injunction to this effect.

VII. PUBLIC FOUNDATIONS

By a joint order dated 13th April 1956, the Ministers of the Interior and of Justice set up a Committee to advise the Government whether the jurisdiction of the Foundations Act should be extended to public foundations, i.e. those foundations in which national, provincial, local or other branches of Government have acted as the sole founder or as cofounder. The Chairman of the Committee was Professor W. C. L. van der Grinten.

At the inaugural meeting of the Committee, the Minister of the Interior, Professor L. Beel, mentioned some of the *pros and cons* in the use of private foundations by public authorities. Foundations had been found to be a very manageable form for those branches of public service which are designed to operate independently, and for projects in which the Government and private persons co-operate on equal footing. The main disadvantage is that publicity and control, two essential conditions of Government, suffer when the Government makes use of foundations.

The Minister asked why these objections had not been raised with regard to Government participation in commercial companies. He ventured the opinion that this might be due to the fact that companies were further removed from the political sphere. In the case of projects entrusted to foundations, the Government wanted to 'keep a finger in the (political) pie'. Moreover, company law is completely codified. As regards the provisions governing public foundations, he thought there were three possibilities: (1) to make the law on private foundations fully applicable to public foundations; (2) to create entirely new bodies (under a new name) for public institutions; or (3) to establish additional rules for public foundations.

The Committee conducted a survey of 876 public foundations and instituted an enquiry into the reasons why they had been established in the first place. The majority of the organisations stated that this was the best way to ensure the active participation of private persons and private organisations and that even in respect of co-operation between public bodies, the establishment of a foundation was sometimes the only solution, for instance co-operation between branches of Government at different levels, e.g. a province and a *waterschap*. Only since 1st April 1950, has the Joint Projects Act (*Wet Gemeenschappelijke Regelingen*) made it possible for public organs to undertake joint ventures such as the setting up of inter-municipal bodies.

The Committee considered the question whether Government should be permitted to continue its practice of using foundations for public purposes. In the Netherlands governmental bodies are generally authorised to use the services of enterprises incorporated under private law. The Committee concluded, therefore, that only for special reasons should public departments be denied this right. There was no reason to deny them the use of foundations.

The Committee found that, in general, there were few objections to the full application of the Foundations Act to public foundations. Some members of the Committee objected to the possibility of extending judicial control and intervention—as foreseen in the Foundations Act—to public foundations because this might lead to a constitutional anomaly where the judiciary and the executive powers (which appoint the members of the board of the public foundations) would be at cross-purposes. These members were also of the opinion that the cases in which the Court can intervene in private foundations —inactivity of the board, mismanagement or incorrect application of the terms of reference—would be most unlikely to occur in the case of public foundations, which are kept under close surveillance by the authorities in any case.

A question of practical importance which the Committee considered in its deliberations was whether staff members of public foundations should and/or could be regarded as having a legal status identical with, or equivalent to the status of public servants (*ambtenaren*). This question was raised in particular with regard to the application of the Public Servants Act 1929 (*Ambtenaren-wet*) and the Pensions Act 1922 (*Pensioenwet*). It appeared that the Public Servants Tribunals and the Central Council of Appeal, to which labour disputes involving civil servants are submitted, sometimes agreed but sometimes refused to grant *locus standi* to staff members of public foundations. Their main criterion was the extent to which a public foundation was under the effective control of the Government.

The Report of the Van der Grinten Committee was published in 1958. On 4th December 1961, the Government proposed that Parliament should drop the exemption clause of Art. 29 of the Foundations Act. In the Provisional Report submitted by the Second Chamber of the States-General, opposition to the exemption clause was much less unanimous. The Report put on record an objection raised by the Association of the Netherlands Municipalities of 12th December 1962, against the proposal of the Van der Grinten Committee and against the Chamber's original intention of bringing public foundations under the 1956 Foundations Act because '...judicial control may interfere in a disturbing fashion with administrative and political policy'. Some members of the Chamber supported this view and were also afraid that public authorities, out of fear of judicial control, would avoid using foundations in future even when these would be appropriate.

The Minister of Justice replied in a memorandum dated 14th January 1963 that the main reason why the State made use of foundations was that in such matters it preferred treatment on equal footing with private citizens or groups. The consequence should be full and loyal acceptance of private law. The Minister did not expect that judges would arrogate to themselves opinions on political matters.

The Minister did not mind a slight change of the Foundations Act so that Church foundations, which so desired, could be brought under the jurisdiction of the Act. In a Notice of Alteration, he introduced an amendment to that effect on 14th January 1963.

In this form, Parliament accepted the amendments to the Foundations Act on 10th July 1963 (*Staatsblad* No. 197—*Wet tot wijziging van de Wet op Stichtingen met betrekking tot kerkelijke stichtingen en overheidsstichtingen*). In Art. 28 b, the Foundations Act was made applicable to those Church foundations whose statutes contain a provision to that effect.

Art. 29, which had excluded public foundations from the Act, was deleted.

VIII. SUBSEQUENT LEGISLATION AND REGULATIONS

Further rules regarding the Register of Foundations were laid down by an Order in Council of 18th October 1956 (*Staatsblad* No. 510).

Foundations submitted for registration are marked with a serial number. Moreover, those foundations which are brought to the notice of the Registrar (for example, by a Court judgment), although they have not been officially reported for registration, are included in the file system (the 'red' files). The registered foundations are card-indexed. One index classifies foundations by municipality, another by name. In addition, it was intended that an index would contain the names of the members of the boards, but this instruction has not been carried out in practice so far.

The system of registration has helped to fill the loopholes in the law, but is still incomplete. Registration of foundations is not compulsory. Polak's sample test showed that many foundations known to exist have not been officially registered. After the enactment of the Foundations Act in 1956, a number of sporadic and apparently insufficient efforts were made in order to induce foundations to register. The same holds true for the registration of public foundations subsequent to the amendment of 10th July 1963.

The Act requires that a foundation must have an official seat, but that need not be its usual address. The Register mentions the municipality in which the foundation has its seat. If the foundation does not appear in the telephone or 'giro' directory of that municipality, the tracing of its address is a cumbersome procedure, and one that is usually effected via the notary public who has recorded the deed. There is, however, neither an obligation on the part of the notary public to keep track of his one-time client, nor an obligation on the part of the founder or the board of a foundation to keep the notary public informed.

Various other instruments affecting foundations should be mentioned at this point. On 1st June 1956, a Convention was drafted at The Hague for the recognition of the legal personality of foreign societies, associations and foundations (*Convention concernant la reconnaissance de la personnalité juridique des sociétés, associations et fondations étrangères*). The Convention (*Tractatenblad* 1956, No. 131) was approved by a Law of the Realm of 25th July 1959 (*Staatsblad* No. 255) and submitted to the seventh session of The Hague Conference of Private International Law. The purpose of the convention was to secure recognition in law of the personality of juridical persons, including foundations, in the signatory States. It has not yet acquired sufficient signatories to become effective.

Another act which has not yet entered into effect is Book Two of the new Civil Code of the Netherlands. It was passed by the States General on 12th May 1960 (*Staatsblad* No. 205). The Book regulates all categories of legal persons: the State, provinces, municipalities, other public bodies, Church societies, limited companies, foundations, partnerships and associations. For the first time, foundations have been incorporated into the Civil Code.

Title 4, consisting of 17 articles, elaborates the foundations, It contains no startling novelties after the 1956 Act, but amounts to a summary of this law.

IX. THE PRESENT SITUATION

The greatest obstacle to gaining insight into the rôle of foundations in the public life of the Netherlands is the lack of a comprehensive survey. Foundations are divided into two broad categories:

a. foundations subject to the 1956 Foundations Act,
b. foundations exempted from the jurisdiction of that Act (Art. 28).

The group of foundations proper (category a.) can be subdivided into:

1. Foundations which have been duly registered,
2. Foundations which have not been registered.

A sample survey has been carried out by Professor J. M. Polak on the foundations proper. We shall cite *some* of his findings below. To our knowledge, no attempt has so far been made to examine non-registered foundations.

Registered foundations

In 1963, at the request of the '*Broederschap van Notarissen in Nederland*', Professor J. M. Polak wrote a survey on his experiences with the Foundations Act. His survey was based, *inter alia*, on a random test of foundations registered in the Foundation Register until 1st October 1962.

The results were classified in 13 tables. By the date of enquiry, the Register contained approximately 15,000 files. The random test concentrated on 566 files.

Table 1 showed the 'density' of foundations per province, and quoted the following global results:

Number of Foundations per 10,000 Inhabitants	Provinces
16.1	Utrecht
14.5	Groningen
14.5	Friesland
13.2	Noord-Holland
13.2	Zeeland
12.6	Zuid-Holland
12.4	NETHERLANDS (Average)
12.3	Gelderland
11.7	Overijssel
11.3	Noord-Brabant
11.2	Drenthe
8.0	Limburg

Professor Polak put forward the hypothesis that a high 'foundation density' was to be found in provinces with a religiously mixed population; in other words, that foundations may be partially explained as a symptom of the Dutch social phenomenon of compartmentalisation (*verzuiling*). A different view was taken by a member from the South of the country (where the foundation density is lowest). He ascribed a high foundation density to those parts of the country where people show the strongest penchant for organisation.

Table 5 shows the growth curve. In the third column the total number of foundations has been divided by the number of years per period under review in order to obtain the annual average:

Period of Establishment	Number of Foundations	
	Total	per year
1900 and before	14	—
1901–1920	16	0.8
1921–1940	69	3.5
1941–1945	9	1.8
1946–1950	64	12.8
1951–1955	110	22.0
1956	17	17.0
1957	43	43.0
1958	45	45.0

Table 5 (*continued*)

1959	50	50.0
1960	45	45.0
1961	48	48.0
1962 (first 9 months)	36	48.0

The growth curve particularly brings out the rapid growth in foundations during the postwar period. The lower figure in 1956 is probably the result of certain misgivings in view of the impending promulgation of the Foundations Act.

Table 7 classifies the foundations in accordance with their activities:

Social Work	76
Education	65
Culture	47
Savings	43
Youth welfare	39
Recreation	36
Staff funds	34
Co-ordination of commercial interests	33
Medical care	31
Religion	23
Family interests	19
Science	17
Industrial welfare	13
Community centres	13
Housing	6
Politics	4
Miscellaneous	67

Table 8 classifies foundations by beneficiaries. They are subdivided both according to the percentage of interest groups and according to territorial sphere of influence. (We cite only the percentage breakdown):

Interest Groups	Total	Territorial Sphere of Action		
		Whole Country	Regional	Local
	%	%	%	%
Society as a whole	24.6	3.5	5.3	15.8
One social category	39.2	7.4	12.5	19.3
A social group not directly related to purpose of foundation	12.4	4.6	4.8	3.0

Table 8 (*continued*)

A social group directly related to purpose of foundation	23.8	7.6	4.4	11.8
Total	100.0	23.1	27.0	49.9

The survey shows that about one half of the foundations under review are active at local level, just over a quarter at regional level and less than a quarter at national (or international) level.

Other details investigated by Professor Polak's survey were certain legal questions such as the extent of a board's competence, the amount of internal and external control over financial management, etc.

The report reveals that the scale of a foundation's initial property varies considerably in practice. Of the 566 cases investigated, 299 dated from before the Foundations Act and 267 from the time thereafter. The sums of initial capital of 522 foundations noted in the notarial act are as follows:

	Number	%
less than f 100,–	160	31
f 100,–	158	30
more than f 100,–	141	27
no amount specified	63	12

Professor Polak further investigated to what extent judges and public prosecutors have made use of their new powers of intervention as laid down by the Foundations Act. The results of the enquiry showed that during the first six years after the enactment of the Foundations Act, both judges and public prosecutors made very little use of their powers of intervention.

The author was not quite sure whether this was necessarily a good thing since the fact that foundations may not have members means that the boards of foundations are very powerful and unhampered by the kinds of control that members of an association exercise over their board. Judicial control is one of the modern methods which ought to be used to guarantee the proper management of foundations.

He added, however, that the statutes of many foundations introduced voluntary supervision, particularly over their financial management. In 50% of the cases investigated, the financial management of foundations was found to be subject to control by outsiders, viz. by (a) submission of financial reports to certain persons or bodies, or (b) requirement to furnish an auditor's

S

report; or (c) requirement to obtain approval of financial management from certain persons or bodies.

Professor Polak's main conclusion was that the Foundations Act is a contribution to closing the loopholes in the law without impairing the traditional freedom of operation of the foundations. Problem cases are, in his view, the following:

(1) *Foundations exempted by Art. 28 from the jurisdiction of the Foundations Act.* In the case of these foundations the *status quo* that existed prior to the promulgation of the Act was maintained. The major category in this group was the Church foundations. The appropriateness of excluding Church foundations from the Act remained questionable and, in fact, the amendment of 1963 made it possible for Church foundations to submit themselves voluntarily to statute law.

(2) *Foundations with an incorrect structure.* The most conspicuous border cases were the foundations which administer commercial enterprises. The provision in Art. 1 para. 3 that foundations may not make payments to their founders or boards has not prevented a number of foundations from assuming the form of business enterprises. Polak found that at least 251 foundations had been registered in the commercial registers kept by the Chambers of Commerce in compliance with the Commercial Registers Act of 26th July 1918 (*Handelsregisterwet*). This provides that every enterprise must be registered. It was noted, moreover, that a large number of these foundations had not been entered in the Foundation Register. Conversely, many foundations which run commercial enterprises had not been entered into the commercial register. In 1964, Professor Polak wrote an article to warn against the abuse of foundations by enterprises. The public may be fooled by an enterprise camouflaged as a foundation. Moreover, uncertainty may arise as to what legislation is applicable in such a case[9].

(3) *Non-registered foundations.* The Foundations Act does not oblige foundations to register, nor does the Act restrict the use of the appellation 'foundation' to registered foundations. Thus, third parties have no direct control over the quality of a body presenting itself as a foundation.

The Polak Report was discussed at the annual meeting of the Association of Notaries Public in the Netherlands on 6th June 1963. The discussion confirmed that the law of foundations is for a large part moulded by the notaries public, but that the notaries are hampered by one obstacle in particular: they can only influence their clients to a certain degree as it is their job to give written shape to the wishes of their clients, the founders of these institutions.

[9] J. M. Polak, De stichting in het bedrijfsleven.

The excluded foundations

The 'excluded foundations' are listed in Article 28:
(1) Church societies and subdivisions thereof;
(2) Church foundations, the statutes of which have not declared the Foundations Act to be applicable;
(3) Foundations referred to in the Royal Decrees of 26th December 1818, 2nd December 1823, and 12th February 1829;
(4) Vicarage estates referred to in the Act of 29th October 1892;
(5) Charitable institutions;
(6) Pension and savings funds;
(7) The Notaries Public Pension Fund.

Church societies, Church foundations and vicarage estates

There are a considerable number of Church societies, Church foundations and vicarage estates. When the Foundations Act was under discussion in Parliament and general consensus was reached that the religious foundations should remain outside the jurisdiction of the Act, the Churches consulted each other about what should be done.

If a Church foundation is not an ordinary foundation, how should it be classified? The Government explained that what it had in mind were those foundations which had been instituted or taken over by a Church and implementing tasks immediately connected with that Church. The reason for the abstention of the State from supervision was the traditional separation between Church and State and the supposition that the Churches would exercise supervision over their own foundations, although the latter point was nowhere specified in the Bill or its memorandum of explanation.

Most Church societies have drawn up their own rules on Church foundations. These rules fulfil a function not only with regard to the internal organisation of the Churches, but also with regard to the external recognition of Church foundations as such.

On behalf of the Secretariat of the Roman Catholic Church in the Netherlands at s'-Hertogenbosch, Professor J. J. Loeff informed the author that the Secretariat disposes of data on a large number of ecclesiastical, religious-charitable and socio-religious institutions, associations and foundations. A catalogue has not been compiled, because the number fluctuates too much: new organisations are frequently founded and some institutions which in the past have been regarded as religious, are no longer considered as such for a number of reasons.

A basic decision was taken by the Archbishop of Utrecht on 23rd April 1942 in his Rules on *'Vereenigingen en Stichtingen'* (Associations and Foundations):

> 'I. In accordance with the provisions of Art. VII of the provisions governing the administration of the Roman Catholic Church in the Netherlands, we shall henceforth recognise as parts of the Roman Catholic Church the following associations, institutions or foundations: 1. ...' (there follows a list of 24 categories)
>
> 'II. The following are not parts of the Roman Catholic Church: 1. ...' (there follows a list of 19 categories)
>
> 'Any association, institution or foundation which is not mentioned under I or II shall have to be separately recognized by Us.
>
> This applies in particular to charitable institutions such as hospitals, etc. and foundations established by youth associations.'

On 2nd September 1964 the Catholic Church issued a new set of rules on Catholic institutions in the charitable and social fields (*Algemeen Reglement van Katholieke Instellingen op Charitatief en Maatschappelijk gebied in de Nederlandse R.K. Kerkprovincie*).

The largest Protestant Church, the Dutch Reformed Church (*Nederlands Hervormde Kerk*), appointed a special committee and in March 1959 it announced the criteria governing its religious foundations. At a meeting on 20th November 1962, the General Synod of the Church issued its General Regulations on Church Foundations (*Generale Regeling voor Kerkelijke Stichtingen*). Art. 5 stipulates that the Central Committee for the Supervision of the Church must maintain a list of Church foundations. In practice, this article has proved to be unworkable, both in view of the large number of congregations and the wide measure of independence each of them enjoyed. A conservative guess puts the total number of Church foundations at 1,500. A special difficulty, as the Special Committee found out, are the inter-Church foundations since these are not instituted by 'a Church'.

Foundations belonging to the second largest Protestant Church, the Reformed Churches in the Netherlands (*Gereformeerde Kerken in Nederland*), are governed by Art. 98 of the Church Order.

We have not attempted to examine the rules governing other Church societies. As for an indication about their total number, it should be mentioned that Van Alphen's handbook of Churches lists 110 registered Protestant Church societies. It may be safely assumed that each of these societies has at least several foundations attached to it.

The vicarage estates (Cat. 4) have successfully withstood the Reformation and the French Revolution and equally well the implementation of rules and regulations for Church and secular foundations. The only legal provision by which these estates are bound is the Act of 29th October 1892 requiring royal consent for property transactions. Such transactions are, however, unusual. In other respects the day-to-day routine of such estates remains hidden from view. Nominally they are supervised by the Church. Some vicarages have been converted into scholarship funds and they are registered and supervised as such (see below).

Scholarships and bursaries

The category of foundations referred to in the three Royal Decrees (Cat. 3) consists of the independent scholarship funds which were confiscated by the State under Napoleon. The first Royal Decree of 26th December 1818, applicable only in the Belgian part of the Netherlands, returned these scholarship funds and their proceeds to '...those who are entitled to them' (whoever that may be) and terminated the administration of these ancient funds (*stichtingen der beurzen of kollegiën*), as of 1st January 1819, by the State administrators of domains, *bureaux de bienfaisance* or committee of hospitals. The second Decree of 1st December 1823, laid down rules on the administration of the scholarship funds. The administrators of each fund have to submit accounts to *provisoren* who, in turn, have to report to the Provincial Governments. The permission of these authorities is required for certain legal transactions. The Decree of 12th February 1829, declared the foregoing decrees to be applicable throughout the Netherlands to all scholarship funds established since 1823 and to the ancient foundations in Friesland known as *lenen*.

The author attempted to ascertain to what extent provincial authorities today actively exercise their powers of supervision. The Deputy Estates of the Province of Zuid-Holland informed him in a letter dated 14th February 1968, that they confine themselves mainly to the auditing of accounts and authorisations for the investment of funds. Their activities are hampered by the fact that many trustees of these foundations seem to be ignorant of the contents of the ancient Royal Decrees or unwilling to comply with them. The Province is forced to acquiesce in this situation since the Decrees do not contain any sanction against non-compliance.

A fairly comprehensive survey of scholarship funds was published in a catalogue entitled *Studiebeurzen*.

We have compiled a table of 497 scholarship funds from this survey, leaving aside those scholarships and bursaries which do not constitute a separate legal entity but are part of

either (a) the national budget, for example the scholarship and study
loans awarded by the Ministry of Education, the provinces or
the municipalities;

or (b) the general programme of expenditure drawn up by a foundation, association or enterprise.

In many cases the terms of reference read:

'The municipality may award a scholarship...', or
'The foundation may render financial assistance to a student of...', etc.

In these cases, the scholarship has not a separate existence, but forms part of
a foundation governed by the general Foundations Act.

It was noted that enterprises very seldom create independent scholarship
funds. They either finance scholarships direct out of their own funds, or out
of their allocations by foundations or associations for professional or in-
service training.

Independent scholarships and study funds appear under a variety of names:
(*studie-*) *fonds, stichting, leen, legaat, vicarie, fundatie, instelling, alumniaat,
praebende,* etc.

In the majority of cases, these scholarships are of the trust type. They are
funds at the disposal of a person, committee or other body (for example, a
municipality, curators of a university, etc.), who make the appropriations.

The table below has been compiled on the basis of the above-mentioned
work.

| | *Name and Purpose of Fund* | | | | | | | |
| | (*Studie*)- | | | | | | *Other* | |
	Fonds	Stichting	Leen	Legaat	Vicarie	Fundatie	name	Total
BENEFICIARY	*General or multi-purpose*							
Countrywide	10	6						16
Regional	7	3	1					11
Local	158	13		2		2	1	176
Certain families			3					3
								206
	Higher Education: General							
Countrywide	6	5	3				1	15
Regional or local	4	3	2				1	10
Certain university	17	5	1				1	24
Certain family		4	10	2				16
								65

Table (*continued from previous page*)

Higher Education: Theology								
General	2					1		3
Protestant	45	10	2	2	2	1	8	70
Roman Catholic	10	55						65
								138
Higher Education: Other Facilities								
	44	17	2	2		1	1	67
Other Studies								
	9	3	5				4	21
							Total	497

The largest number of scholarships, 176, are those administered by the municipalities. Most of these funds have been instituted by the municipality itself (*studiefonds van de gemeente*). Some funds are private endowments, the administration of which has been entrusted to local government bodies.

Many municipalities in the Netherlands, however, do not keep separate funds but simply pay for scholarships out of their current budget. The same can be observed with regard to the provincial funds. Whereas most of the rural provinces (for example *Groningen, Friesland, Gelderland, Limburg*) have a special scholarship fund (*Provinciaal Studiefonds voor...*), the urban provinces like North and South Holland, and Utrecht grant scholarship out of their general budget ('...a scholarship may be awarded from the provincial treasury...').

The most commonly used name for scholarship foundations is *fonds* (fund).

We also noted that the largest number of specially earmarked scholarships are available to students of theology. Most of these scholarship foundations are ancient.

The relatively low number of scholarships earmarked for other faculties does not mean that students in these faculties are less favoured. They generally derive their scholarships either from the general Ministry of Education budget (excluded from our study) or from the budgets of countless special funds, foundations or associations which aim at a wider purpose than scholarships alone and have therefore been excluded from the present survey.

Other excluded foundations

The keeping of an inventory of charitable institutions (Cat. 5) is a task for the town councils. In 1956, the State Printing Office of the Netherlands published a complete list, which consists at present of about one thousand separate lists drawn up by the municipalities (*Lijst van Instellingen van Weldadigheid*).

The pension and savings funds (Cat. 6) are registered with the Insurance Chamber (*Verzekeringskamer*) in Amsterdam. This body is entrusted by law with the supervision at all institutions of life insurance. The Chamber does not publish a list or provide information about these funds to outsiders. Since their nature is somewhat outside the scope of what is ordinarily understood by foundations, we may disregard them for the purpose of this study. The same applies to the Notaries' Pension Fund.

The non-registered foundations

In 1964, the National Council of Social Welfare (*Nationale Raad voor Maatschappelijk Welzijn*) appointed a Committee to study the problem of 'dormant funds'. On 13th December 1967 their findings and recommendations were published. In its report, the Committee recommended that the Minister of Justice should amend the Foundations Act to the effect that Art. 28 of the Act would be abolished so that all foundations should be registered. Secondly, they pointed out the necessity of changing the terms of reference of certain foundations whose purpose has become meaningless today. The Committee cited the example of a foundation whose purpose was to distribute rye-bread among the poor at Christmas. Today, there is no need for this kind of charity. On the other hand, the Committee noted that there are foundations which are so fast asleep that no-one can wake them from their slumber. They accumulate interest on the capital, year after year, owing to bankers' professional discretion and notaries' secrecy, it is impossible to mobilize them for new social purposes. The report cited an interesting case of a charitable institution at Breda which is endeavouring to obtain permission from the Court to change its statutes in order to pursue a more meaningful purpose.

X. FINANCIAL RESOURCES

There are no overall surveys or estimates of the financial resources of foundations in the Netherlands, nor is there any general requirement for foundations to publish reports on their finances or activities. In exceptional cases, the President of a District Court may order a foundation to surrender its books for inspection to the public prosecutor (Art. 11 of the Foundations Act). Some foundations, particularly the great national foundations, publish an account of their activities on a voluntary basis. Moreover, institutional contributors usually make their grants to foundations subject to auditing and reporting.

Real estate is an important component of foundation property, particularly in the case of 'institution' foundations. There are comparatively few foundations based on capital endowment. This phenomenon has a historical and sociological background. Conspicuous display of wealth by private citizens, either during their lifetime or after their death, does not fit into the Dutch social pattern.

In medieval Dutch society, donations by wealthy individuals—rich merchants, or noblemen—were invariably given to the Church or clothed in the form of works of art or architecture. During the time of the Republic of the United Netherlands, private charity was frequently bestowed as 'institution' foundations: alms houses, *hofjes* (social welfare settlements), etc. The donation of assets was mainly found in the case of scholarship and relief funds, but the real value of the latter has depreciated in the course of time.

In the nineteenth century and the twentieth century, the establishment of privately endowed foundations has been rare. Emphasis has gradually shifted from the private founder to the institutional founder. This has caused a change in the financial pattern itself. A regular income from periodical contributions has become more important than income from fixed capital. Periodical benefactors want to see their contributions spent. On the one hand this has induced foundations to practice greater publicity; on the other hand it has prevented them from forming capital.

Apart from the revenue from capital, the main financial resources of foundations are annual contributions, donations, legacies and endowments, proceeds from special appeals, proceeds from foundation activities and Government subsidies.

(a) *Contributions, donations, legacies and endowments*

Many foundations, particularly in the field of social welfare and medicine, derive substantial revenue from annual contributions and from donations (i.e. unique gifts). A technical obstacle is raised by the Foundations Act, which prohibits foundations from having 'members'; the principle of membership is reserved to associations. Various ways of obviating this rule have been found. Some foundations replace the term 'member' by 'benefactor', 'contributor', or 'participant'. Other foundations are supported by a related association. For example, the *Residentie Orkest*, a symphony orchestra organised as a foundation, is supported by a society of friends, the '*Vereeniging van Vrienden van het Residentie Orkest*'.

A certain amount of support for foundations is given by industry. In general, commercial companies are reluctant to commit themselves to recurrent expenditure or to the creation of separate foundations. In recent years, however, there have been new departures, such as the foundations for science and culture established by the concerns of Heineken and Stuyvesant, as well as a number of company-sponsored cultural awards and study funds.

In most cases corporate giving is but one of the many forms of industrial support to society. There are a few instances in which enterprises as such are controlled by foundations: i.e. the entire block or a majority of shares are owned by a foundation. The most conspicuous examples are the *Van Leer Foundation* (an international foundation with its executive headquarters in Holland) and the *Levi-Lassen Foundation* at The Hague.

Legacies and endowments are still important sources of revenue for foundations. The main technical difference with straightforward donations is that legacies and endowments are often earmarked for particular aspects of a foundation's activity, and, for that reason, invested in capital. A private person wishing to further a certain charitable cause does not necessarily want to go to the trouble of setting up a foundation. More often than not, he will find the board of an existing foundation willing to administer his endowment subject to special instructions. There are a fairly large number of study funds set up under this system and these funds are very much akin to an English trust.

(b) *Proceeds from special appeals*

Special appeals are widely used in various forms, such as street collections, house-to-house collections, mail campaigns (for example addressed to holders of postal accounts) and individual 'drives'. This form of fund raising is very effective in the relief and social welfare field. A notable example is the case of the village for the handicapped *Het Dorp* near Arnhem, a foundation for which the Dutch raised the sum of 21 million guilders in one day.

The collection system has several advantages. For example, there is no need to report to the benefactors. Its limitations are twofold. Firstly, the system is applicable only to nation-wide and manifestly charitable purposes. It is unlikely that the public will be interested in donating to a foundation for scientific research. Secondly, the 'collection market' is oversaturated. Crash appeals may override campaigns planned a long time ahead. A central coordinating organisation (*Stichting Collecteplan—Centraal Archief voor het Inzamelingswezen*) at Amsterdam is trying to create some order in the system of collections.

More sophisticated foundations, such as those in the field of culture, arts and science, are supported by the public indirectly, through lotteries, prize contests, sales of special postage stamps, and the proceeds from sports totalisators. In the Netherlands, where there is a traditional bias against lotteries and games of hazard, this indirect support of a worthy cause may help the public to overcome its guilty conscience. These fund-raising activities are strictly supervised and regulated by the authorities.

(c) *Proceeds from foundation activities*

There are foundations which obtain a considerable revenue from their own activities. Many of these foundations render services or furnish certain facilities on payment. It is open to question to what extent these bodies qualify as foundations in the internationally accepted sense of the word, and to what extent foundation status is compatible with profit-making. The official view is that profit-making is permissible, but there still remains some uneasiness about it.

(d) *Government subsidies*

In the Netherlands today, the Treasury is the most general source of finance for community projects, even in the private sphere. The budgets of the various departments of central, provincial and local Government include countless subsidies for foundations. Many of these have resulted from the Government taking over financial responsibility for activities which, in their pioneering or initial stages, were financed entirely out of private funds. In the welfare State, a new division of work has evolved between foundations and the Government, the former contributing expertise, a flair for handling the public (very important in the social sphere), goodwill, voluntary work, and so forth, and the latter contributing the funds.

XI. THE FISCAL REGIME

The fiscal aspect of foundations in the Netherlands is not as important as in some other countries, where the very existence of foundations hinges on the fiscal issue. The reason for this is that, as explained above, the decisive element of Dutch foundations is their activity and their structure, rather than their financial conditions. It is significant, in this respect, that foundations as such do not receive any special treatment in Dutch tax laws. However, foundations and their benefactors benefit from a certain number of general fiscal facilities extended to organisations serving the community.

Legacies and donations

It has been mentioned before (pp. 247–8) that some legal issues have arisen in connection with foundations created and/or endowed by last will. Fiscal legislation was changed several times, in accordance with the changes of the *Hoge Raad's* jurisprudence. While the *Hoge Raad* originally held—in its decision of 30th June 1882—that a foundation could be created and endowed by the same last will, it reversed this opinion in its decisions of 1894–6. In 1932, in the famous *Paul Tetar Van Elven-fonds* case, the *Hoge Raad* reverted to its 1882 position, although it left open the question whether the foundation created and endowed by one testament was, or was not, an heir.

The Succession Act abstained from choosing sides in the legal controversy and construed its own theory. Art. 16 of the present (1956) Act, as amended in 1907, reads:

'The estate set aside by the deceased person in his last will and testament as the property of the foundation which he has created in the said last will and testament, shall be considered, for purposes of the application of this Act, to have been acquired by inheritance.'

Only the new Civil Code, now being introduced, has finally and definitely settled the question. Art. 4.4.4.-1 provides:

'The foundation is heir if the property bequeathed to it fulfils the prerequisites of a legacy.'

The Succession Act contains since 1917 a similar provision with regard to foundations created *inter vivos* (Art. 17, present text):

'The estate set aside in other ways than by a last will and testament in order to create a foundation, shall be considered, for purposes of the application of this Act, to have been acquired by gift."

In principle, the death and gift duties due by foundations for legacies and donations received are rather steep, 36% to 54%, *inter alia* because foundations cannot qualify for the lower rates applicable in case of blood-relationship. However, under Art. 24 of the Succession Act, a special reduced tariff of 10% is applicable for the inheritance or gifts received by those foundations within the Realm which aim exclusively, or almost exclusively, at a general public interest, inasfar as the particular donation or inheritance is not given subject to a condition which invalidates the general social purpose. If the inheritance is f 10,000.- or less, or if the donor gives f 5,000.- or less every two years, total exemption from the payment of gift or death duty will be granted (Art. 32).

Under Art. 33, payment of gift duty is also remitted for (a) gifts received from the Queen or from members of the Royal House, and (b) donations to foundations promoting the material or spiritual interest of employees, or widows and orphans of employees, of the donor's enterprise. Many companies have benefited from this provision with regard to the payments made to their staff welfare funds.

A 'snag' in the Succession Act is that if a foundation is created by several donors, they are regarded as one donor for purposes of the application of the gift duty rate. Since this works out unfavourably in view of the progression of the scale, it is advisable for one donor to act as founder and the other donors to make their contributions at a later stage.

Under the terms of Art. 47 of the Income Tax Act 1964, founders and donors may deduct from their taxable income up to a maximum of 10% their gifts to foundations in the Kingdom, which have aims promoting religious, charitable, cultural or scientific activities or the general interest, inasfar as such donations exceed f 120.- and 1% of the donor's gross income per year. The interpretation of the notion of 'general interest' has generated much discussion, particularly since there is no central authority (like the French *Conseil d'Etat*) to lay down a definite policy. Decisions are taken by the various tax inspectorates and tend to vary from one inspectorate to the other. Important judicial precedents are contained in the decisions of the *Hoge Raad* of 12th February 1958 and of the 's-Hertogenbosch District Court of 15th June 1962.

Under the terms of Art. 16 of the Company Tax Act of 1970, corporate gifts to foundations outlined above are deductible inasfar as they exceed f. 500.-, and up to 6% of the profit.

The general rule for private and corporate donations is that the donations must have been given voluntarily and may not result in a quid pro quo claim.

The 'fiscal regime' of foundation activities

It is recalled that one of the objects of the 1956 Foundations Act is to draw a clear demarcation line between foundations and companies. However, this

line, if it exists at all, is by no means congruous with the demarcation between
'profit' and 'non profit'. Many foundations are in practice involved in a
great variety of business activities. Fiscal legislation takes this reality into
consideration. It should be noted, in this connection, that the fiscal laws are
oriented chiefly by the nature of the product or service produced, rather than
by the status of the taxpayer.

The 1954 Turnover Tax Act (*Wet Omzetbelasting*) stated in so many words
that it was also applicable to institutions furthering public purposes. Certain
exemptions would be possible for social or cultural services rendered by
enterprises promoting a non profit aim, '. . . inasfar as these do not interfere
seriously with the competitive situation of enterprises aiming at the making
of profit'. One can hardly imagine a more elastic formula to distinguish
between 'profit' and 'non profit'.

The 1968 Value Added Tax Act (*Wet B.T.W.*), which superseded the
Turnover Tax Act, no longer contains any reference to the legal character of
the taxpayer (Art. 7 '. . . whoever exercises a trade or enterprise'), but the
Secretary of State issued on 16th April 1969 certain directives to the Tax
Inspectorates with regard to the application of the Act to foundations and
other non-profit bodies. Particular attention was drawn to the fact that
under VAT system, not only services rendered, but also those received by
foundations should be taken into account (the 'cascade' principle). For practical
purposes, the VAT Act provided the same exemptions for certain social and
cultural services as the Turnover Tax Act, but it allowed foundations the
possibility to participate in the VAT cascade system, if it found this to be to its
advantage. A Circular of 12th January 1970 gave an important ruling with
respect to organisations raising funds for social and cultural purposes by
means of the sale of objects (Christmas cards etc.). Under certain conditions,
such sales would be exonerated from VAT, up to a business of f.100,000.-
per year.

The Company Tax Act (*Wet Vennootschapsbelasting*) of 1st January 1970,
follows the same pragmatic approach as the VAT Act. In principle, foundations with commercial activity are fully taxable. However, Art. 5 of the
Act indicates certain non-profit activities which may be exempted. Art. 6
contains a general clause for exempting institutions aiming at a general social
interest and which are either purely non-profit, or profit-making in a very
limited sense.

Other taxes

Dividend tax, levied from legal persons established in the Netherlands (including the foundations) is refunded upon request, in accordance with Art. 8 of the Dividend Tax Decree of 1941 (*Besluit Dividendbelasting*), if the amount of tax is more than f. 10.-.

No property tax is levied on foundations. The tax on land and buildings is not levied on Churches, schools (boarding schools excepted), almshouses, and non profit-making hospitals or homes for invalids.

International problems

The Tax Arrangement for the Kingdom (*Belastingregeling voor het Koninkrijk*), concluded on 28th October 1964 between the Netherlands, Surinam and the Netherlands Antilles provides for the mutual application of most favoured nation treatment for institutions promoting religious, cultural, scientific or other general social purposes.

Of a wider international importance is Art. 50 of the Succession Act Tariff which provides:

'In case of legacies or donations to organisations not domiciled in the Kingdom of the Netherlands which serve the public interest in the international sphere (for example international organisations for development aid) it will in general be possible to grant a reduction or exemption of tax by Decree of the Minister of Finance.'

In 1964, the question was raised in the Dutch Parliament why it would not be possible to extend the fiscal regime for donations and legacies to institutions serving the public interest irrespective of their country of domicile. The Government answered that its only, but effective, objection to such general clause was that it would not be possible to control the accounts of foreign institutions.

LITERATURE

Bosch, J. H. De Stichting 'Pape-Fonds' te 's-Gravenhage (The Hague, 1932).

Bosch Kemper, Jhr.mr. J. De Ontwerp van het Burgerlijk Wetboek voor het Koninkrijk der Nederlanden, met eene voorrede (Leiden, 1864).

Braakman, A. Het is moeilijker te geven dan te vragen (Het subsidiebeleid van de onderneming), in: Tijdschrift voor Efficiency en Documentatie (The Hague, October 1965).

Bregstein, M. H. Enige beschouwingen over de stichting in verband met het ontwerp van wet van 29 April 1954, in: WPNR 4404/6.

Coopmans, J. P. A. De rechtstoestand van de Godshuizen te 's-Hertogenbosch voor 1629 ('s-Hertogenbosch, 1964).

Correspondentieblad van de Broederschap der Notarissen in Nederlands, Vol. 66, 10th Reprint (The Hague, 1963).

Duynstee, J. A. Th. M. Beschouwingen over de stichting naar Nederlands privaatrecht (Deventer, 1970).

Duynstee, W. J. A. J. and Punt, C. Prae-advies over het rechtskarakter en vertegenwoordiging van kerkgenootschappen en kerkelijke instellingen, te behandelen in de algemene vergadering der Broederschap van Candidaat-Notarissen (The Hague 1935).

Feenstra, Robert Le concept de fondation du droit romain classique jusqu'à nos jours: théorie et pratique, in: Revue internationale des Droits de l'Antiquité (3e série, Tome III, 1956).

Feenstra, Robert L'histoire des fondations, in: Tijdschrift voor Rechtsgeschiedenis (Vol. 24, 1956, p. 381 et ss.).

Fikkert's, G. Jaarboek voor Notarisambt en Registratie 1968-9 (Arnhem, 1968).

Groenendaal, J. Het gebruik van Stichtingen door publiekrechtelijke bedrijfslichamen, in: Sociaal-Economische Wetgeving, Afd. Nederland (1961).

Hondius, Frits W. Le régime fiscal des fondations privées culturelles et scientifiques en droit néerlandais, in: Faculté internationale pour l'Enseignement du Droit Comparé (Strasbourg, 1970).

Joubert, C. P. Die Stigting in die Romeins-Hollandse Reg en die Suid-Afrikaanse Reg (The Hague, 1951).

Lijst Instellingen van weldadigheid, opgemaakt ingevolge artikel 3 van de Armenwet (Staatsdrukkerij, The Hague, 1956).

Nederlandse Fondsen voor de Wetenschap (ZWO, The Hague, 1965).

Poelje, G. A. Van Osmose (Alphen aan de Rijn, 1959).

Polak, J. M. Ervaringen met de Wet op Stichtingen (Prae-advies voor de Jaarlijkse Algemene Vergadering van de Broederschap der Notarissen in Nederland) (The Hague, 1963).

Polak, J. M. De stichting in het bedrijfsleven, in: De Naamloze Vennootschap (1964, No. 2).

Stichting, De—V.V.S. Vol. B. (Kluver, Deventer, 1964).

Studiebeurzen welke van overheidswege en door particuliere stichtingen en fondsen beschikgbar worden gesteld (Purmerend, 1961).

Tricht, F. J. B. Van De rechtstoestand der stichtingen (Leiden, 1884).

Verslag van de Commissie van Advies inzake Overheidsstichtingen (The Hague, 1958).

Versteeg, Th. A. Het nieuwe wetsontwerp inzake stichtingen, in: De Naamloze Vennootschap (1954, XXXII, p. 125).

Wet op Stichtingen en de aan een kerkgenootschap gelieerde stichting, De (The Hague, 1959).

Portugal*

José Blanco

I. THE LEGAL PROVISIONS GOVERNING FOUNDATIONS IN PORTUGAL

1. *Introduction*

Under Portuguese law, a foundation may be defined as the dedication of capital for the pursuance of a lasting goal.

A foundation is a juridical person subject to private law. It is constituted when the State bestows legal personality on a private enterprise whose organisation and management are left completely, or at least to a large degree, to the will of the founder.

If the aim of a foundation is to promote the public weal and not to make a profit for the founder or persons of his choosing—even if the profit is to be used for non-commercial purposes—the foundation is said to be in the interest of public welfare (charitable foundation). However, a foundation for private purposes is also conceivable: its aims would be to serve interests closely connected with the founder or persons designated by him. This would be the case with a foundation established to commemorate the founder or his family, etc.

This account will only deal with charitable foundations which serve the interest of the general public. The Calouste Gulbenkian Foundation is, by virtue of the magnitude of its assets and the range of its aims and activities, the most important foundation in Portugal and we shall refer to it each time that we need to illustrate an example of the practical application of the general laws on foundations.

The underlying principles of the legislation governing the organisation and management of foundations were defined in the new Civil Code which came into force in 1967. Nevertheless, the provisions of the Code are of a

* Translated from the French.

general nature and the specific arrangements in respect of each foundation are to be found in its statutes and the special laws which approve them.

2. The establishment of foundations

A foundation is established by the declaration of intent on the part of the founder who at the same time appropriates a sum of money for the attainment of a certain goal of lasting public interest.

It may be established during the founder's life by a disposition *inter vivos* or, after his death, within the framework of a will.

The establishment of a foundation by means of a disposition *inter vivos* has to be done in proper legal form, duly authenticated by a notary and published in the official gazette.

If a foundation is set up under the terms of a will, the founder's heirs may not have it annulled unless the execution of the Will would reduce the portion of a person's assets prescribed by law for certain heirs and which the testator may not dispose of at his own discretion.

In the trust instrument, a founder must indicate the aim of his foundation and specify the assets with which he is going to endow it. Moreover, he may also indicate the address of the registered offices, the organisational pattern and the administrative arrangements of the foundation. In addition, he may set out the conditions subject to which it may be reorganised or dissolved and stipulate the future use of the assets in the latter case[1].

[1] The declaration of intent which set up the Calouste Gulbenkian Foundation was contained in Mr. Calouste Sarkis Gulbenkian's Will from which we now quote the tenth and eleventh clauses.

Clause 10

By this Will a Foundation is formed in accordance with Portuguese law, which shall bear the name of Calouste Gulbenkian Foundation. The essential principles of such Foundation shall be the following:

(a) it is a Portuguese permanent Foundation, its domicile shall be at Lisbon, but it may have any such branches as may be considered necessary at any place in the civilised world;

(b) its purposes shall be charitable, artistic, educational and scientific;

(c) its activities shall be exercised not only in Portugal, but also in any other country where its managers may think fit;

(d) it shall be directed and administered by the trustees appointed hereunder and by any other persons selected by them or in such manner as may be prescribed by the relative Articles.

Clause 11

The property of the Calouste Gulbenkian Foundation shall consist of:

(a) all such property of the estate of the Testator, of whatever nature and wherever

3. *The recognition of foundations*

It is essential if a foundation established by a disposition *inter vivos* or by the terms of a testament is to acquire legal personality that it should be recognised by the competent authorities.

A. The qualifications for applying for recognition

The following may apply for recognition:
(a) the founder himself;
(b) the heirs or executors of the testament;
(c) the authorities which, *ex officio*, are competent in cases (a) and (b).

Once recognition has been requested or the procedure for implementing the recognition has been commenced, the establishment of a foundation by means of a disposition *inter vivos* becomes irrevocable[2].

B. The competent authorities for granting recognition

The right of bestowing recognition on foundations belongs to the Government or, if the activities of the foundation are to be confined to a limited geographical area, to the local Government representative (the *Governador Civil do Distrito*).

The decision as to which Minister is competent depends on the connection between the aim of the foundation and the different ministerial functions. A foundation with educational aims would have recognition granted to it by

situated, as may not be otherwise disposed of by the Testator under this Will or any subsequent Will;
(b) all the property and securities forming the capital of the trusts so far created by the Testator, or which may form the capital of the trusts established by him under this Will or which he may establish in future in favour of any persons of his family, or who may not be members of his family, whether singly or collectively, as and when the said trusts may expire for any reason whatsoever, particularly owing to the death or extinction of the relative beneficiaries; and
(c) any other property which the Testator may specifically allot in his lifetime in any way whatsoever, to the Foundation to be formed by his testamentary executors or with which he may endow the Foundation to be formed by his testamentary executors or with which he may endow the Foundation if he should succeed in creating it himself in his lifetime as is his intention.

[2] The recognition of the Calouste Gulbenkian Foundation was contained in Decree No. 40,690 of 18th July 1956 which states the following:

Art. 1. The Calouste Gulbenkian Foundation, established by Calouste Sarkis Gulbenkian, in his Will dated the 18th June 1953, is a private institution of general public utility, having its seat in Lisbon. The Foundation is in perpetuity and is endowed with legal personality. It will be governed by the Statutes attached to this Decree and which form an integral part hereof, and also by appropriate Portuguese law.

the Minister of National Education. A foundation set up to realise various goals—such as the Calouste Gulbenkian Foundation which pursues charitable, educational, artistic and scientific ends—would receive recognition by Government decree.

The only purpose of Government intervention is to verify that the pre-conditions laid down by law for the granting of legal personality and recognition as a charitable foundation have been fulfilled.

C. Preconditions for the recognition of a foundation

If a foundation is to be given official recognition,
(a) it must have as its object a charitable and public service; and
(b) the assets allocated to the foundation must be sufficient to realise the object envisaged by the founder.

If recognition is withheld owing to the inadequacy of the endowment, the establishment of the foundation will not take place if the founder is still alive. If the foundation has been set up by testament and the testator has not made any other arrangements, the Government must choose a similar association or foundation and transfer the funds to it.

4. *The statutes of the foundation*

The foundation must be governed by statutes which have been approved by the Government and published in the official gazette. No standard form of statutes has been prescribed by the authorities and, in principle, they have to be established by the founder himself in a disposition *inter vivos* or in the testament.

If the founder has not drawn up statutes or if they are insufficient or in-complete, a distinction has to be drawn between the following two cases. If the establishment of the foundation resulted from a disposition *inter vivos*, the right to draw up the statutes devolves upon the Government; if the founda-tion was set up by the provisions of a testament, it is for the founder's execu-tors to formulate the statutes. This has to be done within 12 months of the founder's death. If the executors of the will have not drawn up the statutes within one year after the founder's death, this right passes to the Govern-ment. In both cases, the founder's presumed or known wishes have to be taken into account[3].

[3] Clause 10 (e) of Mr. Calouste Gulbenkian's Will states that: 'at once on the death of the Testator, in the event of his not having done so prior thereto, the testamentary execu-tors and trustees shall draw up and cause to be approved by the Authorities the Articles of the said Foundation and shall carry out any acts which may be necessary either for the legality of the Foundation created by this Will (. . .) or for its establishment and operation.'

In certain cases, the statutes may be modified by the Government. However, the following prior conditions have to be fulfilled before this can happen:

(a) the modification must be proposed by the directors of the foundation;
(b) the modification must not involve any essential change in the aim of the foundation; and
(c) the modification must not be contrary to the founder's wishes.

5. The organisational structure of the foundation

The statutes must specify the organisational structure of the foundation and this must include a board of directors and a supervisory board. There must be an odd number of members on the board of directors and on the supervisory board[4].

The statutes of the foundation were drawn up by the executors and trustees, and approved by the above-mentioned Decree No. 40,690.

[4] The administration of the Calouste Gulbenkian Foundation is carried out by a board of directors comprising three to nine members, one of whom is the Chairman. The majority of members must be of Portuguese nationality.

The first members of the board were chosen by the founder himself in his Will and they retain their membership for life. Other members exercise their functions for periods of five years, but they can always be re-elected for further terms of office.

The vacant seats and those which may become vacant before the nine members provided for in the statutes have been nominated for the first time are filled exclusively by the life-members. Any vacancies which may occur after all the seats on the board have been taken are filled by resolution of the members.

As the founder's Will stipulates, the board of directors has the widest powers of representation of the Foundation, of free management and disposal of its endowment and for the realisation of the aims for which the latter was instituted.

The members of the board of directors are remunerated in accordance with the terms of the Will.

A binding engagement for the foundation requires the signatures of two members of the board, or the signature of one or several representatives, or of one or several nominees of the board authorised to sign on their behalf in accordance with their rights as representatives or duly appointed agents.

The supervisory board which is known as the Accountancy Checking Commission is independent of the board of directors.

As prescribed by the statutes, it consists of five members: the Director General of Public Accounts; the Director General of Public Assistance; one member nominated by the Lisbon Academy of Sciences; one member named by the Lisbon Academy of Fine Arts; and a third by the National Board of Banks.

The fact that the Accountancy Checking Commission contains two members belonging to the Ministry of Finance and the Ministry of Health and Public Assistance merely reflects the wish of the executors (who drew up, and applied for approval of, the statutes) to have auditing and welfare specialists on the Commission.

6. The legal capacity of foundations

Generally speaking, this is governed by the law regulating the legal capacity of juridical persons. This law covers all the rights and duties which are necessary for, or related to, the realisation of the object of the foundation other than those rights and duties which are clearly appropriate only to physical persons. One of the most important aspects of the legal capacity of foundations is their power to acquire and dispose of landed property. The general rule in the Civil Code is that, in their capacity as juridical persons, foundations may acquire landed property gratuitously. However, if they wish to buy landed property, they require Government permission, as indeed they also do for its sale.

However, the laws which approved and sanctioned the statutes of most of the major Portuguese foundations permit the latter to acquire landed property either gratuitously or for payment[5].

7. Supervision of foundations

In order to subject foundations to control by governmental authority (which exercises a kind of administrative tutelage), it is necessary for them to be defined in the declaration of recognition as being charitable foundations of an administrative character serving the public welfare.

This designation is given by the Government to institutions whose objects are social service or education, founded by individuals and whose activities are confined to promoting the wellbeing of the population within a limited geographical area. It may be said that charitable foundations of an administrative character serving the public welfare are entirely local in character and they discharge their functions in a defined area (a commune, district or province).

If, on the other hand, a foundation is recognised as serving the public

---

[5] According to its statutes, the Calouste Gulbenkian Foundation can acquire landed property and not only that necessary to set up its registered offices or branches and charitable, artistic, educational and scientific institutions which the foundation may create or maintain, but also that which the board of directors may deem expedient to acquire with a view to realising a more productive or less hazardous use of the assets of its endowment.

The foundation can also accept outright donations and legacies or those which are subject to certain conditions or charges provided that, in the latter case, the conditions or charges are not opposed to the aims of the institution.

The expropriation of landed property which may be deemed indispensable for the realisation of the foundation's aims is considered as being an act of public welfare.

welfare in general in that its activities embrace several regions, the supervision may assume various forms—from the total absence of any Government interference in the affairs of the foundation (which is the case with the Gulbenkian Foundation) to subjection to the general rules of administrative tutelage.

Thus, there is no clearly established general principle for the control of Portuguese foundations. In the light of the new Civil Code, it may be said that Portuguese law inclines more towards a Government policy of non-interference in the life of foundations[6].

8. The alteration of a foundation's purpose

In certain circumstances, the Government may, after consulting the board of directors, change the objects of a foundation. This modification of its aims may take place in the following circumstances:

(a) when the original aim of the foundation has been entirely attained and accomplished;

(b) when it becomes impossible for the foundation to achieve its aims; and

(c) when the foundation's assets have become insufficient to realise its goal.

Nevertheless, it is essential that the new object of the foundation should be similar to the one originally stipulated by the founder.

9. The dissolution of foundations

The board of directors of the foundation must approach the Government

---

[6] Article 5 of Decree no. 40,690 stipulates that the annual verification of the assets of the Calouste Gulbenkian Foundation and of the statement of the revenue and expenditure of the previous year, as well as verification of the allocation of the income according to the purposes set out in the Statutes, is the duty of the Accountancy Checking Commission, constituted in the manner established in the Statutes.

The board of directors establishes annually a meticulous inventory of the foundation's endowment and draws up a balance sheet. To this end, it organises and keeps constantly up to date the necessary book-keeping procedures under permanent auditing, as laid down in the testament, of an accredited firm of chartered accountants (Thomson McLintock & Co. of London). The Accountancy Checking Commission has to check the inventory of the foundation's assets and the balance-sheet for the preceding twelve months prior to 30th June in each year: in doing so it refers to the reports prepared by the auditors and the documents on which these reports were based. It also confirms whether or not the foundation's assets are being used in conformity with the aims of the institution.

There is a statutory requirement that the Commission's annual report shall be published at the expense of the foundation.

so that the latter may announce the dissolution of the foundation and take measures to liquidate the assets:

(a) if the period of time for which the foundation was established has expired;

(b) if there is another reason for the dissolution envisaged by the founder when it was established;

(c) if a Court has declared the foundation to be insolvent.

Moreover, it is possible for a foundation to be dissolved by the Government:

(d) if the original aim of the foundation has been entirely exhausted or has become impossible to realise;

(e) if the real aim which the foundation is pursuing is not the one envisaged by the founder when it was established;

(f) if the aim of the foundation is being systematically pursued by the board of directors by illegal or improper means; and

(g) if the very existence of the foundation has become contrary to the maintenance of public order.

II. THE FISCAL PROVISIONS GOVERNING FOUNDATIONS IN PORTUGAL

When a foundation is recognised as charitable and serving the public welfare, it enjoys very considerable fiscal concessions:

(a) total exemption from payment of the tax on landed property and the tax on income from agricultural undertakings (*Código da Contribuição Predial e do Imposto sobre a Indústria Agrícola* approved and sanctioned by Decree No. 45,104 of 1st July 1963, Art. 7, No. 4);

(b) total exemption from the tax on personal property (*Código do Imposto de Capitais* approved and sanctioned by Decree No. 44,561 of 10th September 1962, Art. 11, No. 4);

(c) total exemption from the income tax (*Código do Imposto Complementar*) approved and sanctioned by Decree No. 45,399 of 30th November 1963, Art. 85, No. 3);

(d) total exemption from the tax on the transfer of landed property (*sisa*) provided that it is to be used for the direct and immediate purpose of carrying out the aims of the foundation (*Código da Sisa e do Imposto sobre as Sucessões e Doações*) approved and sanctioned by Decree No. 41,969 of 24th November 1958);

(e) total exemption from the tax on inheritances and gifts in regard to such legacies and donations as are granted to the foundation (*Código da Sisa e do Imposto sobre as Sucessões e Doações*).

Sweden*

Klas Herrlin

I. FOUNDATIONS IN CIVIL LAW

1. *The legal nature of a foundation*[1]

A foundation is a legal entity whose sole indispensable characteristic is that its organisational structure must be reasonably sound. This characteristic is considered to be fulfilled if the foundation has a board of directors.

Generally speaking, the same rule may be said to apply to endowments which are restricted funds entrusted to an existing organisation. However, if the stated aim of such a fund, i.e. as specified in the declaration of intent, is identical with that of the organisation concerned, misgivings may arise as to the legal nature of the trust fund. This is particularly true if there is no provision for the funds in question to be administered separately from the recipient organisation's other assets.

2. *The establishment of foundations*

A foundation is considered to have come into existence when assets are earmarked for a specific, constant purpose and subjected to an administering body of their own. No approval on the part of a public authority or entry into a register is needed to obtain legal capacity.

However, pursuant to the terms of the Law on the Supervision of Foundations, the District Administration (known in Sweden as the *länsstyrelse*) is obliged to approve the statutes of a foundation serving the public welfare if the latter submits an application to this end. Nonetheless, such approval is of no direct significance in civil law. Nor are there any other regulations which stipulate that foundations must be organized in a special way.

* Translated from the German.

[1] As regards its civil law content, this account is largely based on H. Hessler: *Om stiftelser*, Stockholm, 1952.

Thus, the assumptions underlying the setting up of a foundation are:
(1) that a declaration of intent is made in respect of the establishment of a foundation and that the aim of the foundation is stated;
(2) that assets are transferred and earmarked for specific purposes; and
(3) that an administrator (or a board of directors) is appointed and that he or they undertake to effect the business of the foundation in the prescribed manner.

(a) The setting up of a foundation

(a)(i) *The declaration of intent*—Natural or juristic persons who possess the capacity for making a legally valid declaration of intent may set up a foundation.

No formalities need be observed when a foundation comes into being. Even though the facts are usually set out in writing, there is no stipulation to this effect.

One should perhaps qualify this statement by pointing out that dispositions *mortis causa* are limited by the general rules on the drawing up of wills. These state that the dead person's wishes must in some way or other be expressed in the form of a will.

It is nevertheless sufficient if the aim of the foundation is stated in general terms in the will, whilst the more detailed provisions, without which the declaration of intent is not valid, can be determined at a later date. The testator may, for example, instruct the proposed board of directors or the executor of the will to elaborate the various points constituting the statutes of the foundation.

(a)(ii) *The aim of the foundation*—The aims of a foundation must be defined in so precise a manner as to enable the foundation to be instituted solely on the basis of this statement of aims. Hence, no recognition would be granted to, for example, foundations 'for the promotion of piety' or 'for the advancement of mankind' or 'for charitable purposes'.

If the objectives of a foundation are defined in imprecise terms, the declaration of intent may be declared invalid. This is not the case where a founder has left it to a third party to define explicitly the aim of a foundation which he himself has only stated in vague and general terms. The process of instituting a foundation is only complete when its aims are quoted with the requisite degree of accuracy.

Nevertheless, the question arises as to how one should assess objectives such as the erection of a statue or the provision of pensions for a limited number of persons or the creation of a collecting charity. It is doubtful whether foundation-type entities of this kind—whose purposes are largely of a temporary nature—may be regarded as foundations. Even though they may not be considered as such in the eyes of the law, their legal position *vis-à-vis* third parties is probably the same as that of foundations with long-term aims.

Concerning the objectives of foundations, it is not necessary to choose aims which will promote the public weal. It is possible to have both private family foundations and foundations which serve the founder's own personal interests. By the same token, little importance is attached to the fact that the aim appears to be frivolous or useless. On the other hand, if an aim appears to be blatantly frivolous or useless in the extreme, it will probably not be recognised. The aim must not violate the provisions of a law or be subversive to public morals. Furthermore, the attainment of the objective must be feasible. There is, however, no requirement for the aim to be directly realisable. For example, if it has been shown during the genesis of a foundation that the available capital is insufficient to implement the aim of the foundation, then the only consequence of this is usually that the assets have to be invested and the interest accumulated until the necessary capital is available.

Where the stated aim is inadmissible, the declaration of intent is invalidated from the outset. However, if merely a part of the stated aim is unacceptable, it is probably safe to say, at least in the case of dispositions *mortis causa*, that the founder's instructions in their entirety will only be invalid if the inadmissible provision would appear to constitute an essential or indispensable element in his eyes. If this does not appear to be the case, one is probably justified in considering that the provision in question does not exist, and to accept the remainder of the trust instrument as valid.

(b) Transfer of assets

Under current law, a foundation only comes into being if and when assets are transferred into its possession. For this reason, the declaration of intent containing a statement to the effect that the necessary assets will be earmarked at a later date is not recognised in law.

As regards the form in which the earmarking of funds has to be carried out, the general rules governing the transfer of property and funds have to be observed. A disposition *mortis causa*, for example, has to be effected by means of a testament. It is also interesting to note that the transfer of assets is regarded as completed when the promise of a gift, which is binding under the general provisions of the law, has been made.

However, it is not necessary to earmark certain assets in order to acquire legal capacity in the case of foundations whose funds are to be raised by third parties (usually the general public) in the form of organised fund-raising.

Notwithstanding, specific obligations undertaken by the board of directors to support a fund-raising drive are valid and such sums may perhaps be deducted from the assets which later accrue to the foundation.

(c) The board of directors

The circumstance that no board has been appointed or that an appointed board refuses to accept the appointment does not mean that the trust instrument is thereby invalidated. The Law on the Supervision of Foundations stipulates that the district authorities have to be informed if a board of trustees has not been appointed when a foundation is set up *mortis causa* or if the appointed person refuses the office. These authorities then appoint a board themselves. This provision is usually only applied to a foundation whose establishment has to be notified to the competent authorities.

This is thus one way in which foundations can secure their board of directors. The other way is for the Government to appoint a board. The prevailing climate of opinion is that this is also possible in the absence of any explicit legal fundament.

3. *The supervision of foundations by the State*

(a) The 1929 Law on the Supervision of Foundations

Apart from a number of significant exceptions, it is laid down in the Supervision Law that the boards of directors of all foundations have to register with the Chief Regional Administrator in whose area the foundation has its business seat.

The statutory requirement does not apply to charitable endowments at private schools, private family foundations, foundations with assets of less than 10,000 crowns or to foundations which, pursuant to the founder's wishes, are not subject to the supervision of the public authorities. Such provision by founders that their foundations are not to be liable to inspection is very frequent.

A registered foundation is usually supervised by the regional authorities unless special circumstances render this unnecessary. The Chief Regional Administrator is obliged to ensure that the various bodies of a foundation subject to his supervision are observing the provisions of the Law on the Supervision of Foundations and the foundation's own statutes. The superintendence is implemented by checking the books and the annual report which a foundation has to submit to the regional administrative authorities each year. The main point for the supervisory body to verify is that the funds are not being used for any other purpose than the stated one and that the assets are being invested in a reasonable way.

Of the other provisions in the law, mention should be made of the board's liability to be held for damages, the possibility open to the Court of appointing a substitute board if there are any irregularities in the running of the foundation and the rule against mixing foundation funds with other assets.

The regional administrative authorities have the right to impose fines in the event of an infringement of certain provisions and stipulations.

(b) Alteration of the aims of a foundation (permutation)

Any change in the provisions stipulated by the founder in his declaration of intent requires Government approval. Even though such a decision is taken through administrative channels, an alteration of the objectives of the foundation must be regarded as an encroachment upon a private legal relationship. This may be seen, for example, in the fact that the Government must first wait for the board of directors to submit an application and that they are then bound by the latter.

Permutation always means that a foundation's funds are being used for a fresh purpose. This should be as close to the original aim as possible.

The preconditions governing the procedure for changing the aims of a foundation are as follows: an application for permutation is accepted if the realisation of the aim has become impossible, if the foundation has become pointless, or if its functions are now contrary to the founder's intentions. The preconditions for a change in aims are also present when the fulfilment of such aims has become a responsibility of the public authorities.

Approval may be granted to a change involving a purely technical point of the statutes if a fresh set of circumstances have rendered the provision in question inconvenient or impracticable.

A change in the investment of the capital is permitted if the requirement for safe investment is met in full.

As regards the accumulation of interest on a foundation's capital, the rule is that a higher level of reservation will always be approved if such a step is deemed expedient. On the other hand, urgent reasons must be adduced before reservation is decreased.

4. *The relationship between foundations and non-profit associations*

Mention should perhaps first be made of non-profit associations who use their funds to promote the weal of the general public. The basic difference between such associations and foundations is that, in the former, paying members are in a position to influence a legal entity once it has been created. This is typical of an association, whose members enjoy far-reaching powers. They have the right to check all the work of the board of directors (and if necessary to install a new board), change the aims of the association, terminate it, and distribute the assets.

The creator of a foundation has none of these powers. However, there is probably no essential difference in the preconditions governing the setting up of a foundation or association, the one exception being that in the case of an association no funds have to be transferred to the newly established legal entity. An association acquires legal capacity when its statutes are drawn up and approved, and when a board of directors which is willing to assume office has been elected by the members.

The dividing line between associations and foundations is not always clear-cut. The position in law of a legal entity created as a foundation or association may be rendered almost identical by means of certain provisions in the statutes. But the general criterion for a foundation is that only one person or a small number of persons should be involved in its formation. An association consists of a larger number of people who co-operate in raising the funds needed for their organisation. These are, of course, also the characteristics of a foundation whose aim is to acquire resources by fund-raising drives. For an association to be constituted it is, however, necessary that, in addition, the group of donors should be given a certain organisational framework. To this end, nothing more is required than for the donors to be known as 'members' and for their organisation to be called an 'association'.

In cases of doubt as to whether a certain body is a foundation or an association, the actual designation or name chosen for the legal entity will probably be of decisive significance.

II. TAX LAWS GOVERNING FOUNDATIONS

1. *Death duties and taxes on gifts*

The provisions on the taxation of grants *mortis causa* or *inter vivos* are contained in the Government Ordinance of 1941 on death duties and taxes on gifts. This states that anyone acquiring such assets is liable to pay taxes thereon.

Foundations and associations are exempt from both death duties and taxes on gifts if their aim is:

(1) to increase the defensive capability of the nation by cooperation with the armed forces or other authorities;

(2) to promote the care and education of children or adolescents;

(3) to further the care of indigent persons who are either old, sick or handicapped;

(4) to promote scientific education or research.

In the last named case—the promotion of research—the foundation is
normally required to work closely with an academy or similar institution so
as to exclude low-calibre and non-academic research. There is no need, however, for the foundation to pursue such activities itself: to obtain tax privileges,
it is sufficient if the organisation in question is according financial assistance
for this purpose. The same applies to the purposes specified under (2) and
(3) above.

But it is always essential that the aim should be the 'main' aim. This
means that, even though other goals may be pursued without prejudice to
tax-exemption, the principal object of the organisation must dominate in
terms of its extent in relation to the other activities and the latter should in
fact be of secondary importance.

The promotion of the aims named in (2) and (3) above should not be
limited to the support of the members of only one or a few families.

A foreign foundation or association cannot claim tax-exemption. However, if an agreement has been concluded with another State to the effect that
juristic persons pursuing non-profit aims are to enjoy tax-exemption or
relief, the Government may decide to reduce the amount of taxation
payable.

The regulation that the aim of a foundation must not consist in assisting
foreigners living outside the territorial limits of the country was abolished in
1963. Donations or bequests to foundations implementing international aid
programmes are tax-free if the above-mentioned prerequisites are fulfilled.

Gifts to foundations or associations which pursue religious, social, charitable, political (but not party-political), artistic, sporting and similar aims, or
to foundations and associations whose object is to promote the economic life
of the nation are tax-free. However, tax exemption cannot be accorded if the
founder has reserved the right to claim or to enjoy the interest on transferred
property during his life-time or for a certain period of time.

Corresponding dispositions *mortis causa* must be taxed. Nevertheless, they
benefit from a more favourable rate of taxation than is applicable in other
cases. The lowest rate is 4%, levied since 1971 on sums of over 3,000 crowns
(any sum below this is tax-free). The highest rate of taxation is 30%: this is
raised on amounts exceeding 60,000 crowns. If these special concessions were
not granted, the lowest rate of taxation would be 20% and the highest 65%
(i.e. for amounts of over 50,000 crowns).

Here again, the precondition is that the organisation in question is a juristic person established under Swedish law and that the object being pursued is, in fact, the organisation's main aim.

Death duties are generally assessed on the basis of an inventory of the deceased's estate drawn up after his death whilst the tax on donations is computed on the basis of the person's tax return. If a gift is tax-free under valid law, no special tax return need be made.

2. Income tax

The provisions on income tax are to be found in the Law on Municipal Taxes (1928) and the Government Ordinance on State Income Tax (1947).

(a) Income from real estate

An income derived from landed property is subject to income tax. This even applies to the following institutions:

(1) Academies and general educational establishments such as private bodies set up to promote teaching, research and the education of children in private institutions (the equivalent State facilities are liable to pay a limited amount of tax);

(2) pension funds set up by corporations (or joint-stock companies);

(3) foundations established by joint-stock companies to support unemployed and sick persons or to help the victims of accidents;

(4) the *Nobel Foundation* and *Dag Hammarskjöld Memorial Foundation*; and

(5) a number of other specified foundations, mostly of a public nature.

These bodies are exempt from the payment of income tax with the exception of the tax on landed property and the tax on the guaranteed sum[2] payable in respect of landed property. However, foundation premises are exempt from the payment of taxes on the guaranteed sum if they directly serve the declared aims of the foundation in question. One exception to the liability to pay tax on the guaranteed sum is parks and spaces belonging to non-profit institutions which are open to the general public.

(b) Income from business operations

The largest group of non-profit organisations only pay national and local income tax on the income from their business operations and municipal taxes on their income from landed property and, subject to the above-

---

[2] The idea of the guaranteed sum is to ensure that the community in which landed property is located enjoys a basic tax fundament. At present, the rate is 2% of the value of the property for tax purposes. The tax must also be paid if the profit derived from the property is small or even non-existent.

mentioned conditions, on the guaranteed sum for an estate. This does not include the parishes belonging to the Church of Sweden and other religious communities. In its capacity as the Established Church, the Church of Sweden is only liable to taxation to a limited extent as are associations devoted to the care of the sick and whose activities are not conducted with a view to making a profit, and charitable and benevolent societies, foundations and non-profit associations whose main aim is:

(1) to strengthen the defence of the nation in co-operation with military and other authorities;

(2) to promote the care and education of children;

(3) to advance tuition or training;

(4) to assist needy persons; or

(5) to promote scientific research.

A foundation whose aim is the advancement of Nordic co-operation can be classified as having limited tax liability, although the highest tax authority (*riksskattenämnden*) has to give the final decision in this case.

It is also interesting to note that a foundation whose aim is the promotion of art, music or literature is not exempt from taxation if it does not come under (3) above. On the other hand, the maintenance of cultural monuments is regarded as scientific research.

A comparison reveals that the above-mentioned aims are more or less the same as the ones which serve as the preconditions for exemption from death duties and the tax on gifts. Notwithstanding, there are certain differences. The care and education of adolescents is not recognised as being 'beneficial to the community' for the purpose of income tax[3].

However, an organisation with such an object is often classified under (3) above. In Income Tax Law, adult education is accorded preferential treatment whilst the requirement in respect of death duties and the tax on gifts is that a suitable education is being given to children or adolescents only. For the purpose of income tax, it is sufficient if needy persons are receiving aid and no limits are imposed in this case whereas the provisions governing death duties and the tax on gifts stipulate that the persons concerned must be indigent old people, sick persons or invalids. The Income Tax Law states that the institutions concerned must furnish the aid themselves whilst it is sufficient in the case of death duties and the tax on gifts if such institutions give financial support.

It is also interesting to note that there is no equivalent in income taxation to the highly liberal provisions of the legislation governing the taxes on gifts

---

[3] The dividing-line between children and adolescents is usually put at approximately 16 years of age.

U

which stipulate that grants to non-profit foundations and associations in the widest sense of the word shall be tax-free.

The rules on the main purpose and possible subsidiary purposes are approximately the same as those in the laws on death duties and the taxes on gifts. The principal aim must predominate *vis-à-vis* other activities to such an extent that the latter are of secondary importance. The Courts have decided in a number of cases that a reduction in tax liability is justified if the sum of the amounts spent for the above-mentioned purposes under (1) to (5) above together with appropriate administrative costs and possible taxes total at least 80% of the income available to the foundation.

Some foundations may not be able to use their income in full for their stated object within a certain period of time: be it that there are difficulties in finding a suitable field of activity for the foundation or that the board of directors may deem it more appropriate to accumulate the income, or that complications may have arisen in interpreting certain regulations in the declaration of intent. The rule in such cases is that the tax privileges are, in principle, only granted to juristic persons who really pursue—in practice—an activity which is non-profit making and beneficial to the community. There are no consequences in Civil Law if a foundation does not exercise any functions at all, and any temporary formation of reserves from profits will not normally affect the non-profit status of the organisation. Nevertheless, a less generous attitude is adopted towards foundations which are in a position to pursue subsidiary aims than towards those whose declaration of intent or statutes do not permit any other activities than those which enjoy preferential tax treatment.

A provision in the declaration of intent of a foundation to be set up as charitable, according to which a life-annuity is to be paid to certain persons does not interfere with the non-profit status of this foundation. However, tax exemption is not granted if the aims of the foundation only favour the members of a certain family, several families or a number of specified persons. The lower limit is a group of perhaps 75 to 80 beneficiaries.

Finally, there are no provisions which limit tax privileges if the foundation plans to implement its aims partly or wholly abroad.

(c) Unlimited liability to taxation

Foundations and comparable institutions whose aims cannot be classified under the last two headings are liable to taxation in respect of their whole income.

The national rate of income tax for foundations (i.e. with the exception of family foundations) and associations is 15% of their taxable income. The tax imposed on family foundations is computed in the same way as that for natural persons in line with a table comprising a progressively rising scale of tax rates. The latter extend from 10% to 65% (on incomes in excess of 150,000 crowns).

The rate for municipal income tax is roughly 20%. Hence, the overall burden of income tax on foundations liable to unlimited taxation or on corresponding income of any kind of foundation with the exception of family foundations is about 35%.

Finally, reference should be made in any discussion of the income tax situation to the fact that the legislation of 1943, which stipulated the way in which foundations and associations are to be taxed and which is still more or less valid, was formulated by the lawmakers in a very restrictive manner. This attitude is still seen to a certain extent today in the interpretation of the various provisions[4].

3. Property tax

The relevant provisions are to be found in the Government Ordinance of 1947 on property tax.

The liability to taxation in respect of the property of a foundation (except family foundations) and of an association only applies to assets whose profits attract national income tax. Thus, foundations with non-profit aims are solely taxable for property which may be regarded as a business enterprise.

A family foundation is subject to tax on the same scale as a natural person. The rate of property tax for foundations that are not family foundations is 0.15% on property worth more than 5,000 crowns. The rate for family foundations is 0.8% on property worth 100,000 to 150,000 crowns and 1.8% on property worth more than a million crowns.

4. The statutory requirement to file tax returns

The provisions on the statutory requirement to make a tax return are to be found in the Ordinance on Tax Assessment of 1956.

This stipulates that family foundations are obliged to file tax returns. Other

---

[4] And according to press statements of the summer of 1970 this attitude is to be intensified. In order to avoid the accumulation of major property holdings in one hand the Government intends to withdraw tax exemption from charitable foundations. In addition, during the election campaign of 1970 it was proposed to have Government representatives in the boards of directors of foundations (comparable to the situation of private banks in Sweden) and to influence the flow of payments. (The Editors)

types of foundations and associations are subject to this obligation if profits during the tax year amount to 100 crowns or over or if the assets exceed 5,000 crowns by the end of the budgetary year. In assessing the question as to whether an organisation must make a tax return or not, no account is taken of tax-free income or assets which are not subject to the property tax.

The tax returns submitted by foundations pursuing non-profit aims must indicate the receipts and expenditure effected during the financial year and draw up an initial and final balance-sheet. A report must also be rendered of any circumstances which affect the charitable status of the foundation. However, the tax authorities may grant exemption from the general requirement to submit a report. The papers submitted for tax purposes are not accessible to the general public.

5. Tax levied on founders

Natural persons are not allowed to deduct from their tax returns either the money spent on the establishment of a foundation or any grants they may have made to others.

Companies may, however, deduct grants made to a pension or welfare fund for employees. In other respects, donations to foundations etc. are only deductible if they may be regarded as operating costs. The rule applied is that expenditure on technical and scientific research is deductible if it is related to the industry, and is thus of indirect benefit to the enterprise concerned.

The question as to whether a grant is deductible depends on whether the recipient exercises or promotes an activity whose cost would be deductible for the promoter if he himself had exercised the activity. Excessive claims to prove a direct and immediate usefulness for the business activities of the donor are not made.

6. Tax on recipients of foundation funds

The recipient of support granted by a foundation or non-profit association is not subject to taxation if the sum of money involved is spent on implementing the object of the foundation.

III. THE CURRENT SITUATION OF FOUNDATIONS IN SWEDEN

Although foundations have played an important part in Swedish life for a long time, there is a considerable lack of information on the actual state of such organisations. There is no central register of foundations nor any statistical surveys[5] nor any systematic account of Swedish foundations in modern times. As a result, one has to make do with an approximate picture of the circumstances of foundations, their programmes and their financial means.

An attempt was made in 1966 (and again in 1969) to ascertain the number and condition of foundations in Sweden but both the objectives and the scope were limited[6]. This handbook set out to tell the recipients of funds something about the donors: it listed 440 (698) foundations or comparable institutions (both public and municipal) which promote scientific, artistic and cultural aims in general. The following account is largely based on this selection of cultural foundations.

1. The number of foundations

No precise figures can be quoted to indicate how many non-profit foundations there are, but there can be little doubt that the number is a substantial one. According to information furnished in 1961, the number of foundations under the superintendence of district administrations and cathedral chapters amounted to 6,000. The number of foundations which are not subject to supervision is probably much higher since. The possible order of magnitude may be seen in the fact that there were already 12,600 foundations in 1910. Most of the existing foundations appear to have been formed since then.

As far as the available material shows, the number of new foundations created in the 1940s and 1950s was much larger than in previous decades. It would also appear that founders were much more active in the 1960s than ever before[7].

2. The assets of foundations

There is no available evidence on which to make an assessment of the financial position of Swedish foundations. However, it can be assumed that the overwhelming majority of foundations dispose of a relatively modest fortune and thus have little money with which to make grants. The number of foundations set up by private individuals and possessing real significance—with an annual expenditure of several hundred thousand or million crowns—can be put at about 40. A handful of them possess assets of over 40 million crowns.

Most of Sweden's private foundations have been set up by one person

[5] The last statistical survey relates to the situation as it was in 1910.

[6] Kurt Lehsman—Wilhelm Odelberg: *Svenska kulturfonder*, 2nd Ed., Stockholm 1967 (3rd Ed., Stockholm 1970).

[7] This statement is based on information published about the cultural foundations.

only or by a small number of persons, and their wealth stems from these founders. But there are foundations whose funds are raised by public collections. An example is the group of funds for charitable and scientific purposes whose capital was raised in order to pay tribute to Swedish Kings or other prominent personalities on their anniversaries. Public money is never used to subsidise the activities of private foundations.

3. The objects and programmes of foundations

The basic duties of a foundation are to administer assets and to use the profits on the latter to realise concrete projects within the framework of general aims. Examples are poor relief and scientific research etc. Although the other legal entities such as joint-stock companies could do such work, foundations as such appear to have achieved something like a monopoly in this field. Cases occur where a certain project such as the erection and administration of a student hostel represents the original aim and the financial means for achieving it are given less and less prominence. In other cases where there are no assets to serve as the basis for the activities of a foundation, the latter's operations depend on a continuous stream of grants in money or kind. In this situation, another legal entity—the non-profit association— seems to be particularly suitable.

In former times, foundations were usually most active in the fields of poor relief, children's welfare and education. It was not unusual for such welfare to be restricted to a certain category of persons such as unmarried women from 'better-class families'.

Now that the State has taken over these tasks, the aim behind grants by private individuals and the setting up of large new foundations has been to look continuously for ways and means of supplementing and improving inadequate public services. The process has not yet been completed.

In recent times, foundations have tended to concentrate their efforts on scientific research, literature and art. The following figures from a survey conducted at the beginning of the 1960s will serve to illustrate the relatively major importance attached to private promoters of scientific, medical and technical research. A total of 148,100,000 crowns was spent on research and development at universities, technical colleges, agricultural and forestry schools, academies and various industrial research institutes. The Government's share of this sum was about 124,300,000 crowns. Swedish and foreign foundations contributed 17 million and industry 5.2 mill. 1,600,000 crowns came from the various research institutions' own funds[8].

[8] These figures are taken from Provisional Report No. I published in December 1962

In view of the modest volume of available material on this subject, it would not be expedient to classify foundations on the basis of their aims. However, the list of organisations we have appended to this report will be a useful guide.

The majority of foundations, i.e. above all smaller foundations, appear to operate within a geographically carefully defined area. They usually have local ties, for example with a town, a community or a school etc. However, generally speaking there are no regional restrictions within Sweden on cultural foundations. Be this as it may, most of them are in fact located in Stockholm.

Occasionally, the statutes stipulate that only persons from a certain region or researchers from a specified university etc. may be considered as beneficiaries, or that such a person must be given precedence if several people compete.

A decade ago, there were hardly any foundations whose aim it was to grant help to foreign States or to foreigners. Nowadays, the special requirements of the developing countries are playing an ever greater rôle in foundation programmes.

The Swedish student associations, for example, have created scholarship foundations whose funds are used to assist foreign students who have no opportunity to study in their own country. In addition, there are a number of similar foundations.

A noticeable trend at present is for foundations and funds in the Scandinavian countries to implement 'inter-Nordic' programmes and to disregard the nationality of the recipients of grants.

4. *Organisation*

Only a small number of foundations are administered by their own board of directors: the majority are connected with an institution of some kind or other. It is true to say that many foundations, indeed most of them, are administered by Government and above all by municipal authorities.

by the Committee for Research Organisation and Economics at the Scientific Research Council. This report is one of the many duplicated papers prepared by the Committee for Research Planning on 'The Use of Funds for Research in the Postwar Period' (March, 1963).

The committee had the following to say about the accuracy of the figures: 'The data quoted should be regarded as provisional. As soon as time permits, the attempt will be made to increase the accuracy of our statistics'. Moreover, the report in question is now out of date.

Our intention in quoting these figures is not to present an accurate picture of the financing of research: it is merely an attempt to give the reader some idea of the relative importance of private funds in this context.

Appendix: List of Cultural Foundations (1966)
(classified according to their stated aims)

Pursuant to the criteria applied here, a foundation may be entered under more than one heading and at least as regards 4 below under several sub-headings. This is because our list was intended as a guide for scholarship applicants and it makes no attempt to offer a complete survey.

Aim of the foundation	*Number*
1. General humanitarian aid	15
2. Public health, hygiene, questions pertaining to alcohol	13
3. Education and training	52
— Child and youth welfare, popular education (28)	
— Teaching at schools for further education (8)	
— Training of skilled workers and craftsmen (16)	
4. Research and higher education	273
— University and college studies, scientific research of a general nature (49)	
— Mathematics and sciences without medicine (37)	
— Medicine, pharmacology, odontology, veterinary studies (91)	
— Psychology, pedagogics, teachers' training (11)	
— The humanities (23)	
— Jurisprudence (16)	
— Political science, politics and social questions (26)	
— Theology (5)	
— Research into the history of the press, journalism (8)	
— Monument preservation, local history (7)	
5. Literature, art, music, etc.	78
— Music, theatre, literature, films (34)	
— Industrial art, painting, sculpture, architecture (44)	
6. Economics	100
— Political economy, modern trading (28)	
— Engineering, technology, advanced technical training (31)	
— Mining, iron finishing (8)	

— Agriculture, forestry (26)
— Insurance questions (7)
7. International Affairs   42
— International questions, cultural
co-operation (14)
— General international studies &
research (17);
for specified spheres of interest,
foundations may be found under the
relevant category of aims and objects
— Nordic questions and cultural
co-operation in Scandinavia (11)

573

LITERATURE

Bratt, J. Deklaration och beskattning, Stockholm 1967.

Bratt, J. and Fogelklou, L. Skatt på arv och skatt på gåva, Stockholm 1964 (1969).

Geijer, E., Rosenqvist, E., Sterner, H. Skattehandbok, Part I, Stockholm 1964.

Hessler, H. Om stiftelser, Stockholm 1952.

Karlgren, H. Ändamalsbestämmelse och stiftelse, Lund 1951.

Lehsmann, K. and Odelberg, W. Svenska kulturfonder, 2nd Ed., Stockholm 1967; 3rd Ed., Stockholm 1970.

For magazine articles, the reader can consult:

Regner, N. Svensk juridisk litteratur 1865–1965. Stockholm 1957 (with supplements in Svensk Juristtidning).

Notes on the Authors

A	AUSTRIA	Dr. Gunter Beinhauer: Then assistant at the Institute for State and Administrative Law at the University of Vienna.
B	BELGIUM	Maître Pierre Ansiaux: Lawyer with the High Court, Brussels. Maître Francis Allard: Lawyer with the High Court, Brussels.
CH	SWITZERLAND	Dr. Uwe Pavel: Then member of the staff of Deutsche Treuhand-Gesellschaft AG, Frankfurt/Germany. Dr. Hans G. Wirz: Vice-Director of Julius Bär & Co., Bankers, Zurich.
D	GERMANY	Dr. Ernst-Joachim Mestmäcker: Professor of Civil and Commercial Law at Bielefeld University. Dr. Dieter Reuter: Assistant to Professor Mestmäcker.
DK	DENMARK	Dr. Klaus Neuhoff: Consultant on Foundations with the Stifterverband für die Deutsche Wissenschaft (Donors' Association for the Promotion of Sciences and Humanities), Essen.
E	SPAIN	The Spanish entry has been compiled by members of the staff of the Fundación Juan March, Madrid.
F	FRANCE	Michel Pomey: Maître des requêtes with the Conseil d'Etat, Paris, Director of the Fondation de France (established in 1969).
GB	ENGLAND AND WALES	Christopher P. Hill: Former Chief Commissioner of the Charity Commission, London (until 31st December 1965).
I	ITALY	Professor Alberto Predieri: Director of the Institute for Public Law at the University of Florence.
NL	NETHERLANDS	Dr. Frits W. Hondius: Former Secretary General of the International Institute of Social Studies, The Hague; Principal Administrator at the Council of Europe in Strasbourg since 1969; in this function also charged with questions pertaining to foundations in Europe.
P	PORTUGAL	Dr. José Blanco: Assistant Director at the Office of the Chairman of the Board of Administration of the Calouste Gulbenkian Foundation, Lisbon.
S	SWEDEN	Jur.kand. Klas Herrlin: Since 1970 member of the staff of the Kungl. Kammarrätten, an Administrative Court dealing mainly with tax matters, Uppsala.

Legal Committee of the Atlantic Co-ordinating Committee of Foundations:

Dr. Reinhard Goerdeler (Chairman): Lawyer and Certified Accountant, Frankfurt, Germany.

Pierre Ansiaux (*infra*).

J. D. Livingston Booth, M.A.: Chief Executive of the Charities Aid Fund of the National Council of Social Service, Tonbridge, England.

Michel Pomey (*infra*).

Sture Petrén: President of the Royal High Court, Stockholm, Sweden.

Currency Table

Country	National currency	(as at end of 1970)		(as at end of 1971)*	
		£	$	£	$
A	100 Schilling	1.60	3.85	1.65	4.30
B	100 Francs	0.80	2.00	0.87	2.25
CH	100 Franken	9.55	22.90	10.00	26.05
D	100 DM	11.40	27.35	11.90	31.05
DK	100 Kroner	5.55	13.35	5.54	14.30
E	100 Pesetas	0.60	1.45	0.59	1.50
F	100 Francs	7.50	18.00	7.50	19.55
GB	1 Pound	—	2.40	—	2.60
I	1000 Lire	0.65	1.60	0.66	1.70
NL	100 Gulden	11.50	27.65	12.04	30.80
P	100 Escudos	1.45	3.50	1.44	3.65
S	100 Kronor	8.05	19.30	8.07	20.80

* based on London Selling Rates for currency 31.12.71.